Enemies of Mankind

The Erik Castrén Institute Monographs on International Law and Human Rights

General Editor

Martti Koskenniemi

VOLUME 18

The titles published in this series are listed at brill.com/ilmc

Enemies of Mankind

Vattel's Theory of Collective Security

By

Walter Rech

MARTINUS NIJHOFF PUBLISHERS

LEIDEN • BOSTON
2013

Library of Congress Cataloging-in-Publication Data

Rech, Walter.
Enemies of mankind : Vattel's theory of collective security / by Walter Rech.
pages cm. -- (The Erik Castren Institute monographs on international law and human rights ; volume 18)
Revised version of thesis (Ph.D.)--University of Melbourne, Melbourne Law School, 2012.
Includes bibliographical references and index.
ISBN 978-90-04-25434-3 (hardback : alk. paper) -- ISBN 978-90-04-25435-0 (e-book) 1. Vattel, Emer de, 1714-1767. Droit des gens. 2. International law--History. 3. War (International law)--History. I. Title.
KZ2414.R43 2013
341--dc23

2013018787

This publication has been typeset in the multilingual "Brill" typeface. With over 5,100 characters covering Latin, IPA, Greek, and Cyrillic, this typeface is especially suitable for use in the humanities. For more information, please see www.brill.com/brill-typeface.

ISSN 1568-2765
ISBN 978-90-04-25434-3 (hardback)
ISBN 978-90-04-25435-0 (e-book)

This book is printed on acid-free paper.

For Amandine, Annamaria and Luciano

CONTENTS

ABSTRACT

Swiss international lawyer Emer de Vattel (1714–1767) has been regarded by authoritative legal historians as the advocate of a classical conception of international law grounded on sovereignty and the *ius in bello*. In the mid-eighteenth century, as the just war doctrine based on canon law and moral theology became inadequate to regulate warfare in a growingly secularised international society, Vattel distinguished legality from legitimacy and (re)asserted the formalist argument that war between sovereign entities must be considered as legal on both sides regardless of the justice of the cause. The mutual acknowledgment of the opponent as a lawful combatant constituted the primary condition for the development of the modern *ius in bello* as a body of norms regulating the conduct of warfare irrespective of the war guilt.

Far from contesting the above, this book attempts to unveil Vattel's 'other face' by exploring his notion of the 'enemy of mankind'. Besides asserting the right of all sovereigns to have recourse to force in conformity with the laws of war, Vattel pointed out that if they either abused this right or carried out unrestricted warfare, whether against foreign nations or their own population, they should be repressed as common enemies of all by an international coalition. This had to be done for the sake of collective security, and to preserve the laws of war themselves in the long run.

The book critically analyses this doctrine and contextualises it in the history of international law. It investigates the meanings and functions of the enemy of mankind concept in early modern international legal thought, and particularly in Vattel's *Droit des gens* of 1758 as its culminating point. The present work describes Vattel's enemy of mankind doctrine as a theory of collective security and international law enforcement, and spells out the implications of this theory within the Vattelian system and for the history of international law.

FOREWORD

The notion of "enemies of mankind" rose to prominence in the aftermath of the attack on the World Trade Center in New York in 2001 and the consequent "war on terror". At that point the argument was sometimes heard that because terrorists attack innocent civilians and destroy their property they should be regarded as "enemies of humanity" or "enemies of mankind" to be fought by all available means. They ought not to enjoy protections provided by law to "normal" actors complying with certain minimal criteria of civilized adversity. Against this reasoning concerns were raised regarding the arbitrary nature of categories such as "terrorist" and "enemy of mankind." Might the use of such morally condemnatory language operate simply as a strategy of "lawfare" – that is to say, designed to liberate powerful actors to take whatever action they wish against their inevitably weaker opponents?

This 21st century problem is not the direct subject of this work. Instead, Dr. Walter Rech has chosen to discuss the use of the category of "enemy of mankind" in early modern international law, especially in the writings of the most influential of 18th century international jurists, the Swiss Emer de Vattel. For it appears that concerns quite similar to contemporary ones were present in early modern law where issues of formal legality and civilizational difference as well as ideas about appropriate and inappropriate conduct in warfare and government turned out important for the treatment of certain international activities. Rech begins by focusing on the way the legal treatment of pirates acting on their own and "privateers", endorsed by states, depended on the identity of the endorsing State – that is to say, whether it was "civilized" or "barbarian". But when Vattel advocated that Barbary corsairs should "be exterminated like ferocious and pernicious beasts", he was conveniently forgetting that the behaviour of European nations differed often in no way from that of their Muslim opponents. Rech then turns to the way European rulers were sometimes regarded as "enemies of mankind" on the basis of their aggressive behaviour, their disturbance of the balance of power or their "tyrannical" policies. By a close reading of Vattel's letters and essays, as well as his activity in the service of Elector Augustus of Saxony, Rech expounds the way he came to indict Prussia's Frederick II as an unscrupulous aggressor and as such, an enemy of mankind. Frederick's notorious attack on Silesia at the commencement of the War of Austrian Succession (1740–1748) seems even to impel Vattel to come out as an early exponent of individual criminal responsibility, less on moral grounds, however, but to maintain European order and civility. In both situations, outside and within Europe, Rech argues, Vattel chose his positions on the basis of pragmatic, anti-moralist and anti-legalist views that nevertheless reflected a Eurocentric civilizational bias and a concern over security and good order among European States.

This erudite book is a fine example of contextual history of legal and political thought. It provides a many-sided description and analysis of the notion of "enemy of mankind" during Vattel's lifetime and later legal rhetoric. Then, like now, it has seemed available both to mark a civilizational hierarchy as well as to castigate adversaries who seemed to violate norms of civilized behaviour. It has operated as a motivation for enlisting the collective – in this case, the collective of (European) States – to take action against an enemy whose actions have condemned it as an outsider or even an outlaw. Rech situates Vattel's views in the context of his professional activities as well as within the doctrines of international law in the early modern period. The views of Bodin, Grotius, Gentili, Pufendorf, the two Coccejis and Bynkershoek are compared with that of the book's main protagonist. Then, as now, jurists differed on the use of the qualification and the treatment to be accorded to unconventional actors.

This is a very well-written study with obvious contemporary relevance. Its source-material is wide and the secondary literature comes in many languages. Through an analysis of an early moment in the development of "modern" international law, Rech has been able to elucidate the way legal language can be used in ways to erect and operate civilizational barriers, to arouse moral opprobrium in order to castigate one's adversaries and to enlist political support for one's foreign policy goals. This is a methodologically sophisticated and politically relevant contribution to the burgeoning literature of history of legal and political thought.

Helsinki
MK

ACKNOWLEDGMENTS

This book is the outcome of a PhD project conducted at Melbourne Law School, University of Melbourne, and the Max Planck Institute for European Legal History of Frankfurt. I am grateful to both institutions, which hosted me for around two years each, for their financial support, the opportunity to use their first-class facilities and the kindness of their staff.

I particularly wish to thank Anne Orford of Melbourne Law School for her supervision and invaluable comments on these chapters. Her insightful remarks greatly contributed to the development of my argument. I further express my gratitude to Kevin Heller, Jan Klabbers, Martti Koskenniemi, Sundhya Pahuja, Peter Rush and Greg Taylor, who at different points provided me with essential feedback on my work.

I am very much indebted to Michael Stolleis, whose supervision I benefited from as I was affiliated with the Frankfurt Max Planck in the first part of my research. The whole project owes much to his support and advice. I extend my thanks to all professors who together with Michael Stolleis animated the weekly seminars of the International Max Planck Research School for Comparative Legal History: Albrecht Cordes, Bernhard Diestelkamp, Gerhard Dilcher, Susanne Lepsius, Guido Pfeifer and Joachim Rückert. Special thanks go to Luigi Nuzzo and Miloš Vec, whose expertise in the history of international law I profited from, and whose friendliness and cordiality I much appreciated. Further, I am obliged to Michele Nicoletti and Diego Quaglioni of the University of Trento for their mentorship as I first ventured into the fields of political philosophy and the history of international law. Their guidance has been fundamental for my research prior and during the writing of the book.

Debts are also due to my fellow PhD students as well as administrative staff at Frankfurt and Melbourne. I am thinking especially of Juan Cañizares Navarro, Olivia Barr, Domi Cordoba, Sara Dehm, Maria Elander, Mas Generis, Bec Goodbourn, Laura Griffin, James Muldoon, Darren Parker, James Parker, Connal Parsley, Saw Tiong Guan and Hao Zhang. I would like to thank all of them for their assistance, friendship and countless stimulating conversations.

Most of all I am grateful to my wife Amandine and to my parents, Annamaria and Luciano, for their help, patience and constant encouragement.

INTRODUCTION

This book explores the meaning and function of the 'enemy of mankind' concept in Emer de Vattel's international legal doctrine, particularly in his *Droit des gens* of 1758.[1] It argues that in calling for all states to join forces to repress 'enemies of mankind' egregiously violating the law of nations, Vattel put forward an innovative theory of the collective enforcement of international law grounded on collective security and utility.[2] In advancing this claim, the book demonstrates that the enemy of mankind theory is of significance both for Vattel's international legal project and for the history of international law.

Vattel characterised as enemies of mankind mainly those belligerents who gravely abused the right to make war or carried out unrestricted warfare, whether against foreign nations or their own population. He stated that such international criminals should be repressed by a coalition of states relieved from any obligation to observe the laws of war in retaliation.[3] In this case of international emergency, Vattel posited, the civilised usages of war prescribed by the 'voluntary law of nations' provisionally ceased to be mandatory, while strict natural law re-entered into force. As a result, the coalition was entitled to take any measures necessary to stop and punish the enemy of mankind to deter him and others from further offending. This had to be done to preserve the civilised laws of war themselves, and the voluntary law of nations more generally, in the long run.

The originality of Vattel's perspective especially lay in the fact that he did not plead for the enforcement of international law for moral purposes, that is, to implement inherently 'just' rules and a righteous world order, as was held by just war doctrinarians.[4] Nor did he raise the issue of enforcement for theoretical purposes, that is, to define international law as law 'proper', which was the concern of his master, Christian Wolff, under the

---

1 Emer de Vattel, *Droit des gens, ou principes de la loi naturelle appliqués à la conduite des nations et des souverains* (London, i.e. Neuchâtel, 1758) (hereinafter referred to as *DG*).

2 *DG*, IV, 7, § 81.

3 See, for instance, *DG*, II, 4, § 53; II, 5, § 70; II, 15, § 222; III, 8, § 155.

4 On the just war doctrine, see the seminal works of Frederick H Russell, *The Just War in the Middle Ages* (CUP, 1975) and Peter Haggenmacher, *Grotius et la doctrine de la guerre juste* (Paris, PUF, 1983).

'world state' theory.[5] Instead, Vattel endorsed a straightforwardly pragmatic approach and called on all nations to enforce international law uniquely to preserve a minimum level of international order. For Vattel, here obliterating the classical just war doctrine, international law should be enforced collectively, not by unilateral action, and only to pursue the 'common security and well-being of nations', not for the sake of retribution against the wrongdoer.[6] He put forward a utilitarian and 'enlightened' doctrine of the repression of international crimes, in accordance with his fundamental theoretical assumption that all law is ultimately based on the principle of utility.[7] The doctrine played a central role in his broader project of rationalising, universalising, and enforcing the European law of nations.

Literature Review

The enemy of mankind concept has recently been investigated with reference to a set of interrelated topics such as piracy, terrorism, crimes against humanity and universal jurisdiction. However, to date no thorough historical analysis has been made of the emergence and significance of this concept in modern international legal discourse.[8] The Vattelian enemy of mankind concept has indeed been discussed by a few scholars, who have mostly regarded it as evidence of his continuing reliance on the just war

---

[5] Christian Wolff, *Jus gentium methodo scientifica pertractatum* (first published 1749, Joseph H Drake trans, Oxford, Clarendon, 1934) Prolegomena, § 21.

[6] *DG*, II, 12, § 162; II, 15, § 222.

[7] Emer de Vattel, 'Essai sur le fondement du droit naturel' [in *Pièces diverses, avec quelques lettres de morale, et d'amusemens* (Paris, 1746)], reprinted in *DG* (Paul Pradier-Fodéré ed, Paris, 1863) 1–32, § 29. Vattel's utilitarian approach clearly emerged also in his book review on Rousseau's *Discourse on Inequality*: Emer de Vattel, 'Réflexions sur le Discours de M. Rousseau touchant l'origine de l'inégalité parmi les hommes' (first published 1755) in Emer de Vattel, *Amusemens de littérature, de morale et de politique* (The Hague, 1765) 79.

[8] Accounts of the enemy of mankind concept have been given by Alfred P Rubin, *The Law of Piracy* (first published 1988, Irvington-on-Hudson, NY, Transnational Publishers, 1998) 91–95; David Luban, 'A Theory of Crimes against Humanity' (2004) 65 *Yale Journal of International Law* 85, 140–141; Gerry Simpson, 'Enemies of Humankind', in Jennifer Gunning et al (eds), *Law, Ethics and Society* (Aldershot, Ashgate, 2006) 85; Gerry Simpson, *Law, War and Crime. War Crimes Trials and the Reinvention of International Law* (Cambridge, Polity, 2007) 159–177; Daniel Heller-Roazen, *The Enemy of All* (New York, Zone Books, 2009). Dan Edelstein has provided a brief history of the *hostis humani generis* concept, but has not gone into detail about the legal ramifications of the concept: Dan Edelstein, *The Terror of Natural Right. Republicanism, the Cult of Nature, and the French Revolution* (University of Chicago Press, 2009) 26–42.

doctrine and of his unwillingness or incapability to depart from a moralist paradigm of warfare.[9]

Yet this book maintains otherwise. It contends that far from elaborating on the just war doctrine, Vattel dismissed its basic assumptions to put forward a modern idea of the enforcement of international law in analogy with the Hobbesian domestic security paradigm.[10] Vattel's enemy of mankind theory constituted an essential element of his realist and utilitarian international legal theory in open rejection of the just war doctrine. In his view, the sole aim of the repression of international crimes was to grant a minimum level of international order and thus create the conditions for the long-term preservation of the 'voluntary law of nations' when the latter was egregiously violated and under threat. Vattel did not advance his enemy of mankind theory to relativise his doctrine of the 'voluntary law of nations', but to underpin it. In the face of grave and systematic violations of the 'voluntary law of nations', it was imperative that strict natural law re-enters into force and allows the coalition to repress the enemy of mankind by any means available. This punitive action was necessary if the 'voluntary law of nations' itself was to be preserved and observed in the long run.

A pertinent comment on the Vattelian enemy of mankind doctrine has recently been given by Dan Edelstein in *The Terror of Natural Right*. Elaborating on Reinhard Koselleck's view of Enlightenment political and legal theory, Edelstein has rightly remarked that by outlawing enemies of mankind, 'Vattel authorised and encouraged the temporary suspension of lofty liberal principles in the name of these very principles'.[11] However,

---

9 Simone Zurbuchen, 'Vattel's *Law of Nations* and Just War Theory' (2009) 35 *History of European Ideas* 408; Gabriella Silvestrini, 'Justice, War, and Inequality. The Unjust Aggressor and the Enemy of the Human Race in Vattel's Theory of the Law of Nations' (2010) 31 *Grotiana* 44, 46 and 67; Gabriella Silvestrini, 'Vattel, Rousseau et la question de la justice de la guerre' in Vincent Chetail and Peter Haggenmacher (eds), *Vattel's International Law in a XXIst Century Perspective* (Leiden – Boston, Nijhoff, 2011) 110. Francesco Mancuso's reading of Vattel's enemy of mankind doctrine is more balanced and accurate: Francesco Mancuso, '*Le Droit des gens* come apice dello *jus publicum europaeum*? Nemico, guerra, legittimità nel pensiero di Emer de Vattel' (2009) 38 *Quaderni Fiorentini per la storia del pensiero giuridico moderno* 1277. In earlier scholarship, Albert de Lapradelle already drew attention to the idea of a war in humanity's name in his 'Introduction' to the *Droit des gens* (Washington, Carnegie Institution, 1916) XXV, XXVI.

10 Thomas Hobbes, *Leviathan* (first published 1651, Richard Tuck ed, CUP, 1991) II, 17. On Vattel's use of Hobbes' notion of security see also Peter Haggenmacher, 'Le modèle de Vattel et la discipline du droit international' in Chetail and Haggenmacher (eds), *Vattel's International Law in a XXIst Century Perspective* 1, 36 and 41.

11 Edelstein, *The Terror of Natural Right*, 39.

Edelstein has not provided a convincing analysis of the enemy of mankind concept from the legal perspective. He has rashly concluded that Vattel 'came close to codifying natural right in such a way that the 'enemy of the human race' could become an effective legal category liable of being used in courts and introduced into legislation'.[12] While the strengths of Edelstein's reflections are mainly in the description of the enemy of mankind concept as a literary topos, the present work sets out to analyse its legal implications.

As it addresses the legal ramifications of the enemy of mankind theory, this book engages with Vattel scholarship on the broader issue of the significance of Vattel's work, notably of his masterpiece, the *Droit des gens*, for the general history of international law. Opinions on the subject have traditionally been divided.[13] Whilst commentators have generally recognised that Vattel enjoyed considerable authority, in particular among diplomats and practitioners, from the publication of the *Droit des gens* until the late nineteenth century, there has been disagreement as to the implications of this long-standing influence. Vattel's admirers have highlighted his innovative contribution to the modern law of nations, notably to the doctrines of sovereign equality, neutrality, self-determination, and to the laws of war.[14] From the late eighteenth century, these scholars have

---

[12] Ibid 38.

[13] As to Vattel's enduring impact, especially on international legal practice, see August Bulmerinck, *Die Systematik des Völkerrechts* (Dorpat, 1858) 40; Alphonse Rivier, *Lehrbuch des Völkerrechts* (2nd ed, Stuttgart, Ferdinand Enke, 1899) 58–59; Charles Fenwick, 'The Authority of Vattel' (1913) 7 *The American Political Science Review* 395; Francis S Ruddy, 'The Acceptance of Vattel' in Charles H Alexandrowicz (ed), *Grotian Society Papers: Studies in the History of the Law of Nations* (The Hague, Nijhoff, 1972) 177.

[14] William Oke Manning, *Commentaries on the Law of Nations* (first published 1839, London, Sweet, 1875) 39–41; Travers Twiss, *The Law of Nations Considered as Independent Political Communities* (2nd ed, Oxford, Clarendon, 1875) 429–431; de Lapradelle, 'Introduction'; John Westlake, *Chapters on International Law* (first published 1894) in *The Collected Papers of John Westlake on Public International Law* (Lassa Oppenheim ed, CUP, 1914) pt 1, XVIII–282, 77; Paul Fauchille, *Traité de droit international public: 8ème édition du Manuel de droit international public de M. Henri Bonfils* (Paris, Rousseau et Cie, 1922) vol 1, pt 1, 134. Specifically on the importance of Vattel for the development of the idea of sovereign equality, see Ernst Reibstein, 'Die Dialektik der souveränen Gleihheit bei Vattel' (1958) 19 *Zeitschrift für ausländisches öffentliches Recht und Völkerrecht* 607, 608. Further, Vattel's contribution to the formulation of the principle of self-determination has been discussed by writers emphasising the authority that Vattel enjoyed in debates among the Founding Fathers of the United States in the end of the eighteenth century. On this point, see Jesse Reeves, 'La communauté internationale' (1924) 3 *Recueil des cours de l'Académie de droit internationale de La Haye* 1, 37–39. Further, Arthur Nussbaum emphasised the innovative character of the Vattelian doctrine and argued that Vattel was more 'humanitarian', 'cosmopolitan' and 'democratic' than Christian Wolff: Arthur Nussbaum, *A Concise History of the*

described the Vattelian theory as a dynamic force in a history of international law on the whole characterised by progressive advancements.[15]

Such confidence in historical progress has meanwhile been discarded, but the modernist paradigm on which this confidence relied is still alive. It is recognisable in the opinions of several contemporary commentators. In the best Vattel monograph to date, *Emer de Vattel et l'émergence du droit international classique*, Emmanuelle Jouannet stresses Vattel's role in the development of 'classical international law' as a potentially civilising normative order based on sovereign freedom and equality.[16] In a similar vein, Christoph Good draws attention to the development of an enlightened human rights and humanitarian international law discourse in the *Droit des gens*.[17] From a different yet still modernist perspective, Anthony Carty acknowledges Vattel's contribution to the idea of self-determination and to the secularisation of politics to overcome

---

Law of Nations (2nd ed, New York, Macmillan, 1954) 157. Finally, and more problematically, Vattel's alleged role in the construction of a 'non-discriminating' international order based on state sovereignty was stressed by Carl Schmitt, *The Nomos of the Earth* (1st published 1950, New York, Telos, 2003) 165–168. Reinhart Koselleck in his *Critique and Crisis* followed in Schmitt's footsteps, but delivered a more balanced judgement as he stressed that while Vattel pleaded for a sovereignty-centred international legal order, he also remained a moralist in many respects: Reinhart Koselleck, *Kritik und Krise. Eine Studie zur Pathogenese der bürgerlichen Welt* (Frankfurt am Main, Suhrkamp, 1973) 36.

15 This kind of judgement was already made by Robert Plumer Ward, *An Inquiry into the Foundation and History of the Law of Nations in Europe, from the Time of the Greeks and Romans, to the Age of Grotius* (London, Strahan and Woodfall, 1795) vol 2, 625–627. The same view was reiterated, for instance, by Coleman Phillipson, 'Emer de Vattel' in John Macdonell (ed), *Great Jurists of the World* (Boston, Little, Brown, & Company, 1914) 477, 504.

16 Emmanuelle Jouannet, *Vattel et l'émergence doctrinale du droit international classique* (Paris, Pedone, 1998); Emmanuelle Jouannet, *Droit international libéral-providence. Une histoire du droit international* (Brussels, Bruylant, 2011) 125–130. On Vattel as a theorist of sovereignty and the *ius in bello*, see also Anthony Carty, *The Decay of International Law* (Manchester University Press, 1986) 7, 71; Horatia Muir-Watt, 'Droit naturel et souveraineté de l'État dans la doctrine de Vattel' (1987) 32 *Archives de philosophie du droit* 71; Peter Haggenmacher, *Grotius et la doctrine de la guerre juste*, 609; Peter Haggenmacher, 'L'état souverain comme sujet du droit international, de Vitoria à Vattel' (1992) 16 *Droits* 11, 20; Francesco Mancuso, *Diritto, stato, sovranità. Il pensiero politico-giuridico di Emer de Vattel tra assolutismo e rivoluzione* (Naples, Edizioni Scientifiche Italiane, 2002) ch 3; Stéphane Beaulac, *The Power of Language in the Making of International Law. The Word Sovereignty in Bodin and Vattel and the Myth of Westphalia* (Leiden, Brill, 2004); Robert Kolb, 'La validité du modèle de Vattel après 1945' in Yves Sandoz (ed) *Réflexions sur l'impact, le rayonnement et l'actualité du 'Droit des gens' d'Emer de Vattel à l'occasion du 250e anniversaire de sa parution* (Brussels, Bruylant, 2010) 137, 159–163.

17 Christoph Good, *Emer de Vattel (1714–1767): Naturrechtliche Ansätze einer Menschenrechtsidee und des humanitären Völkerrechts im Zeitalter der Aufklärung* (Baden-Baden, Nomos, 2011).

confessional struggles.[18] While Carty appears more sceptical than Jouannet and Good of Vattel's overall project, all of these authors view the Vattelian theory of sovereignty as key in the transition from pre-modern moralist paradigms of law and politics to legal and political modernity.

Critics of Vattel have been equally vocal, particularly since the mid-nineteenth century. 'Positivist' writers reproached Vattel for a lack of systematicity and a tendency to mix law, philosophy, and politics, which prevented him from developing a 'scientific' system of international law.[19] This critique was frequently associated with the characterisation of Vattel as a mere populariser of Christian Wolff's work, and an abuser of the eclectic method.[20] According to this view, Vattel both forfeited Wolff's speculative yet coherent methodological rigour and failed to replace it with the positivist approach necessary to lay the basis for the modern law of nations. By the beginning of the twentieth century, an opposing critical view emerged. It pointed at the key role of the notion of sovereignty in Vattel's system and blamed him for actually contributing to the

18 Anthony Carty, *Philosophy of International Law* (Edinburgh University Press, 2007) 114; Anthony Carty, 'Vattel, 17th Century Wars of Religion and the Present' in Yves Sandoz (ed), *Réflexions*, 181, 181–188.

19 Early criticism from a natural law perspective already pointed to the contradictions inherent in Vattel's system. See, for instance, Jean Pierre Chambrier d'Oleires, *Questions de droit des gens et observations sur le traité du Droit des gens de M. de Vattel* in *Mémoires de l'Académie royale des sciences et belles-lettres depuis l'avènement de Fréderic Guillaume II au trône, 1788–1789* (Berlin, Georg Decker, 1793) 436–459; Jean Pierre Chambrier d'Oleires, *Questions de droit des gens. Suite des observations sur le traité du Droit des gens de M. de Vattel* in *Mémoires de l'Académie royale des sciences et belles-lettres depuis l'avènement de Fréderic Guillaume II au trône, 1790–1791* (Berlin, Georg Decker, 1796) 419–430. The critique of Vattel as an ambiguous and contradictory writer became more common in the central decades of the nineteenth century. The most significant expression of the latter critique was given by Baron Karl Kaltenborn von Stachau in his *Kritik des Völkerrechts* (Leipzig, Mayer, 1847) 78–85.

20 Vattel first conceived his *Droit des gens* as a compendium of Christian Wolff's *Jus gentium* designed to extend the influence of the Wolffian philosophy beyond the boundaries of academic circles. Although Vattel ended by writing an autonomous work that essentially diverged from the Wolffian *Jus gentium* on key issues, early commentators nevertheless highlighted his debt to Wolff. Ompteda even compared the structures of Wolff's *Jus gentium* and of Vattel's *Droit des gens* to demonstrate the strict relationship between the two works: Ludwig von Ompteda, *Litteratur des gesammten sowohl natürlichen als positiven Völkerrechts* (Regensburg, Montag, 1785) 338–347. Wheaton did the same in his *Histoire des progrès du droit des gens* (4th ed, Leipzig, Brockhaus, 1865) 238. As to eclecticism, it was indeed a characteristic feature of Vattel's narrative and has been pointed out by commentators unanimously. See, for instance: André Mallarmé, 'Emer de Vattel' in Antoine Pillet (ed) *Les fondateurs du droit international* (Paris, Giard & Brière, 1904) 481, 482; Antonio Truyol y Serra, *Histoire du droit international public* (Paris, Economica, 1995) 89–90; Jens Bartelson, *A Genealogy of Sovereignty* (CUP, 1995) 194.

establishment of a positivist international order doing away with Grotian and Wolffian universalism.[21] While nineteenth century critics acknowledged Vattel's emphasis on sovereignty and simply accused him of shrinking from developing a positive system of the law of nations based upon it, early twentieth century critics charged him with granting a central role to sovereignty in the first place.[22] For these critics, Vattel's focus on sovereignty represented an essential precondition for the development of international legal positivism properly so-called in later scholarship.

Such attacks launched by publicists engaged in the struggle between positivism and naturalism have gone out of fashion in recent times. The dichotomy naturalism/positivism has been disputed and deconstructed, as it no longer accounts for the dimension of power and says little about the concrete modalities through which the law operates. The moralist tone of critics engaged in the naturalism/positivism debate has today been replaced by historical surveys of Vattel's legal and political project at the border between intellectual history and history of international law. Emmanuelle Jouannet's seminal study of Vattel as a theorist of classical international law belongs to that historical approach. Yet while Jouannet in her Vattel monograph follows a modernist perspective and tends to emphasise the progressive aspects of Vattel's theory, other contemporary commentators take a more critical view by emphasising the ambiguities of his discourse. In *From Apology to Utopia*, Martti Koskenniemi deconstructs Vattel's doctrine and presents him as a typical proponent of international legal liberalism perpetually oscillating between the ideas of individual sovereignty and international community, freedom and order, will and reason.[23] Incidentally, Jouannet herself, while maintaining a

---

[21] Cornelius van Vollenhoven, *The Three Stages of the Law of Nations* (The Hague, Nijhoff, 1912) 27–37; Louis Le Fur, 'La théorie du droit naturel depuis le XVIIe siècle et la doctrine moderne' (1927) 18 (3) *Recueil des cours de l'Académie de droit international de La Haye* 259, 330–331. This view was later reasserted by James L Brierly, *The Law of Nations. An Introduction to the International Law of Peace* (first published 1928, Oxford, Clarendon, 1963) 40, and by Charles Rousseau, *Principes de droit international public* (Paris, Sirey, 1953) 8.

[22] Peter P Remec reaffirmed this critique as he set Vattel's state-centred conception of international law against Grotius' individual-centred paradigm: Peter P Remec, *The Position of the Individual in International Law* According to Grotius and Vattel (The Hague, Nijhoff, 1960) 242, 243. A similar critical approach can also be found in today's cosmopolitan literature which discards the Vattelian model as the one still underpinning present international politics and hindering the advance of constitutional cosmopolitanism. For this cosmopolitan critique, see Rafael Domingo, *Gaius, Vattel, and the New Global Law Paradigm* (2011) 22 (3) *European Journal of International Law* 627.

[23] Martti Koskenniemi, *From Apology to Utopia. The Structure of International Legal Argument* (2nd ed, CUP, 2005) 108–122.

modernist perspective, has recently underlined the structural ambiguities of the Vattelian narrative in a piece eloquently entitled *Les dualismes du Droit des gens*.[24] Most commentators now stress the incoherence of Vattel's theory, and in this connection they particularly highlight his discriminatory attitude towards native populations and his role in the legal apology of Western expansion.[25]

This work takes a critical stance as it draws attention to the problematic assumptions and biases underpinning Vattel's international legal project, especially his doctrine of the repression of international crimes. While it accepts the modernists' claim that Vattel put forward a number of progressive and emancipatory arguments, it points out that his *Droit des gens* also contained a number of counter-emancipatory theses. Such emancipatory and counter-emancipatory arguments implied each other and belonged to the same discourse. They co-operated in the doctrinal formation of classical international law and determined its structural contradictions.

Other contemporary scholars, however, go beyond this moderate critique overtly to oppose any modernist reading of Vattel. Ian Hunter puts forward the radical suggestion that because Vattel's arguments were often inconsequential and easily manipulable, his *Droit des gens* can be described as a mere 'diplomatic casuistry'.[26] Hunter claims that the characterisation, put forward by Emmanuelle Jouannet, of the *Droit des gens* as a doctrine of international law based on theoretical principles is misleading as it seeks to establish coherence where there was none originally. In fact, Hunter's statement that Vattel did not advance any doctrinal project or principles does not seem to be tenable. As this investigation shows, defining the *Droit des gens* as a theory of international law based on principles does not imply that such principles were coherent, coherently applied, or independent from international politics and diplomatic practices. It is contended that Vattel did pursue a doctrinal project, however flawed and politically-loaded it was.

---

24 Emmanuelle Jouannet, 'Les dualismes du droit des gens' in Chetail and Haggenmacher (eds), *Vattel's International Law in a XXIst Century Perspective*, 133–150, 133, 148.

25 Alexis Keller, 'Vattel, la tradition du droit des gens et la question des peuples autochtones' (2006) 56 (4) *Schweizerische Zeitschrift für Geschichte* 387; Antony Anghie, 'Vattel and Colonialism' in Chetail and Haggenmacher (eds), *Vattel's International Law in a XXIst Century Perspective*, 237.

26 Ian Hunter, 'Vattel's *Law of Nations*: Diplomatic Casuistry for the Protestant Nation' (2010) 31 *Grotiana* 108, 111; Ian Hunter, 'Law, War, and Casuistry in Vattel's *Jus Gentium*' (2011) 28 (2) *Parergon* 87, 88.

This research contextualises Vattel's doctrine and reads it in light of the political events that drove him to lay down the enemy of mankind theory. Through an analysis of Vattel's and other relevant narratives on universal enmity, the research stresses that the enemy of mankind concept never constituted an immutable entity, but rather a rhetorical tool that has undergone a number of transformations and served disparate aims from Cicero until the present day.[27] This investigation situates the enemy of mankind discourse historically and unveils the political and theoretical projects behind it. This is significant not only as a historical exploration of a topic inadequately analysed as yet, but also as a preliminary step for criticising the ideological use of the enemy of mankind concept at present. It thus challenges contemporary attempts to bend the concept to the justificatory exigencies of today's political rhetoric.

In focusing on Vattel's writings, in particular on the *Droit des gens*, the present work explores international law at a stage in which it was not yet an autonomous discipline or 'science'. It is a period before the age of international law's systematic positivisation and internal differentiation. By 1750, international law, which Vattel programmatically defined as natural law 'applied to the conduct and affairs of nations and sovereigns', might have emancipated itself from theology but not yet from philosophy, even less from politics, history, and economics.[28] Nor had international law yet been divided into international humanitarian law, human rights law or international criminal law. This inquiry reflects the multidisciplinary character of international legal doctrine at that stage. It intervenes in the field of international law while working at the intersection of jurisprudence, political philosophy, legal history and history of international relations.

Main Arguments

Collective Security and the Necessity of International Law Enforcement

While often neglected by commentators, the issue of international law enforcement played a fundamental role in the *Droit des gens*. Vattel's conception of the international order rested on the idea that if 'polished'

---

[27] Cicero, *De officiis* (Walter Miller trans, London, Heinemann, 1913) III, 29.

[28] As the law applying to sovereign entities, Vattel's 'law of nations' was clearly a much narrower and more specific concept than the Roman *ius gentium*, and indeed coincided with what later writers following Bentham would call international law. See Jeremy Bentham, *Principles of International Law* in John Bowring (ed), *The Works of Jeremy Bentham* (Edinburgh, William Tait, 1838–1843) vol 2, 535–572.

eighteenth century international law was to survive in the long term, all nations had to be coerced to respect its basic rules. Though he praised some powers of his day – especially Britain and France – for their general compliance with the law of nations, Vattel believed that the situation might change due to new conflicts and changing stakes in the international arena.[29] He stressed that for the law of nations to be consistently observed in present and future scenarios it must be enforced and those responsible for grave or systematic offences had to be punished. Warlike 'barbarian' nations, egregious violators of the *ius ad bellum* or the *ius in bello*, disturbers of the balance of power, and tyrants had to be repressed as enemies of mankind as they directly or indirectly threatened the 'common security and well-being of nations'.[30]

It is of paramount importance that Vattel grounded the repression of international crimes not on retribution, or on the moral duty to rescue victimised nations, as had been held by the just war doctrine since Cicero.[31] Instead, Vattel based international law enforcement on collective security and utility, and he accordingly added that enforcement measures should be taken collectively rather than left to individual avengers. The collective security concept had recently been developed by Christian Wolff in analogy to Hobbes' domestic security paradigm, and was picked up by Vattel as he believed that collective security and international law enforcement represented two faces of the same coin.[32] Both played a central role in furthering states' interests in the international sphere. By grounding punishment on security as opposed to retribution, Vattel integrated the principles of enlightened criminal law theory in his system and put forward a utilitarian and 'enlightened' doctrine of international law enforcement.[33]

Pluralism, Universality, and Natural Law

The enemy of mankind theory fulfilled a central function in the project of rationalising, universalising and enforcing the European law of nations

---

[29] Vattel explicitly praised Britain and France for their conduct of warfare in *DG*, III, 8, § 150.

[30] *DG*, II, 4, § 53; II, 5, § 70; III, 3, § 49; III, 9, § 168; II, 5, § 62.

[31] Cicero, *De officiis*, I, 7.

[32] Hobbes, *Leviathan*, II, 17; Wolff, *Jus gentium*, VI, § 652.

[33] 'Enlightened' though it was, the bare move from retribution to security as the ground for punishment did not warrant any progress in the enforcement of international law, any improvement depending on the manner in which the security principle was enforced. The book actually shows that in Vattel's case, his relying on security did not prevent him from maintaining a biased and discriminatory doctrine especially penalising 'barbarian' international criminals.

that Vattel carried out in his *Droit des gens*. The project involved providing a theory of the collective repression of international crimes in Europe and, in theory, outside Europe as well. To be sure, Vattel was aware that the latter was hardly feasible in the mid-eighteenth century as European powers were not militarily capable nor politically willing to take on law enforcement responsibilities in distant African and Asian countries. Yet he insisted on the civilised nations' moral duty to repress international villains. He demanded that European powers at least take action against warlike robber peoples at Europe's doorstep, such as the Barbary corsairs and the Tartars.

Vattel's criminalisation of the Barbary corsairs in the name of a universal and civilised international law was of great historical significance. It entailed rejecting the international legal pluralism of the laws of war as established in doctrine and practice from the late sixteenth century.[34] Within the pluralist framework, most early-modern jurists, including Bodin, Grotius and Bynkershoek, posited that Barbary warfare had to be tolerated as it qualified as lawful privateering justified through letters of marque by legitimate sovereigns. In addition, pluralist writers maintained that the corsairs were not bound to the European rules of war, the nature of which was deemed mostly customary.[35]

Vattel opposed the pluralist argument by recourse to a naturalist paradigm. This became apparent as he criminalised the corsairs by declaring their customs of war to be absolutely contrary to natural law. More importantly, he contended that corsairs' criminal conduct gave rise to their enemies' right to take any measures necessary to annihilate them. This meant that in such a case of international emergency as the struggle against the

[34] Here, specific reference is made to an international legal pluralism of the laws of war, not to international legal pluralism as such. Indeed, international legal pluralism of the laws of war in early-modern times coexisted with universalist narratives which might dominate in other domains, for example in the issue of colonisation, and which might be tolerant or not depending on the circumstances and on the publicists' political projects. The present claim differs from Charles Alexandrowicz's, who asserted that early-modern law of nations as a whole was characterised by a tolerant spirit thanks to the universalist foundations of natural law at that time. See Charles H Alexandrowicz, 'Doctrinal Aspects of the Universality of the Law of Nations' (1961) 37 *British Yearbook of International Law* 506, 513. Alexandrowicz's argument has been relativised by Martti Koskenniemi in *The Gentle Civilizer of Nations. The Rise and Fall of International Law 1870–1960* (CUP, 2001) 130.

[35] This was one of these historical instances in which the 'exclusion' of the barbarian from the European international legal order actually fulfilled an emancipatory function and was asserted against an intolerant universalist discourse grounded on a misrepresentation of the European customs as rational and universalisable. On this point, see Koskenniemi, *The Gentle Civilizer*, 131.

enemy of mankind, strict natural law fully re-entered into force and superseded the voluntary law of nations. Under such circumstances, natural law would come into effect on a provisional basis, and should be replaced by the voluntary law of nations as soon as the crisis was over. Natural law thus constituted the condition of possibility of the preservation of international law, particularly of the civilised laws of war.

The Two-Tiered Approach to International Law Enforcement

As much as Vattel stigmatised the Barbary corsairs, they did not constitute the central target of his enemy of mankind theory. Rather, attacking the corsairs represented an intermediate step in a rhetorical crescendo that culminated with the stigmatisation of other and most dreadful enemies of mankind, that is, European sovereigns who seriously jeopardised the international order by abusing the right to make war, trampling upon the laws of war, disturbing the balance of power, or tyrannising their subjects. The heyday of Barbary privateering were long gone as Vattel wrote his *Droit des gens* in the 1750s, and the European powers were not interested in embarking on colonial wars in North Africa for commercial and colonial reasons yet. At that stage, Vattel was less concerned with the Barbary corsairs giving up their quasi-harmless maritime expeditions than with European sovereigns observing the laws of war in large-scale international conflict in Europe.

Indeed, the criminalisation of the corsairs itself fulfilled a specific function in respect to the criminalisation of European sovereigns. Criminalising the corsairs was convenient for Vattel to establish a connection between the classical doctrine on the repression of piracy and his novel doctrine on the punishment of state-sanctioned international crimes. If Barbary privateering, though state-sanctioned, could be treated as an international offence, then an analogy might be drawn to argue the same with reference to state-sponsored violations of the law of nations in Europe. As Vattel drew this analogy, he was the first writer to extend the enemy of mankind label, usually attached to pirates and robbers only, to European sovereigns violating the law of nations.

Vattel did not push the analogy between Barbary corsairs and European sovereigns any further. As regards punishment, he maintained that European sovereigns, even when liable for international crimes, deserved a gentler treatment than barbarian offenders. He stated that while irredeemable barbarian pirates and robbers could be harshly punished and even exterminated, European sovereigns responsible for breaches of the law of nations might at most be compelled to provide compensations or forfeit some of their countries' provinces, as was ordinarily done through peace treaties.[36] While Vattel made a progressive move by arguing that barbarians were not the only enemies of mankind, he ended by discriminating against them as far as punishment was concerned.

Structure of the Book

The book starts off with a brief biographical section on Vattel and then turns focus on the enemy of mankind concept and the repression of international crimes. These central topics are analysed with respect to Vattel's entire work, including his correspondence and minor political, philosophical and literary works. Particular attention is paid to his masterpiece, the *Droit des gens*, in which he laid down his international legal theory and accorded the enemy of mankind concept a specific function within it. Although he did not define the concept systematically, he did provide a number of examples of enemies of mankind and came to general conclusions regarding all nations' right to repress them. He thus established what can be fittingly described as a typology of offenders. This is well illustrated in relevant paragraphs of the *Droit des gens* specifically referring to the measures to be adopted against 'he who destroys the equilibrium', against 'a mischievous people', or 'against one who openly despises justice', or yet 'against him who disrespects the faith of treaties'.[37]

The book is structured so as to highlight the typology of the enemies of mankind as it appears in the *Droit des gens*. It discusses warmongers, violators of the laws of war, disturbers of the balance of power, and tyrants, as well as the traditionally stigmatised pirates and robber nations. It may be remarked that Vattel charged certain enemies of mankind, such as Philip II of Spain, Louis XIV of France and Frederick II of Prussia, with multiple offences, thereby characterising them as warmongers as well as violators of the laws of war and disturbers of the balance of power in the same breath. Accordingly, the typology suggested in the present work is not aimed to determine invariable and autonomous offender types, but to

---

36 See, for instance, *Treaty of Peace and Amity between France and the Netherlands, signed at Utrecht*, 11 April 1713, 28 CTS 39–60; *Treaty of Peace and Amity between France and Savoy, signed at Utrecht*, 11 April 1713, 28 CTS 125–134; *General and Definitive Treaty of Peace between France, Great Britain and the Netherlands, signed at Aix-la-Chapelle*, 18 October 1748, 38 CTS 301–323.

37 *DG*, II, 3, § 53; II, 5, § 70.

spell out the principal offences which Vattel intended to criminalise. Individual criminals might definitively be responsible for several of these forms of misconduct at once.

In addition to accounting for the main enemy of mankind types, the structure of the book calls attention to Vattel's two-tiered approach to the enforcement of international law. As he patently put forward a dichotomy between uncivilised enemies of mankind deserving harsh punishment and civilised enemies of mankind to be subject to milder penalties, the main body of the book is divided into two parts. Part One deals with the uncivilised enemies of mankind outside Europe, that is pirates and robber nations, while Part Two investigates the civilised enemies of mankind inside Europe, that is warmongers, violators of the laws of war, disturbers of the balance of power, and tyrants.

Part One is devoted to the pirate/robber as a broad and paradigmatic type of enemy of mankind. This is to account for the fact that early-modern writers, Vattel included, did not essentially distinguish piracy from robbery and simply considered piracy as robbery on the high seas. Chapter One opens this part by providing a historical and critical introduction to the enemy of mankind concept, beginning with Cicero's paradigmatic definition of the pirate as the 'common enemy of all'. Emphasis is put on the characteristic ambiguity and manipulability of this concept, in Cicero's as well as in later narratives. Account is given of the apparent move towards universalism that occurred in the first centuries AD as Christian theologians abandoned Cicero's notion of a common enemy of all and introduced the enemy of mankind concept to name the devil. Whilst this discourse remained confined to theology and had little political relevance, the enemy of mankind concept took on concrete implications in the mid-eighteenth century as Enlightenment writers, including Vattel, characterised individuals or peoples not complying with the dictates of Reason as universal foes who should be fought and, in situations of civil war or international conflict, might be rightfully annihilated. The chapter shows that the enemy of mankind concept then proved a powerful device in political and legal rhetoric. It was used by Vattel to criminalise pirates and warmongers, and by revolutionaries to disqualify royalists and other political opponents.

Chapter Two explores some of the most significant accounts of the enemy of mankind concept in early-modern legal doctrine. These views, all differing from each other to some extent, are here selected as models of the doctrine of piracy that Vattel took issue with and either rejected or adhered to, or both. The most significant result of this analysis is that the greater part of these doctrinal accounts belonged to a similar tolerant and pluralist paradigm, inaugurated by Bodin, who by strictly applying the distinction between piracy and privateering legalised Barbary warfare as it was performed under sovereign commission.[38] Typical of the argumentation by Bodin and his followers was a tendency to separate the moral and legal planes: as much as privateers, including the Barbary corsairs, carried out indiscriminate attacks without a just cause and could thus be defined as morally blameworthy enemies of mankind, they were not legally liable as long as such attacks were state-authorised. These writers also claimed that because the Barbary corsairs did not belong to the European international legal order, they could not be criminalised for failing to observe the European law of nations. While the enemy of mankind concept might retain a rhetorical function in this strand of the doctrine, it ultimately had scarce or no legal ramifications. Vattel, for better or worse, was to innovate on this point.

Chapter Three returns to the *Droit des gens* to assess Vattel's position on Barbary warfare in light of the alternative doctrinal paradigms examined in Chapter Two. Chapter Three contends that by advocating harsh repressive measures against the Barbary Regencies under the banner of humanity and civilisation, Vattel broke with the traditional international legal pluralism of the laws of war. He thus prepared the ground for nineteenth century narratives justifying Western interventionism in North Africa based on the twofold argument of the repression of international crimes and the civilising mission. The chapter stresses Vattel's bias against barbarian international offenders, who in his opinion deserved a harsher treatment than civilised criminals and might rightfully be annihilated and even exterminated. He alleged that barbarians could not be deterred otherwise.

Part Two explores Vattel's extension of the enemy of mankind concept to European sovereigns. In opening this part, Chapter Four deals with sovereigns responsible for grave violations of the *ius ad bellum* and the laws of war. As far as the *ius ad bellum* was concerned, Vattel contended that while sovereigns occasionally waging unjust wars should be excused under the voluntary law of nations, those systematically resorting to blatant aggressions as a normal instrument to fulfil hegemonic or imperialist ambitions could not be pardoned. The latter practice would inevitably escalate the size and intensity of conflicts and thus jeopardise the preservation of

---

38 Jean Bodin, *Six livres de la République* (first published 1576, Aalen, Scientia, 1977) bk I, ch 1, p 2.

international order in the long run. Based on Vattel's private correspondence, Chapter Four demonstrates that the main concrete target of his enemy of mankind doctrine around 1750 was alleged warmonger Frederick II of Prussia. In this regard, the chapter illustrates the (unsuccessful) attempts made at the time to hold Frederick in check through the Holy Roman Empire's collective security system. It shows that despite its chronic malfunctioning, this system represented a relevant pattern from which Vattel could take inspiration to formulate his theory of the repression of international crimes. The chapter then discusses the violators of the laws of war. It argues that the punishment of these offenders was of particular importance for Vattel, as he accorded a key role to the laws of war in the long-term maintenance of international security. While predecessors like Gentili, Grotius, Pufendorf, Bynkershoek and Wolff granted belligerents a broad licence to exceed the boundaries of the customary laws of war, Vattel demanded a much stricter observance of the *ius in bello* to prevent all-out conflicts and secure long-term international stability. Chapter Four however emphasises that Vattel did contemplate exceptions to the compulsory observance of the laws of war, either due to reasons of military necessity or to punish an enemy of mankind guilty of trampling upon the laws of war in the first place.

Chapter Five focuses on the disturbers of the balance of power. It demonstrates that the balance of power principle still played a central role in Vattel's system although the principle by 1758 had already been criticised by some writers pointing out its hegemonic implications. Critics included Christian Wolff, who had developed the modern concept of collective security in analogy to Hobbes' domestic security paradigm and thereby intended (but hardly managed) to furnish an alternative to the balance of power theory. The chapter shows why and how Vattel re-integrated the traditional balance of power principle into the Wolffian collective security paradigm through his enemy of mankind doctrine.

Chapter Six turns to the tyrant, an enemy of mankind whose conduct was relevant to both public and international law. It illustrates that Vattel's position on the right of resistance and of intervention represented the catalyst and culminating point of political and legal modernity. Here, just as in the repression of international crimes, natural law played an essential role. Following Hobbes, Vattel first maintained that intolerable tyranny dissolved the civil state and precipitated the commonwealth into a state of nature in which the people re-gained possession of its natural rights based on the principle of legitimate self-defence. This was grounded on the assumption that natural law re-entered into force as soon as the positive laws, be they municipal or international, ceased to fulfil their fundamental function of protecting those over whom they had authority. According to this paradigm, tyranny represented a state of domestic emergency analogous to the state of international emergency caused by the presence of an enemy of mankind, with natural law coming into effect in both circumstances to supersede the positive laws. Vattel also stated that if no other means was available to topple the tyrant and prevent him from doing further harm, he might be rightfully assassinated. This theory displays once again the centrality of security as the ground of punishment in Vattel's system and highlights his assumption that natural law may supersede any positive law in the face of grave threats to domestic or international security.

VATTEL'S LIFE

Emer de Vattel was born in Couvet, in the Principality of Neuchâtel, Switzerland, on 25 April 1714.[1] His father David, a Calvinist pastor and member of the *Vénérable Classe*, the local consistory, had been influential in endorsing Frederick I of Prussia's successful claim to the sovereignty of Neuchâtel upon the death of Marie de Nemours in 1707. Emer's mother, Marie, equally came from a filo-Prussian and well-off family. She was the sister of Emer de Montmollin, who served as the Chancellor of Neuchâtel and a diplomatic envoy for Fredrick I at Utrecht in 1713.[2]

Prussian rule in Neuchâtel had inaugurated a time of economic prosperity, especially in the clock industry, as well as intellectual activity. Although it was not until 1838 that the city saw the birth of its long-awaited academy of sciences, an animated scholarly debate had been thriving there since the first decades of the eighteenth century. At the centre of this development were theologian Jean-Frédéric Ostervald, who was to become one of Emer de Vattel's closest friends, as well as polymath Louis Bourguet, who gave lectures on philosophy, law and mathematics and founded the reviews *Mercure Suisse* and *Journal Hélvetique*, with which Vattel was to publish several pieces.[3] Though not as celebrated as natural lawyers Jean Barbeyrac in Lausanne or Jean-Jacques Burlamaqui in Geneva, Ostervald and Bourguet nevertheless were intellectuals of Europe-wide renown, and their presence in Neuchâtel certainly benefited the early evolution of Vattel's thinking.

A brilliant young student, Vattel commenced his university studies in 1728, at the age of fourteen. As Neuchâtel still lacked an *académie* at the time, he moved to Basel, where thanks to his uncommon talents he was admitted to the faculty of theology prior to reaching the minimum age required.[4] However, this experience in the field of theology largely

---

1 Edouard Béguelin, 'En souvenir de Vattel' in *Recueil de travaux offert par la Faculté de Droit de l'Université de Neuchâtel à la Société Suisse des Juristes* (Neuchâtel, Attinger, 1929) 35–176, 35.

2 Albert de Lapradelle, 'Introduction' in Emer de Vattel, *Droit des gens, ou principes de la loi naturelle appliqués à la conduite des nations et des souverains* (first published 1758, Washington, Carnegie Institution, 1916) III.

3 Béguelin, 'En souvenir de Vattel', 38.

4 Ibid 40.

disappointed him as he questioned orthodox theological dogmas and teaching. It was probably at this stage that he began to feel close to contemporary deist doctrines and develop a certain anticlerical attitude not only towards Roman Catholics, but also towards the Calvinist Church. In a letter sent to Ostervald a few years later, Vattel denounced the alleged greed and lust for power of the Neuchâtel consistory in the following terms:

> There is good reason to believe that the greater part [of the *Vénérable Classe*] pays much more attention to preserving their own rights than to protecting their sheep from the Devil; indeed, they regard the Devil himself but as a scarecrow very much suitable for them to dominate over the inane. Good apostles, who preach the Gospel to others and apply very well themselves the maxims of secular politics.[5]

As Vattel grew critical of the role of ecclesiastical hierarchies and tended to reject orthodox theology he set out to quit the faculty. Probably pressured by financial issues too, he moved to Geneva, where he worked as a preceptor and enrolled at the Academy, in 1733. There he was initiated, perhaps through Burlamaqui's lectures, to natural law and political philosophy, and became acquainted with the works of Leibniz and Wolff.[6] Both Burlamaqui's utilitarianism and Leibniz-Wolffian rationalism were to become primary sources of inspiration for the Vattelian system of natural law later on.[7]

Still, Vattel's first literary endeavours did not consist of any systematic treatises, but of brief essays, often on trivial topics, as well as poetry, his life-long passion.[8] Even in later stages of his life, when he delved more deeply into legal theory and international law, he never ceased to compose verses and dialogues. So he recurrently published miscellanea of short pieces of different literary genres, such as the *Pièces diverses, avec quelques*

---

[5] Emer de Vattel, Letter to Frédéric Ostervald, 19 December 1746, quoted in Béguelin, 'En souvenir de Vattel', 37. Translation by the author. Original text: 'On n'a pas tort de croire que le grand nombre [des membres de la *Vénérable Classe*] est bien plus attentif à conserver ses droits qu'à défendre leur brebis contre le Diable; c'est qu'ils ne regardent le Diable lui-même que comme un épouvantail fort propre à les faire dominer sur les sots. Bons apôtres, qui prêchent aux autres l'Évangile et pratiquent fort bien eux-mêmes les maximes de la politique du siècle.' Given Vattel's hostility towards Calvinist pastors and theologians, Alfred Dufour's stress on the Protestant motifs behind Vattel's theory of public law seems somewhat hazardous: Alfred Dufour, 'Religion, Eglise, Etat dans la pensée d'Emer de Vattel' (2002) 3–4 *Revue historique neuchâteloise* 169, 172.

[6] Béguelin, 'En souvenir de Vattel', 41.

[7] Bernard Gagnebin, *Burlamaqui et le droit naturel* (Geneva, La Frégate, 1944) 245–251.

[8] Béguelin, 'En souvenir de Vattel', 42.

lettres de morale, et d'amusemens of 1746, and the *Mélanges de littérature, de morale et de politique* of 1760.[9] Though most of these creations are of scarce literary and theoretical value, they remain interesting documents as they highlight some significant features of Vattel's character. Together with the love letters he sent to his unofficial fiancée Ester Marguerite de Merveilleux, these writings have been taken by some apologists of old as a testimony to Vattel's morality and sensibility.[10] However, virtue and morals do not seem to be Vattel's main concern in these pieces. What really dominates there is the fashionable eulogy of frivolity and hedonism, sometimes evoked against the rigour of religious ethics. Here he first revealed utilitarian arguments which would characterise much of his later philosophical and legal work, and which he strove to reconcile with rationalist thinking.[11]

Vattel published his first scholarly treatise, the *Défence du système Leibnitien*, in 1741, after (presumably) completing his studies at the Academy of Geneva.[12] In this book, through which he attempted to make a name for himself in the republic of letters, he defended Leibniz's *Theodicy*, in particular the pre-established harmony doctrine, against the critiques of Calvinist theologian Jean-Pierre de Crousaz. In an attempt to take advantage of the traditional ties of his own family to the Prussian monarchy, Vattel dedicated this work to Frederick II in hopes of obtaining a post in Prussia's diplomatic service or, alternatively, a professorship of philosophy at the new academy of sciences that His Majesty might wish to establish in Neuchâtel.[13] Yet His Majesty, who was busy handling more impending issues and had recently started a continental-scale conflict, the War of the Austrian Succession, did not show any interest in Vattel's spontaneous candidature.

In 1743, as Vattel became disillusioned about his career as a Prussian civil servant, he 'defected' to the enemy. He left Berlin for Dresden to seek

---

9 Emer de Vattel, *Pièces diverses, avec quelques lettres de morale, et d'amusemens* (Paris, 1746); Emer de Vattel, *Mélanges de littérature, de morale et de politique* (Neuchâtel, 1760).

10 Virgile Rossel (ed), 'Lettres intimes d'Emer de Vattel' (1902) 25 *Bibliothèque universelle et revue suisse* 36–54.

11 On Vattel's utilitarianism, see Philippe Meylan, *Jean Barbeyrac (1674–1744) et les débuts de l'enseignement du droit dans l'ancienne Académie de Lausanne. Contribution à l'histoire du droit naturel* (Lausanne, Rouge, 1937) 193; Simone Goyard-Fabre, 'Barbeyrac et la théorie du droit naturel' in Jean Barbeyrac, *Ecrits de droit et de morale* (Simone Goyard-Fabre ed, Paris, Duchemin, 1996) 1–74, 58–63.

12 Emer de Vattel, *Défense du système Leibnitien contre les objections et les imputations de M. de Crousaz* (Leiden, Jean Luzac, 1741). There is evidence that Vattel enrolled at the Academy, not, however, that he was awarded a degree: Béguelin, 'En souvenir de Vattel', 40.

13 Béguelin, 'En souvenir de Vattel', 45.

his fortune at the court of the Prince-Elector of Saxony and King of Poland, Augustus III, who in the ongoing War of the Austrian Succession had just turned on Frederick to align with Austria and Great Britain.[14] In Dresden Vattel enjoyed good relations with premier minister Count Brühl, but because of the chaotic situation of Saxon affairs during wartime he had to allow some time for a definitive response to his application. Vattel's insistence was eventually rewarded in 1747, when he was hired as a diplomatic envoy to Bern and Neuchâtel. This appointment did not entirely relieve him from financial hardships, given the meagre and irregular pay, but at least was little absorbing.[15] It left him with time off to carry on philosophical investigations and envisage the drafting of a major treatise on the law of nations, the *Droit des gens*, which was to become his masterpiece.[16] During this period Vattel also had the opportunity to enjoy the company of the aristocratic and bourgeois society, and earn a reputation as a man 'very polite and holding good and agreeable conversation', a man highly respectable for the 'candour of his soul and the wisdom of his spirit'.[17] How these statements can be reconciled with Vattel's penchant for frivolity and utilitarianism will likely remain an open biographical question.

As Vattel first planned his treatise on international law he conceived of it as a mere compendium of the Wolffian *Jus gentium*, which he regarded as the most insightful work ever written on the topic but which, he regretted, had never made it out of the academies. So he wished to abridge and translate Wolff's book to popularise its key ideas, beginning with the state-centred definition of the *ius gentium* as the exclusive law of 'nations and sovereigns'.[18] Still, while working on Wolff's *Jus gentium* Vattel became critical of some of its central elements, notably the theory of the world state, the justification of the patrimonial state, and the absence of any

---

14 Ibid 45.

15 Ibid 49.

16 Lapradelle, 'Introduction', V.

17 Lettre de Mlle Prévost à Isabelle de Zuylen (1758), quoted in Philippe Godet, *Madame de Charrière et ses amis* (Geneva, Jullien, 1906) vol 1, 19, and in Béguelin, 'En souvenir de Vattel', 57. Translation by the author. Original text: 'très poli et d'une conversation bonne et agréable'; Lettre de Pierre-Michel Hennin à Voltaire (1766), quoted in Voltaire, *Œuvres complètes* (Paris, Garnier, 1882) vol 44, 312, and in Béguelin, 'En souvenir de Vattel', 64. Translation by the author. Original text: '… M. de Vattel, auteur d'un bon ouvrage sur le droit des gens, mais plus estimable encore par la candeur de son âme et la sagesse de son esprit'.

18 *DG*, Préliminaires, § 3; Peter Haggenmacher, 'L'état souverain comme sujet du droit international, de Vitoria à Vattel' (1992) 16 *Droits. Revue française de théorie juridique* 11–20, 19.

binding laws of war protecting civilians and war prisoners.[19] Vattel did not hesitate to discard the Wolffian opinion in these and other matters and to pursue his own line of argument instead. As a result, the *Droit des gens* was a largely independent work as it came out in 1758. It earned Vattel immediate and wide notoriety, as well as the appointment to *Geheimrat* by Augustus III the following year. It was printed in several editions and languages, and would remain the most authoritative international law textbook until the mid-nineteenth century.[20]

Among the causes of Vattel's instantaneous and worldwide success, mention should be made of his plain and sometimes even pleasant French prose, so different from the dry, pedantic Latin of earlier writers, especially of his master Wolff.[21] Vattel opted for a clear and comprehensible language as he intended to speak to statesmen and diplomats, not only to scholars, and with a pragmatic intent. Here lay an essential reason for his celebrity, that is, his ability to formulate readily usable arguments that could be concretely put to work in international affairs, without excessive abstractions and lengthy demonstrations.[22] Further to his credit, Vattel in his discussion of concrete legal issues managed to be somewhat exhaustive without being overly detailed. He touched on all sensitive international legal problems of the time, and accounted for state practice far better than did philosophical natural law treatises that dwelt on the foundations of the law of nations and sometimes missed the point of actual international disputes.[23]

Vattel's popularity among diplomats and practitioners can additionally be explained by his skill at constructing legal grounds for nearly any type of conduct. Indeed, he did not take a firm stance on a number of issues, since he assumed that the legal principles he defended might justify different courses of action based on context and circumstances. This did not mean that Vattel turned into a mere casuist, but he was certainly less systematic and formally coherent than Wolff, and deliberately so. In Vattel's

19 *DG*, Préface, XVI.

20 Charles Fenwick, 'The Authority of Vattel' (1913) 7 *The American Political Science Review* 395; Dominique Gaurier, *Histoire du droit international: auteurs, doctrines et développement de l'Antiquité à l'aube de l'époque contemporaine* (Rennes, Presses Universitaires de Rennes, 2005) 174–176.

21 Lapradelle, 'Introduction', VIII.

22 Commentators have often stressed the centrality of this point. Arthur Nussbaum, for instance, defined the *Droit des gens* as a mediocre work and put down its success only to its suitability for diplomatic use in a time when reference books on international law had become indispensable tools for any official involved in foreign policy: Arthur Nussbaum, *A Concise History of the Law of Nations* (2nd ed, New York, Macmillan, 1954) 160.

23 Paul Guggenheim, *Emer de Vattel et l'étude des relations internationales en Suisse* (Geneva, Librairie de l'Université, 1956) 20.

view, some leeway in terms of accuracy and logical strictness was necessary to establish an international legal doctrine valid not only in the republic of letters but also, and more important, in the society of princes. In the *Droit des gens* he did not aim to build an irrefutable theoretical system, so much to deliver a few realistic guidelines for the maintenance of international legal order.

Vattel's pragmatic concern about international politics became especially visible during the Seven Years' War (1756–1763), as he relentlessly defended Saxony's and the Empire's right to collective security against aggressive Prussia, thereby putting to work his enemy of mankind theory.[24] At that time he took on further diplomatic responsibilities and was also engaged in an advocacy for the claim of Augustus III's son, Frederick Christian, to the Duchy of Courland and Semigallia.[25] However, owing to the intensification of his professional activity, and to his increasingly precarious health, Vattel was no longer to produce any significant scholarly work after the *Droit des gens*, though he still devoted some of his time to study.[26] In 1762 he published the *Questions de droit naturel*, a commentary on the Wolffian *Jus naturae* that he had drafted in the 1740s.[27]

At this stage Vattel might rejoice in seeing his career goals fulfilled, yet his private life had not given him the same satisfactions. His inadequate financial situation had always prevented him from formally asking for the hand of his unofficial fiancée, Ester de Merveilleux, who died after long illness soon before Vattel achieved international fame through the *Droit des gens*. Only in 1764 did Vattel get married, with a younger woman, Marie de Chêne, a descendant of a noble family of French refugees in Dresden.[28] The following year they had a child, Charles Adolphe Maurice, whom Emer wished could at some point become a notable and an illustrious member of the republic of letters too.[29] Charles was to meet some of these expectations as he entered a political career culminating with the position of councillor of state in Neuchâtel, and he also published a few literary works. However, Emer did not bear witness to these accomplishments. His health steadily worsened from the early months of 1765, and he died on 28 December 1767.

---

24 Béguelin, 'En souvenir de Vattel', 56; Ernst Reibstein, *Völkerrecht. Eine Geschichte seiner Ideen in Lehre und Praxis* (Freiburg – Munich, Alber, 1957) vol 1, 582.

25 Emer de Vattel, *Mémoire sur les affaires de Courlande* (Warsaw, 1763).

26 Lapradelle, 'Introduction', VI.

27 Emer de Vattel, *Questions de droit naturel* (The Hague, 1763).

28 Béguelin, 'En souvenir de Vattel', 62.

29 Ibid 65.

PART ONE

ENEMIES OF MANKIND OUTSIDE EUROPE

CHAPTER ONE

PIRATES AND ROBBER NATIONS

This chapter provides a historical and critical introduction to the enemy of mankind concept. It begins with Cicero's definition of the pirate as the 'common enemy of all' and further discusses the recourse of other Roman writers to the universal enemy concept in legal and political texts. It demonstrates that since its inception, the concept possessed various meanings and was used to achieve disparate ends. This was confirmed by medieval theologians resorting to the enemy of mankind concept to characterise the devil, and later, more relevantly, by Enlightenment writers employing the concept in ideological debates on law and politics. It was in the second half of the eighteenth century that the enemy of mankind took on a major political significance and was used, by Vattel as well as by the French revolutionaries, to call for wars in humanity's name against those acting against Reason, both in the domestic and the international sphere.

After this general overview of the enemy of mankind concept, the chapter focuses on the concept's legal ramifications. Here, attention is paid to the idea of the pirate as the enemy of mankind and this characterisation's influence on the notion of piracy. The chapter outlines the transformations of the law of piracy from the thirteenth century with the distinction, more doctrinal than practical, between piracy and privateering. At this point Vattel's stance is examined closely. His justification of (European) privateering and stigmatisation of (non-European) piracy is criticised in light of examples from early-modern international relations and warfare. The chapter in particular evaluates Vattel's attack on the Barbary corsairs, whose practice of enslaving war captives – a practice actually resorted to by Europeans as well – he deemed an egregiously unlawful behaviour deserving of harsh punishment by all states. As he set out to make a case for the collective enforcement of international law, he took a hard line against the Barbary Regencies and labelled the corsairs as pirates and enemies of mankind.

Vattel on Heinous Crimes and the Preservation of Human Society

In the first book of the *Droit des gens* Emer de Vattel held that a criminal had to be punished by the organs of the state in which they had committed the crime, and not by foreign authorities.[1] He assumed that the right to punish, which naturally rested with the victim of an offence, passed to state institutions following the establishment of civil society and was relinquished by states only in cases in which a state allowed extradition.[2] Yet Vattel pointed out that the territoriality principle did not necessarily apply to cases of poisoning, murder, arson, or piracy. Every nation was called on actively to participate in the repression of crimes of such gravity, even if those crimes were committed beyond its own boundaries, if the state having territorial jurisdiction over the offence was unable to mete out the appropriate punishment. Those responsible for such heinous crimes qualified as enemies of mankind subject to the common jurisdiction of all nations.

> [A]lthough the justice of each nation ought in general to be confined to the punishment of crimes committed in its own territories, we ought to except from this rule those villains, who, by the nature and habitual frequency of their crimes, violate all public security, and declare themselves the enemies of the human race. Poisoners, assassins, and incendiaries by profession, may be exterminated wherever they are seized; for they attack and injure all nations by trampling under foot the foundations of their common safety. Thus, pirates are sent to the gibbet by the first into whose hands they fall.[3]

The 'heinousness' of the above-mentioned crimes constituted the main reason for Vattel to plead for universal jurisdiction. Piracy under international law might elicit universal jurisdiction for the further reason that it was committed on the high seas, hence outside national jurisdictions, and was directed against citizens regardless of their nationality.[4] Yet offences such as poisoning, murder, arson – and indeed piracy inside territorial waters – were committed within state jurisdictions and therefore could not be assimilated with piracy *iure gentium*. The gravity of these offences here came into play. Vattel maintained that while crimes such as poisoning, murder or arson rarely concerned the international community directly, they did so at least indirectly due to their heinous character. These mostly violent crimes challenged the fundamental rules of human society

---

[1] *DG*, I, XIX, § 232.

[2] Ibid I, XIII, § 169.

[3] Ibid I, XIX, § 233.

[4] Today's lawyers tend to assume that universal jurisdiction applies to piracy *iure gentium* mainly because piratical attacks occur on the high seas, whereas the 'heinousness' traditionally attributed to piracy is not decisive: Eugene Kontorovich, 'The Piracy Analogy' (2004) 45 *Harvard International Law Journal* 183, 223; Vaughan Lowe and Christopher Staker, 'Jurisdiction' in Malcolm D Evans (ed), *International Law* (3rd ed, OUP, 2010) 313–39, 327.

and were therefore noxious to mankind as a whole. They were therefore condemned both by natural law, the end of which was to preserve the minimum conditions for peaceful human coexistence, and by the positive laws of all nations.[5] These crimes made peace and tranquillity impossible domestically as well as internationally. Vattel clarified this point in a later chapter devoted to the *ius in bello*, in which he argued that assassination and the use of poison were illicit means of warfare as they would escalate hostilities beyond all boundaries, prevent reconciliation, and thus harm human society at large.[6] Vattel required that those responsible for such grave misconduct be punished by all nations as enemies of mankind. In his utilitarian view, the repression of the enemies of mankind was necessary to preserve a minimum level of security and tranquillity both at the domestic and international level.

Cicero's Invention of a Common Enemy of All

When Vattel drafted his *Droit des gens* in the 1750s, the enemy of mankind concept already had a long history. In particular, the definition of pirates and robbers as universal enemies had proved a long-standing topos in legal scholarship since Cicero, Vattel's favourite classical author.[7] Cicero first introduced the definition in his orations *In Verrem*, in which he aimed at ensuring the conviction of Gaius Verres, governor of Sicily. Cicero did not deal with piracy directly; however, in a celebrated and much-quoted statement he did accuse the defendant of acting just as pirates did, whom he

5 Vattel defined natural law in Ciceronian terms as a means to safeguard the elementary rules of human society. See 'Essai sur le fondement du droit naturel' in *DG* (Paul Pradier-Fodéré ed, Paris, 1863) 1–32, § VIII; Cicero, *De officiis* (Walter Miller trans, London, Heinemann, 1913) III, 5. Vattel further emphasised that by contributing to the preservation of human society natural law assisted human beings in attaining their true end, that is, happiness: Vattel, 'Essai sur le fondement du droit naturel', § XXIV.

6 *DG*, III, §§ 155–156. A similar argument was later asserted by Immanuel Kant in *Zum ewigen Frieden* (first published 1795, Wilhelm Weischedel ed, Frankfurt am Main, Suhrkamp, 1977) Sixth Preliminary Article.

7 Cicero, *In Verrem* (Albert C Clarck ed, Oxford, Clarendon, 1917) II, IV, 8, § 21; Cicero, *De officiis*, III, 29. On the importance of Cicero for Vattel, see Emer de Vattel, Letter to Frédéric Ostervald, 7 November 1746 in Edouard Béguelin, 'En souvenir de Vattel' in *Recueil de travaux offert par la Faculté de Droit de l'Université de Neuchâtel à la Société Suisse des Juristes à l'occasion de sa réunion à Neuchâtel, 15–17 Septembre 1929* (Neuchâtel, Attinger, 1929) 35–176, 64; Emer de Vattel, Letter to Johann Heinrich Samuel Formey, 14 December 1764 in *Varnhagen Collection* (Jagiellonian Library, Kraków) 270; Emer de Vattel, Letter to Johann Heinrich Samuel Formey, 21 September 1765 in *Varnhagen Collection* (Jagiellonian Library, Kraków) 270.

defined as *communes hostes omnium*, 'common enemies of all'.[8] He defined pirates in such terms because they acted for profit rather than political motives and therefore tended to attack ships indiscriminately. As they despised all law and morality and refused to live in a well-ordered commonwealth, they formed unlawful robber states for the sake of crime.[9] Unlike the 'just and lawful enemies' (*iusti et legitimi hostes*)[10] against whom war should be waged according to the rituals of the *ius fetiale*, pirates were right-less criminals undeserving of mercy.[11] In a famous and influential passage in the *De officiis*, Cicero pursued a similar argument by contending that since pirates did not observe either the laws of war or any moral standards, oaths taken with them do not have to be observed.[12]

Although Cicero characterised pirates as 'common enemies of all' triggering universal hostility, he certainly did not imply that all nations were authorised or bound to repress them. Nor was there any need to call on all nations to co-operate in anti-piracy measures, for the Romans already dominated the Mediterranean and did not require any assistance to prevail over the pirates. Quite the contrary, Cicero was not interested in calling for large-scale mobilisation of all nations against piracy because once general alliances had been formed, they could be used to challenge not only the pirates but also the Romans. Moreover, Cicero did not mention any form of collective action as he did not consider piracy as a special offence with ramifications at the international level, but simply as robbery on the high seas, and hence in his eyes the repression of piracy remained a matter for the individual polities to deal with.[13] Further, pirates, even if

[8] According to Cicero, Verres had broken his allegiance to the Roman Republic and had committed grave crimes both in Italy and the Asian provinces: Cicero, *In Verrem*, II, IV, 8, § 21 and I, I, 1, § 3.

[9] Cicero, *Philippicae* (David R Shackleton Bailey trans, Harvard University Press, 2009) IV, 6; Cicero, *De finibus* (Leighton D Reynolds trans, Oxford, Clarendon, 1998) III, 67, 69.

[10] Cicero, *De officiis*, III, 29.

[11] The dichotomy pirate *versus* lawful enemy was later consolidated by Pomponius and Ulpian in the following terms: 'Those are enemies (*hostes*) who declare war against us, or against whom we publicly declare war; others are robbers (*latrones*) or brigands (*praedones*)' (*Digesta* 50.16.118) [Pomp. *lib. II ad Q. Mucium*]; 'Enemies are those against whom the Roman people have publicly declared war, or who themselves have declared war against the Roman people; others are called robbers, or brigands' (*Digesta* 49.15.24) [Ulp. *lib. I inst.*]. The standard Latin edition of Justinian's *Digest* is *Digesta Iustiniani Augusti* in *Corpus iuris civilis* (Paul Krüger and Theodor Mommsen eds, Berlin, Weidmann, 1911) vol 1. An English translation of this edition has been provided by SP Scott, *The Civil Law, Including the Twelve Tables* (Cincinnati, Central Trust Company, 1932).

[12] Cicero, *De officiis*, III, 29.

[13] Roman lawyers indeed characterised the 'pirate' (*pirata*) as a mere 'robber' (*latro* or *praedo*) on the high seas. In legal texts, piracy and robbery were frequently associated as

organised as outright criminal societies or pirate states, might be hostile to many but in fact were no enemies of mankind in its entirety. They actually enjoyed strong support at least from those who provided shelter to them and bought or sold their booty. Cicero himself admitted that many coastal communities lived on or drew some income deriving from piratical activities, and that piracy was thus intertwined with local political and economic powers.[14]

The Latin genitive *omnium* in the expression *communes hostes omnium* may well be translated as 'of all humans', especially in Cicero's philosophical and universalist prose. This is indeed the meaning that *omnium* bore when he argued that there are things and duties common 'to all'. Later, Roman jurists familiar with Stoic philosophy in the same vein defined the sea and the air as 'things common to all' (*res communes omnium*), that is, common to all humans, under the law of nature.[15] However, notwithstanding the general and abstract meaning of the term *omnium*, the concrete meaning remained problematic as it could be interpreted differently according to the circumstances and Cicero's agenda.[16] When speaking of the pirate as the enemy of 'all', he might mean all human beings; or all citizens of the Roman Republic and its provinces, most of which had access to either the Mediterranean or the Black Sea and were familiar with piracy; or simply all seafarers. The meaning of Cicero's concept of a 'common enemy of all' remained uncertain, and so were its legal implications, if any.

What is safe to say is that although Cicero put forward a notion of universal hostility he did not invent or even hint at universal jurisdiction, for he never mentioned the issue of jurisdiction over the crime of piracy or a moral duty to repress pirates. With hindsight, it can be contended that the Romans de facto exercised what today is called universal jurisdiction in their struggle against the pirates, in particular after Pompey was granted extraordinary powers through the *lex Gabinia* of 67 BC, but Cicero did not

essentially constituting the same kind of offence. See, for instance, *Digesta* 13.6.18pr (Gai. *lib. IX ad ed. prov.*); *Digesta* 49.15.19.2 (Paul. *lib. XVI ad Sab.*).

14 Cicero, *In Verrem*, II, IV, 8, § 21. Cicero argued that Verres 'behaved just as the pirates are wont to behave. They are the general enemies of all mankind; but nonetheless, there are some people whom they make friends, not only sparing them but enriching them with stolen wealth. They select, for this purpose, the inhabitants of conveniently situated towns, where it is often desirable and sometimes necessary for them to put in'.

15 Cicero, *De officiis*, I, 16. See also Justinian's *Institutiones*, 2.1.1.

16 The ambiguity of the term *omnium* with reference to 'things common to all' in the Roman law has been stressed by Martin Josef Schermaier, '*Res communes omnium*. The History of an Idea from Greek Philosophy to Grotian Jurisprudence' (2009) 30 *Grotiana* 20, 21.

deal with the legal ramifications of these practices.[17] Plausibly, he regarded anti-piracy operations more as a measure to safeguard Roman interests rather than as an attempt to protect all nations from international offenders.

A further problem with Cicero's concept of a 'common enemy of all' is that in the first century BC pirates were not necessarily outlaws or mavericks acting for profit. From a military viewpoint, in times when a sharp legal differentiation between 'regular' and 'irregular' warfare was not conceivable, piracy was hardly condemnable as illegal. It is well known, and it has been emphasised in legal scholarship at least since Grotius and Hobbes, that ancient peoples actually tended to view pirates as heroes rather than as offenders.[18] In addition, pirate organisations in ancient times might claim political legitimacy and possess a military strength such that allowed them to challenge the Roman navy in open battles. Those who Cicero branded as maritime bandits might well be seen from a different angle as fighters against Roman hegemony. These struggles sometimes escalated into outright wars, as is witnessed by the use of the word *bellum*, meaning 'public war', and *hostes*, meaning 'public enemies', even by Roman historians reporting on the conflicts. The term they employed to refer to these events was indeed 'piratical wars', and this indicated that they at least differentiated between pirates acting for private gain (straightforwardly assimilated with common robbers, or *latrones*) and pirates acting for political motives (partly assimilated with lawful public enemies, or *hostes*).[19] For instance, Mithridates, the King of Pontus, clearly remained a legitimate king and public enemy of the Romans although Roman historians called him a pirate.

---

[17] For a detailed discussion of the *lex Gabinia*, see Lucia Monaco, *Persecutio piratarum* (Naples, Jovene, 1996).

[18] Philip de Souza, *Piracy in the Graeco-Roman World* (CUP, 1999) 17; Hugo Grotius, *De iure belli ac pacis libri tres* (first published 1625, Francis W Kelsey trans, Washington, Carnegie Endowment, 1913) III, 3, § 2; Thomas Hobbes, *De cive* (first published 1642, Richard Tuck ed, CUP, 1998) III, 14.

[19] The term *bellum piraticum* was used for instance by Marcus Velleius Paterculus, *Historiarum ad M. Vinicium consulem libri duo* (Frederick W Shipley trans, Harvard University Press, 1979) II, 33; Plutarch, *Agesilaus and Pompey* in *Parallel Lives* (Bernadotte Perrin ed, London, Heinemann, 1914–26) vol 5, XXX; Tacitus, *Annales* (John Jackson trans, London, Heinemann, 1925–37) vol 4, XV, 25; Lucius Annaeus Florus, *Epitome de Tito Livio bellorum omnium annorum DCC libri* (Edward S Forster trans, London, Heinemann, 1929) I, 41. This tradition persisted in the Middle Ages, for instance in the definition of war by Isidore of Sevilla: 'Bella itaque dicuntur interna, externa, servilia, socialia, piratica' [Isidore of Seville, *Etymologiarum sive originum libri XX* (Stephen A Barney ed, CUP, 2010) XVIII, 1].

Despite Cicero's frequent use of a cosmopolitan vocabulary and his attempt to pass himself off as the advocate of all nations, his cosmopolitanism remained abstract and ambiguous. And in any case it was of little practical significance for international relations as Cicero's cosmopolitanism was situated less at the level of law and politics than that of ethics and metaphysics. Statements like 'we must conceive of this whole universe as one commonwealth of which both gods and men are members', and 'there is no human being of any race who ... cannot attain to virtue' demanded commitment from humans as moral, not political subjects.[20] Incidentally, when Cicero discussed moral obligations he made clear that nearness, benevolence, and solidarity were due primarily to relatives, friends, and fellow-countrymen, in that order,[21] but not necessarily due to foreigners. Also, in his view, assistance to foreigners and compliance with foreign allegiances constituted less of a duty than a means of pursuing glory and greatness, especially in the international sphere, where the Roman people 'by defending [their] allies had gained dominion over the whole world'.[22] Whereas Cicero thought of mankind as a unified whole, it was structured as a hierarchical order of which the Romans had turned out to be the legitimate rulers thanks to 'just wars' and the favour of the gods.[23]

The issue of war made clear that although he depicted himself as a 'citizen of the world' (*civis totius mundi*),[24] Cicero was actually far away from conferring any legal and political relevance to cosmopolitan arguments. He partly seemed to implement his idea of a 'universal society of mankind' as he demanded that belligerents wage war in a civilised manner, particularly by complying with the customs of the *ius fetiale* such as *rerum repetitio* and *belli declaratio*.[25] He also affirmed that 'the only excuse for going to war is that we may live in peace unharmed',[26] and that 'those wars are unjust which are undertaken without provocation. For only a war

20 Cicero, *De legibus* (Clinton W Keyes trans, London, Heinemann, 1928) I, 23 and 31; Cicero, *De finibus*, III, 19.

21 Cicero, *De officiis*, I, 17; III, 17.

22 Cicero, *De re publica* (Clinton W Keyes trans, London, Heinemann, 1928) III, 23.

23 Cicero, *De legibus*, I, 23.

24 Ibid I, 61.

25 For a survey on the *ius fetiale* with an exhaustive bibliography see Karl-Heinz Ziegler, *Das Völkerrecht der Römischen Republik* in Hildegard Temporini (ed), *Aufstieg und Niedergang der Römischen Welt* (Berlin – New York, de Gruyter, 1972) vol 1, 68–114. An investigation of the use of the *ius fetiale* by modern lawyers has been provided by Virgilio Ilari, *L'interpretazione storica del diritto di guerra romano fra tradizione romanistica e giusnaturalismo* (Milan, Giuffrè, 1991).

26 Cicero, *De officiis*, I, 11.

waged for revenge or defence can actually be just'.[27] Yet these statements represent pure rhetorical concessions considering what Cicero often envisaged when addressing the topic of war, that is, furthering the imperialist policy of the Roman republic for the benefit of the *equites*.[28]

> Those, then, whose office is to look after the interests of the state ... must strive, too, by whatever means they can, in peace or war, to advance the state in power, in territory, and in revenues.[29]

Beyond all rhetoric, the Ciceronian ideal of war was represented by the struggle for empire between great powers, and this was the only form of conflict that he believed should be regulated.[30] Yet he did not really believe that regulation could occur through the observance of outdated legal or religious rituals like the *ius fetiale*, which had long fallen into disuse and which he only mentioned for the record, but rather through a common ethic of war grounded on military honour and shared by the restricted club of those who could afford to compete for glory. True, Cicero was aware that this ethical code was not enforceable and sometimes must be overridden, as in the wars against Carthage; that the *pax Romana* was imposed to a large extent by unlawful violence; and that these imperial wars had been the very cause for the once effective *ius fetiale* to turn into a literary relic. Cicero clearly admitted all of this. Nevertheless, engaged as he was in defending the interests of the Romans, of the *equites*, and of his clients, he was not at pains to leave aside the moral principles he proclaimed to judge imperialist policies simply depending on who carried them out.[31]

From a conceptual viewpoint, two main factors can be identified in Cicero's definition of a 'common enemy of all': first, that he waged war without legitimate authority; second, that he mainly acted for profit and did not choose his victims depending on political, social or ethnic criteria. For Cicero, the figure of the pirate was symbolic of all those who encroached upon justice and law, endangering the security and safety of the 'society of mankind', which tended to coincide with the Roman people and his allies. This conception was instrumental and highly flexible. Whilst Cicero

[27] Cicero, *De re publica*, III, 35. This otherwise lost passage is reported by Isidore of Seville, *Etymologiarum sive originum libri XX*, XVIII, I, 2–4.

[28] Peter Rose, 'Cicero and the Rhetoric of Imperialism. Putting the Politics back into Political Rhetoric' (1995) 13 (4) *Rhetorica* 359.

[29] Cicero, *De officiis*, II, 24.

[30] Ibid I, 12.

[31] Rose, *Cicero and the Rhetoric of Imperialism*, 388–90.

labelled Verres as a universal enemy, he was defending Marcus Fonteius, a contested governor of the Gallia Transalpina, along with other notorious exploiters of the provinces who took care not to annoy Roman citizens.[32]

From Common Enemies of All to Enemies of Mankind

Equating the good of mankind with the political and economic interest of Rome became commonplace in Roman historiography on the *bella piratica*, for example in Appian's *Roman History* and Florus' *Epitome*, where pirates were branded as those who broke the natural bond uniting the entirety of humankind.[33] Appian and Florus were less interested in making a point about the universal threat of piracy than in disqualifying Mithridates, implacable rival of the Romans in the East Mediterranean, whom they accused of supporting piracy and hence of being a foe of the 'society of mankind'.[34] Given that recent research has indicated that the allegation about Mithridates' piratical warfare is dubious,[35] his case confirms that the main aim of writers in using the universal hostility argument was to push their agenda and deprive their adversaries of political legitimacy and acknowledgment.[36]

Partisanship, polysemy, and ambiguity affected the universal enemy concept from the outset. Appian and Florus aside, a certain vagueness also characterised similar narratives by Pliny the Elder, who labelled Nero as an enemy of mankind due to his tyrannical rule, and by the Roman emperor Constantius II, who applied the same label to magicians and predictors as he ordered them to be tortured and crucified to prevent them from spreading misbelief and superstition.[37] In these accounts, the enemy of mankind was seen as an enemy of the citizens of Rome rather than an actual universal enemy. Semantic complexity grew further in the first centuries AD as writers perceived humankind no longer as a mere philosophical idea,

---

32 Ibid 371.

33 Appian, *Roman History* (Horace White trans, London, Heinemann, 1912–3) XII; Florus, *Epitome*, I, 40–41.

34 Florus, *Epitome*, I, 41.

35 de Souza, *Piracy in the Graeco-Roman World*, 116–118.

36 Ibid 36 f.

37 Pliny the Elder, *Natural History* (Harris Rackham trans, London, Heinemann, 1942) vol 2, VII, 46; *Codex Theodosiani* (Theodor Mommsen and Paul M Meyer eds, Berlin, Weidmann 1905) 9.16.6, a. 358. These instances have been reported by Marie Theres Fögen, '*Inimici humani generis*. Menschheitsfeinde und Glaubensfreunde in der Spätantike' in Laurent Mayali and Maria M Mart (eds), *Of Strangers and Foreigners* (Berkeley, Robbins Collection, 1993) 4, 12.

but a real entity in light of Christology. They began to merge the Ciceronian notion of a 'common enemy of all' with that – by then markedly Christian – of an 'enemy of mankind' proper (*hostis humani generis*). Authors such as Lactantius and John Chrysostom began to discuss the enemy of mankind concept in a moral-theological sense with reference to the devil, thereby giving rise to a commonplace of the Middle Ages.[38] Such readings conferred a religious and universalist imprint on the concept and raised its polemical character, for the enemy of mankind now constituted an existential threat to the human community and its normative order as instituted by God. It is not surprising that one of the first to employ the enemy of mankind notion in the modern period was a religious personality like Cardinal Reginald Pole in his refutation of Machiavelli.[39] In the eyes of the Archbishop of Canterbury, the Florentine deserved being characterised as a foe of the entire humanity as he denied all law, morals, and religion.

The convergence of theological, philosophical, and juridical elements used with discriminatory function had repercussions for the modern vision of piracy, beginning from the first definition of the pirate as a *hostis humani generis* in sixteenth century admiralty law – a definition resorted to by Sir Edward Coke in his *Institutes*.[40] And the same theological background can be recognised in the use of the enemy of mankind concept by another English writer, John Locke in his *Second Treatise of Government*, in which the universalist discourse merged with the theoretical foundation of domestic political power. It is significant that Locke defined not pirates, but tyrants and anarchists as the enemies of mankind.[41] So by 'enemy of mankind' he meant less a truly universal enemy than the enemy of a given society or polity. To be sure, using the vocabulary of universal enmity for the sake of internal politics was not a novelty, and it was not surprising in a time in which, despite increasing geographic discoveries, mankind as such largely remained an object of confused or incoherent speculation. This seemed to be the case for Locke, who had little difficulty practising slave trade while preaching universal human rights.[42]

---

38 Lactantius, *Divinae institutionae*, II, 16, §§ 20–21, cited in Marie Theres Fögen, *'Inimici humani generis'*, 14; John Chrysostom, *Expositiones in psalmos*, XLIV, 1, cited in Marie Theres Fögen, *'Inimici humani generis'*, 15.

39 Reginald Pole, *Apologia ad Carolum Quintum*, XXX, cited in Heinrich Lutz, *Ragione di stato und Christliche Staatsethik im 16. Jahrhundert* (Münster, Aschendorff, 1961) 55.

40 Edward Coke, *Institutes of the Lawes of England* (first published 1628, Clark, NJ, Lawbook Exchange, 2001) Third Part, XLIX.

41 John Locke, *Two Treatises of Government* (first published 1690, Peter Laslett ed, CUP, 1988) Second Treatise, II, 11.

42 Barbara Arneil, 'Trade, Plantations, and Property: John Locke and the Economic Defense of Colonialism' (1994) 55 *Journal of the History of Ideas* 591.

Conceptual ambiguity around the enemy of mankind concept even increased in the mid-eighteenth century as the term 'mankind' or *humanité* gradually lost its link to ancient ethics and to Christology to be recovered by Enlightenment thinkers, who upheld the universalist implications of the term while dropping the theological aspect.[43] It was at that stage that the Latin expression *hostis humani generis*, translated into vernacular as 'enemy of mankind', *ennemi du genre humain*, or *Feind der Menschheit*, drew the attention of engaged writers and was commonly used in political and literary debates. Enlightenment philosophers, pamphleteers, and politicians anxious to overthrow fallacious philosophical doctrines as well as tyrannical governments by the power of universal human reason proved particularly eager to brandish the enemy of mankind label against their political and private adversaries.[44] Those making use of the label in this way included Rousseau and Robespierre.[45] Yet as much as these purported 'friends of humanity' found the enemy of mankind label rhetorically appealing and effective, they shrank from dealing with its problematic aspects, which revolved around the question of who was entitled to declare someone a universal enemy. Just as Cicero assumed that the enemies of the Romans were enemies of all, Enlightenment writers took for granted that the enemies of, say, revolutionary France must be the advocates of tyranny and thus the enemies of humanity as a whole. This was the logic applied by Diderot in his 1775 statement that those rising against the general will of the nation should be regarded as 'enemies of mankind'.[46] A similar argument grounded on the allegedly absolute right of revolution lay behind the 1793 declaration by the *Convention nationale* of William Pitt as an 'enemy of mankind'.

It was in this scenario, largely dominated by the faith in universal reason and morals, that Vattel, like his contemporaries, asserted that those

---

[43] Hans Erich Bödecker, 'Menschheit' in Reinhard Koselleck (ed), *Geschichtliche Grundbegriffe* (Stuttgart, Klett – Cotta, 1982) vol 3, 1087–90; Henri Duranton, 'Humanité' in Rolf Reichardt and Hans-Jürgen Lüsebrink (eds), *Handbuch politisch-sozialer Grundbegriffe in Frankreich 1680–1820* (Munich, Oldenbourg, 2000) vol 8, 1–51.

[44] On the use of the enemy of mankind concept in revolutionary rhetoric, see Dan Edelstein, *The Terror of Natural Right. Republicanism, the Cult of Nature, and the French Revolution* (University of Chicago Press, 2009) 40–42.

[45] Jean-Jacques Rousseau, Letter to Jean le Rond d'Alembert, 20 March 1758 in Jean-Jacques Rousseau, *Œuvres complètes* (Bernard Gagnebin ed, Paris, Gallimard, 1995) vol 5, 1, 34; Maximilien Robespierre, *Rapport fait au nom du Comité de salut public sur la situation politique de la République*, 27 brumaire an II (17 November 1793) in Marc Bouloiseau and Albert Soboul (eds), *Œuvres de Maximilien Robespierre* (Ivry, Phénix, 2000) vol 10, 167, 176.

[46] Denis Diderot, 'Droit naturel' in Denis Diderot and Jean-Baptiste le Rond D'Alembert (eds), *Encyclopédie, ou Dictionnaire raisonné des sciences, des arts et des métiers* (first published 1751–80, Elmsford, NY, Pergamon Press, 1985) vol 5, 116, §§ 8 and 9.

who breached the most elementary moral and legal rules shared by all reasonable beings, in particular as these rules were laid down in the law of nature and nations, ought to be treated as enemies of mankind. However, Vattel used the enemy of mankind concept in a far more systematic and rigorous manner than the *philosophes* and pamphleteers, for he, as a jurist, attempted to construct a rationale for the concept by establishing an analogy between the violation of the most elementary rules of the law of nations and the crime of piracy. To this end, though, Vattel needed stronger arguments than Cicero could provide.

The Dichotomy of Piracy and Privateering and Its Problematic Implementation

In the first two centuries of the Imperial Age piracy remained confined almost exclusively to the Red and Black Seas due to the strong control exercised in the Mediterranean area by the Roman fleets.[47] It proliferated again at the beginning of the third century AD as Sarmatians and Goths started raiding the Mediterranean, announcing the incipient decadence of the Empire. After the collapse of Roman rule, by contrast, it was especially coastal populations of Italy, Southern France, and Spain, who preyed on the ships involved in the trade with Africa and the Orient.[48] Subsequently, between the eighth and the eleventh centuries, Arab and Saracen piratical actions in the Western Mediterranean took on the form of outright military expeditions with incursions into the hinterland. Such large-scale piracy was to become a constant during the Crusades, although in the first stages it was contained by Italian and Provencal ships patrolling the Mediterranean; on the other hand, crusaders' warfare also occasioned the escalation of maritime war and a consequent revival of piracy on both sides.[49]

At the very time of the Crusades there occurred the most important development in the history of the law of piracy: the differentiation between piracy and privateering. It emerged in the early thirteenth century as jurists attempted to regulate the conflicts between Italian maritime republics struggling for commercial predominance.[50] To this end, the

---

47 Cesare Maria Moschetti, 'Pirateria' in Francesco Calasso (ed), *Enciclopedia del diritto* (Milan, Giuffrè, 1958–95) vol 33, 873, 874.

48 Ibid 875.

49 Ibid. See also Fernand Braudel, *La Méditerranée et le monde méditerranéen à l'époque de Philippe II* (first published 1949, Paris, Armand Colin, 1966) vol 2, 195.

50 Moschetti, 'Pirateria', 891.

Roman law dichotomy between lawful enemies (*hostes*) and unlawful enemies (*piratae, latrones, praedones*) was reasserted to back the argument that whereas piracy committed for private gain in principle is unlawful, it becomes a lawful act of public war if commissioned by political authorities.[51] Hence, the maritime republics might grant special commissions to private ship-owners for them to organise military operations, and these entrepreneurs were allowed to retain part or the whole of the prize in return for the service provided. In due course, a doctrine developed according to which privateering in wartime fell within 'general reprisals', while privateering in peacetime was categorised as a form of 'special reprisal'. The latter occurred when private citizens were attacked and robbed by strangers and, after having unsuccessfully asked the aggressors' prince for reparation or satisfaction, were authorised by their own sovereigns to retaliate by assaulting any ship flying the flag of the wrongdoer's home country. Whilst the doctrine of special and general reprisal gradually fell into disuse, the essential distinction between piracy and privateering would be retained for centuries until the abolition of privateering by the Paris Declaration of 1856.[52] Vattel also upheld the distinction in his *Droit des gens*.[53]

Yet because abuses of sovereign commissions were frequent in the Middle Ages and Early-Modern Times, privateering, in its form of general as well as special reprisal, easily degenerated into mere piracy despite the monitions of the legal doctrine. Some regulation was provided by custom and by the rules collected in the *Consolato del mare*, but they were scarcely effective given the political and economic stakes of privateering warfare at the international level.[54] Later, in a more favourable political scenario, the matter was addressed in Louis XIV's *Ordonnance de la marine*, which reasserted the differentiation between the crime of piracy and lawful privateering under a prince's commission (*lettre de marque ou de représaille*).[55] Abuses still occurred at that stage, but with the nation state now taking on

51 Ibid.

52 *Declaration Respecting Maritime Law, signed at Paris*, 16 April 1856, 115 CTS 1–3, art 2.

53 DG, III, 15, § 229.

54 Giuseppe Maria Casaregi (ed), *Il consolato del mare* (Lucca, 1720) chs 80, 99, 137, 225–9, 287. The *Consolato del mare* was a collection of ancient and medieval maritime laws compiled since the eleventh century. Originally written in Catalan, the *Consolato del mare* was translated into several languages and became an authoritative text on maritime law in all European countries.

55 *Ordonnance de la marine* (first published 1681, Paris, Les Libraires Associés, 1755) bk III, tit IX–X.

the monopoly of the use of legitimate force, the traditional distinction between piracy and privateering rested on a firmer footing. Moreover, the distinction gained additional significance in the Modern Age: thanks to developments in the laws of war, privateers might enjoy belligerent rights like regular troops in land warfare.[56] The *Ordonnance* also set out important rules on prize, notably the provision that even neutral ships could be rightfully seized if they were loaded with goods belonging to the enemy.[57] The rules of prize had indeed become a thorny matter because of the escalation of piracy/privateering in the Atlantic within the great powers' colonial struggle.

On the other hand, the relevance of piracy/privateering to the struggle for colonial power made the international legal settlement of piracy disputes highly problematic. Interference of politics in the international law of piracy grew acute in the late sixteenth century as the English, French, and Dutch privateers preying on Spanish shipping claimed to be waging lawful warfare, while the Spaniards treated them as pirates. Still, writers on international law usually upheld a normative stance and insisted on the general principle that a sovereign commission was a necessary and sufficient requirement for waging war.[58]

Vattel on the Law of Piracy

As Vattel dealt with piracy and privateering while drafting his *Droit des gens*, he left aside the problematic aspects and the geopolitical ramifications of the issue. He took a traditional formalist line and maintained a neat distinction between piracy and privateering. In his view, an official authorisation by the sovereign sufficed for civilians involved in sea warfare to qualify as public enemies and acquire the corresponding rights, including the right to retain a part of the booty.[59]

Vattel's justification of privateering can be put down to three factors that go beyond a simple reiteration of the classical formalist argument based on the requirement of the letter of marque. First, he justified war on the basis of a perfect 'right to security', which in turn stemmed from the nation's absolute duty of self-preservation.[60] Vattel argued that when the

56 *DG*, III, 15, § 226.
57 Ibid III, 9, §7.
58 See below Chapter 2.
59 *DG*, III, 15, § 229.
60 Ibid II, 4, § 49.

nation's self-preservation was at stake the entire population, usually to be spared from hostilities, may be required to take part in military operations, and in this case civilians might rightfully engage in privateering.[61] He welcomed the modern custom of protecting civilians from war operations and viewed this as a sign of civilisation. And yet, as a Swiss national, he put forward an idea of the domestic commonwealth as a nation at arms and maintained that the civilian population should join in war if military necessity so demanded.[62] This reasoning led Vattel not only to declare the lawfulness of privateering but also to vindicate the rights of partisans to take up arms in case of civil war or foreign invasion.[63] He saw privateering and partisan resistance as necessary means for small principalities and republics to defend themselves from the imperialist ambitions of the big international players. War might have turned into a game for the big powers of Europe, but remained an existential threat for the lesser states.

There was a second reason why Vattel justified privateering. Historically, privateering reached its climax in popularity and military success between the sixteenth and seventeenth centuries, during which privateers supported and authorised by the Protestant powers and France would assault Spanish vessels in the Atlantic. In the eyes of many contemporaries and historians, and later Vattel, privateering at the end of the sixteenth century represented the only way to tackle Spanish hegemony both in the colonies and on the Continent and prevent Spain from turning into a despotic 'universal monarchy'. This instance of a common struggle against alleged tyranny, religious extremism, and imperialism deeply impressed Vattel, who placed tyrants and warmongers like Charles V and Philip II into the bad lot of the 'enemies of mankind'.[64] Vattel believed that privateering represented an indispensable device to counter the overwhelming military force of despotic nations threatening international peace and freedom.

The pattern of a European coalition created for the sake of the equilibrium on the Continent as well as in the colonies was repeated in another event mentioned by Vattel, the Grand Alliance against Louis XIV in the Nine Years' War. Here again, a monarch was blamed by much of international public opinion for ruling despotically and promoting religious

---

[61] Ibid III, 15, § 226.

[62] By the 1750s, civilians' massive involvement in warfare was a far off memory and was recalled just by some obsolete expressions such as *courir sous*, which was still used in war declarations but no longer meant that all nationals were urged to attack the enemy. See *DG*, III, 15, § 227.

[63] Ibid III, 15, § 224; III, 18.

[64] Ibid II, 4, § 53; IV, 7, § 84.

radicalism. Louis' bad reputation since the revocation of the Edict of Nantes played a great part in the general hostility against him, but the Grand Alliance in itself was mainly politically motivated. The Sun King's expansionist foreign policy, be it truly imperialist or actually defensive in its purpose, triggered common concern throughout Europe, as French expansionism might jeopardise the territorial integrity of France's neighbours and Europe's balance of power altogether. As a result of this expansionist policy, the Sun King gained a place of honour in the *Droit des gens* among the 'enemies of mankind' and 'disturbers of the peace'.[65] Conversely, the allies were depicted as defenders of the freedom of Europe authorised to resort to any means necessary to counter Louis, including, in theory, privateering.

Yet, unlike in the anti-Spanish struggle, it was now the disturber of the peace himself, that is, Louis XIV, and not the members of the coalition, who mostly relied on privateering. He had to adopt this policy due to the precarious state of the French navy. Despite consistent financial and logistical efforts led by Jean-Baptiste Colbert, then finance minister and secretary of the navy, to make France a naval power, the imposing French navy was still broadly ineffective militarily at the end of the seventeenth century, and could hardly rival the English in sea warfare.[66] The Sun King thus began to employ corsairs systematically from the Nine Years War onwards.[67] They proved in fact a precious asset and constituted a threat to England until their main base, Dunkirk, was deprived of its fortifications with the Peace of Utrecht in 1713.[68] Even after 1713, privateers continued playing a significant role in French warfare under Louis XV's reign as the French navy was falling apart due to mismanagement, lack of funds, and the burden of the colonial struggle.

Louis' strategy of warfare indicated that privateering might be employed not only by weak and peaceful nations for the sake of self-defence and the preservation of international equilibrium, but also by great powers engaged in aggressive wars. This relativises the first point about Vattel's justification of privateering as a weapon of the lesser states: he certainly assumed that privateering mainly constituted an option for the militarily weak, but had no difficulty admitting that powerful monarchs might also use privateering whenever they needed, especially when the existence of their own state was at stake. The primary argument for legalising privateering

65 Ibid III, 3, § 44.

66 Derek McKay and Hamish M Scott, *The Rise of the Great Powers 1648–1815* (London – New York, Longman, 1983) 48, 95.

67 Ibid 48.

68 Ibid 65.

remained the right of every nation to self-preservation. Piratical acts instead were systematically unlawful because they were committed for the sake of private gain.

The third reason used by Vattel to justify privateering was its being practised by 'civilised nations', which thereby distinguished themselves from 'uncivilised' nations practising mere piracy. Here he was referring in particular to the Barbary corsairs, who had embodied a constant threat for Christian vessels in the Mediterranean for centuries. Historically, North African privateering appeared as a significant phenomenon as early as the eight century with Arab and Saracen raids in the Western Mediterranean, and developed throughout the time of the Crusades and of the *Reconquista*. In the aftermath of the Crusades most Mediterranean pirates were Christian – predominantly Italians, Spaniards, and Frenchmen – assailing both Muslim and Christian ships, but North African privateers regained momentum and made an important contribution to the Ottoman expansion in the aftermath of the Battle of Lepanto in 1571.[69] Their enterprises impressed generations of Europeans and remained a *topos* in European narratives even after the Great Turkish War, which signalled the beginning of Ottoman and Barbary decline.[70] Attacks by North African privateers then became more sporadic but continued throughout the eighteenth century until the French conquest of Algiers in 1830.

Barbary Corsairs

It was by reflecting on the Barbary issue that Vattel developed his enemy of mankind concept, which he thereafter applied to warmongers and other violators of the law of nations. More than fifty years after the Great Turkish War, however, the Barbary issue as described in the *Droit des gens* was no longer about sea-robbery proper but, more generally and more importantly, about enforcing international law and order. Vattel's main argument regarding North African privateers was that they intolerably threatened international peace and security and could not be stopped once and for all unless collective action was taken to punish them harshly. He thus called on all European nations to form a coalition with the task of annihilating the corsairs and re-establishing safety and security for traders and travellers in the Mediterranean. Moving beyond Cicero, he clearly

---

69 Moschetti, 'Pirateria'.

70 See below Part 1, Chapter 2.

stated that since pirates offended all nations and jeopardised international security, every state was allowed to repress and exterminate them if necessary.

> The Christian nations would be no less justifiable in forming a confederacy against the states of Barbary, in order to destroy those haunts of pirates, with whom the love of plunder, or the fear of just punishment, is the only rule of peace and war.[71]

It may be stressed that by calling on the 'Christian nations' to take action against Barbary Vattel was not reasserting traditional arguments about hostility and warfare between Christians and Muslims, or Europeans and Ottomans.[72] This once much-discussed hostility was no longer a source of concern for writers on international law around 1750. In mid-eighteenth century Europe, the Ottomans were more likely to be at the centre of public attention and curiosity for their culture and lifestyle than for their military power. This was particularly true in the French-speaking world, as the traditional alliance between the Ottomans and the French had favoured cultural exchange and contamination (*turqueries* were much fashionable around 1750, and Vattel himself seemed to follow the trend as he wore a turban in one of his portraits).[73] More importantly, Vattel in his *Droit des gens* gave the Ottomans a fairer treatment than they had received in many classical writings of the European tradition. If he remained critical of some specific aspect of the Ottomans' law of war, he preferred not to criticise them systematically on this point; nor did he deal with other delicate issues such as their 'dreadful despotism', already described by Montesquieu.[74] Vattel actually took trouble to understate the differences between Ottomans and Europeans and thereby give credibility to his project of a rational and universal law of nations.

A further reason for Vattel not to take issue with Ottoman responsibilities in North African privateering was that although the Barbary corsairs nominally were vassals of the Sublime Porte, they in fact enjoyed political

[71] *DG*, II, 6, § 78.

[72] Vattel's lay and universalist conception of international law can be seen at *DG*, II, 12, § 162.

[73] Fatma Müge Göçek, *East Encounters West. France and the Ottoman Empire in the Eighteenth Century* (OUP, 1987) 85; Frank Matthias Kammel, 'Gefährliche Heiden und gezähmte Exoten: Bemerkungen zum europäischen Türkenbild im 17. und frühen 18. Jahrhundert' in Ronald Asch, Wulf Eckart Voß, and Martin Wrede (eds), *Frieden und Krieg in der Frühen Neuzeit* (Munich, Wilhelm Fink, 2001) 503.

[74] Montesquieu, *De l'esprit des lois* (Victor Goldschmidt ed, Paris, Garnier-Flammarion, 1979) XI, 6.

autonomy.[75] Traditionally, they had waged war and signed international agreements beyond the Porte's commission, and had not shrunk from acting to the detriment of the Porte, sometimes by disrupting the relations between the Porte and the Christians. That the corsairs even made outright peace treaties – and not just truces – with the Europeans, is clear evidence of their political autonomy. It also shows a disregard for the Islamic international law principle, maintained by the Ottomans, that any cessation of hostilities with infidels cannot be stipulated for longer than ten years.[76] It is curious that, to preserve the Ottoman-French friendship, the Sultan Ahmet I explicitly allowed Henry IV to wage war against his vassals Algiers and Tunisia in the event that they assaulted France's shipping.

To be sure, the North African corsairs were not alone in terrorising the Mediterranean. Christians likewise practised piracy and made considerable profits from it, even in the heyday of the Barbary Republics. The Knights of Malta and St Stephen were highly organised and competed against the North African corsairs, who in turn established a flourishing exchange of captives and goods with the Europeans through the markets of Livorno and other coastal cities. This trade of slaves and prizes had far-reaching consequences and gave rise to a characteristic form of interdependency within the entire Mediterranean economy. In this context, Christian and Muslim pirates/privateers did not necessarily act based on religious and political motives, and often assaulted both Christian and Muslim ships indifferently.[77]

Privateering in the Mediterranean in the sixteenth and seventeenth centuries cannot be simplistically defined as a product of Ottoman expansion, nor as a result of the clash between Christianity and Islam. Rather, privateering spread thanks to the prosperity of Mediterranean commerce and the suspension of the *grande guerre* in this area following the Battle of Lepanto.[78] In the absence of large military confrontations, privateering turned frequently into piracy, being carried out from single towns rather than states, and much more for economic profit than political, religious,

75 Salvatore Bono, *Corsari nel Mediterraneo. Cristiani e musulmani fra guerra, schiavitù e commercio* (Milan, Mondadori, 1993) 23.

76 Jörg Manfred Mössner, *Die Völkerrechtspersönlichkeit und die Völkerrechtspraxis der Barbareskenstaaten* (Berlin, de Gruyter, 1968) 109–110.

77 The rich Venetian vessels were often the most coveted by both Christian and Muslim pirates (Braudel, *La Méditerranée*, 203), while the Venetians committed in turn acts of piracy in the Mediterranean. On the latter point see Daniel Goffman, *The Ottoman Empire and Early Modern Europe* (CUP, 2002) 157.

78 Braudel, *La Méditerranée*, 190.

or ideological interests. This was also true for Algiers, Tunis or Tripoli, which contributed to and benefited from the Ottoman expansion but clearly pursued an independent policy.[79]

Furthermore, since the focus of European politics was moving away from the Mediterranean to concentrate on other fronts or domestic religious strives, piracy in the Mediterranean area was by then perceived as a secondary problem by Europe's powers. The latter also hesitated to crack down on the Barbary corsairs, let alone engage in a collective struggle to this end, due to internal rivalries and the awareness that the strength of the North African fleets and the endemic nature of piratical activity in the Mediterranean made any plans of large-scale repression expensive and uncertain. As a consequence, the European states usually applied tolerant policies with North African privateering and privileged indirect means and negotiations over open military confrontations. Peace treaties were signed after every significant conflict, especially between the Regencies and the French, although they were recurrently broken on either side.[80]

The main actors in this scenario were merchants, both Christian and Muslim, unofficial intermediaries, and diplomats who had good connections both in Europe and Africa and earned large profits from trading captives and goods. The French consulate of Tunis was established as early as 1577, and the consuls were renowned by contemporary European observers for seeing to it that some captives be quickly returned and others not be returned at all.[81] The situation altered only by the end of the 1580s, when the diminishing ascendancy of the Porte over Algiers, evidenced by the weakness of the pashas and the growing power of the Janissaries, led to long-term political instability.[82] Piratical attacks then increased and France itself became a target for pirates acting outside of the pashas' control.

In general, beyond the rhetoric of the holy war popular both in Europe and North Africa, the confrontation in the Mediterranean in practice occurred on the footing of mutual recognition.[83] As long as the Barbary States maintained their political autonomy, European nations had to negotiate with them in complex ceremonials and ensure their agreement by means of allowances. To be sure, from the age of Louis XIV onwards the European powers began to claim a higher status, as can be inferred from

---

79 Ibid 194.

80 Heinz Duchhardt, *Balance of power und Pentarchie* (Paderborn, Schöningh, 1997) 193.

81 Mössner, *Die Völkerrechtspersönlichkeit*, 7; Braudel, *La Méditerranée*, 211.

82 Mössner, *Die Völkerrechtspersönlichkeit*, 10.

83 Christian Windler, *La diplomatie comme expérience de l'autre. Consuls Français au Maghreb (1700–1840)* (Geneva, Droz, 2002) 227–230.

new rituals and drafting of treaties, but there is evidence that this was a lengthy process. For instance, the custom of the Europeans conceding tributes (or 'presents', as the French and the British called them) to the North African republics maintained considerable political significance far into the eighteenth century and even later.[84] However much the political survival of the republics might have been facilitated by inter-European dissent, they long remained regarded as equal contractual partners of the European nations.

Vattel spoke out against this state of affairs. He complained that the North African corsairs not only committed piracy, but specifically targeted shipping flying flags of militarily weak states which were not able to retaliate. He also hinted at the open secret that some European states had been maintaining ambiguous relations with the corsairs to ensure a privileged position in the Mediterranean to the detriment of other powers.[85] These states did not care about attacks launched by the corsairs on other Christian states' shipping, and rather promoted such attacks. Nevertheless, Vattel did not dare explicitly denounce any European power. Especially interested in the perspective of a diplomatic assignment at the court of Louis XV, he did not mention France's traditional links to the Ottomans and the Barbary Republics.[86] To avoid displeasing any power, Vattel restrained himself to a brief and apparently harmless notation in which he remarked that the corsairs were 'wise enough to respect those who are most able to chastise them', and that some nations which knew well how to protect their commerce were 'not sorry' to see other nations being prevented from trading.[87] However critical of those European powers which sponsored and took advantage of North African privateering, Vattel put a purely moral blame on these powers. Legal responsibility uniquely lay with the corsairs despite European sponsorship.

Vattel thus focused on the Barbary corsairs' criminality. In his opinion, they were liable for piracy as they performed their attacks solely for profit, without any political motive, legal ground or any pretext whatsoever. Regardless of whether they acted under sovereign commission, they qualified as common robbers, committing brigandage instead of waging war.

---

84 Ibid 485 f.

85 Great Britain and the Netherlands especially benefited from the Barbary corsairs' attacks on Spanish shipping. Accordingly, Godfrey Fisher has reported that Great Britain had relatively peaceful relations with Barbary from 1682 onwards: Godfrey Fisher, *The Barbary Legend: War, Trade, and Piracy in North Africa, 1415–1830* (Oxford, Clarendon, 1957) 11.

86 On Vattel's professional expectations, see Béguelin, *En souvenir de Vattel*, 52.

87 *DG*, II, 6, § 78.

> Legitimate and formal warfare must be carefully distinguished from those illegitimate and informal wars, or rather predatory expeditions, undertaken either without lawful authority or without apparent cause, as likewise without the usual formalities, and solely with a view to plunder. Grotius relates several instances of the latter. Such were the enterprises of the *grandes compagnies* which had assembled in France during the wars with the English,—armies of banditti, who ranged about Europe, purely for spoil and plunder: such were the cruises of the *buccaneers*, without commission, and in time of peace; and such in general are the depredations of pirates. To the same class belong almost all the expeditions of the Barbary corsairs: though authorized by a sovereign, they are undertaken without any apparent cause, and from no other motive than the lust of plunder. These two species of war, I say,—the lawful and the illegitimate,—are to be carefully distinguished, as the effects and the rights arising from each are very different.[88]

To some extent, Vattel's argument about the lack of political motives behind Barbary privateering might sound more tenable in the eighteenth century, given that the corsairs by then acted entirely on their own and no longer committed to Ottoman policies, than it was until the Great Turkish War. However, the fact remains that the Barbary republics around 1750 were sovereign states, entitled to issue letters of marque, and contending that they still were at war with all Christians although the Ottomans no longer were. Legally, no more arguments were required to justify the corsairs' position. As the two fundamental conditions for lawful military action at sea, that is, state authorisation and political motives, were allegedly present, attacks by North African vessels counted as privateering, not piracy. From their perspective, Vattel's charges could be dismissed as based on a double standard discriminating against them: while he justified European privateering as an instrument of rightful self-preservation, he qualified Barbary privateering as a heinous international offence to be punished by all nations. Vattel maintained this view despite its incoherence, as he needed a notorious example of, say, piracy to support his broader theory of the repression of international crimes. With the Ottoman Empire declining and the Europeans taking over the Mediterranean, the Barbary corsairs had become an easy target.

[88] Ibid III, 4, § 67 (emphasis in original).

CHAPTER TWO

THE BARBARY ISSUE IN EARLY-MODERN LEGAL DOCTRINE

This chapter gives an account of the doctrinal alternatives available to Vattel in developing the enemy of mankind concept and his doctrine of the repression of international crimes. To this end, the chapter presents a set of relevant views on the Barbary issue from the late sixteenth century until the mid-eighteenth century. It demonstrates that publicists in that period nearly unanimously embraced a tolerant and pluralist international legal paradigm which accorded the Barbary corsairs lawful enemy status. The paradigm first emerged when French jurist Jean Bodin, in his *Six livres de la République* of 1576, declared Barbary warfare to be legal and essentially different from piracy as it was carried out under sovereign commission.[1] In the view of Bodin and his followers, the Barbary corsairs might be morally responsible for assaulting Christian vessels without a just cause, and even be labelled as 'enemies of mankind' as a result, but they nevertheless qualified as lawful belligerents in point of law. This widely acknowledged opinion attests to the existence of an international legal pluralism of the laws of war in early-modern doctrine. When Vattel put forward his doctrine of the repression of international crimes for the sake of the 'common security of nations', he moved away from this pluralist tradition.

The chapter begins by illustrating Bodin's paradigmatic legalisation of Barbary warfare, which largely fitted with the traditional policies of France, in particular its alliance with the Ottomans. It then presents Gentili's ambiguous position, which lay in between stigmatisation and tolerance towards Barbary, in the context of his activity as a practitioner. Gentili oscillated between sovereignty-based arguments apologetic of Barbary warfare, and the just war doctrine which disqualified it from being a legitimate form of warfare on the basis that it lacked a just cause. The chapter then describes Grotius' original attempt to circumvent Gentili's recourse to the just war doctrine by means of historical arguments. Grotius postulated that the conflict between the Barbary corsairs and the Europeans followed the rules of the 'ancient law of nations', according to

1 Jean Bodin, *Six livres de la République* (first published 1576, Aalen, Scientia, 1977).

which all warring parties had the right to enslave captives. Therefore, the corsairs qualified as lawful belligerents although they appeared to lack a just cause for war.

The chapter goes on to analyse Pufendorf's approach. It argues that while Pufendorf tended to legalise Barbary warfare based on the sovereignty-argument, this argument became largely ineffective within his natural law system as a result of his idea of the just enemy's 'unlimited right' to harm the unjust enemy. This was problematic because, lacking a common superior, both the Barbary corsairs and their opponents might claim to be fighting a just war and push hostilities to extremes. The chapter then turns to Heinrich and Samuel von Cocceji, authors of an influential commentary on Grotius' *De iure belli ac pacis*.[2] Heinrich was among the few writers radically to disqualify Barbary privateering, yet his son Samuel responded by providing an insightful treatment of the concept of piracy in which he aligned himself with Bodin and Grotius. However, the potential of Samuel von Cocceji's, like Pufendorf's, tolerant stance was conditioned by the 'unlimited right' concept, which might justify total warfare and obliterate any restraints on the conduct of hostilities. Samuel von Cocceji however attempted to evade this problem by arguing that between the Barbary corsairs and the Christians there existed a state of 'perpetual war' within which the warring parties' responsibilities could not be determined. Here, the notions of just cause and just enemy, and hence of 'unlimited right' as well, could hardly apply. The chapter further presents the tolerant view of Cornelius van Bynkershoek, who, like Grotius, legalised Barbary warfare based on sovereignty and historical arguments. Both a scholar and a practitioner, Bynkershoek took a pragmatic approach and straightforwardly discarded any consideration of the corsairs' lacking a just cause for war.

Bodin and the Sovereignty Argument

Bodin's Initial Reliance on a Thick Definition of the 'Well-Ordered Commonwealth'

As Vattel pleaded for collective military measures against the Barbary corsairs he simultaneously took issue with former scholars who had put forward a more tolerant view on the topic. In general, earlier scholars morally

[2] Heinrich von Cocceji, *Grotius illustratus, seu Commentarii ad Hugonis Grotii libros tres* [4 vols, Samuel von Cocceji ed, Wrokław (Breslau), 1744–52].

condemned Barbary warfare, particularly the practice of enslaving captives, but added that it was state-authorised and thus legal. Further, some among them contended that North Africans belonged to a different legal order with their own laws of war and thus they could not be compelled to observe the European customs of war; hence Europeans might at most retaliate, as they actually did. In making such arguments, these writers legally sanctioned the current state of affairs and provided a justification for the incapability (until around 1700) and later unwillingness of the European states to repress the corsairs effectively. European powers indeed preferred to pay tributes to the corsairs to protect themselves and would rather encourage them to assault other powers' shipping than embark on their own costly and counterproductive anti-piracy operations.[3]

Not surprisingly, the first authoritative legal justification of Barbary warfare came from France, whose traditional friendship with the corsairs' suzerains, the Ottomans, dated back to the Franco-Ottoman treaties of the early Middle Ages – a friendship which was reaffirmed by the alliance between Francis I and Suleiman the Magnificent against the Habsburgs in the first half of the sixteenth century.[4] This justification of Barbary warfare was given by Jean Bodin, who dealt with piracy and Barbary privateering in the first chapter of his *Six livres de la République* of 1576.[5] In that chapter, he compared the 'well-ordered government' with its opposite, meaning the criminal organisation or robber state. Here the question was whether pirate societies may be governed by some principles of justice even though they are not lawful commonwealths. Following an argument of Cicero's, Bodin first suggested that pirates might indeed observe some kind of justice or fairness, for instance when sharing out a prize, but Bodin added that because such division derived from criminal activities, it could not be defined as 'fair' in the legal sense. In support of his thesis, Bodin relied on

---

[3] The interdependence of Europe and Barbary in early modern times has been stressed by Anne Pérotin-Dumon, 'The Pirate and the Emperor: Power and the Law on the Seas, 1450–1850' in James D Tracy (ed), *The Political Economy of Merchant Empires. State Power and World Trade 1350–1750* (CUP, 1991) 196–227.

[4] Political and commercial treaties based on the principle on the equality of the parties between the Mamluks and the French reached back to the thirteenth century. See Peter M Holt, 'The Treaties of the Early Mamluk Sultans with the Frankish States' (1980) 43 (1) *Bulletin of the School of Oriental and African Studies* 67, 71. On the Franco-Ottoman friendship, see also Karl-Heinz Ziegler, 'The Peace Treaties of the Ottoman Empire with European Christian Powers' in Randall Lesaffer (ed), *Peace Treaties and International Law in European History* (CUP, 2004) 342 ff.

[5] Bodin, *République*, bk I, ch 1.

a passage from Justinian's *Digest* in which the Roman jurist Ulpian declared the division of booty by pirates and robbers to be void.[6] Bodin stressed that the illegal seizure and detention of booty nullified any successive possession right, regardless of whether the division itself was actually performed according to commutative justice.

Expanding on this, Bodin argued that robbers and pirates had to be distinguished from the category of 'lawful enemies' and excluded from any form of treaty or alliance.[7] Drawing on the Aristotelian conception of the state, he contended that while the 'rightly ordered commonwealths' were legitimately sovereign – as they aimed to facilitate the happiness of their members and the whole – robber and pirate societies aimed to facilitate crime and must therefore be regarded as illegal.[8] Rather than political entities, criminal associations represented the complete obliteration of the political.[9] Thus, unlike the lawful princes who maintained their states and republics 'by means of justice', the leaders of pirate states were categorised as unlawful enemies deprived of the right to make treaties, alliances, settle boundaries, or declare war.[10]

The Justification of Barbary Warfare through a Formal Notion of Sovereignty

Bodin however added that in the case of a 'compelling necessity', political authorities of a 'well-ordered commonwealth' might be urged to acknowledge a pirate leader as a lawful sovereign.[11] After all, Bodin argued, even pirates might turn from 'enemies of mankind' into good princes in due course. History had demonstrated that capable pirate chiefs sometimes deserved the title of king more than legitimate yet ineffective monarchs.

> Sultan Suleiman [the Magnificent] called to his council the two noblest corsairs in living memory, Hayreddin Barbarossa and Dragut Reis, and made them both admirals and pashas, to clear other pirates from the seas as well as protect his state, and maritime trade. Such a manner of attracting pirate chiefs to the haven of virtue is, and always will be, laudable, with a view to

---

6 *Digesta* 10.3.7.4 [Ulp. *lib. XX ad ed.*].

7 Bodin here referred to *Digesta* 50.16.118 (Pomp. *lib. II ad Q. Mucium*) and 49.15.24 (Ulp. *lib. I inst.*). He literally employed the expression 'corsairs' but thereby meant both privateers and pirates. Incidentally, at the end of the sixteenth century the term *guerre de course* was still commonly used to indicate both privateering and piracy.

8 Aristotle, *The Politics* (Stephen Everson ed, CUP, 1988) I, 2, 1252b.

9 Bodin, *République*, bk I, ch 1, p 2.

10 Ibid.

11 Ibid.

> prevent such people from taking a chance to attack not only one's own state, but also other states, thus behaving like enemies of mankind.[12]

This passage might sound problematic to the non-French readers of Bodin, especially to those from Spain and the Italian states who were at war with the Ottoman Porte and its Barbary vassals. Bodin commended the Barbary corsairs Hayreddin Barbarossa and Dragut Reis as 'the noblest corsairs of all times'. He also praised the Sultan Suleiman the Magnificent for attracting these corsairs to the 'haven of virtue' and appointing them admirals and pashas at Algiers and Tripoli respectively. The tone of Bodin's argumentation clearly indicated his favourable disposition towards the Sublime Porte, and towards Barbary privateering as a weapon available to the Franco-Ottoman alliance in the struggle against the Habsburgs.

The most relevant idea behind the above statement was that although Hayreddin Barbarossa and Dragut Reis acted immorally and illegally in the first place, their position was fully legalised by the Sultan's formal acknowledgement of their lawful combatant status and political authority. The statement proved that as Bodin was moving towards a modern theory of sovereignty, he was willing to leave aside the just war theory in favour of a realist doctrine of lawful commonwealth and lawful belligerent status. To be sure, Bodin, as an heir to the medieval legal tradition, did not take the realist approach to extremes.[13] Indeed, he did not contend that pirates by the sole fact of being politically autonomous become sovereigns, but rather that they may be regarded as sovereigns despite their criminal conduct only if foreign powers recognised them as such.

Bodin believed that it was for its own interest that the Porte recognised the Barbary corsairs as lawful belligerents, as it feared that they might otherwise turn into rogues. When Bodin himself described the Sultan's legalisation of the corsairs' position as an act justified by 'compelling necessity', he made it clear that the Sultan's motivation was not to rehabilitate the corsairs, but to preserve the Ottoman Empire from a potential threat.

---

12 Ibid bk I, ch 1, p 3. Translation by the author. Original text: 'Sultan Suliman appela à son conseil les deux plus nobles corsaires de mémoire d'homme, Ariadin Barberousse, & Dragut Reis, faisant l'un & l'autre Amiral, & Pacha, tant pour nettoyer la mer des autres pirates, que pour assurer son Etat, & le cours de la trafique. Ce moyen d'attirer les chefs des pirates au port de vertu, est, & sera toujours louable, non seulement à fin de ne réduire point telles gens au désespoir d'envahir l'Etats des princes, ainsi aussi pour ruiner les autres, comme ennemis du genre humain'.

13 On Bodin's relationship with the Medieval legal tradition, see Margherita Isnardi Parente, 'Introduzione' in Jean Bodin, *I sei libri dello stato* (3 vols, Margherita Isnardi Parente and Diego Quaglioni eds, Turin, Utet, 1964–1997) vol 1; Diego Quaglioni, *La sovranità* (Rome – Bari, Laterza, 2004) 49–69.

Therefore, Bodin put forward a sketch of a constitutive theory of recognition that withdrew attention from whether the political authorities to be recognised complied with any obligations towards their subjects or the international community. The corsairs needed the external sanction of the Sultan to clear their criminal record, but they did not actually have to become a 'well-ordered commonwealth' before being recognised as such. Indeed, while here Bodin on the one hand was moving away from classical Aristotelian and Ciceronian theories of government, on the other hand he was simply implementing the legal distinction between piracy and privateering as it had developed during the late Middle Ages. The distinction justified piracy-like warfare on the basis of state sanction and completely disregarded whether the state in question could be seen as a rightful commonwealth.[14]

In his *République*, Bodin first treated piracy and pirate states according to the traditional canons of moral and political philosophy. Eventually, he put forward a realist and pragmatic position that would become paradigmatic in the later doctrine, also because it reflected the state practice of most European states until the late eighteenth century. His sovereignty argument justifying Barbary warfare would be taken up by practising legal scholars like Gentili (if only in part) and Bynkershoek, who particularly esteemed Bodin's political realism, as well as by natural law theorists like Grotius, Pufendorf and Samuel von Cocceji, who each turned sovereignty into a fundamental principle of their doctrinal systems. Vattel was the first to move away from the tolerant and pluralist paradigm. While he emphasised the centrality of sovereignty on a number of occasions, he maintained that the 'common security' of all nations may require the restriction or even obliteration of sovereignty when the latter is exercised in a way that imperils international law and order.[15]

Manipulating Universal Enmity: Gentili

The Delegitimation of Barbary Privateering in De iure belli

Alberico Gentili in his *De iure belli* seemed to draw similar conclusions to Bodin by privileging legality over legitimacy in defining war and statehood. Gentili famously characterised war as a *publicorum armorum iusta*

---

[14] On Bodin's treatment of the just war doctrine, see Quaglioni, *I limiti della sovranità. Il pensiero di Jean Bodin nella cultura politica e giuridica dell'età moderna* (Padua, Cedam, 1992) 129 f.

[15] On the 'common security' of nations see, for instance, *DG*, II, 12, § 162; II, 15, § 222.

contentio, where *iusta* meant not morally 'just', but 'legal' in the sense of being waged by a prince.[16] In his view, the first requirement for war to be just was that it be waged by sovereigns, as they have no common judge on earth and are endowed with an absolute right to use force to defend their country and subjects.[17] Gentili specified that the adjective *iustus* signified not only 'legal' but also that which is perfect in all of its parts, as allegedly was the Roman public war, formally declared and conducted according to a 'just custom of war' (*iustum mos belli*).[18] This confrontation was a 'regular war' between sovereign states. However, the observance of the customary law of war – the main principle of which was constituted by the prohibition of harming the innocent – was not essential for Gentili. It remained a secondary requirement for lawful warfare compared with the criterion of sovereignty. Also, if one party did not comply with the customs of war, the opponent might do the same in retaliation, and even take punitive measures if necessary to obtain security and reparations.[19] Gentili believed belligerents to be under no legal duty to restrain their conduct of war if they could not obtain redress otherwise. In his view of war as a trial in which the verdict was pronounced on the battlefield, enemies stood in front of each other as judges entitled to carry on a potentially unlimited war.[20] This he concluded because each sovereign prince's judgement over the causes and the conduct of war could not be questioned. Only illegal combatants such as pirates and robbers could be held liable for violating the law of nations and waging 'unjust wars'. Here Gentili, following Balthazar Ayala, took Bodin's theory of sovereignty to extremes and interpreted the distinction in Roman law between legal and illegal combatants as a cornerstone of the law of nations.[21]

---

16 Alberico Gentili, *De iure belli libri tres* (first published 1598, Coleman Phillipson ed, Oxford, Clarendon, 1933) bk I, ch 2, p 12.

17 Ibid bk I, ch 3.

18 Livy, *Ab urbe condita* (Benjamin O Foster trans, London, Heinemann, 1919) I, 15.

19 Gentili, *De iure belli*, bk II, ch 18.

20 Ibid bk I, ch 6, p 33. On Gentili's departure from the just war doctrine and his emphasis on the belligerents' equality, see Diego Panizza, 'Political Theory and Jurisprudence in Gentili's *De iure belli*' (Working paper No 15, New York, Institute for International Law and Justice, 2005) 13–19, <http://www.iilj.org/newsandevents/documents/Panizza.pdf>.

21 See Balthazar Ayala, *De iure belli et officiis bellicis et disciplina militari libri tres* (first published 1582, John Westlake ed, Washington, Carnegie Endowment, 1912) I, 2; I, 5, § 38; I, 6, § 8. Gentili criticised Bodin for not offering a systematic treatment of the law of war, but largely agreed with his theory of sovereignty and its consequences on the international plane (Gentili, *De iure belli*, bk I, ch 1, p 4). On Gentili's recovery of the Bodinian theory of sovereignty in relation to the dichotomy between lawful and unlawful belligerents, see Peter Schröder, 'Vitoria, Gentili, Bodin. Sovereignty and the Law of Nations' in Benedict Kingsbury and Benjamin Straumann (eds), *The Roman Foundations of the Law of Nations* (OUP, 2010) 163, 174.

While Ayala was mainly concerned with rebels, Gentili was more interested in piracy, to which he dedicated an entire chapter of his *De iure belli*.[22] Faithful to the terminology originally employed by Cicero and Florus, he defined pirates as 'common enemies of every human being', who broke off every bond with the society of mankind as a whole and should be considered as common criminals, not lawful belligerents.[23] By cutting themselves off from human society, pirates might not entertain diplomatic relations and enter into any private legal agreement or public treaty. This view, echoing Cicero's argument that nobody is obliged to keep their word with robbers and pirates, was brought forward particularly against François Hotman's claim that pirates enjoy the rights of embassy and freedom of contract. Gentili, who as a fervent Bartolist was particularly hostile to Hotman, straightforwardly rejected his opinion that pirates and rebels may avail themselves of any rights under the law of nations.[24]

> Neither brigands or pirates are entitled to the privileges of international law. Since they themselves have utterly spurned all intercourse with their fellow-men and, so far as in them lies, endeavour to drag back the world to the savagery of primitive times. ... How can men who have withdrawn from all intercourse with society and who ... have broken the compact of the human race, retain any privileges of law, which itself is nothing else than a compact of society?[25]

Like his predecessors, Gentili spoke of the 'common enemies of all' in a rhetorical sense. Although he mentioned the Stoic idea of a 'society of mankind' and stated that all human law rested on it, he saw the universal human society as a mere gathering of sovereign states and maintained that natural law, though common to all, was either instrumental or irrelevant in the foundation of the law of nations, in particular of the law of war. Distancing himself from Scholastic as well as Protestant natural law theorists, Gentili merely equated natural reason with a kind of common sense.[26]

As a realist and pragmatic writer not inclined to speculations about the universal human society, Gentili did not draw radical conclusions from the universal enemy concept. He rather grounded his anti-piracy doctrine on the Roman dichotomy between lawful and unlawful belligerents.

---

[22] Gentili dwelt on piracy in *De iure belli*, bk I, ch 4.

[23] Gentili, *De iure belli*, bk I, ch 4, p 22.

[24] François Hotman, *Quaestionum illustrium liber* (Geneva, 1573) VII.

[25] Alberico Gentili, *De legationibus libri tres* (first published 1585, Ernest Nys ed, OUP, 1924) II, 8.

[26] Coleman Phillipson, 'Introduction' in Gentili, *De iure belli*, 24a.

The problem with this approach was that when he turned to the Roman tradition he had to deal with those views which, unlike Cicero's, did not exactly fit in with his own as they complicated the opposition between pirates and lawful belligerents. Historians like Velleius Paterculus, Plutarch, and Florus indeed defined the conflicts between the Romans and the pirates as outright wars (*bella piratica*).[27] The historians' terminology conveyed the significant point that if pirates or pirate states were in a condition to engage in open naval battles and hold the Roman navy in check, they could hardly be characterised as common criminals. This characterisation would have been both unjustified and misleading in terms of an historical understanding. Moreover, qualifying pirates as lawful combatants (*hostes*) did not necessarily encroach upon Roman interests, for lawful combatants under the ancient law of nations of the late Republican and early Imperial Age did not enjoy any particular rights, except the right of postliminy.[28] By that stage, the rules of the *ius fetiale* which once regulated conflicts between the Italic peoples had long been shelved: Rome had grown into a great military power and no longer needed to comply with these rules. Finally, the Roman use of terms such as *bellum* and *hostis* was not yet loaded with implications in terms of sovereignty and international recognition, as would become the case during the modern age. Early-modern writers like Bodin, Ayala and Gentili published in times of domestic and international confessional strife and put a strong emphasis on state sovereignty as a means to neutralise conflict. For them, the dichotomy between lawful and unlawful belligerents was practically more relevant than it was for the Romans.

At the end of the sixteenth century, with the modern state emerging, lawyers and theorists of sovereignty began systematically to make use of the term *bellum* specifically to indicate 'public war' between states, and *hostis* to refer to lawful and internationally recognised 'public enemies' in the context of public war. Gentili sanctioned this process by defining war as *publicorum armorum iusta contentio*. It was on this basis that he rejected the idea that pirates be deemed lawful enemies and sovereigns. He denied both that pirates may be defined as lawful combatants and that they may be treated as such.

---

27 See above Chapter 1, 32.

28 By the right of postliminy (*ius postliminii*), military returning home after captivity might revert their rights and properties. For a detailed historical analysis of the right of postliminy, see Alberto Maffi, *Ricerche sul postliminium* (Milan, Giuffrè, 1992); Maria Floriana Cursi, *La struttura del "postliminium" nella repubblica e nel principato* (Naples, Jovene, 1996).

However, had he clung to his own doctrinal principles, Gentili could not have responded to the challenge represented by the terminology of the Roman historians, for it belonged to the same theoretical framework as his own doctrine. The historians' argument that large-scale conflicts must be defined as wars proper simply followed from Roman political realism – the same realism that the humanist Gentili pursued as he defined war as a contest between public enemies to get rid of theologians' speculations on just and unjust causes.[29] In fact if large-scale piratical warfare, largely analogous to state warfare and therefore called by historians *bellum piraticum*, was to be criminalised, there was no other way to do so except by reclaiming the just war doctrine and the thick concept of the state as bequeathed by the Aristotelian and Ciceronian tradition.

Here Gentili fell back on the just cause argument. He contended that regardless of whether pirates were able to wage state-like warfare or not, they remained criminals because they waged war for private gain alone and lacked legitimate institutions comparable to those of well-ordered commonwealths established with a view to increasing the citizens' happiness. While Gentili jettisoned any use of the notion of just cause as a useful criterion to evaluate the legitimacy of wars between sovereigns, he recovered it to disqualify pirates and thus maintain the dichotomy between lawful and unlawful belligerents within the realist framework. If legitimate princes were defined as lawful enemies largely regardless of the justice of the cause, pirate leaders by definition could not claim that same status. They remained ordinary criminals even if they ruled over state-like entities.

> Charles Martel said of the Saracens, that because they roved about in great numbers and had leaders, camps, and standards, they were none the less brigands, since they had no motive for war. ... Pirates may follow the customs of war, and not those of brigands, as Paterculus writes of those against whom Pompey made his campaign; yet they do not wage war. Even those pirates did not carry on war like a regular enemy (*iusti hostes*), although Pompey was sent against them with most unusual powers and with extraordinary equipment.[30]

In this excerpt, Gentili referred to a fundamental document in the history of piracy. It was Valleius Paterculus' statement that the reason why Pompey was given extraordinary powers by the *lex Gabinia* was that pirates were

[29] On Gentili as a representative of politically realist early-modern humanism, see Richard Tuck, *The Rights of War and Peace: Political Thought and the International Order from Grotius to Kant* (OUP, 1999) 16–50.

[30] Gentili, *De iure belli*, bk I, ch 4, p 22.

terrorising the Mediterranean 'not as heretofore by furtive marauding expeditions but with fleets of ships in the manner of regular warfare (*cum belli more*)'.[31] According to Velleius, pirates were harshly repressed not due to the irregular and illegal character of their warfare – on the contrary, piratical raids had largely been tolerated until then – but because they had turned from occasional robbers into public enemies (*hostes*) due to the scale of their warfare and the political legitimacy of the pirate leaders. According to Velleius, the conflict in question was an outright public war between lawful enemies, as is clear also from his portrait of the King of Pontus Mithridates in later paragraphs.

Gentili responded that pirates remained ordinary robbers even if they waged large-scale warfare, observed the customs of war and, most importantly, even if they were sovereigns. By criminalising all 'those against whom Pompey' made war, Gentili was implying that Mithridates himself was a pirate. Gentili's argument was ambiguous and weak, as it did not clarify why Mithridates should be deemed a pirate although he was a legitimate sovereign. Gentili took trouble to restate the Ciceronian definition of the lawful enemy as he who has 'a state, a senate, a treasury', but Mithridates certainly fell into this category.[32] As for Mithridates allegedly lacking a just cause for war, this simply warranted the characterisation of him as an unjust enemy, and not a pirate.

Gentili particularly insisted on the requirement for just cause as it was the only argument he could oppose to Bodin's claim that the Barbary corsairs, who certainly waged large-scale warfare in Velleius' terms, were lawful combatants. Gentili had to admit that like Mithridates, the pashas of Algiers and Tripoli qualified as legitimate sovereigns. If this point was contested, they must be regarded at least as Ottoman vassals waging war in the name of the Sultan. Hence, the only way for Gentili to delegitimise the corsairs was to accuse them of waging war unjustly and for private gain, like pirates. On this account, he could argue that the Sultan's acknowledgment of the corsairs, although it had effects on the constitution of the Ottoman Empire, was irrelevant under the law of nations.

The Justification of Barbary Warfare in Hispanica advocatio

Gentili published *De iure belli* in the late 1580s, at the moment when the Barbary corsairs began to assault not only Spanish ships, but French,

---

[31] Marcus Velleius Paterculus, *Historiarum ad M. Vinicium consulem libri duo* (Frederick W Shipley trans, Harvard University Press, 1979) II, 31.

[32] Cicero, *Philippicae* (David R Shackleton Bailey trans, Harvard University Press, 2009) IV, 6.

English, and Dutch vessels as well. These developments, which might induce many Europeans to view the corsairs as 'common enemies of all', partly explains Gentili's critique of piracy and privateering too. However, his doctrine on piracy changed over time, conditioned very much by his activity as a practitioner, especially as a counsel to the Spanish embassy at the English Court of Admiralty from 1605 onwards.[33] In the *Hispanicae advocationis libri duo*, a posthumous work composed of legal opinions from that period, Gentili complicated the criminalisation of piracy as laid down in his *De iure belli* to admit that sometimes pirates may be regarded as lawful combatants, and lawful combatants as pirates.[34] He thus retraced the path of Bodin, who first neatly differentiated pirates from legitimate princes and then conceded that the former may turn into the latter, as had been the case with Hayreddin Barbarossa and Dragut Reis.

The discussion on piracy in the *Advocatio* still commenced with an argument resonating with *De iure belli*. Gentili put it forward at Chapter 15 of the *Advocatio*, where he gave an opinion on the ownership of merchandise stolen from a Spanish vessel by North African corsairs and then sold to English merchants through the treasury of the King of Barbary. The English argued on the basis of a constitution of the Roman emperor Zeno that they had bought the goods from a political authority who had legitimately owned them.[35] In contrast, Gentili declared this constitution unjust and inapplicable. He stated that the English merchants were wrong and had acted in bad faith, for they knew that they were buying stolen merchandise when they made the purchase.[36] Moreover, he maintained that any sale by the public functionaries of Barbary was illegal in the first place, because the transaction was not effected with honesty and, further, because no treasury official specifically in charge of public sales had been appointed. Gentili asserted that it was merely a 'custom of this kingdom [i.e. Barbary] that the king buys everything and that everything is bought of the king – or through him – as a temporary owner.'[37] This depicted the Barbary Regencies as unlawful states by reiterating the widespread idea that Algiers, Tunis, and Tripoli, as well as all other countries of the Ottoman

---

33 Phillipson, 'Introduction', 14a.

34 Alberico Gentili, *Hispanicae advocationis libri duo* (first published 1613, Frank F Abbott ed, OUP, 1921) I, 22–3. For a comment on this work, see Lauren Brenton, 'Legalities of the Sea in Gentili's *Hispanica Advocatio*' in Kingsbury and Straumann (eds), *The Roman Foundations*, 270.

35 *Codex Theodosiani* (Theodor Mommsen and Paul M Meyer eds, Berlin, Weidmann, 1905) 7.37.2; Gentili, *Hispanicae advocationis*, bk I, ch 15, p 70.

36 Ibid bk I, ch 15, p 71.

37 Ibid.

Empire or under Ottoman influence, were despotic patrimonial states governed by rulers pursuing their own interests instead of the public good.[38] Here Gentili drew the conclusion that he had merely hinted at in *De iure belli* when he mentioned Cicero's definition of the lawful state and enemy: the Barbary Regencies could be deemed unlawful enemies not just because they waged war unjustly, but also because they did not qualify as well-ordered commonwealths grounded on the principle of the common good and run by leaders acting responsibly towards nationals and foreigners. Gentili sarcastically commented that if the King of Barbary exerted such absolute rights upon his subjects' ownership and acted as a receiver of stolen goods, his country would constitute an ideal place in which corsairs could take refuge after plundering the Spanish vessels and to meet English merchants waiting for the booty.[39] In his view, this was no fair arrangement of buying and selling but organised crime.

In Chapters 22 and 23 of the *Advocatio*, Gentili advanced a completely different opinion. He addressed a case of English merchants who through the prefect of Tunis had bought booty taken from Venetian vessels by English pirates. Gentili first denied any Venetian claims to restitution by resorting to Zeno's constitution – which he had rejected in Chapter 15 as unjust and inapplicable – and claiming that the Prince of Tunis was entitled to the sale by both civil law and Tunisian custom.[40] Second, Gentili maintained Ayala's opinion that the *lex Atinia*, which took the original owner of a stolen good as the unique subject having rights over it, only applied to citizens of the same state.[41] Having been robbed by foreign pirates, the Venetians could not demand any restitution or compensation towards either the English merchants or the treasury of Tunis.[42] Gentili dismissed the Venetians' virulent accusations against Barbary as he argued that those accusations simply originated from disappointment that the Regencies' foreign policy favoured the rise of English commerce in the Orient. This was a highly significant point as it stressed the fact, often omitted by European writers, that Barbary warfare actually benefited some European powers, and that no general war existed between Europe and Barbary.

38 Ann Thomson, *Barbary and Enlightenment* (Leiden, Brill, 1987) 119.

39 Gentili, *Hispanicae advocationis*, bk I, ch 15, pp 71–72.

40 Ibid bk I, ch 23, p 108.

41 Ayala, *De iure et officiis bellicis*, I, V, § 40; *Digesta* 41.3.4.6 (Paul. *lib. LIV ad ed.*); Gentili, *Hispanicae advocationis*, bk I, ch 23, p 109.

42 Gentili, *Hispanicae advocationis*, bk I, ch 23, p 111.

In support of his thesis justifying Tunisian privateering, Gentili did not hesitate to repeat Alciati's provocative assumption that 'pirates commit a lesser crime, since they commit it at sea', and even Hotman's opinion that agreements with pirates are lawful.[43] More importantly, Gentili said that the Venetian argument that Tunis was a 'den of brigands' was of no consequence as the Tunisians were 'infidels' and belonged to a different legal order. Therefore, Tunisian corsairs ought to be considered 'lawful enemies' entitled to acquire and own booty when at war against Christians.[44] This view relied on the opinion of medieval jurists Bartolus de Saxoferrato and Baldus de Ubaldis.[45] They argued that in their day, Turks and Saracens were regarded as lawful enemies of the Emperor in the sense of the Roman public war (*bellum Romanum*), as they were organised in independent polities ruled by legitimate authorities.[46] This meant that they had the same status at war as Christians, including the right to enslave captives. To be sure, the *bellum Romanum* was such a harsh form of warfare that being part of it was not necessarily an advantage, but the main point for Gentili in recovering Bartolus' and Baldus' argument was that the Barbary corsairs, not unlike the 'Turks and Saracens' of old, could be placed on a footing of equality with the Christians. Indeed, Gentili did not think much of restraints on the conduct of hostilities, as he assumed, like most other writers in his age, that they might rightfully be neglected for the sake of military necessity and the punishment of perfidious enemies.[47] His main concern here was with the formal status of the Barbary corsairs.

Gentili appeared somewhat innovative in his *Advocatio* as he specified not only that pirates may be regarded as lawful enemies, as Bodin had already argued, but also that lawful enemies may be deemed pirates. He advanced this thesis largely because he, as a counsel of the Spaniards, had to find arguments to delegitimise privateering against Spanish vessels. It was at this point that Gentili brought to bear his observations on the 'just

---

[43] Alciati, *Responsa* (first published 1561, Frankfurt am Main, Vico, 2004) XI, 2; Hotman, *Quaestionum illustrium*, VII.

[44] Gentili, *Hispanicae advocationis*, bk I, ch 23, p 112.

[45] In a note Gentili said to be taking up such conclusion from the *Decisiones rotae Genuae de mercatura et pertinentibus ad eam* (Marcantonio Bellone ed, Genoa, Ternoni, 1582) CI, § 1. In this decision, however, further reference was made to Alciati's entry '*hostes*' in *De verborum significatione* (Lyon, Sebastiano Grifo, 1530) in which he qualified Saracens and Turks as 'lawful enemies' of the Europeans according to Bartolus' and Baldus' teaching.

[46] Bartolus de Saxoferrato, *Commentaria* (Giovanni Polara ed, Rome, Il Cigno Galileo Galilei, 1996–98, reprint of 1526 Venice edn) vol 6, f 146^{r}; Baldus de Ubaldis, *In infortiatum, digestum novum, et instituta commentaria* (1577 Lyon edn) f 175^{r}.

[47] Gentili, *De iure belli*, II, 18.

customs of war' briefly mentioned in his *De iure belli*. In one opinion relating to privateers' attacks on Spanish ships, he condemned privateering as a form of disguised piracy contrary to the law of war, particularly because it targeted harmless people.

> The man who captured a Spanish ship is, of course, a Dutch enemy; but, in this case, he is also an unscrupulous belligerent, since he is more truly committing piracy under letters of marque than carrying on war. ... This predatory warfare is waged in accordance with no discipline or custom of war, a war against non-combatants (*inermes*) and harmless merchants, and others situated far from the battle lines, although it is only what takes place at the front that really seems to be done in war.[48]

Gentili here referred to the case of a Dutch corsair ship which had been seized by the English off the coast of England after it had captured a Spanish vessel, and for which the Dutch owners demanded compensation. After dismissing the Dutch claim with reference to international treaties and the doctrine of state jurisdiction at sea, Gentili added that the ship-owners had no rights upon the booty as it was derived from privateering, which as a piracy-like activity could not be employed in a 'just', that is, legal or regular war. Gentili's argument against privateering on the basis that it violated the customs of war might sound strange to readers familiar with his work. On many occasions, especially in *De iure belli*, he had given evidence that he did not think much of these customs, all of which could be overruled by the 'right of war', so his delegitimation of privateering in the *Advocatio* was at least problematic. Moreover, Gentili's point was questionable as privateers authorised by letters of marque were considered as lawful combatants nearly unanimously by general opinion. They would continue to retain this status until the late eighteenth century, when navies dominated the seas and maritime warfare was regulated more effectively. It was not until that stage that publicists systematically began to equate privateering with piracy.[49]

In *De iure belli*, which Gentili wrote before becoming an advocate of Spain, he had indeed taken the general view that privateering was entirely legitimated by letters of marque. There he had stated that French corsairs fighting for António and against Philip II in the Portuguese dynastic crisis

48 Gentili, *Hispanicae advocationis*, bk I, ch 8, p 37.

49 Gérard de Rayneval, *Institutions du droit de la nature et des gens* (2nd ed, Paris, Leblanc, 1803) III, 16, §§ 3–4; Ferdinand de Cussy, *Phases et causes célèbres du droit maritime des nations* (Leipzig, Brockhaus, 1856) vol 2, bk I, tit III, § 20. A critical view of privateering had earlier been taken by Gabriel Bonnot de Mably, *Le droit public de l'Europe* (Geneva, 1746) vol 2, 300.

of the 1580s qualified as lawful combatants. This held true irrespective of whether Antonio was a usurper or a legitimate ruler, since the corsairs had been granted letters of marque directly from their king, Henry III.[50] As a result, Gentili argued, the Spanish claim that French privateers could be treated as pirates was groundless.

It is hard to see how these arguments could be put together to form a consistent doctrine of piracy, much less of universal enmity and international crimes. Despite his frequent recourse to universalist expressions such as 'society of mankind', 'common law of mankind', and 'common enemy of all', Gentili's case proves once again how the doctrine of universal enmity could be easily instrumentalised. Here, originality and incoherence went hand in hand. What could be seen as insightful intuitions and complications of the traditional doctrine, such as Gentili's argument that piracy might turn into legal warfare and vice-versa, actually represented mere tricks to serve particular interests. If Gentili demonstrated some coherence in *De iure belli*, his incoherence – indeed a common feature in the civilist tradition from which he took inspiration – became apparent later in connection with his practical activity. At that point he had to defend the Spanish while at the same time demonstrating reverence to the English, who accorded him hospitality and protection from the Roman Inquisition. He was urged to shape his doctrine in a way that could both appease his magnates and support his clients.

Grotius and the Recovery of the 'Ancient Law of Nations'

Reasserting the Sovereignty Argument

Grotius upheld in principle the Roman dichotomy between lawful and unlawful belligerents, and yet, not unlike Bodin and Gentili, he ended by dismantling it in fact. Grotius maintained the Ciceronian point that 'a gathering of pirates and brigands is not a state', for while 'pirates and brigands are banded together for wrongdoing; the members of a state … have been united for the enjoyment of rights, and they do render justice to foreigners.'[51] This dichotomy might be questioned by the historical evidence that many ancient nations, most notoriously the Greeks, deemed pillaging and plundering permissible. For learned humanists like Grotius the

50 Gentili, *De iure belli*, bk I, ch 4, p 26.

51 Hugo Grotius, *De iure belli ac pacis libri tres* (first published 1625, Francis W Kelsey trans, Washington, Carnegie Endowment, 1913) III, 3, § 2.

question then arose whether there existed any real difference between sovereign nations and pirate states. Grotius answered that the difference still persisted because whilst sea-robbers entirely disregarded the law of nations, legitimate polities which engaged in piracy nonetheless observed some of the rules of the law of nations and fulfilled some obligations towards the enemy. For example, as Thucydides noticed, 'the Greeks refrained from murder and raids by night, and from the seizure of the cattle of ploughmen', while Strabo reported that other nations living on piracy, 'upon returning home after being at sea, sent word to the owners in order that these might, if they wished, recover their stolen property at a fair price.'[52]

Grotius supported the dichotomy between lawful and unlawful belligerents by asserting the authority of Roman law, stating that captives taken by pirates remained free, while those captured by public enemies, such as the German nations, forfeited their freedom.[53] This was to stress that under Roman law, and in general under the ancient law of nations, public enemies had a licence to plunder and enslave prisoners of war, but pirates had no entitlement whatsoever. Grotius agreed with Roman sources that while free nations were lawful enemies, pirates were 'common enemies of all' and should be viewed as ordinary criminals.[54] In his view, there existed an essential difference between a nation, warlike though it was, and an association formed for the sake of illicit activities.[55]

In so arguing, Grotius adopted a realist concept of sovereignty and got rid of Cicero's and Bodin's thick notion of state, according to which the well-ordered commonwealths are only those in which justice and customs are observed.[56] After all, Bodin himself had already relativised that notion when he defined the Barbary corsairs as lawful combatants. Grotius' realist approach here was hardly surprising. Moreover, he was concerned with the thick notion of state being unsuitable for the Dutch Republic and other states that were effectively sovereign but the independence of which

52 Ibid.

53 *Digesta* 49.15.5 (Pomp. *lib. XXVII ad Q. Mucium*).

54 Grotius, *De iure belli ac pacis*, II, 3, § 1; Grotius, *De iure praedae commentarius* (written 1604, first published 1868, Gwladys L Williams trans, Oxford, Clarendon, 1950) XIV, 1, p 327. When affirming that oaths with pirates had to be accomplished, Grotius was not legitimating piracy but simply taking up the argument that whoever gave his word had to keep it insofar as God had been invoked as witness and insofar as natural law itself required that promises be honoured (Grotius, *De iure belli ac pacis*, II, 13, § 15; III, 19, § 2).

55 Grotius, *De iure belli ac pacis*, III, 3, § 3.

56 Bodin, *République*, bk I, ch 1, p 2.

might be legally contested.[57] Once the Dutch Republic could be defined as a lawful commonwealth, Dutch privateering was justified in the same breath.

Grotius' definition of the state as 'a complete Body of free persons, associated together to enjoy peaceably their rights, and for their common benefits' might sound traditional, but it was broad enough to be interpreted in different ways.[58] In his discussion of lawful and unlawful societies, Grotius clearly neglected the issue of justice and focused on the end of the commonwealth, not on the means of attaining it. Echoing Bodin, he thus affirmed that there had been several historical instances of pirates turning into lawful enemies simply by renouncing crime and entering regular armies.[59] Grotius maintained that as long as pirates acted in small groups they must be repressed through police operations,[60] but the situation changed in the case of large criminal organisations such as the Barbary corsairs. If these organisations possessed a military power sufficient to allow them to confront regular forces and potentially defeat them, sovereigns should avoid open clashes and rather neutralise the threat by pardoning the criminals and integrating them into the state's political and military hierarchies.[61]

The 'Ancient Law of Nations' Re-enters into Force

Grotius was aware that while a realist justification of Barbary warfare might only circumvent the characterisation of the corsairs as 'unjust enemies', a further argument was required if this characterisation was to be refuted straightforwardly. That is why he resorted to historical narratives attesting to the fact that piracy was legal in ancient times. Yet if Grotius' narratives were reliable, he still had to explain the reason why piracy was permissible under the ancient law of nations. If this reason remained unclear, it would be hard to see how Grotius might claim that the old view could be of any contemporary relevance. He thus elucidated that after the Flood, widespread moral corruption generated 'evil customs' and made

[57] On Grotius' attempts to justify the lawfulness of the Dutch Republic, see Cornelis G Roelofsen, 'Grotius and the International Politics of the Seventeenth Century' in Hedley Bull, Benedict Kingsbury, and Adam Roberts (eds), *Hugo Grotius and International Relations* (Oxford, Clarendon, 1990) 95, 102–3.

[58] Grotius, *De iure belli ac pacis*, I, 1, § 14.

[59] Ibid III, 3, § 3.

[60] Had they committed piracy abroad they could be extradited and tried under foreign law, especially when bilateral agreements to this effect were in place (ibid II, 21, § 5).

[61] Ibid II, 21, § 4.

peoples insensitive to the immutable principles of justice.[62] Over time, the natural law prohibition against harming one's neighbour lost its force, while pillage and plunder became such a common practice that it grew to be accepted as a righteous and laudable means of warfare.[63] General consent upon inherently immoral practices then brought about a perverse conception of the law of nations that asserted itself throughout antiquity.[64]

Grotius affirmed that the harshness of the ancient law of nations (*vetus ius gentium*) had been gradually abandoned by the most civilised nations largely due to economic and political interests as well as the diffusion of religious feelings. From the Middle Ages onwards, both Christians and Muslims, at least when not fighting against each other as purported defenders of the 'true faith', preferred to hold prisoners as hostages and ask for ransom, rather than slay or enslave them.[65] This meant, said Grotius, that peoples had become mindful again of the original bond linking mankind together and were no longer willing to deal with each other as wild beasts. Nevertheless, the ancient law of nations was still in force when a 'civilised' nation was confronted with unscrupulous 'barbarians' who waged war only for the sake of profit, without any legal ground and without formally opening hostilities, as the Algerian corsairs did. In this case, the enslavement of captives was permitted, as was the seizure of booty. As a consequence, either party to this warfare had the right to sell prisoners and spoils on the market, and this sale would be lawful, as had been confirmed by a recent sentence of the highest chamber at Paris.

> In our times, ... not only among Christians but also among most Mohammedans, both the right of captivity apart from war (*ius captivitatis extra bellum*), and likewise that of postliminy, have disappeared. ... Nevertheless that ancient law of nations (*vetus illud ius gentium*) could be applied if there should be an affair with a people so barbarous that without declaration or cause it should consider it lawful to treat in a hostile manner all foreigners and their possessions. While I was writing these words, a

62 Ibid I, 1, § 10.

63 Research has actually demonstrated that early-modern writers' belief in a diffused and 'natural hostility' among all ancient peoples was fallacious. German historian Alfred Heuss first contested the 'natural hostility' thesis in *Die völkerrechtlichen Grundlagen der Römischen Aussenpolitik in republikanischer Zeit* (first published 1933, Aalen, Scientia, 1968) 4–5. See also Ziegler, *Das Völkerrecht der Römischen Republik*, 68–69; Maffi, *Ricerche sul postliminium*, 151.

64 Grotius maintained that the law of nations should not be confounded or assimilated with natural law. The former was the product of human will and customs and could be proved 'uso continuo & testimonio peritorum' (Grotius, *De iure belli ac pacis*, I, 1, § 14).

65 Ibid III, 7, § 9.

> judgement to that effect was rendered in the highest chamber at Paris ... The decision held that goods which had belonged to French citizens, and had been captured by the Algerians, a people accustomed in their maritime depredations to attack all others, had changed ownership by the law of war (*belli iure*), and therefore, when recaptured by others, became the property of those who had recovered them.[66]

Grotius maintained that by dismissing the formalities required by the modern law of war the Algerians implicitly appealed to the ancient right to enslave foreigners in peacetime (*ius captivitatis extra bellum*). This argument found its justification in a doctrine stated by Roman jurists Pomponius and Proculus in the title of the Digest *De captivis et postliminio*. Here they stated that the right to enslave and the right of postliminy were enjoyed not only by the Romans and their public enemies (the *hostes* in the narrow sense, now meaning the European nations). Those rights were equally enjoyed by free and independent peoples (the Barbarians and other *hostes* in a broader sense, now meaning the Barbary corsairs) which might have no bonds of friendship or hospitality with the Romans (and now with the Europeans). Such peoples would attack Roman civilians or troops without a prior declaration of war, and hence without officially putting an end to peacetime. As a consequence, it was argued, there had to apply a 'right of postliminy during peacetime' (*postliminium in pace*), as opposed to the 'right of postliminy during wartime' (*postliminium in bello*), which only came into effect in times of open and declared public war between *hostes* proper.[67]

These opinions departed from other classical discussions of the enemy concept in Roman law, most importantly from the definitions of *hostes* as public enemies of the Romans. In these definitions, stated by Ulpian and Pomponius himself, all enemies who committed hostilities without formally declaring war fell into the category of robbers (*piratae* and *latrones*).[68] Those declaring war, the Romans included, qualified as public enemies proper (*hostes*). Yet the above quoted statements by Proculus and Pomponius diverged from this dichotomic approach and expressed a

---

[66] Ibid III, § 9, 19.

[67] *Digesta* 49.15.5.2 (Pomp. *lib. XXXVII ad Q. Muc.*); 49.15.7.1 (Proc. *lib. VIII Ep.*). On the *postliminium in pace*, see Ferdinando Bona, 'Postliminium in pace' (1955) 21 *Studia et documenta historiae et iuris* 249.

[68] 'Those are enemies (*hostes*) who declare war against us, or against whom we publicly declare war; others are robbers (*latrones*) or brigands (*praedones*)' (*Digesta* 50.16.118) [Pomp. *lib. II ad Q. Mucium*]; 'Enemies are those against whom the Roman people have publicly declared war, or who themselves have declared war against the Roman people; others are called robbers, or brigands' (*Digesta* 49.15.24) [Ulp. *lib. I inst.*].

more pragmatic account of hostility. In these statements, independent robber nations were presented as particular international legal subjects that could not be categorised either as ordinary robbers or as public enemies proper. This doctrine moved away from the dichotomy of robbers and public enemies to establish a threefold differentiation of belligerents into bands of robbers; peoples engaged in publicly declared wars against the Romans; and peoples with which the Romans were involved in a non-formally-declared war. Robber nations here enjoyed those rights that they were otherwise denied based on the dichotomy of robbers and public enemies.

The dichotomy of robbers and public enemies was rigid and abstract. It hardly reflected the reality of war. While the jurists asserting the dichotomy idealised the declaration of war as a means to establish lawful belligerency, they were well aware that the Romans themselves would hardly open a war by formal declaration. This was true at least since the Romans began to expand outside Italy and struggle against peoples who did not acknowledge the fetial law, under which the declaration of war was compulsory.[69] As the Romans themselves no longer observed the fetial law, they certainly did not pretend that their enemies did so. Proculus and Pomponius sanctioned this situation as they attributed certain rights to robber nations. Their accounts translated into legal language a reciprocity which already existed de facto.[70] Grotius pursued a similar goal when advancing his theory of the 'ancient law of nations' and conferring upon Algerian corsairs the right to own booty. Not unlike Proculus and Pomponius, he attempted to depart from the dichotomy of robbers and *hostes* to provide a pragmatic account of hostility.

Grotius deserved credit for explaining the lawfulness of Barbary warfare by means of both sovereignty and historical arguments in an original way. In resorting to the sovereignty argument he came close to Bodin, who argued that the Barbary corsairs had been lawful enemies since the Porte

69 Cursi, *La struttura del "postliminium"* 138; Adam Watson, *International Law in Archaic Rome* (Johns Hopkins University Press, 1993) 54. The Hellenistic-Roman international legal order declined in correspondence to Rome's march towards world domination and definitively collapsed in 168 BC, when the Romans defeated Perseus of Macedon and forced Antiochus IV Epiphanes to withdraw from Egypt (Ziegler, *Das Völkerrecht der Römischen Republik*, 82).

70 Maffi, *Ricerche sul postliminium*, 165. While the term 'robbers' (*latrones*) was indeed used to label the populations that raided the frontiers of the Roman Empire, they were not identified with common criminals and deprived of the right to make war as a result. See Egidio Forcellini, 'Latro' in *Lexicon totius Latinitatis* (first pubslished 1771, Jacopo Facciolati and Egidio Forcellini eds, Padua, 1871) vol 3, 40.

had endowed them with political legitimacy. By clearly taking Bodin's line, Grotius distanced himself from the ambiguous Gentili, who had maintained a discriminatory attitude towards piracy/privateering in *De iure belli* before changing his view in the *Hispanica Advocatio*. Yet if it was enough for Bodin to demonstrate that the Barbary corsairs were sovereigns in order to discard any charges of piracy, this did not suffice for Grotius. Because Grotius believed in universal jurisdiction and explicitly called on every state and individual to punish grave violations of natural law including piracy, he was required to provide additional theses to justify why the Barbary corsairs should not be subject to repression by all nations.[71] Also, even if the corsairs had been declared public enemies, they might still be labelled as unjust enemies under the just war doctrine for lacking a just cause for war. Grotius' historical argument from the ancient law of nations was meant to rule out the application of both the universal right to punish and the just war doctrine to the corsairs. His advocacy of the corsairs' customs of warfare represented an insightful attempt to reconcile universalism and particularism, natural law and customary law, within the law of nations.

As for Vattel, he would dismiss both Bodin's and Grotius' arguments. Based on universalist assumptions, he insisted that the sovereign authorisation did not excuse the corsairs, and that their corrupted mores, far from being tolerated, should be eradicated by means of harsh punishment.[72] In Vattel's view, international law had to be enforced properly if collective security was to be safeguarded in the long term. There was still a historical element to his doctrine, like in Grotius' theory, yet Vattel was oriented to the future, not the past. While Grotius aimed to perpetuate the 'barbarian' law of nations of ancient times, Vattel intended to perpetuate the civilised law of nations as it had been established in the age of politesse.

Belligerent Equality and Its Collateral Effects: Pufendorf

Pufendorf's Definition of the 'Enemy of All'

In accordance with the Ciceronian and Bodinian tradition, natural lawyer Samuel Pufendorf declared bands of robbers and pirates as unlawful bodies and their members as common enemies of all.[73] But what did it

---

[71] Grotius, *De iure belli ac pacis*, II, 21, § 5.
[72] *DG*, III, 9, § 167.
[73] Samuel Pufendorf, *De jure naturae et gentium* (first published 1672, Charles H Oldfather and William A Oldfather trans, Oxford, Clarendon, 1934) III, 6, § 11; VII, 2, § 23.

actually mean for robbers and pirates to be 'common enemies of all'? Pufendorf, unsatisfied with the ambiguous use of the term by his predecessors, took the trouble to settle this neglected issue.

> Now a robber is called a common enemy (*communis hostis*) because he does not declare war upon any particular person as other enemies do, but threatens with violence any and every person who falls into his hands. For this reason there is no need for a declaration of war, the formation of an army, or a call to arms, to put down such a person, but nature herself allows every man the right to take up arms (*licentia militiae*) against him.[74]

Pufendorf was the first scholar to flesh out the universal enemy notion and attempt to establish its precise meaning, and his effort stood out in comparison with the approach of former humanists who used the notion without bothering to define what they thereby meant. In his natural law theory, Pufendorf was able to define the 'common enemy of all' also because the term 'all' in his natural law theory had a precise meaning, signifying all human individuals in the primeval state of nature or rather, in the current world order, all nations in the international state of nature. The 'common enemy of all' thus meant an enemy hostile to all and exposed to potential repression by literally all nations.[75] If Pufendorf had criticised his inspirer Hobbes for hypothesising a 'war of all against all', there might however exist a 'common enemy of all' as long as his presence did not disprove Pufendorf's thesis of universal sociability.[76] Actually, the existence of a common enemy of all confirmed that all individuals and nations in the state of nature had some interests in common.

Pufendorf, however, assumed that those fighting universal enemies acted out of self-interest, not for the common interest of humanity, and indeed it was significant that he referred to 'common enemies of all' instead of 'enemies of mankind'. Since humanity was not a political entity, it was not able to have enemies and wage war. Particularly illuminating of Pufendorf's position is his statement that 'against pirates and freebooters, inasmuch as they are enemies of all (*hostes omnium*), every man is a soldier *of his own country*.'[77] Pirates may be universal enemies, but this was a mere statement of fact without any legal consequences: the repression of

---

74 Pufendorf, *De jure naturae*, III, 6, § 11.

75 Samuel Pufendorf, *Elementorum jurisprudentiae universalis libri duo* (first published 1660, Edwin H Zeydel trans, Oxford, Clarendon, 1931) I, 9, § 1.

76 For an exhaustive analysis of Pufendorf's recovery and critique of Hobbes' theses, see Fiammetta Palladini, *Samuel Pufendorf discepolo di Hobbes* (Bologna, Il Mulino, 1990).

77 Pufendorf, *De jure naturae*, VIII, 3, § 13. Emphasis added.

piracy remained a state matter and those engaged in it acted to protect their fellow citizens, not mankind.

It is also significant that Pufendorf never called on international coalitions to stop piracy; neither did he argue that states were under an international legal or even moral obligation to repress piracy. He limited himself to recommending that sovereigns release letters of marque for civilians intending to pursue freebooters so as to regularise the pursuers' position before foreign governments and thus prevent international disputes.[78] In Pufendorf's eyes, states were bound to prosecute piracy only when it was committed by their own nationals.[79] This fitted well into state practice as the countries repressing piracy *iure gentium* at that time acted autonomously and rarely set up collective measures.

Among the common enemies of all Pufendorf placed not only pirates and robbers but also other violent offenders such as 'assassins, cutthroats, and the like' who received capital punishment under domestic law.[80] All of these offenders were indeed listed among those deserving of the death penalty in the *Constitutio Criminalis Carolina*, the criminal law statute enacted by the emperor Charles V in 1532 and still in force, at least as a subsidiary source, in many German territories when Pufendorf wrote his *De jure nature et gentium*.[81] His expansion of the universal enemy concept to the class of violent offenders deserving of capital punishment represented a significant move, as it allowed him to attribute a legal character to the previously abstractly formulated concept of a universal enemy. He thus gave inspiration to later writers like Vattel who would likewise go beyond the traditional anti-piracy rhetoric and use the enemy of mankind concept with reference to poisoners, assassins, arsonists, as well as warmonger and war criminals.[82]

---

[78] Ibid VIII, 3, § 13; Grotius, *De iure belli ac pacis*, II, 20, § 14. Also, nationals had the possibility to address the offender's sovereign and ask for reparation (Pufendorf, *De jure naturae*, VIII, 6, § 8).

[79] Pufendorf, *De jure naturae*, VIII, 6, § 8. Regarding extradition, Pufendorf relied on contemporary European praxis and said that no strict obligation could be imposed upon states to concede extradition, unless it had been requested to pursue political crimes or unless specific international agreements had been stipulated (ibid VIII, 6, § 13). Pufendorf did not explicitly refer to piracy in the crimes justifying extradition. He was more restrictive than Grotius, who considered this procedure as mandatory not only for state offences but also for any violent and atrocious crime (Grotius, *De iure belli ac pacis*, II, 21, § 5).

[80] Pufendorf, *De jure naturae*, VIII, 4, § 5.

[81] *Constitutio Criminalis Carolina* (first published 1532, Osnabrück, Biblio-Verlag, 1973) §§ 126 and 137. For a discussion of the *Constitutio Carolina*, see Carl Ludwig von Bar, *History of Continental Criminal Law* (Thomas S Bell trans, Boston, Little Brown, 1916) 220 [trans of *Geschichte des deutschen Strafrechts und der Strafrechtstheorien* (first published 1882)].

[82] *DG*, I, 19, § 233.

In addition, restraining universal enmity to violent offences, and hence to the province of law proper, allowed Pufendorf to discredit the tendency of various contemporary moralisers to categorise what he believed to be lesser wrongs as offences against mankind to be harshly repressed. Among the representatives of this strand were Francis Bacon and Grotius, who defined those who committed so-called *crimina contra naturam* such as sodomy and bestiality as enemies of mankind deserving of punishment by literally everyman.[83] Similarly moved by moral and religious zeal, German jurist Benedict Carpzov in the section devoted to sorcery in his celebrated criminal law treaty *Practica nova rerum criminalium* reasserted Roman emperor Constantius II's statement that sorcerers must be viewed as 'enemies of mankind' (*humani generis inimici*).[84] Carpzov, who like many of his contemporaries was convinced that witchcraft was an exceptional crime (*crimen exceptum*) to which the normal rules of evidence did not (and indeed could not) apply, accordingly argued that because witches constituted a threat to the Christian society which they exited upon stipulation of a pact with the devil, they no doubt deserved capital punishment.[85] In opposition to such views, Pufendorf put forward a narrower enemy of mankind concept and contended that deviance must be subject to penalties only when it concretely threatened citizens' safety and security, hence only in case of violent crimes.[86] Moreover, he argued against Grotius that punishment was a prerogative of the sovereign, not of any individual.

By 'common enemies of all' Pufendorf meant only the offenders who clearly trampled on the most elementary rules of the human community, and he particularly stigmatised the repeat offenders who by their conduct lost all reputation and 'esteem' and were regarded by the law, as well as broader society, as infamous and indecent individuals. They qualified as degraded humans with no rights associated with citizenship or the human condition, and might thus be considered as banished from their own polity and from mankind. Vattel would refer to the same typology of criminals when speaking of those 'villains, who, by the nature and habitual frequency

83 The objects of Pufendorf's polemic were Bacon and, implicitly, Grotius (*De iure belli ac pacis*, VIII, 6, § 5). Pointing to this issue, Andreas Roth has asserted that in the Pufendorfian secularised theory of crime 'there is no longer a *crimen contra naturam*'. See Andreas Roth, '*Crimen contra naturam*' in Lorraine Daston and Michael Stolleis (eds), *Natural Law and Laws of Nature in Early Modern Europe* (Farnham – Burlington, Ashgate, 2008) 89, 102.

84 Benedict Carpzov, *Practica nova imperialis Saxonica rerum criminalium in tres partes divisa* (first published 1638, Leipzig, 1709) pt I, q 48, § 2.

85 Ibid pt I, q XLIIX, § 46.

86 Pufendorf, *De jure naturae*, VIII, 3, § 8 f.

of their crimes, violate all public security, and declare themselves the enemies of the human race'.[87] However, whilst Vattel would conceive of these individuals as international offenders and straightforwardly link universal enmity to universal jurisdiction, Pufendorf still thought of them mainly as domestic offenders. Pufendorf certainly admitted that pirates, robbers, and murderers infringed upon the common laws of humanity and could thus be deemed, in an abstract sense, its enemies. Yet as he advocated for a thick notion of sovereignty he remained sceptical of universal jurisdiction.[88] As a result he viewed the 'common enemies of all' primarily as enemies of the domestic commonwealth, at least as far as their punishment was concerned. He contended that because such individuals were in violation of the social contract, which strictly obliged them not to harm their fellow citizens, they must be treated more harshly than external enemies and therefore should be subject to severe penalties, including torture, to deter them and others from further offending.[89] If they did not attempt to redeem themselves, they might be exterminated like beasts.

Pufendorf's Theory of Punishment and the Repression of the Enemy of All

When dwelling in or entering a sovereign country, individuals were supposedly subscribed to the social contract implying forfeiture of natural freedom, which comprised the right to use force pre-emptively, and the requirement of submission to common superiors. Enemies of mankind plainly violated this contract, but no citizen was permitted to take personal action against them beyond the limits of self-defence. Pufendorf believed, like Hobbes, that punishment was by definition a harm inflicted by a superior,[90] and that the repression of crime was exclusively a matter for civil authorities to deal with.[91] In terms of the law of nations, it is worth remarking that as penalties in the earthly life could be administered only by the state against its own nationals (because in the afterlife this task appertained to God), it was hard to see how Pufendorf could justify the punishment of foreigners, most importantly when they qualified as enemies of mankind. The question could be evaded relatively easily in case of

---

87 *DG*, I, 19, § 233.

88 See also Pufendorf's position on the right of intervention: *De jure naturae*, VII, 8, § 9.

89 Ibid VIII, 4, § 5. See also Pufendorf, *Elementorum*, I, 9, § 1.

90 Pufendorf, *De jure naturae*, VIII, 3, §§ 4 and 7.

91 Ibid VIII, 4, § 5. Pufendorf referred in particular to 'harlots, panders, sturdy and vagabond beggars' as well as 'professional thieves'.

state-like criminal entities, such as the buccaneer communities. While on the one hand these communities could not be punished under any domestic law as they qualified as independent entities living in the state of nature with the rest of mankind (and according to Pufendorf no penalty was thinkable in the state of nature, which lacked a common superior), well-ordered states might still take military action against them, if merely by virtue of the right of war, not of the right to punish.[92] While states preserved the right to punish piracy committed within their territory according to municipal law, anti-piracy action on the high seas took the shape of war proper.

> [W]hatever punishment is inflicted in such places and upon such persons as are not under the jurisdiction of certain courts of justice, such as pirates, belongs to the right of war (*jus belli*), which is something different from the power to exact penalties (*potestas poenas exigendi*).[93]

In this passage, Pufendorf attributed to independent pirates the status of free natural individuals, who could not be 'punished' by foreign authorities but only countered by the right of war. To be sure, this did not imply that pirates should be treated any more gently than domestic criminals. On the contrary, since pirates egregiously disregarded the law of nature and nations, their opponents were allowed to do the same against them based on the principle of reciprocity.[94] Under natural and international law, pirates remained aggressors and unjust enemies of the worst kind, and should be treated as 'wolves and other ferocious beasts.'[95]

The 'Unlimited Right' of the Just Enemy

It was precisely Pufendorf's thesis that pirates lived in the state of nature and that their opponents acted against them *iure belli* which justified their annihilation beyond any doubt. Certainly, punishment of the common enemies of all on the footing of national jurisdiction (Pufendorf did not contemplate universal jurisdiction) might generally be harsher than retaliatory measures taken by the right of war. Yet Pufendorf himself warned against excessively harsh domestic penalties, above all if they

92 Those unwilling to subscribe to the social covenant could not be compelled to do so by the contractors and might persist in the state of nature (ibid VII, 2, § 7).

93 Ibid VIII, 3, § 13.

94 As robbers and pirates first dismissed the law of war, their opponents were allowed to do the same on the basis of the natural legal principle of reciprocity (ibid VIII, 6, § 7).

95 Ibid VIII, 4, § 5.

were measured after the law of talion, and recommended indulgence as long as it was not detrimental to the public security.[96]

But at war, when the existence of the commonwealth or at least of many of its members was at stake, indulgence became risky. The unjust enemy in the state of nature, unlike the domestic criminal, was 'protected by no law ... against suffering the extreme consequences'.[97] Here, Pufendorf reasserted the Hobbesian idea that in a state of uncertainty such as the state of nature the slightest offence or even the appearance of a threat justified recourse to 'extreme means' to neutralise the threat.[98] This point allowed Pufendorf to develop his doctrine of the 'unlimited right' of the just enemy against the unjust enemy – a doctrine commented upon until the late eighteenth century.[99] According to the doctrine, the mere occurrence of an injury caused the offender to forfeit any right and the victim to acquire a limitless 'right' (*ius in infinitum*) or 'licence'[100] to use force against him.[101] If an individual in the state of nature committed even the slightest offence, he could not expect clemency from the victim. The latter might rightfully opt for annihilating the offender for the sake of future security.

By arguing so, Pufendorf attempted to propose a normative framework alternative to the classical doctrines of the *ius belli* as laid down by Pierino Belli, Balthasar Ayala and Alberico Gentili. These authors emphasised the realist motives of the Romanist tradition to state that war is a condition of nearly absolute licence in its own right (notwithstanding the few restraints recommended by customs and state interests). Yet Pufendorf maintained that the just enemy possesses a *ius in infinitum* only if an aggression or

---

96 Ibid VIII, 3, §§ 23 and 27; *Digesta* 50.17.155.2 (Paul. *lib. LXV ad ed.*).

97 Pufendorf, *De jure naturae*, II, 5, § 16.

98 Pufendorf, *De jure naturae*, II, 5, § 16; Thomas Hobbes, *Leviathan* (first published 1651, Richard Tuck ed, CUP, 1991) I, 13.

99 Heinrich Köhler, *Juris socialis et gentium ad jus naturale revocati specimina VII* (2nd ed, Jena, 1737) § 1807; Johann Ernst Gunnerus, *Vollständige Erklärung des Natur- und Völkerrechts nach den Grundlagen des Herrn Hofrath Darjes* (first published 1752, Vienna, 1786) ad § 334; Giovanni Maria Lampredi, *De licentia in hostem liber singularis, in quo Samuelis Cocceji sententia de infinita licentia in hostem exponitur et confutatur* (Florence, 1761).

100 Quite problematically, Pufendorf used both 'right' and 'licence' to indicate the just belligerent's faculty to injure the enemy. See, for instance, Pufendorf, *De jure naturae*, II, 5, §§ 3 and 12.

101 Ibid VIII, 6, § 18. Some years before, in the *Elementorum jurisprudentiae universalis*, Pufendorf had been more moderate and had recalled the traditional opinion that those who exceed the limits of self-defence and demand a disproportionate reparation or satisfaction abused and consequently lost their right, so the former aggressor became the just enemy (Pufendorf, *Elementorum*, I, 21, § 2).

threat has occurred. For Pufendorf, a belligerent might exercise an absolute right not as a *iustus hostis* in Ayala's or Gentili's terms, that is, as a sovereign legally entitled to wage public war, but as the victim of an injury compelled to react for the sake of self-preservation. Pufendorf also put forward this argument to reconcile the classical just war doctrine – which focused on the justice of the cause – with the Hobbesian account of the state of nature – which linked war to fear. Indeed, although Hobbes, along with Grotius and Locke, had already hinted at the idea of an 'unlimited right' of the defender against the attacker, it was Pufendorf who made it a central category of the law of nature and nations.[102] Through his work, the 'unlimited right of the injured against the injurer' (*ius infinitum laesi in laedentem*) became a pivotal point in the discussion of belligerent rights and the permissible means of harming the enemy.

Pufendorf's *ius infinitum* theory was grounded on the assumption that natural law assigned to just belligerents the faculty to do whatever it took to achieve justice. They were entitled to carry on the fight until they obtained reparation for losses and damages caused by the unjust enemy and to make sure that he no longer constituted a present or future threat, in the fulfilment of which he might be totally annihilated.[103] Pufendorf clearly disclaimed the hypothesis that some proportion should be observed in retaliating against unjust combatants. Sparing the enemy might be advised by Christian ethics, but might at the same time jeopardise the nation's security. Charity had to be left aside because the fundamental perfect obligation of individual humans and nations remained self-preservation.[104] Instead of wasting time on the rhetorical provision that armed response shall be proportionate to the offence suffered, Pufendorf preferred to encourage sovereigns to listen to prudence and to make preparations for upcoming wars.[105] On the basis of the just enemy's absolute right and duty to security and self-preservation, Pufendorf also came to the conclusion that this enemy was allowed to kill or

102 Thomas Hobbes, *De cive* (first published 1642, Richard Tuck ed, CUP, 1998) I, 10 (where an absolute right of injuring the enemy flows from the *ius omnium in omnia*); Hobbes, *Leviathan*, II, 28; Grotius, *De iure belli ac pacis*, II, 1, § 10; John Locke, *Two Treatises of Government* (first published 1690, Peter Laslett ed, CUP, 1988) Second Treatise, III, 20; XVI, 182.

103 Pufendorf, *De jure naturae*, II, 5, § 3.

104 Ibid II, 5, § 16.

105 Ibid II, 5, § 6. Other writers, less influenced by Hobbes, clearly stressed the necessity of respecting some proportion between the injury and the licence to harm the enemy. See, for instance, Johann Wolfgang Textor, *Synopsis juris gentium* (first published 1680, Carl Ludwig von Bar ed, Washington, Carnegie Institution, 1916) ch 18.

mutilate innocent people even in peacetime if this was necessary to survive.[106]

Pufendorf's *ius belli* came down to a *ius ad bellum*. It singled out the righteous reasons for war and left to the conscience of the adversaries the question of how to conduct and terminate hostilities. It would be euphemistic to say that Pufendorf did not think much of the role of the customs of the 'civilised nations' in humanising warfare. To him, customary international law was only a device for belligerent parties to embellish the game of war.[107] In Pufendorf's view, all such customs might be disregarded by the just enemy, especially if they stood in the way of victory.[108]

Right to Make War versus Right to Punish?

A point in which Pufendorf appeared original compared with the tradition of the *ius belli* was represented by his spelling out the ends of warfare, which he categorised as self-defence, reparation, and safety for the future.[109] These ends of warfare had certainly been mentioned in former scholarship, but had not been systematically linked together and conceived of as a threefold end thus far. In particular, while self-defence and the pursuit of reparation or satisfaction had usually been presented together as central requirements for just war, future security as a goal of war in its own right was a specifically modern addition.[110] It constituted a natural outgrowth of the proliferation of warfare in early-modern times and of Machiavellian and Hobbesian anthropological pessimism. In medieval theories of warfare, the reflection on post-war scenarios came into play only in moral and theological discussions on the just enemy's 'righteous intention' (*recta intentio*), or when scholars called on victors to use clemency and moderation in the aftermath of conflicts in order to abide by the Gospel.[111] A modification of this perspective first occurred in

[106] Pufendorf, *De jure naturae* II, 6, § 4.

[107] Ibid VIII, 6, § 15.

[108] Ibid II, 3, § 23.

[109] These three goals might be independent from or imply each other depending on the situation. See also Gentili, *De iure belli*, III, 2; Grotius, *De iure belli ac pacis*, II, 1, §§ 1–2.

[110] The combination of self-defence and reparation was inaugurated by Cicero's famous statement that 'extra ulciscendi aut propulsandorum hostium causam bellum geri nullum potest'. See Cicero, *De re publica* (Clinton W Keyes trans, London, Heinemann, 1928) II, 23, 25. For the sedimentation of this account in the medieval thought see Frederick H Russell, *The Just War in the Middle Ages* (CUP, 1975).

[111] An attempt to resume and rationalise the complex of authoritative opinions on these issues was made by Grotius in his *De iure praedae commentarius*, ch IX.

sixteenth century modern historiography and political science, when questions such as whether or not to take vengeance on the defeated and raze to the ground their fortresses was seen as one of prudence and state interest, not of justice and charity.[112] Within this framework the primary goal was to prevent the defeated from regaining military strength and seeking vengeance, hence it might be necessary to annihilate his troops and tear down his cities. This realist approach was then approved by jurists such as Bodin, Ayala, and Gentili, and found its way into that stream of the natural law tradition which was emancipating itself from Scholasticism. Eventually, once Hobbes had stated that natural individuals were characterised by mutual fear and will of hurting, and that they lived in an inherently perpetual state of war, safety for the future began to be accepted as a key objective of warfare.[113] In concrete terms, this implied the legalisation of pre-emptive war.[114]

Pufendorf, like Hobbes, justified pre-emptive warfare. Pufendorf contended that anticipation was rightful in the imminence of a threat, especially when a peaceful approach would be unlikely to dissuade the adversary from attacking.[115] In his view, the adversary could be defined as an aggressor for the fact alone of having conceived an attack and preparing himself to execute it, regardless of whether any military aggression was actually carried out. According to Pufendorf, a pre-emptive strike aimed to avert a likely aggression qualified as an act in self-defence.[116]

This doctrine did not lean on earlier scholarship. When Vitoria, Gentili, Suárez, or Grotius talked about safety for the future, they still intended it, following Seneca, as a form of penalty and not as an autonomous goal of war.[117] Gentili devoted an entire chapter of his *De iure belli* to this issue, and gave valuable insights into the conception that traditional legal doctrine had of security and punishment. Building on Seneca's *De clementia*, Gentili claimed that punishment (*ultio*) pursued two goals: compensation

---

112 Niccolò Machiavelli, *Il Principe* (first published 1513, Delio Cantimori ed, *Il Principe e altre opere politiche*, Milan, Garzanti, 1976) XX; Niccolò Machiavelli, *Discorsi sopra la prima deca di Tito Livio* (first published 1513–21, Delio Cantimori ed, *Il Principe e altre opere politiche*, Milan, Garzanti, 1976) II, 24.

113 Hobbes, *De cive*, I, 1, §§ 2–3; I, 1, § 13.

114 Hobbes, *Leviathan*, I, 13.

115 Pufendorf, *De jure naturae et gentium*, II, 5, § 6.

116 Ibid.

117 Francisco de Vitoria, *Relectio de iure belli* (first published 1539, Anthony Pagden and Jeremy Lawrance eds, CUP, 1991) XVIII; Gentili, *De iure belli*, III, 13; Francisco Suárez, *De triplici virtute theologica* (first published 1621, Gwladys L Williams trans, Oxford, Clarendon, 1944) disp XIII, sec VII, § 5; Grotius, *De iure belli ac pacis*, II, 20, §§ 8 and 9.

for injury, and security for the time to come. He also specified that, in the narrow sense, punishment was a chastisement for past injuries, while vengeance (*vindicta* or *vindicatio*) aimed to avert the enemy from committing further misdeeds in the future.[118] But whether such an account precisely corresponded to the general or technical legal meaning of these terms in ancient Rome was of negligible importance for Gentili.[119] He and most writers up to Grotius rather argued on a normative plane that revenge, that is, any forceful action taken against the perpetrator beyond the limits of self-defence, should not be sought out of acrimony but in the pursuit of justice and, more importantly, state utility (*utilitas reipublicae*).[120] While justice was achieved through reparation, utility was secured by the guarantee of future peace and, under national criminal law, by the correction of the wrongdoer.

Whether based on judicial practice, common sense or authoritative sources, the great majority of legal theorists in early modern times considered penalty as an instrument to educate the offender and ensure the victim's and the whole community's security. Their conceptualisation of the ends of warfare was accordingly based on the following, threefold temporal sequence: 'self-defence', which was a response to a present threat; 'restitution', 'reparation', 'compensation', or 'satisfaction', all of which served to re-establish justice after a past injury; and 'punishment', which was meted out to ensure future tranquillity. This temporal and functional differentiation went along with the classification of war into defensive, reparative, and punitive.[121]

However, when Pufendorf listed the ends of warfare, he proposed an alternative three-fold categorisation differentiating self-defence; restitution or satisfaction; and reparation. He dropped punishment on the

---

118 This Gentili claimed on the basis of the *De differentiis vocabulorum*, a work by an unknown Latin grammarian which he erroneously ascribed to Fronto (Gentili, *De iure belli*, III, 13).

119 For a philological analysis of these terms see Egidio Forcellini, 'Vindicta' in *Lexicon totius Latinitatis* (first pubslished 1771, Jacopo Facciolati and Egidio Forcellini eds, Padua, 1871) vol 4, 998.

120 Frank Grunert, 'Theologien der Strafe. Zur Straftheorie von Thomas von Aquin und ihrer Rezeption in der Spanischen Spätscholastik: das Beispiel Francisco de Vitoria' in Hans Schlosser and Dietmar Willoweit (eds), *Neue Wege strafrechtsgeschichtlicher Forschung* (Cologne – Weimar – Vienna, Böhlau, 1999) 313, 327.

121 This distinction can already be somehow perceived in Baldus de Ubaldis, *Super toto Codice* (1545 Lyon edn) ad *Codex* 3.34 (De servitutibus et de aqua), n 71, f 197r. As for the moderns, see Diego Covarruvias, *In regulae peccatum: De regulis iuris, lib. VI admodum breves commentarji* (first published 1554) in Diego Covarruvias, *Opera Omnia* (Turin, 1594) vol 2, II, § 10, 3; Grotius, *De iure predae*, 69.

ground that it cannot exist in the state of nature without a common authority. He thus replaced the right 'to punish' (*punire*) by the right to 'extract assurance' (*cautionem extorquere*) from the unjust enemy.[122] The name was different but the meaning remained the same, as Norwegian theologian Johann Ernst Gunnerus put it some years later. Gunnerus rightly pointed out that 'Pufendorf actually admits of a punitive war as a matter of fact, only he does not like the word punishment.'[123] Indeed, with regard to the civil sphere Pufendorf had taken a classical Grotian line by defining punishment as a measure aimed to correct the criminal and deter him and his fellow citizens from infringing upon the law.[124] The deterrent function of penalty so described corresponded to security for the future, to which Pufendorf's *cautionem extorquere* was aimed as well. The dispute was merely terminological. Following Hobbes, Pufendorf assumed that punishment was a harm inflicted ('with respect of the future good', specified Hobbes) by a superior, and hence it was unconceivable in the state of nature.[125] This being so, any forceful action taken by a state against its public enemies – and against all those who, within or without, did not recognise or were not submitted to its authority – constituted an act of war, not a punitive measure.

That this controversy was purely about names is patently clear, considering Hobbes' foundation of the right to punish. Hobbes argued that the right to punish proper first originated when natural individuals turned all their rights over to the sovereign. The right to punish did not exist prior to the creation of sovereignty, 'for the Subjects did not give the Sovereign that right; but only in laying down theirs, strengthened him to use his own, as he should think of it, for the preservation of them all.'[126] Therefore, the right to punish was not something essentially different from the right of war: it represented the aggregate product of all natural individuals' rights of war as concentrated in the sovereign person upon stipulation of the social covenant. For this construction to be effected, contractors to the social covenant did not need to declare that they would not resist to publicly sanctioned penalties – indeed an impossible

122 Pufendorf, *De jure naturae*, VIII, 6, § 3.

123 Gunnerus, *Vollständige Erklärung*, ad § 365, n 3.

124 Grotius, *De iure belli ac pacis*, II, 20, §§ 7–9. Despite some criticism, Pufendorf basically stuck to Grotius' definition of the aims of punishment. See Pufendorf, *De jure naturae*, VIII, 3, § 9.

125 Hobbes, *Leviathan*, II, 28.

126 Ibid.

obligation according to Hobbes – but only that they would abstain from acting on behalf of any third party against the civil authority.[127]

That the right to punish was a subspecies of the right to make war is confirmed by the fact that Hobbes substantially assimilated internal and external enemies. The right to punish accordingly represented the right of war that civil authorities exercised against nationals. Domestically, this right might be subject to some restrictions as rulers were bound to punish their subjects according to municipal laws and equity, but internationally they were allowed to use force arbitrarily, against legitimate states as well as pirate states. With respect to the domestic sphere it is, however, significant that all of the limitations on the right to punish mentioned by Hobbes were purely descriptive, not normative. He certainly contended that harms which were inflicted without public hearing, which exceeded penalties prescribed by the law, or which were inferior to the benefit of the transgression could not be defined as forms of punishment. Yet by arguing so he was by no means denying the legal validity of such acts, but instead differentiated them from penalties proper for the sake of definition. In Hobbes' view, a prince might well take measures which went beyond those described, only they no longer fell within the category of punishment, but rather within that of hostile act. Again, it was a matter of terminology.

If Pufendorf did place some clear restraints on the exercise of domestic power, he wholly shared the Hobbesian opinion that sovereigns may act with absolute discretion in foreign affairs.[128] This became patent in the doctrine of the just enemy's 'unlimited right' to repress the unjust enemy. As much as some commentators attempted to understate the real scope of this doctrine in the work of Pufendorf and other natural lawyers making use of the 'unlimited right' notion, such as Heinrich Köhler and Christian Wolff, the real meaning of the notion could hardly be mistaken. Gunnerus endeavoured to explain that whilst Pufendorf, Köhler and Wolff spoke of an 'unlimited right' (*ius infinitum, unendliches Recht*) they in fact meant a mere 'indefinite right' (*ius indefinitum, unbestimmtes Recht*).[129] That is, they did not accord the just enemy an unrestricted licence of war, but only granted him full discretion in the choice of the means necessary to obtain safety and reparation from an aggressor who had no rights of his own. Yet this attempt to minimise the validity of the *ius infinitum* was not

[127] Hobbes, *De cive*, II, 18; Pufendorf, *De jure naturae*, VIII, 3, § 1.

[128] Pufendorf discussed the limitations to the exercise of civil power in *De jure naturae*, VII, 6.

[129] Gunnerus, *Vollständige Erklärung*, ad § 334.

convincing. The 'unlimited right' was surely 'indefinite', but also much more than that. Pufendorf left no doubts on this point when he discussed the issue of duelling and stated that even a slap in the face authorised the offended to kill the offender. Committing an injury meant forfeiting any rights of one's own and throwing oneself at the injured party's mercy. The injured party might still spare the attacker or treat him fairly as a consequence of moral principles, but he was not obliged to do so by the law.[130] To Pufendorf, the *ius infinitum* clearly meant the right to annihilate the unjust enemies and exterminate them if necessary.

This should apply especially against enemies of mankind such as pirates and robbers. Such criminals, claimed Pufendorf, could not be excused by the argument that even noble peoples of ancient times would pillage and plunder, since all of them, the Greeks included, did so out of corrupt mores and not of right.[131] Interestingly, however, Pufendorf pointed out that only pirates assailing foreigners indiscriminately ought to be labelled as enemies of mankind. Indeed there existed pirates who, although they were accustomed to attacking and violating covenants stipulated with certain peoples, respected and maintained good relationships with others. As Jean Barbeyrac remarked, Pufendorf here was referring to the Barbary corsairs, who attacked Christian vessels while living in peace with most Muslims.[132] As much as the behaviour of the North African corsairs might reveal a perpetual hostile sentiment against Christianity, it did not amount to general enmity against mankind.

In Pufendorf's eyes, even the principle of reciprocity could be brought forward in defence of the Barbary corsairs. Hypothetically, the corsairs could be seen as just enemies acting in retaliation, because among Christians themselves 'there are those who have the task of waging an implacable war on the Muslims.'[133] Remarkably, this opinion only appeared in Pufendorf's dissertation *De existimatione* but was absent in his major works such as *Elementorum jurisprudentiae universalis*, *De iure naturae et gentium*, and *De officio hominis et civis*. Pufendorf's caution was understandable, since his statement represented the first admission by a European international legal scholar that Muslim privateering might be

[130] Pufendorf, *De jure naturae*, II, 5, § 12.

[131] Samuel Pufendorf, *De existimatione* in Samuel Pufendorf, *Dissertationes academicae selectiores* (Lund, 1675) § 7, 203.

[132] Samuel Pufendorf, *Le droit de la nature et des gens* (Jean Barbeyrac ed, Amsterdam 1706) vol 2, VII, 4, § 5, n 3. See also Samuel Pufendorf, *De officio hominis et civis juxta legem naturalem libri duo* (Gottlieb Gerhard Titius ed, Leipzig, 1709) ad II, 14, § 3.

[133] Pufendorf, *De existimatione*, § 7.

equivalent to Christian privateering legally as well as morally. To be sure, Grotius had already stated in a similar tone that the struggle between Muslims and Christians in the Mediterranean was conducted legally by both sides under the *vetus ius gentium*, but in his eyes this only occurred because the Algerians' barbarous warfare had forced Europeans to get even, therefore the Algerians alone were responsible for the persistence in modern times of primitive practices such as the enslavement of war prisoners. At the basis of this view lay the assumption that Europeans, as heirs of the Greek and the Roman culture and as believers of the true religion, were the bearers of the highest civilisation and had a deep insight into the principles of natural law and of the law of nations. If the Greeks and the Romans practiced the *vetus ius gentium*, this was so because they lived at the dawn of civilisation and had to deal with barbarous peoples unaware or neglectful of the laws of humanity. In a similar way, Grotius assumed that in the medieval and modern period the Knights of Malta and of St Stephen had to wage a nearly lawless war on the Saracens and the Barbary corsairs to protect Christianity aggressed and in danger.

Pufendorf thought, conversely, that the confrontation between the Christians and the Muslims in the Mediterranean was one between two different standards of civilisation of which none might claim superiority over the other. In his view, the Greek and Roman anti-barbarian rhetoric as well as the European civilising discourse indicated nothing but haughtiness and overconfidence.[134] Pufendorf clearly dismissed European lawyers' pretension of speaking in the name of humanity and labelling North African privateers as 'common enemies of all'.

Yet, despite its emancipatory potential, Pufendorf's cultural openness and his criticism of the European monopolisation of the law of nature remained of little use to the Barbary corsairs. The very principles which enabled Pufendorf to raise the international legal status of Algerians and Tunisians were at the same time used to their detriment. That he relieved them from their condition of universal enemies and targets of (indeed improbable) international coalitions did not mean that they should regain their innocence and receive a better treatment. Rather, they fell into a state of nature in which they could be regarded as unjust enemies and exterminated by recourse to the *ius infinitum* (the corsairs might label their opponents as unjust enemies in turn, but nonetheless remained in an unenviable position). Because one had to assume that customs and

134 Pufendorf, *De jure naturae*, VIII, 6, § 5.

treaties had no legal force here and that the laws of morality found little consideration among natural individuals, the best way to survive was to strike first and heavily, as Pufendorf argued in his justification of pre-emptive warfare. Such a harsh conception of war as a form of pre-emption and repression, foreshadowed by Pufendorf in the 1670s, was repeatedly implemented by Louis XIV in the following decades, at times against Algiers as well. Apparently, the Barbary corsairs were better off in their heyday as 'common enemies of all' than as sovereigns in the post-Westphalian international arena so well depicted in Pufendorf's *De jure naturae*.

Vattel inherited some significant and problematic elements of the Pufendorfian theory: the extension of the enemy of mankind notion to criminals other than pirates, the idea of punitive war, the 'unlimited right' concept, and (partly) the justification of pre-emptive warfare. All of these aspects, some of which overtly justified total warfare, found application in Vattel's enemy of mankind theory. But while Pufendorf had no difficulties applying those notions in the international sphere, because he saw war as a near feral condition hardly moderated by moral obligations, Vattel, writing in the heyday of 'polished warfare', had to provide further arguments as to why certain sovereigns and public enemies forfeited their belligerent rights and might rightfully be 'punished', or even exterminated. Vattel set out to do so by means of his doctrine of collective security, which Wolff had first elaborated while bypassing Pufendorf to re-read Hobbes. This doctrine was supposed to ground the enforcement of international law on a firmer basis than the classical just war doctrine, of which Pufendorf's theory illustrated both the potentialities and contradictions.

Revisiting the Grotian Paradigm: Heinrich and Samuel von Cocceji

Heinrich von Cocceji's Anti-Utilitarian Natural Law and his Stigmatisation of Barbary Warfare

While the progressive view of the Algerians put forward by Pufendorf in his dissertation *De existimatione* went largely unnoticed, the learned discussion on Barbary privateering in the eighteenth century still pivoted on Bodin's and Grotius' arguments. The most significant contribution to this discussion can be found in the *Grotius illustratus*, a critical commentary on Grotius' *De iure belli ac pacis* initiated by German jurist Heinrich von Cocceji and published by his son Samuel, with extensive additions of his own, between 1744 and 1752.[135] The main tenets of the commentary were based on a rejection of Grotius' assertion that the law of nature was founded on the principle of sociability, and on a denial of the Grotian concept of the voluntary law of nations. Heinrich, as well as Samuel, who shared many of the principles first expounded by his father, also disagreed with Grotius on the way in which certain knowledge of the principles of the law of nations could be attained. They argued that Grotius' reliance on authoritative opinions and the general consent of peoples as a means to find legal norms was unwarranted. In their opinion, the 'empirical' method as well as the Aristotelian principles about human nature as contained in *De iure belli ac pacis* led to ambiguous and unsatisfactory conclusions as to the features of natural and international law. This was so because the unique source of the law of nature was the will of God, they argued, as opposed to sociability.

According to the Coccejis, Grotius' considerations on piracy/privateering, largely based on municipal law and the customary law of nations, exemplified his failure to deliver rational and coherent norms in accordance with divine law. Based on an analysis of the Scriptures, they dismissed his idea of a postdiluvian nomadic existence in which all peoples were accustomed to committing piracy and robbery; and they also denied the hypothesis of a loose law of nations typical of ancient and barbarous times. The Coccejis claimed that a 'society of mankind' as conceived of by Grotius had never existed, so it was pointless to argue that its dissolution had brought about a specific law of war and conception of warfare. In their view, even the harshest international legal institutions such as the enslavement of war captives belonged to the law of nature as given by God, and not to the customary law of nations of old.[136]

---

[135] Heinrich von Cocceji (1644–1719), professor of the law of nature and nations first at Heidelberg, as the successor of Pufendorf, and then at Frankfurt/Oder, was the author of the first systematic textbook on German public law (*Juris publici prudentia*, Frankfurt/Oder, 1695) and of a number of works on international and private law. See Erich Döring, 'Heinrich von Cocceji' in *Neue Deutsche Biographie* (Bayerische Akademie der Wissenschaften ed, Berlin, Duncker & Humblot, 1957) vol 3, 300. He engaged in the debate on the foundation of natural law and argued, against Grotius' and Pufendorf's sociability theory, that the law of nature was grounded on divine will. Samuel von Cocceji (1679–1755) was co-author, with his father Heinrich, of the *Grotius illustratus* [Wrocław (Breslau), 1744–1752, 4 vols], but devoted himself mainly to practical activities. He led an extensive reform of the Prussian justice system under Frederick II. See Erich Döring, 'Samuel von Cocceji' in *Neue Deutsche Biographie*, vol 3, 301.

[136] Samuel von Cocceji, *Introductio ad Henrici L. B. de Cocceji Grotium illustratum* (Halle, 1748) diss IV, § 43. The Coccejis similarly claimed that the right of postliminy belonged to the law of nature: ibid diss XII, § 758; Heinrich von Cocceji, *Theses ordinariae ex jure*

The issue of slavery was extremely relevant in relation to Barbary privateering. To demonstrate that slavery – or at least the kind of slavery that originated from warfare – might be justified by the law of nature, the Coccejis put forward the argument that those who waged a just war had the right to take any action necessary for their security, which might involve the enslavement of war prisoners. The Coccejis thus furthered Pufendorf's argument that the victims of an act of aggression in the state of nature had the right to carry self-defence to its extremes by annihilating the aggressor if this was necessary for the sake of present and future security.[137] Since the aggressor 'disrupted any relations of humanity'[138] with his victims, he consigned himself to their judgement and lost nearly all rights as a human being, notably the right to life, liberty, and property.[139] As a result, he might be enslaved as well.[140]

In some regards, the Coccejis even went beyond Pufendorf. While Pufendorf maintained that the enslavement of war captives had a consensual and customary basis (which he deemed weak, indeed),[141] the Coccejis affirmed that it was inherently rational. They insisted that this form of enslavement arose from the forfeiture of rights by the assailant following his wrongdoing, and from the absolute licence to harm that natural law conceded to those acting in self-defence. The Coccejis thereby put forward a radical version of the 'unlimited right' doctrine.

On the other hand, the Coccejis' radical interpretation of the just enemy's absolute right at war was complicated by their argument that determination of the just cause could not be made by the warring parties themselves. Heinrich von Cocceji, in particular, expressly rejected the Hobbesian view that in the state of nature everyone is judge in his own cause, and he forcefully rejected the 'monstrous idea' of a natural *jus omnium in omnia*.[142]

---

naturae & gentium de jure postliminii (Heidelberg, 1673) § 6–7. Regarding piracy, the Coccejis questioned the Grotian statement that it had been a general consent of all nations which had deprived freebooters of rights at war. They argued that the necessity of a moral and legal condemnation of piracy was evident to all reasonable beings and that the universal criminalisation of piracy stemmed from rational certitude. Pirates were forbidden to enslave their prisoners and were not permitted to enjoy postliminy not because a large majority of peoples agreed on this, as Grotius had put it, but because piracy was contrary to the most elementary principles of natural justice.

137 Pufendorf, *De jure naturae*, II, 5, § 3; VIII, 6, § 7.

138 Ibid II, 5, § 3.

139 Ibid VIII, 6, § 16.

140 Ibid IV, 3, §§ 5–6.

141 Ibid VI, 3, §§ 4–5.

142 Heinrich von Cocceji, *Theses ordinariae*, § 1; Heinrich von Cocceji, *Prodromus iustitiae gentium sive exercitationes duae* (Frankfurt/Oder, 1719) Exercitatio II, § 37.

Advancing an analogy between international and domestic disputes, Heinrich stated that all differences should preferably be settled by arbitration or adjudication by an impartial third party.[143] And this remained true even though the custom of summoning arbitral courts for international legal disputes had long decayed.[144] Regardless of whether human arbiters passed judgment, the actual sentence was pronounced by God.

> [W]e will demonstrate that all wars and battles are decided by the most just and wise advice of the Heavenly Powers, and that no war or battle is indeed decided by accident or with an undue and unjust outcome.[145]

Heinrich von Cocceji's account of warfare as an instrument of divine providence and retribution was no doubt original in a time when the law of nature and nations was emancipating itself from theology. This account was underpinned by a literal interpretation of old-testamentary as well as new-testamentary texts and had allegedly been confirmed by the customs of the Germanic peoples, and by feudal law and warfare.[146] Since God was supposed to intervene directly in human history, waging war was not merely a means to obtain redress, but also always a means to enforce His justice. Indeed, the deepest aim of any war should be to punish the wrongdoer, since God bestowed on the just enemies the right to make war 'not much for them to claim compensation for losses, but for them to invoke the talion, that is, the punishment for an injury inflicted.'[147] This point was confirmed in the dissertation *De sacro-sancto talionis iure*, in which Heinrich von Cocceji resorted to biblical, Greek, and Roman sources to assert that the talion was the only true principle of criminal law.[148] A convinced anti-utilitarian, he believed that punishment ought to be

---

143 Heinrich von Cocceji, *Theses ordinariae*, § 3. See also Heinrich von Cocceji, *De postliminio in pace, et amnestia* (Frankfurt/Oder, 1691) I, §§ 1–2.

144 Wilhelm Grewe, *The Epochs of International Law* (Michael Byers trans, Berlin, de Gruyter, 2000) 199–200 [trans of *Epochen der Völkerrechtsgeschichte* (first published 1984)].

145 Heinrich von Cocceji, *Dissertatio iuris gentium publici de iusto proeliorum exitu* (Frankfurt/Oder, 1706) Summaria, § 6; I, 5. Translation by the author. Original text: '[D]emonstratum dabimus, omnia bella ac proelia justissimo aeque ac sapientissimo summi Numinis Consilio, nullum vero vel fortuito casu, vel indebito injustove exitu decidi.'

146 Heinrich von Cocceji, *Disputatio iuris gentium publici de armis illicitis* (Frankfurt/Oder, 1698) § 6.

147 Samuel von Cocceji, *Introductio*, diss XII, § 740. The conception of war as a judgement did not imply, however, that sovereigns may identify themselves with biblical figures and presume to be the chosen executors of God's commands. Since sovereigns as humans were easily corrupted by passion and interest, they lacked any true insight into the inscrutable will of God. Indeed, the Coccejis stated that modern sovereigns were not addressed directly by God as were the ancient rulers of Israel and therefore could not know with certainty whether war must be waged and to what extent the enemy must be punished.

148 Heinrich von Cocceji, *De sacro-sancto talionis iure* (Frankfurt/Oder, 1705).

inflicted simply because a crime had been committed (*quia peccatum est*), and not to prevent future crimes (*ne peccetur*).[149]

The question arose of whether this pattern could apply to piratical wars as well. Indeed, as Barbeyrac noticed, Heinrich von Cocceji strongly criticized Grotius' tolerant attitude towards Barbary and denied that goods seized by the Algerians became their property by the right of war.[150] He rejected the Grotian hypothesis that because the corsairs belonged to sovereign entities their maritime expeditions should be seen as acts of war by public enemies. He claimed that although the Barbary Regencies were de facto sovereigns, they remained criminal associations (*societates sceleris*), not body politics properly established for the sake of true happiness and justice.[151] Heinrich von Cocceji thus pushed to extremes Bodin's argument on the just aim of a commonwealth – an argument that Bodin himself had already denied could apply to Barbary.

> What if human nature, which prompts human beings to desire a peaceful and stable society ... legalised all societies, including those of robbers and pirates, as if they were stable and peaceful? Rather, there must be admitted another principle of law, according to which pirate societies are prohibited, and thus licit societies can be distinguished from the illicit ones. ... [T]he city of the Algerian pirates ... is so powerful, stable, peaceful internally, completely self-sufficient, and strong militarily that no other city has been able to weaken its power thus far; yet at present the Algerians attack all with impunity, and infest the seas with their depredations, publicly and in front of the whole world.[152]

Heinrich von Cocceji's criminalisation of the Barbary corsairs, first laid down in his dissertation *De postliminio in pace* of 1691, may have originated in the climate of hostility against the Ottomans and their allies common

149 This point would be retained against spreading utilitarianism by Kant as well. See Immanuel Kant, *Rechtslehre* (first published 1797, Wilhelm Weischedel ed, *Kants Werke*, vol 8, Frankfurt am Main, Suhrkamp, 1977) § 49, sec I. Here Kant criticised Seneca's utilitarian position in *De ira*, XIX, 5.

150 Hugo Grotius, *Le droit de la guerre et de la paix* (2 vols, Jean Barbeyrac ed, Amsterdam, 1724) III, 9, § 19, n 1; Heinrich von Cocceji, *De postliminio in pace*, II, §§ 7–8.

151 Heinrich de Cocceji, *De postliminio in pace*, II, § 8.

152 Heinrich von Cocceji, *Prodromus*, Exercitatio I, § 118. Translation by the author. Original text: '[S]i humana natura, quae homines fert ad societatem tranquillam & stabilem appetendam, jus facit ... omnes societates, etiam praedonum & pyratarum, fore Justas, modo id agatur ut stabiles & tranquillae sint; aut admittendum est aliud principium juris, quo quaedam societates prohibitae, adeoque licitae ab illicitis distinctae sunt. ... [C]ivitas Algiriensium pyratarum ... tam potens, & firma, & in suo sinu tranquilla; tanta porro rerum omnium copia, tam validis opibus, ut nulla hactenus potentiam eam concutere potuerit; sed hodieque ipsa omnes impune lacessat, & publice in conspectus orbis terrarum toto mari depredationibus infestet.'

in Europe at the end of the seventeenth century in conjunction with the Great Turkish War. However, by the time he published the *Prodromus justitiae gentium* in 1719, from which the excerpt above is taken, this hostility had largely disappeared: a downsized Ottoman Empire no longer represented a threat to Europe. In those days the Sublime Porte's domestic as well as foreign policies were strongly influenced by a modernist current envisaging closer relations with European powers so as to keep up with their technological and military progress and achieve a favourable position within the 'balance of power' through diplomatic relations.[153] In 1720–1, the Ottomans sent an embassy to France to seek French expertise and improve the traditional friendship with Paris to Austria's detriment. Incidentally, a further aim of the embassy was to exert diplomatic pressure to compel the Knights of Malta to stop raiding Muslim shipping.[154] The Barbary corsairs were certainly not alone in infesting the Mediterranean.

Samuel Cocceji's Reassessment of the Concept of Piracy

Heinrich's son Samuel von Cocceji reversed his father's views on Barbary. Samuel first distinguished between pirates subject to a civil authority and acting within its jurisdiction from those independent of any such authority – a distinction foreshadowing the neat nineteenth century dichotomy between piracy under domestic law and piracy under international law.[155] Cocceji stated that pirates subject to a civil authority should be punished by the sovereign, who also ought to provide redress for the victims. In respect to independent pirates, he further differentiated between rogue pirates without state support and 'pirate nations' exerting sovereignty over a specific territory. According to Cocceji's view, rogue pirates were exemplified by vagrant robbers like the filibusters, who allegedly escaped from the restraints of civil society and held all nations to be potential enemies. Because pirates lived in the state of nature they could righteously be punished directly by their victims and those who came to their rescue.[156] Military action by legitimate political authorities against

153 Heinz Duchhardt, *Balance of power und Pentarchie* (Paderborn, Schöningh, 1997) 193.

154 Fatma Müge Göçek, *East Encounters West. France and the Ottoman Empire in the Eighteenth Century* (OUP, 1987) 9–10.

155 Henry Wheaton, *Elements of International Law, with a Sketch of the History of the Science* (Philadelphia, Carey, Lea & Blanchard, 1836) II, 2, § 16.

156 Pirates had the entire human kind as their enemy ('totum humanum genus pro hoste habent'). See Samuel von Cocceji, *Introductio*, Diss IX, § 166. Pirates were then enemies of mankind not because they actually made war against all but because they had a

such robbers was taken by the right of necessary self-defence (*de jure necessariæ defensionis*).

As far as 'pirate nations' like the Barbary corsairs were concerned, they qualified as public enemies entitled to wage public war. After all, Cocceji said, the Romans had similarly regarded the Cilician pirates as true public enemies, as was confirmed by Pompey being awarded the triumph after his victories over them in the *bella piratica* (this account opposed Gentili's erroneous statement testifying to Pompey being denied the triumph).[157] Cocceji went on to say that, more recently, the war between Charles V and Hayreddin Barbarossa in the first half of the sixteenth century equally qualified as a public war, as Barbarossa fought as an admiral of the Ottoman fleet in the name of the Sublime Porte, obtaining the title of pasha in return. Here Cocceji pointed out that Barbarossa waged war in compliance with the law of nations.

> If pirates form a nation, and observe the law of nations in their relations with neighbouring states, and never infest the seas, then a conflict with them is a true public war. ... Such was the Balearic War ... as well as the war that Charles V waged against Hayreddin Barbarossa. The latter indeed was a commander of the Turk navy and thus waged war on behalf and for the right of the Ottomans.[158]

Samuel Cocceji did not express himself about the current situation, but if he legitimated the Algerians' privateering in the mid-sixteenth century – a time in which their international legal status was dubious, as they were neither politically autonomous nor completely dependent on the Ottomans – he all the more had to justify the Algerians' later wars.[159]

'disposition thereto' (Hobbes, *Leviathan*, I, 13). On this point, Cocceji drew also on John Locke, *Two Treatises*, Second Treatise, VII, § 87: 'Those who are united into one body, and have a common established law and judicature to appeal to, with authority to decide controversies between them and punish offenders, are in civil society one with another; but those who have no such common appeal, I mean on earth, are still in the state of nature'.

157 Samuel von Cocceji, *Introductio*, diss IX, § 166, n 7; Gentili, *De iure belli*, bk I, ch 4, p 25. Pompey's triumph, testified by Florus (*Epitome de Tito Livio bellorum omnium annorum DCC libri* (Edward S Forster trans, London, Heinemann, 1929), III, 6), had not been of much consequence for Heinrich von Cocceji, who had considered the use of the term *bellum* with regard to piratical and civil wars by Roman sources improper. See Heinrich von Cocceji, *Prodromus*, Exercitatio II, § 162.

158 Samuel von Cocceji, *Introductio*, diss IX, § 166, n 7. Translation by the author. Original text: 'Si piratae gentem constituunt, & cum potentis vicinis jura gentium observant, ac maria saltem infestant, verum bellum publicum est. ... Huc quoque pertinet bellum Balearicum, ... item quod cum Barbarossa gessit CAROLUS V. Fuit enim ille praefectus classis Turcicae, adeoque Ottomanorum jure & nomine bellum gerebat.'

159 The brothers Barbarossa seized power in Algiers in 1516 after driving out the Spanish and put to death the Arab sheik Selim ben-Eutemi, who had been called on to rule the city

In the first decades of the eighteenth century, European international lawyers no longer doubted that the Regency of Algiers constituted a sovereign entity, independent from the Porte and from any European state, and did not need any external approval to wage war on the Christians. Samuel Cocceji clearly endorsed Grotius' opinion that the Barbary corsairs were lawful enemies, hence the rights of captivity and postliminy applied to wars between the corsairs and the Christians.[160]

Yet formal acknowledgment of the Barbary corsairs as public enemies did not imply that they should be treated any more humanely than ordinary pirates. As both Heinrich and Samuel Cocceji believed, following in Pufendorf's footsteps, that the right of the just belligerent was limitless, there might be little difference in labelling the attacker as either *hostis* or *pirata*. Samuel literally pleaded for an 'unlimited licence against the [unjust] enemy' (*infinita licentia in hostem*). He argued that even the right to enslave, harsh though it might appear, represented an attempt to put a curb on the exercise of the 'unlimited licence' and thus avert unnecessary slaughters. Yet the 'unlimited licence' came back into force against aggressors who waged unrestrained warfare without any just cause and without formal declaration. The Algerians fell into this category.

> Indeed, by the law of nature, when dealing with such peoples who enslave our nationals, rob them, and arrogate the right of life and death over them, it is licit to treat such peoples as robbers and thieves; thus, those who apprehend these peoples have the discretion to kill them, or spare them to make them slaves.[161]

In an attempt to describe the Barbary corsairs' unlawful conduct, Samuel von Cocceji stated that although they qualified as public enemies they were not lawful enemies proper in the sense of Roman law (*iure Romano hostes*) as long as they refused to declare war before attacking.[162] However, he was aware that this could hardly constitute a fundamental requirement for belligerent rights because the declaration of war had long lost the

---

by its population and had asked the Barbarossas for help against the Christians [Jörg Manfred Mössner, *Die Völkerrechtspersönlichkeit und die Völkerrechtspraxis der Barbareskenstaaten* (Berlin, de Gruyter, 1968) 4–5]. Later on, Algiers' position remained unstable until the disastrous expedition ordered by Charles V in 1541.

160 Samuel von Cocceji, *Introductio*, diss. IX, § 113.

161 Heinrich von Cocceji, *Grotius illustratus* (Samuel von Cocceji ed) vol 3, n *i* ad III, 9, § 18, 1. Translation by the author. Original text: 'Nam jure naturae in tales gentes quae cives nostros servos faciunt, eoque jus vitae & necis sibi in eos arrogant, res eorum rapiunt, &c. tanquam in praedones & fures saevire licet, adeoque in capientium arbitrio est an captos interficere, an servare eos, i.e. servos facere velint.'

162 Ibid vol 3, n *c* ad III, 9, § 19.

compulsory character it was attributed under the Roman *ius fetiale*.[163] At any rate, Cocceji assumed, the Algerians could be deemed unjust enemies as they lacked a just cause for war. As a result, he advanced a binary reasoning in which the corsairs' warfare was both formally 'legal', thanks to their sovereignty and the scarce relevance of the declaration of war, and 'unjust', due to their lack of a just cause. Samuel Cocceji here maintained a legalist and a naturalist approach in the same breath. It was characteristic of his position that he did not agree with the classical pragmatic argument, asserted by Bodin and Grotius, that although the Barbary corsairs waged unjust war and deserved moral blame they should be accorded impunity by the law to avoid the escalation of conflict. Indeed, Cocceji denied the very notion of impunity in international law in the first place: the unjust enemy deserved punishment at any rate, regardless of his sovereign status, by a just enemy bearing a *licentia infinita*.

Cocceji could not categorise the Algerians either as public enemies proper or as pirates and indeed did not draw any significant consequences from such a distinction. He thus sought alternative conceptualisations, philosophical rather than legal, to circumvent the dichotomy of pirates *versus* public enemies when it proved inapplicable. Drawing on Plato's and Aristotle's category of 'natural enmity', Cocceji contended that the Algerians essentially represented the 'natural public enemies' (*naturali ratione hostes*) of the Christians.[164] Although Plato and Aristotle applied the natural enmity concept to the hostility between the civilised Greeks and the 'barbarians', and in doing so clearly discriminated against the latter, Cocceji claimed that he was using the concept in a neutral way. He also delivered an original interpretation of Aristotle according to which Aristotle himself was not despising the 'barbarian' Persians when he argued that a state of 'natural war' existed between them and the Greeks. In Cocceji's view, by 'natural war' Aristotle merely meant a long-lasting

---

[163] For Grotius, the declaration of war was not a matter of justice, but rather of convenience. He argued that the practice of declaring war had been introduced in order to assure that military confrontations qualified as public wars proper and thus produced certain legal effects, especially regarding the ownership of captured goods (Grotius, *De iure belli ac pacis*, III, 3, § 11). This view was opposed by Barbeyrac who considered the claim for satisfaction as a decisive element of the war declaration and stressed the parties' moral duty to seek a peaceful settlement of the dispute (Grotius, *Le droit de la guerre et de la paix*, III, 3, § 11, n 2, 763). For a survey of the declaration of war in early modern theory and practice, see Frederic J Baumgartner, *Declaring War in Early Modern Europe* (New York, Palgrave Macmillan, 2011) especially 115–145.

[164] Plato, *Republic* (Robin Waterfield trans, OUP, 1994) V, 470c; Aristotle, *The Politics* (Stephen Everson ed, CUP, 1988) I, 8, 1256b; Heinrich von Cocceji, *Grotius illustratus* (Samuel von Cocceji ed) vol 3, n *hh* ad II, § 20, 40.

conflict, that is, a 'perpetual' or 'hereditary' war, as Roman historian Florus later said of the Social War of 91–88 BC.[165] Cocceji argued that a similar state of persistent hostility, such as that which was frequent in ancient times, also existed between the Christians and the Barbary corsairs in modern times. This complicated the question of the original responsibility for the war and dimished the importance of the idea of just cause. Also, the concept of 'natural war' blurred the distinction between piracy and privateering, and rendered inapplicable customs such as the declaration of war, with the result that the Barbary corsairs were acting in between lawfulness and unlawfulness.[166]

In practice, this elaborate construction seemed to matter little once the just enemy was accorded an 'unlimited licence' against the unjust enemy. Although Samuel von Cocceji's argument proved emancipatory as regards the international legal status of the Barbary corsairs, it was not altogether a humanitarian argument. His reliance on the Pufendorfian concept of the 'unlimited licence' situated him in a doctrinal tradition which regarded war as a nearly unrestrained exercise of force, hardly moderated by moral prescriptions. While progressive in theory, the position of Pufendorf and Samuel Cocceji on the laws of war did not practically diverge from that of older humanist and realist writers like Pierino Belli, Bodin and Gentili who despite some moralising statements about moderation in armed conflict maintained that almost every means of warfare can be licit *iure belli*. Surely, Pufendorf, Samuel Cocceji and other just war doctrinarians insisted – more than the humanists – on the requirement of the just cause, but still claimed that those fighting for such a cause might nonetheless resort to any means necessary to attain victory.

Not even 'humanitarians' like Vattel entirely abandoned this radical conception of warfare. While Vattel tended to rule out the 'unlimited right' being applied to normal wars, he maintained that it might be resorted to collectively by the 'society of nations' in the face of grave threats to international security. In such cases, when the need for preserving a minimum international order and the laws of war so required, strict natural law

---

165 Florus depicted the Social War as a 'hereditary war' as it outlived the death of his initiator, the tribune of the plebs Livius Drusus: Florus, *Epitome*, II, 5; Heinrich von Cocceji, *Grotius illustratus* (Samuel von Cocceji ed) vol 3, n *g*, *h* ad III, § 9, 19.

166 A further example of 'natural and perpetual war' (*naturale et perpetuum bellum*) was represented by the ongoing conflict between the Spaniards and the filibusters. Even in this case, Samuel von Cocceji focused on the perpetuity of war rather than on the potentially discriminatory character of the natural enmity concept. See Samuel von Cocceji, *Introductio*, diss IX, § 166, n 7.

re-entered into force and justified total warfare. Here, it was Vattel's focus on security and utility that differentiated his contentions from earlier theories. His straightforwardly utilitarian arguments distinguished him from Pufendorf and Samuel von Cocceji, as well as from radical just war doctrinarians like Heinrich von Cocceji, who called for the repression of the Barbary corsairs for purposes of retribution.

The Pragmatic Legalisation of Barbary Warfare: Bynkershoek

To Samuel Cocceji's generation belonged Cornelius van Bijnkershoek, one of the most reputed authorities in the field of international law throughout the first half of the eighteenth century. If Cocceji had still hesitated to confer lawful enemy status upon the Barbary corsairs and notwithstanding such conferral maintained that they must be subject to harsh punishment by a just enemy, Bynkershoek put forward a straightforwardly pragmatic view. The sovereignty of the Barbary Regencies here constituted the key argument to accord the corsairs lawful enemy status and dismiss their lack of a just cause for war. In this connection Bynkershoek criticised the opinion of Gentili, who, just like him, was very much concerned with the concrete legal consequences of the charge of piracy.

> [I] do not think that we can reasonably agree with Alberico Gentili and others who class as pirates the so-called Barbary peoples of Africa, and that captures made by them entail no change in property. The peoples of Algiers, Tripoli, Tunis, and Salé are not pirates, but rather organised states ... The States-General [of the Dutch Republic], as well as other nations, have frequently made treaties with them ... Cicero defines as a regular enemy 'one that has a commonwealth, a senate, a treasury, the unified support of its citizens, and that shows some respect for treaties and covenants of peace when an occasion is offered to make one'. All these requirements they satisfy; they even have some respect for treaties, as other nations have, though nations are usually more concerned about their own advantage than about treaties. That they should have complete respect for treaties, no one could require, since we cannot require that even from other nations.[167]

Bynkershoek gave a somewhat reductive interpretation of Gentili, whose position was far more complex and contradictory than Bynkershoek's treatment of it in the passage above. Bynkershoek did so by interestingly reversing Gentili's reading of Cicero's famous definition of the public

---

[167] Cornelius van Bynkershoek, *Quaestionum juris publici libri duo* (first published 1737, Tenney Frank trans, Oxford, Clarendon, 1930) bk I, ch 17, p 99.

enemy in the *Philippicae*.[168] While Gentili had contended that the Barbary corsairs did not fit into Cicero's framework, Bynkershoek responded that they did, for they had a commonwealth supported by the consent of the governed, political institutions, a treasury, and had some respect for international treaties.[169] If this was more clearly the case in Bynkerhoek's lifetime, when Algiers and the other North African towns had gained total political autonomy, Gentili's position denying the Barbary corsairs' right to make war was already disputable around 1600. Gentili was himself aware that his interpretation of the Ciceronian definition of the enemy might sound overstated. He therefore went on to blame the Barbary corsairs for waging war without a just cause, rather than for being state-less robbers. Instead, Bynkershoek insisted on Cicero's definition and acknowledged the cities of Algiers, Tripoli, and Tunis as sovereign international legal subjects bearing the same dignity as European states.

While one strand of Bynkershoek's argument in favour of the Barbary corsairs was that they fell within Cicero's characterisation of the public enemy, the other strand was that they did not fit into the classical definition of the pirate. Indeed, according to the traditional doctrine, and to Louis XIV's *Ordonnance de la marine*, in which this doctrine was first implemented, pirates were 'those who rob on land or sea without the authorization of any sovereign.'[170] Patently, this definition of piracy under international law did not apply to the Barbary corsairs.

As he dealt with the Barbary issue, and piracy/privateering more generally, Bynkershoek had a clear pragmatic concern. His main aim was to provide clear definitions and guidelines, from whatever relevant sources were available, to settle cases of sea-robbery and prize disputes before the Dutch courts. In the chapter on piracy of his *Quaestiones juris publici*, Bynkershoek attempted to answer key practical questions such as which court should judge cases of piracy; how it should be punished; and whether foreigners could be brought before Netherlands' courts for piracy committed upon non-Dutch nationals.[171] It was owing to these concrete concerns

---

[168] Cicero, *Philippicae* (David R Shackleton Bailey trans, Harvard University Press, 2009) IV, 6.

[169] Gentili, *De iure belli*, bk I, ch 4, p 25.

[170] *Ordonnance de la marine* (first published 1681, Paris, Les Libraires Associés, 1755) bk III, tit IX, art 1 f.; Bynkershoek, *Quaestionum*, bk I, ch 17, p 98.

[171] Bynkershoek, *Quaestionum*, bk I, ch 17, pp 100–3. He came to the conclusion that common courts were competent in matters of piracy unless the indicted were Dutchmen acting under the Admiral's command, in which case the competence passed to the Admiralty. Regarding punishment, Bynkershoek recalled that notwithstanding the judge's discretion in adjudication the customary penalty for pirates consisted of the deprivation of

that Bynkershoek advanced a pragmatic opinion on Barbary privateering and acknowledged the corsairs' lawful belligerent status, which entailed their right to make war and retain booty. Not unlike Grotius, Bynkershoek saw in the legalisation of Barbary warfare a means to settle disputes over the ownership of goods captured by the corsairs and re-sold in Europe.

Yet while in the *Quaestiones juris publici* Bynkershoek stigmatised the equation of Barbary warfare with piracy as totally groundless, he seemed to express a somewhat different view in his early dissertation *De dominio maris*, in a passage in which he dismissed the claim of Genoa to hold dominion over the Ligurian Sea. According to the Genoese, they held an exclusive right over the Ligurian Sea because they protected it from the Barbary 'pirates'. It is noteworthy that instead of declaring Genoa's claim void on the ground that the Barbary corsairs qualified as lawful enemies, Bynkershoek simply resorted to the argument that the Genoese were not permanently patrolling the Ligurian Sea with their fleet as they purported to do. Thereby he accepted by implication the point that the raids from Barbary be regarded as piratical acts and only criticised the Genoese for their unwillingness to implement an effective response to such acts. He then insisted on Genoa's failure to enforce maritime policing as he contended that the Genoese only occasionally took action against Barbary vessels, and thus had no more rights than the Venetians and the Pope, who also took occasional action 'when the pirates infest[ed] the sea.'[172]

Such equation of Barbary warfare with piracy should not be overstated. In Bynkershoek's eyes, it represented a fiction useful for the purpose of rejecting Genoa's claims and was not meant as a broader delegitimation of the Barbary corsairs. He conceded that they may be characterised as pirates for the sake of his own argumentation, but found negligible whether this characterisation corresponded to the facts. His only aim here was to assert—against the Genoese, who had vindicated it in the first place—the principle that sovereignty on the sea derived from effective military control over it. Bynkershoek admitted that the Genoese would have produced a tenable legal argument had they demonstrated their willingness and capacity to keep the Barbary corsairs 'and anyone else they please'[173] out

life and property. As to the indictment of foreigners, Bynkershoek criticised the Dutch civil law system in that it excessively favoured the accusers and hindered a proper defence of the accused captor.

172 Cornelius van Bynkershoek, *De dominio maris dissertatio* (first published 1703, Ralph Van Deman Magoffin trans, OUP, 1923) VI, 74.

173 Ibid VI, 73.

of the Ligurian Sea, but he believed that there was no evidence supporting their claims.

That Bynkershoek otherwise regarded the Barbary privateers as lawful combatants became evident in a passage of the *Dominio maris* in which he questioned their stigmatisation by German jurist Gottlieb Gerhard Titius.[174] On that occasion, Bynkershoek criticised Titius for equating 'robber nations' with ordinary pirates and thus misinterpreting the Roman jurists Proculus' and Pomponius' doctrine of the *postliminium in pace*, formerly analysed by Grotius in his theory of the ancient law of nations.[175] Bynkershoek, like Samuel von Cocceji, conceded that 'robber nations' such as the peoples of Barbary might not be defined as *hostes* in the narrow sense because they did not observe any formalities at war, which the Romans purportedly did. Yet Bynkershoek insisted that the Barbary Regencies were sovereign entities, like the robber nations mentioned by Pomponius, and not ordinary pirates. As state-authorised combatants the Barbary corsairs held the right to wage war, retain the spoils, and even enslave war captives.

As Vattel elaborated his enemy of mankind theory in the 1750s, he had to deal with Bynkershoek's view as one of the most authoritative expressions of the pluralist paradigm. Not only did this view represent a significant re-articulation of Bodin's sovereignty thesis and of Grotius' historical argument in favour of a tolerant approach to Barbary warfare. It was also firmly grounded on state practice. While Vattel might reject both the sovereignty thesis and the historical argument on the *postliminium in pace* from a theoretical perspective, his approach would hardly convince Barbary-friendly European states to invert their policy towards the corsairs. European states would first change their attitudes towards the end of the eighteenth century, when the advantages for trade and colonial policies of getting rid of Barbary privateering outweighed the benefits of using the corsairs as a weapon in the struggle for hegemony in Europe.

The International Legal Pluralism of the Laws of War

The examination of the above sources leads to the conclusion that the early-modern discussion of the Barbary issue was largely dominated by a

174 Ibid I, 39.

175 Titius claimed that 'the decrees of nature and the sanctions of positive law are invoked in vain' against nations who lived on pillaging and perpetuated the corrupt customs of the ancient barbarian tribes: 'Id interim facile liquet, ex moribus Gentium corruptis, frustra repeti vel decreta naturalia, vel sanctiones juris positivi, quae, inter amicos aut cives, dominii acquisitionem vel conservationem dirigant' [Gottlieb Gerhard Titius, *De dominio in rebus occupatis* (Braunschweig, 1704) § 32].

sovereignty-based and tolerant paradigm, initiated by Bodin, which reflected state practice and accorded the corsairs lawful enemy status on the basis that they acted under sovereign authorisation. Those who, like Heinrich Cocceji, and partly Gentili, discarded this general opinion did not deny that the corsairs acted in the name of a legitimate sovereign. These publicists rather resorted to the just war theory to argue that the corsairs – regardless of any formal authorisation – did not qualify as lawful combatants as they waged war without a just cause and without paying respect to the laws of war, especially in their resort to the 'barbarian' custom of enslaving captives. To neutralise such claims, authors such as Grotius, Samuel von Cocceji, and Bynkershoek articulated historical narratives demonstrating the groundlessness of any European discrimination against the Barbary corsairs. Stressing the customary component of the law of nations, Grotius and Bynkershoek contended that the corsairs still followed ancient customs of war, including the enslavement of captives, and nobody could rightfully coerce them to abandon these customs to observe the usages of modern Europe instead. Samuel von Cocceji put forward a similar thesis when he opined that the Barbary corsairs could hardly be characterised as unjust enemies because they had been de facto 'natural' and 'perpetual' enemies of the Christians for centuries, and that in such a 'perpetual' conflict the notion of just cause could hardly apply. As to Pufendorf, he justified Barbary warfare based on Bodin's sovereignty thesis.

All of these writers – Bodin, Grotius, Pufendorf, Samuel von Cocceji and Bynkershoek – put the Barbary corsairs on a footing of equality with their European counterparts and thereby endorsed an international legal pluralism of the laws of war. Not all of these writers presented their doctrines in a systematic and coherent way, but they agreed that Europeans could not discriminate against the Barbary corsairs based on the latter's allegedly unlawful conduct of war. Pluralist writers were aware that far from being 'enemies of mankind' threatening all nations, the Barbary corsairs were ordinary enemies who restricted themselves to attacking the vessels of certain European powers.

The few critiques of the pluralist paradigm appeared either unconvincing or obsolete. Gentili's opinion on the subject was openly contradictory largely because of his incongruous activities as a practitioner. It is significant that after criminalising Barbary warfare based on the Roman dichotomy of pirates and public enemies, Gentili also ended by advancing a pluralist view. In a passage of his *Hispanicae advocationes*, Gentili admitted that the Barbary corsairs, as 'infidels', belonged to a different legal order and could not be forced to respect European customs. Radical just war doctrinarian Heinrich Cocceji instead took a hard line on the Barbary issue as he believed in the necessity of repressing the corsairs for the sake of retributive justice and the divine will. Yet his stance represented a relic of old school just war doctrine and was rejected by later authors.[176]

It may be remarked that the doctrine of international legal pluralism of the laws of war did not arise out of a humanitarian concern. The pluralists did not vouch for the Barbary corsairs' public enemy status to imply that combat should be more humane or that prisoners should be treated more gently. These authors certainly had no such concerns given that they justified the enslavement of war captives both by the corsairs and by Europeans in retaliation. Pluralist and realist writers like Bynkershoek, and partly Bodin, conceived war as a nearly lawless condition in which every means of injuring the enemy and of attaining victory was allowed 'by the right of war'.[177] Their apology for the Barbary corsairs was not in the least meant to protect the corsairs under the 'laws of war'. Rather, Bodin and Bynkershoek articulated his apology for Barbary as they believed that Europeans were by no means morally superior to the Barbary corsairs and were not entitled to discriminate against them at war. These writers made a case for cultural relativism, not however for 'humanitarianism'.

Pluralist jurists – Bynkershoek and Grotius in particular – also had clear practical interests in mind as well when making their apology for Barbary. They accorded the corsairs public enemy status to defend the corsairs' ownership rights over the booty and thus provide a criterion to settle international disputes.[178] Incidentally, Barbary-friendly European traders were supposed to benefit from the corsairs' lawful enemy status too, as the goods seized by the corsairs were often re-sold in Europe. Had these goods been classified as merchandises stolen by pirates, any successive sale would have become void. The stolen goods would have to be returned to the original owners by the buyers without compensation, according to the

---

[176] Reliance on a divine law paradigm, and the idea of a *bellum Deo auctore*, were more popular in the seventeenth century. See, for instance, John Selden, *De iure naturali et gentium juxta disciplinam Ebraeorum libri septem* (London, 1640) bk VI, ch 12.

[177] Bynkershoek, *Quaestionum*, I, 1 (on the idea that everything is licit during wartime) and II, 3 (on the killing of ambassadors); Bodin, *République*, V, 5–6. Bodin's move towards a realist view of war in Machiavelli's footsteps has been discussed by Diego Quaglioni in *I limiti della sovranità*.

[178] The right of postliminy, otherwise obsolete in modern times, was also discussed in light of this pragmatic concern.

principle that pirates cannot claim ownership to the booty.[179] Moreover, Bynkershoek and Grotius as Dutchmen had little difficulty justifying Barbary privateering as it mostly targeted Spanish, Portuguese and Italian shipping.

Pluralist just war theorists like Pufendorf and Samuel von Cocceji were not humanitarians either. They acknowledged the corsairs as public enemies but maintained that despite this status the corsairs might nevertheless be characterised as unjust enemies by their opponents for waging war without a just cause. This turned out to be especially detrimental to the corsairs, as both authors theorised the just enemy's 'unlimited right' or 'licence' (*ius infinitum* or *licentia infinita*) to harm the unjust enemy. Had the corsairs been characterised as aggressors, they would have become literally right-less – their treatment remaining at the discretion of the just enemy – and might have been totally annihilated. To be sure, the Barbary corsairs might label their adversaries as unjust enemies in turn, but this changed little about the position of the corsairs themselves. Moreover, because Pufendorf, in particular, entirely obliterated customary international law and hardly asserted any restraints, except moral ones, on the conduct of war, his formal legalisation of Barbary warfare had scarce practical effects. While Pufendorf and Samuel von Cocceji belonged to the pluralist stream apologetic of Barbary, they did not advocate for a concrete improvement in the condition of the corsairs in the international arena. They eventually perpetuated the classical and humanist vision of war as a feral-like status, scarcely moderated by purely moral obligations.

Luckily for the Barbary corsairs, the pluralist doctrine of the laws of war, far from being monopolised by scholars theorising an unrestrained *ius belli* or the just enemy's 'unlimited right', was rooted in state practice as well. In actual warfare, including the conflict between Barbary corsairs and their European counterparts, the speculative doctrine of the 'unlimited right' found scarce application, at least by 1700. At that stage, sovereigns rarely resorted to total warfare, whether as a result of purely political and economic calculations or of some sense of humanity as well.[180]

By 1758, practical humanitarianism was translated into theory in the *Droit des gens*. Vattel, who had to deal with the 'unlimited right' doctrine as it had been reasserted in the Wolffian *Jus gentium*, generally dismissed it.

---

[179] For a discussion of this principle, see Ben A Wortley, 'Pirata non mutat dominium' (1947) 24 *British Yearbook of International Law* 258, 259.

[180] Christopher Duffy, *The Military Experience in the Age of Reason* (London, Routledge, 1987) 10 and 11; Geoffrey Parker, 'Early Modern Times' in Michael Howard (ed) *The Laws of War. Constraints on Warfare in the Western World* (Yale University Press, 1994) 40, 45 and 52.

He contended that sovereigns occasionally waging unjust wars should not be treated as right-less unjust enemies but only countered in a civilised manner within the framework of the war 'in due form'. Hostilities, regardless of any just cause, should not exceed certain boundaries.[181] However, Vattel retained some aspects of the 'unlimited right' doctrine within his enemy of mankind theory. He maintained that when strict natural law re-entered into force in the event of a struggle against the enemy of mankind, those engaged in the struggle acquired the right to take any measures necessary to re-establish international order and, in principle, might wage a war of annihilation or extermination against the universal enemy.[182] Vattel here departed from contemporary state practice and resumed the 'unlimited right' paradigm to argue that the Barbary corsairs, as enemies of mankind, should turn into a target of European total warfare.

In criminalising Barbary privateering, Vattel rejected Bodin's sovereignty argument, as well as the historical narratives by Grotius, Bynkershoek, and Samuel von Cocceji. Against the sovereignty argument Vattel pointed out that the corsairs, though authorised by their sovereign to wage war, systematically acted in a way that jeopardised the international order as a whole. Therefore, they should be repressed collectively for the higher sake of international security, regardless of their public enemy status – an argument that Vattel analogously advanced to criminalise European international offenders. Against the historicist arguments, Vattel stipulated that barbarian usages of war such as the enslavement of captives could not be pardoned by virtue of their customary nature alone, and should actually be eradicated for the sake of humanity and international tranquillity.[183]

Vattel's utilitarian narrative and his emphasis on the necessity to preserve the 'civilised' customs of war represented a novel approach compared with the theses by former critics of Barbary warfare, such as Gentili (partly) and Heinrich von Cocceji, who entirely relied on the just cause argument. Yet Vattel's attack on Barbary in opposition to the traditional pluralist view remained problematic in terms of doctrine and, most importantly, of state practice around 1750, with many European powers still benefiting from Barbary privateering. This might constitute a key issue for a pragmatic author like Vattel. Yet he did not hesitate to put forward a radical and moralising anti-Barbary critique that openly clashed with the

181 *DG*, III, 8.
182 Ibid III, 8, § 155.
183 Ibid III, 15, § 222.

pluralist doctrine of the laws of war. He did so less to stigmatise the Barbary corsairs themselves than to make a case for the general enforcement of international law and the repression of international crimes. According to Vattel, the traditional tolerance threshold for international crimes had become unacceptable in the age of 'polished' warfare. Impunity should no longer be granted to international criminals violating the civilised laws of war and disrupting the world public order.

CHAPTER THREE

UNIVERSALISING THE EUROPEAN LAW OF NATIONS: VATTEL'S REJECTION OF THE INTERNATIONAL LEGAL PLURALISM OF THE LAWS OF WAR

The foregoing chapter has retraced the main themes in the debate on the Barbary issue from the second half of the sixteenth century up to the first half of the eighteenth century. The present chapter returns to Vattel. It provides a detailed analysis of his criminalisation of Barbary warfare and contextualises it within his broader project of universalising and enforcing the European law of nations. The chapter emphasises the innovative character of Vattel's intransigent attitude towards Barbary privateering compared with former tolerant views of jurists like Bodin, Grotius and Bynkershoek. In opposition to the pluralist tradition, Vattel posited that the Barbary corsairs' warfare, in particular their habit of enslaving war captives, could no longer be tolerated in a civilised age. It had to be punished by a coalition of powers willing to protect collective security and international trade. The great powers did not follow Vattel's advice immediately, but they would do so from the end of the eighteenth century, when France and the United States justified military adventurism in North Africa in the name of the civilising mission and moral duty to repress piracy.

The chapter commences by illustrating the arguments used by Vattel to criminalise Barbary warfare. It expounds the four conditions he requested as requirements for a war to be lawful: sovereign authority; declaration of war; workable pretext, as opposed to just cause; and compliance with the laws of war. Vattel acknowledged the pluralist argument that the Barbary corsairs acted under sovereign authorisation, but pointed out that they failed to comply with all other requirements for lawful warfare. In particular, he blamed the corsairs for not observing the laws of war as they carried on the 'barbarous' custom of enslaving war captives (a custom in fact followed by Europeans too). It was to eradicate this custom and to ensure maritime security and safety in the Mediterranean that Vattel called on all European nations to join forces and punish the Barbary Regencies.

Collective anti-piracy measures had to be set up not only to repress the Barbary corsairs but also to deter others from committing grave breaches of the law of nations. Vattel indeed criminalised Barbary privateering to advance a general theory on the repression of international crimes grounded on the idea of collective security. The theory demanded that the 'civilised' nations take action to preserve the customs of the 'war in due form' as developed from the 'good mores of Europe' in the first half of the eighteenth century. The chapter however questions Vattel's idealisation of the war in due form as opposed to 'barbarian' warfare. It notes that Vattel eventually admitted several exceptions to the war in due form, as he clearly privileged military necessity over humanity. In this regard, he came close to realist writers on the *ius belli* like Gentili, or to just war doctrinarians like Pufendorf, all of whom saw war as a quasi-feral condition hardly restrained by moral obligations, in which every means of injuring the enemy was licit if it was necessary to secure victory. Vattel did not entirely agree with this tradition, but he did not break off from it.

The chapter concludes by problematising the notion of sovereign equality in the *Droit des gens*. Vattel claimed that international offences may be repressed worldwide for the sake of collective security, yet he maintained that European offenders should be punished gently, while irredeemable 'barbarian' offenders, for instance warlike Tartar tribes, might be 'exterminated like ferocious and pernicious beasts'.[1] Allegedly, such warlike peoples could not be deterred by any lesser means. If Vattel began by seeming to put forward an egalitarian approach as he pleaded for all international crimes to be punished, be they committed by 'civilised' or 'uncivilised' offenders, both inside and outside Europe, he ended by discriminating against the 'uncivilised' as far as punishment was concerned.

Vattel's Four Requirements for Lawful Warfare

Vattel addressed the Barbary issue in a more radical fashion than most of his predecessors. He felt that Barbary warfare stalled the progress of the law of nations, especially by perpetuating the idea that war captives may be enslaved. By the 1750s the project of establishing 'civilised' war customs appeared to many to be accomplished within Europe, and Vattel set out to provide a systematic, doctrinal treatment of such customs and to demonstrate their potential universal validity. In his eyes, Barbary privateering could no longer be tolerated as it trampled on the fundamental principles of the modern law of nations.

[1] *DG*, I, 7, § 81.

> Legitimate and formal warfare must be carefully distinguished from those illegitimate and informal wars, or rather predatory expeditions, undertaken either without lawful authority or without apparent cause, as likewise without the usual formalities, and solely with a view to plunder. ... To the same class belong almost all the expeditions of the Barbary corsairs: though authorised by a sovereign, they are undertaken without any apparent cause, and from no other motive than the lust of plunder.[2]

To make a case against Barbary warfare, Vattel had to depart from the idea that sovereignty as such elicited the right to make war, or that the *vetus ius gentium* and the *postliminium in pace* were still in force, all of which entailed that the Barbary corsairs must be treated as lawful enemies. He still engaged with Roman law sources, but suggested a critical reading of them. Vattel commenced his anti-Barbary argument by referring to the classical Roman distinction between lawful and unlawful wars, and although he mentioned Grotius' interpretation on this point, he turned it over by declaring the Barbary corsairs as pirates. As seen above, Grotius justified the conduct of warfare of ancient 'robber nations' because they were permitted to pillage and plunder under the law of nations of old. In addition, he reasserted Bodin's sovereignty argument and argued that pirates and robbers could be viewed as lawful enemies as soon as they set up proper political institutions. History had allegedly provided several examples of such cases.

Vattel instead stigmatised the 'robber nations' and denied that they should be treated as lawful enemies. He equated the wars waged by ancient robber nations (and now by the Barbary corsairs) with analogous robbery-like or piracy-like enterprises such as those of the medieval *grandes compagnies* and the filibusters, who waged war without formalities and for the sake of gain. Vattel claimed that, similarly, the Barbary corsairs did not observe the (European) laws of war and acted *animo furandi*, without 'any other motive than the lust of plunder.'[3] He insisted that for these reasons, Barbary privateering might be treated as piracy, even though it was state-authorised.

As Vattel blamed the corsairs for committing hostile acts for the sake of plunder, he problematically resorted to the just cause argument, which he put aside when describing the 'war in due form' between European sovereigns. Actually, Vattel did not wish to criminalise 'war for the sake of plunder' or 'unjust war' as such. His real concern was with enemies—be they

2 Ibid III, 4, § 67.
3 Ibid.

Barbary corsairs or warlike European sovereigns—who systematically abused the right to make war. Vattel was willing to excuse sovereigns or sovereign-authorised combatants who occasionally resorted to force without a just cause, but did not tolerate them doing so as a habit. While tolerance was recommended in the former case to prevent the demonisation of the enemy and the escalation of conflict, it became detrimental in the latter case, as systematic violations of the right to make war would jeopardise international order as a whole. Vattel's project considerably differed from that of earlier just war doctrinarians. While mainstream just war doctrine spelled out the conditions under which a war was 'just', Vattel focused instead on the formal requirements for a 'war in due form'. He reintegrated the just cause argument only to a limited extent, and with a very specific aim.

Vattel did not provide a list of the requirements for a 'war in due form', but at least four of them clearly emerged at different points in his *Droit des gens*: sovereign's authority; workable pretext, as opposed to just cause; formal declaration; and observation of elementary norms of *ius in bello* relating to the means of injuring the enemy and to the treatment of civilians and war captives.[4] None of these conditions for lawful warfare constituted a novelty, but the fashion which Vattel construed them proved original and influential. His theory of the 'war in due form', elaborating on the Grotian *bellum solemne*, represented an attempt to move away from the traditional just war doctrine by focusing on the modality as opposed to the morality of warfare.

In his paradigmatic systematisation of the just war doctrine, Thomas Aquinas had put forward that for a war to be just it must be waged: under the authority of a sovereign (*princeps*); for a just cause (in the sense of Aristotle's final cause); and with a rightful intention (which corresponded to Aristotle's efficient cause).[5] From the sixteenth century onwards, as a consequence of the emergence of modern statehood, moral theologians and natural lawyers tended to emphasise the authority requirement, given the increasing centrality of sovereignty, and to reduce the significance of the just cause requirement, given the progressive weakening of

---

[4] Ibid III, 3, § 33 (on pretexts); III, 4, § 67 (on authority); III, 4, § 68 (on the declaration of war); III, 8 (on the *ius in bello*).

[5] Thomas Aquinas, *Summa theologiae* (60 vols, Thomas Gilby et al trans, London, Eyre and Spottiswoode, 1964–73) II–II, q 40, a 1. On Aquinas' conception of just war, see Frederick H Russell, *The Just War in the Middle Ages* (CUP, 1975) 258–291.

the universal powers able to sanction it.[6] In this process, Aquinas' idea of 'rightful intention' either entirely disappeared or was conflated with 'just cause'.

A further alteration of Aquinas' doctrine by early-modern lawyers was the renewed emphasis on the declaration of war, a requirement stemming from the Romanist tradition. It had been put forward by Cicero in his statement that 'no war is just, unless it is entered upon after an official demand for satisfaction has been submitted or warning has been given and a formal declaration made.'[7] This approach relied on a statist paradigm, and modern jurists privileged it over Aquinas' moral theology of warfare. While modern jurists reduced the importance of the just cause, they instead stressed the importance of formal requirements such as the official demand for redress and the declaration of war, the fulfilment of which presupposed the presence of a sovereign authority in the first place. In fact, few wars in the early-modern age were waged following an official declaration.[8] Modern lawyers mostly sanctioned this requirement for a declaration of war to support the state's monopoly on the use of force, while simultaneously reminding princes purportedly *legibus soluti* that they were no less bound by international obligations just because they were strong enough to disregard them.

Vattel particularly insisted on a further requirement for war: the observance of the *ius in bello*. He claimed that belligerents should not enslave or kill captives, or harm children, women, the elderly or the sick, that is, all people not directly engaged in hostilities. While these ideas had been proclaimed since at least the Middle Ages, Vattel established them as legal principles proper.[9] Wars justified on the ground of requirements such as the declaration of war and the compliance with the laws of war were no longer 'just wars', but rather 'wars in due form'. The main question for Vattel was no longer why war was undertaken – a question which rather concerned the theologian and the moralist – but instead how, and by whom. Aquinas had also formulated this latter question regarding the

6 At that point the idea of a war which was 'just on both sides' became dominant. On the development of this idea from the sixteenth century, see Peter Haggenmacher, *Grotius et la doctrine de la guerre juste* (Paris, PUF, 1983) 203–223.

7 Cicero, *De officiis* (Walter Miller trans, London, Heinemann, 1913) I, 36.

8 This point was well illustrated by Bynkershoek in his *Quaestionum juris publici libri duo* (first published 1737, Tenney Frank trans, Oxford, Clarendon, 1930) I, 2.

9 See Giovanni da Legnano, *Tractatus de bello, de represaliis et de duello* (written 1360, Thomas E Holland ed, OUP, 1917) pt V, ch 59. For a discussion of the laws of war in the Middle Ages, see Robert C Stacey, 'The Age of Chivalry' in Michael Howard (ed) *The Laws of War. Constraints on Warfare in the Western World* (Yale University Press, 1994) 27, 30 and 37.

agency of warfare in his 'authority of the prince' requirement: where by 'prince' he already meant the sovereign prince who had no superiors on earth and therefore must be deemed *imperator in regno suo*, as a typical thirteenth century formula put it.[10] However, the 'authority of the prince' requirement in Aquinas' writings had no priority over 'just cause' and 'rightful intention'. Also, the prince's competence over matters of war was complicated by the right of resistance, to which medieval doctrine traditionally attributed a wide scope. The authority requirement took unquestionable priority from the sixteenth and seventeenth centuries, as a consequence of the emergence of the princely, later absolutist, states, and of political realism. Bodin, Ayala, Gentili, and Grotius were the first to attest to this shift and put forward the idea of a 'public', 'lawful', and 'solemn war' as distinct from the just war.[11] In an international arena torn apart by ideological strife and endemic warfare between sovereign states, the medieval, thick notion of a 'just cause', premised on the existence of a common legal order, became ineffective as a means to interpret warfare, and might actually escalate conflicts instead of regulating them.[12]

Repressing International Deviance to Perpetuate Moderate Eighteenth Century Warfare

If Bodin, Ayala, Gentili, and Grotius replaced the 'just war' with the 'solemn war' mainly in order to adapt to the exigencies of the rise of nation states and the corresponding *raison d'Etat* paradigm, Vattel had a further reason to theorise his 'war in due form'. This was that the laws of war had made unmistakable progress in the first half of the eighteenth century, with the nations of Europe usually conducting hostilities 'with great moderation and generosity'.[13] That warfare in the eighteenth century was far more humane and moderate than in previous ages was a common belief

---

[10] Diego Quaglioni, *La sovranità* (Rome – Bari, Laterza, 2004) 25–6.

[11] Jean Bodin, *Six livres de la République* (first published 1576, Aalen, Scientia, 1977) V, 5–6; Balthazar Ayala, *De iure belli et officiis bellicis et disciplina militari libri tres* (first published 1582, John Westlake ed, Washington, Carnegie Endowment, 1912) I, 2; Alberico Gentili, *De iure belli libri tres* (first published 1598, Coleman Phillipson ed, Oxford, Clarendon, 1933) I, 3; Grotius, *De iure belli ac pacis* (first published 1625, Francis W Kelsey trans, Washington, Carnegie Endowment, 1913) III, 3.

[12] On the notion of *ordo iuris* in the Middle Ages, see Paolo Grossi, *L'ordine giuridico medievale* (Rome – Bari, Laterza, 1997) 13–5. For an analysis of endemic warfare in early modern times, see Johannes Burkhardt, 'Die Friedlosigkeit der Frühen Neuzeit. Grundlegung einer Theorie der Bellizität Europas' (1997) 24 *Zeitschrift für historische Forschung* 509.

[13] *DG*, III, 8, § 158.

for enlightened writers such as Vattel, Voltaire, or Montesquieu, and later became one of the resilient myths of modern historiography.[14] There was some truth behind this myth. Comparatively speaking, eighteenth century warfare was less lethal, and had a lessened impact on civilians' daily life and on economic activities.[15] This resulted from a series of notable factors: the creation of standing armies; the differentiation between military forces and civilians; the developments of military strategy and of the conception of warfare as oriented to minor territorial acquisitions; the progressive neutralisation of confessional strife; and the formation of a common aristocratic and military ethic among Europe's elites and reigning dynasties. All of this indicates that, essentially, the causes of the moderation of warfare were cultural and, most importantly, economic: deadly battles should be avoided because well equipped armies had become extremely expensive, while civilians should be spared because they alone could contribute to the state's economic wealth.

As Vattel put forward his 'war in due form' theory, he intended to preserve the benefits brought about by these historical developments. In his view, the traditional just war doctrine was absolutely incompatible with contemporary warfare and ought not to be reasserted if conflict was to be restrained and Europe was not to plunge back into the radical hostility characteristic of the confessional age. Recent progress had been possible thanks to the idea, largely mirroring state practice, that sovereign states were free and equal individuals.[16] Based on this idea, Vattel claimed that in principle, sovereigns could not disqualify each other as 'unjust enemies'. They could not be criminalised as aggressors and deprived of their *ius ad bellum*; rather, they might wage war even without an evident 'just cause'.

However, this licence might be abused by warmongers and thus produce international insecurity and instability. Hence Vattel's efforts were directed towards placing some restraints on sovereign rights so as to attain

---

[14] Voltaire, *Le siècle de Louis XIV* (first published 1751, Jaqueline Hellegouarc'h ed, Paris, Librairie Générale Française, 2005) 128; Montesquieu, *De l'esprit des lois* (first published 1748, Victor Goldschmidt ed, Paris, Garnier-Flammarion, 1979) X, 3.

[15] Christopher Duffy, *The Military Experience in the Age of Reason* (London, Routledge, 1987) 10–11. See also Francis S Ruddy, *International Law in the Enlightenment: The Background of Emmerich de Vattel's* Le Droit des Gens (Dobbs Ferry, NY, Oceana Publications, 1975) 249.

[16] The principles of sovereign equality and freedom were systematised by Christian Wolff, *Jus gentium methodo scientifica pertractatum* (first published 1749, Joseph H Drake trans, Oxford, Clarendon, 1934) Prolegomena, § 2. It was Vattel, however, who based on these principles radically questioned the just war doctrine and attributed a truly compulsory character to the laws of war.

the ultimate goal of a minimum level of international tranquillity and the preservation of the laws of war as recently established by the 'civilised' nations. So while Vattel maintained that sovereigns in principle could not be criminalised, they might become criminals when they plainly trampled on the law of nations, on the basis that in doing so they posed an egregious threat to collective security. In this event, all nations were called upon to repress the wrongdoer. In Vattel's view, if the modern rules of warfare were to survive in the long run, they had to become the ethos of the society of nations at large and be enforced collectively.

Vattel's Criminalisation of Barbary Warfare in Opposition to the Pluralists

According to Vattel, Barbary warfare amounted to one such case that should elicit collective repressive measures. Indeed, of the four requirements for lawful warfare – sovereign authority, workable pretext, a declaration of war, and compliance with the *ius in bello* – they seemed to fulfil only one, namely sovereign authority. This at least could not be questioned because the Barbary Regencies qualified as sovereign states and their corsairs acted under letters of marque. As anticipated above, Vattel thus turned to further arguments, first of all those based around the *causa belli*. To be sure, in this respect he made it clear that for a war to be lawful it does not have to be waged for an evident 'just cause', as had been claimed by the greater part of the just war doctrine, but rather for a plausible cause, or at least a workable pretext. Wolff had paved the way for this approach by bluntly admitting that even utilitarian considerations could be brought forward to justify the use of force – an admission that the purists of the just war doctrine abhorred.[17] Yet he had still upheld a moralist façade as he thundered against the practice of artfully constructing pretexts for war, at which contemporary politicians and diplomats were particularly skilled. Vattel jettisoned Wolffian moralism and acquiesced in both the state practice and the principles of contemporary *politique*. He certainly stigmatised extremely trivial excuses for war such as the affair of medals complained of by Louis XIV against the United Provinces in 1672, or the failed salute to Peter I which triggered the Great Northern War.[18] Nonetheless, he argued that even such dubious pretexts as these must be deemed legitimate in the

---

17 Ibid, VI, § 621–623.

18 *DG*, II, 2, § 19; II, 4, § 48.

international state of nature, in which sovereigns could not arrogate the right to judge one another.

By stating that frivolous pretexts had to be seen as acceptable reasons to undertake war, Vattel attained two goals. First, he conformed to European state practice; second, he might still condemn warfare by peoples such as the Tartars and the Barbary corsairs that, allegedly, was totally unmotivated and thus amounted to mere robbery and piracy. In addition, even if the corsairs had had a 'workable' pretext for war, Vattel might still criminalise them based on the systematic character of their aggressions and their posing a threat to international security.

Vattel pointed out that the Barbary corsairs failed to comply with a further requirement for lawful warfare, namely a formal declaration of war. This in turn merged with the 'workable pretext', as war could be declared only after an injury had been committed. Vattel maintained that those who consider resorting to armed force should first notify the enemy of the harm suffered and demand reparation.[19] If reparation was granted, the right to make war decayed.[20] Yet this procedure, called *rerum repetitio* by the Romans, was hardly relevant to contemporary international law and represented a pure homage by Vattel to the tradition.[21] Also, when criticising the Barbary corsairs for not declaring war Vattel overlooked the evidence that they had been waging war on the Europeans, nearly without interruption, for centuries, and hence a formal declaration seemed useless. This had been one of Samuel von Cocceji's points as he described the confrontation between the corsairs and some European states as a 'perpetual war'.[22]

The same idea of 'perpetual war' had been asserted by German scholar Johann Friedrich Weidler in a disputation *De quaestione iuris gentium utrum praeda Salensibus Afris erepta vindicari possit*, discussed in Wittenberg in 1735.[23] Therein, Weidler had explored the historical framework

---

19 Ibid III, 4, § 53.

20 Ibid III, 4, § 54.

21 Already Grotius, who first distinguished between 'conditional' and 'pure and simple' war declarations, held the demand for satisfaction an accessorial element from the point of view of the law of nations, so it is not surprising that Vattel hardly mentioned that requirement in the *Droit des gens*. The *rerum repetitio* would re-emerge in the nineteenth century in the mutated form of the ultimatum. On this point see Stephen C Neff, *War and the Law of Nations. A General History* (CUP, 2005) 105.

22 Heinrich von Cocceji, *Grotius illustratus, seu Commentarii ad Hugonis Grotii libros tres* [Samuel von Cocceji ed, Wrokław (Breslau) 1744–52] vol 3, n *hh* ad II, § 20, 40.

23 Johann Friedrich Weidler, *De quaestione iuris gentium utrum praeda Salensibus Afris erepta vindicari possit* (Wittenberg, Eichsfeld, 1735).

of the hostility between the corsairs of Salé and the Iberians, tracing it back to the Crusades and the Reconquista.[24] He contended that the bulk of the responsibility for this enduring strife – by then clearly a *bellum perpetuum* – lay with the aggressive policies of Portugal and Spain, directed against the Moors in the Iberian Peninsula and on the African coasts.[25] As the privateers of Salé acted in self-defence and with the authorisation of their sovereign, Weidler argued, they were not committing acts of piracy but rather waging a just war against Christian aggressors. Weidler also recalled that Moroccan corsairs were not hostile to all Christians but only towards those who did not care about peace with the Moors (*qui pacem cum illis non colent*), namely Portugal and Spain in the first place.[26] This was proved by the recent peace that the Republic of Salé had signed with the Swedish, and by its respectful demeanour when dealing with dreaded Britain.[27]

Yet Vattel's rejection of the idea of a 'perpetual' or 'natural hostility' was understandable. This idea was fading away in the eighteenth century although it had long fed on the expansionist policy of modern nation states and on the theory of natural boundaries.[28] The natural hostility concept could not resist Enlightenment political philosophy along with its progressive notion of history, and became practically outdated due to developments in international relations, as changing alliances had become one of the favourite activities among European monarchs in the mid-eighteenth century. After the diplomatic revolution of 1756, the idea of 'natural hostility', most famously between Austria and France, lost much of its argumentative force.[29]

As Vattel rejected the 'natural hostility' concept, he was not moved by a spirit of tolerance towards the Barbary corsairs. Conversely, he assumed that designating the Barbary corsairs as 'natural enemies' of the Christians would be unacceptable, as it diminished the corsairs' responsibility for

---

[24] Ibid II–X.

[25] Ibid X.

[26] Ibid II.

[27] Ibid XI and XIII.

[28] For a critical view on the notion of the natural frontiers in the modern age see Peter Sahlins, *Natural Frontiers Revisited. France's Boundaries since the Seventeenth Century* (1990) 95 *The American Historical Review* 1423.

[29] The natural hostility concept would be recovered in the age of nationalism. It was at that point that scholars revived the idea, already discussed by Grotius and his followers, that ancient nations lived in a state of perpetual war with each other. This perspective was later decisively rejected again in the early twentieth century by Alfred Heuss in his *Die völkerrechtlichen Grundlagen der Römischen Aussenpolitik in republikanischer Zeit* (first published 1933, Aalen, Scientia, 1968) 4–6.

committing piratical raids, as Samuel Cocceji and Weidler had indeed concluded. For Vattel, the Barbary Regencies as sovereign entities belonged to the society of nations and must therefore comply with its obligations. If the modern and rational (read European) law of nations was to be universalised, as Vattel wished, deviant conduct like that of the Barbary corsairs was no longer justifiable based on any historical arguments regarding perpetual hostility or the ancient law of nations. He thus insisted that the corsairs should be considered criminal for waging war without a valid motive and without declaring war.

The final and fundamental requirement for a war to be lawful was the compliance with the *ius in bello*.[30] Indeed, Vattel saw the moderation of warfare as the primary task of international law, the prevention of war being largely left to diplomacy, and broader co-operation falling outside the scope of international law in Vattel's time. As the *ius in bello* fulfilled a key role in the *Droit des gens*, it is not surprising that it also became the basis for the main argument against the Barbary corsairs, here especially blamed for perpetuating the barbarian custom of targeting and enslaving civilians. Vattel did not mention that this custom was also practised by Christian privateers preying on Muslim vessels, and emphasised instead that it had long been banished in civilised warfare among Europeans.[31]

Taking a position against the general opinion and especially Grotius, Vattel dismissed the hypothesis that warfare between Barbary Regencies and European states might be conducted according to the ancient law of nations permitting the enslavement of captives. In Vattel's view, the ancient right of postliminy during peacetime entitling all belligerents to enslave captives could not apply in a civilised age for the sole fact that some barbarian nations were unaware of or unwilling to conform with the civilised customs of war. Vattel contended that the right of postliminy in modern times applied in wartime only, not in peacetime or during truces.[32] The *postliminium in pace* was a relic of barbarian times and should no longer arise except in the immediate aftermath of peace treaties, when war captives were released and should have their rights in their homeland restored.[33] Regardless of whether the Barbary corsairs were accustomed to enslaving captives, Europe's nations should neither yield to this practice nor employ it in retaliation, as Grotius had wrongly proposed. Conversely,

---

30 Vattel did not himself use the expression *ius in bello*, but he meant the same as he spoke of the 'right of nations during wartime' (*droit des Nations dans la guerre*): *DG*, III, 8.

31 Ibid III, 8, § 153.

32 Ibid III, 14, § 216; III, 16, § 256; Wolff, *Jus gentium*, VII, § 922.

33 *DG*, III, 14, § 217.

they ought to commit themselves to eradicating it. Vattel admitted that long established customs with which the majority of nations (or the nations affected by them) agreed should normally be observed, and this seemed to be the case with the right to enslavement as claimed by both Christians and Muslims in the Mediterranean. Yet he was adamant that the general consent endorsing these customs was void if they were plainly contrary to the law of nature. He contended that far from conforming to such unlawful and barbarian customs, all nations were bound to 'use their endeavours to effect their abolition'.[34]

When urging the civilised to 'use their endeavours' to achieve the universal abolition of barbarian customs of war, Vattel was not referring to diplomacy. Given that a soft approach, as attempted in a number of negotiations and peace treaties, had not prevented the Barbary corsairs from carrying on hostilities, he decidedly pleaded for a forceful solution. This became glaring in a later section as Vattel discussed the legality of 'ravaging and burning' in cases of necessity for security and deterrence purposes. Here he praised Louis XIV 'for his firmness and just resentment' in ordering two heavy bombardments of Algiers in 1682 and 1683, which resulted in civilian casualties and the destruction of vast parts of the city.[35] What is more, Vattel believed that the measures taken by Louis, although temporarily effective, had not been harsh enough. The total annihilation of the Barbary cities was required to stop piracy once and for all.

> Who can doubt that the king of Spain and the powers of Italy have a very good right utterly to destroy those maritime towns of Africa, those nests of pirates, that are continually molesting their commerce and ruining their subjects?[36]

This opinion attributed full responsibility for war to the Barbary corsairs alone and thus reversed the thesis by Weidler and other Protestant authors imputing the responsibility of the 'perpetual war' to Spanish imperialism. Most importantly, Vattel's statement authorised the European states mostly victimised by Barbary privateering, notably Spain and the Italian states, to take extreme punitive measures and literally raze to the ground those North African cities that harboured the corsairs. Here Vattel gave clear evidence of his bias against the 'barbarians' and in favour of the 'civilised'.

---

34 Ibid III, 15, § 222.

35 Ibid III, 9, § 167. On these episodes, see also Samuel Pufendorf, *Introduction à l'histoire générale et politique de l'univers* (Amsterdam, 1745) vol 7, 538–9.

36 *DG*, III, 9, § 167.

Indeed, while he legitimated Louis XIV's order to heavily bombard Algiers, Vattel strongly criticised him for doing the same to Genoa in 1684.[37] Vattel here stipulated that regardless of whether Genoa as a result of its ties to the Spanish was a political enemy of the French, it did not deserve such a harsh treatment as it was a well-ordered and civilised commonwealth. Its civilian population was not involved in any hostile acts towards France and could not be deemed responsible or punishable for decisions made or acts committed by the Genoese government. Algiers, on the contrary, constituted for Vattel an outright pirate state whose entire economy rested on maritime robbery and whose subjects had been accustomed to plundering and pillaging for centuries. In his opinion, if the Algerians were to abandon their hostile temperament and 'barbarian' habits, they first had to be punished most severely.[38] While Genoa ought to be fought with good manners, Algiers, not unlike Carthage at the time of the Third Punic War, had to be destroyed.

By advocating for harsh repression against Barbary, Vattel clearly deviated from writers like Bodin, Grotius, and Bynkershoek, who endorsed a pluralist conception of the laws of war. As far as the conduct of hostilities was concerned, they rejected universalist arguments and argued that the North African corsairs had the right to enslave war captives on the ground that they did not belong to the European-Christian legal order and could not be compelled to observe its rules. According to this paradigm, the Barbary corsairs qualified as lawful combatants thanks to their Otherness, not unlike the barbarians at the borders of the Roman Empire in the first centuries AD, or the Saracens in the Middle Ages (to be sure, this reasoning also justified Christian privateering as a means of self-help). At the heart of such considerations was the assumption that at the current stage, a universal law of nations, especially a universal law of war, did not exist. For Bodin, Grotius, and Bynkershoek, natural law remained an inter-cultural bridge, but the *ius gentium*, then rapidly turning into the law of the European powers, could not be exported. On the one hand European lawyers were convinced that their own law of nations was the most advanced, and on the other hand they were aware that they could not force non-European nations to accept it.

---

37 Ibid III, 9, § 167.

38 Vattel thought that behaviour was determined by temperament in the first instance and secondarily by education, which might modify the *naturel*: Emer de Vattel, Letter to Samuel Formey, 14 July 1767 in *Varnhagen Collection* (Jagiellonian Library, Kraków) 270.

Vattel opposed his faith in universal Reason to these lawyers' cultural relativism. He contended that Europe's international law could be exported, and also that it should be exported, given its inherent rationality and conformity with the principles of the natural law of nations as could be found among the civilised nations of all times, including the Chinese, the Indians, and the pre-Colombian peoples of America. Vattel pretended to have distilled from the laws and customs of Christian Europe the immutable tenets of natural and international law. In his work, he set himself the task of presenting the European law of nations as the most rational so that it could claim universal validity and be enforced even against non-Europeans, or at least against those at Europe's doorstep like the Barbary corsairs.

Vattel's attitude towards the corsairs and other international offenders was not one of exclusion. On the contrary, he attempted to include the Barbary Regencies as part of the new world order regulated by the universalised European law of nations and to compel them to abide by it. This meant a rejection of 'barbarian' customs in the name of the rational customs of Europe. The novelty of the Vattelian approach when compared with the pluralist tradition was that non-Europeans were now denied the opportunity to play according to their own rules, which were deemed to be contrary to the basic principles of international law, and urged to comply with the laws observed by Europeans among each other. The problem with this doctrine was not 'exclusion', but forced 'inclusion'.[39]

As Vattel advanced a rationalist argument in favour of a universal and 'enlightened' law of nations and did away with the historicist perspective of the pluralist tradition, he justified the hegemony of the civilised. By doing so, he departed not only from historicism, but also from the rationalist critique of historicism formerly elaborated by Wolff, who advocated for a tolerant cosmopolitanism at odds with Vattel's project. While Wolff, though a 'universalist', still belonged to the 'pluralist' tradition in the sense that he used his universalist conception of the law of nations to contest the Europeans' moral superiority over the 'barbarians', notably in the issue of colonies, Vattel's recourse to universalist arguments had the opposite effect.[40] Unlike Wolff, Vattel denied the validity of the pluralists' historical arguments based on the ancient law of nations to call on European powers to punish international crimes committed by 'barbarians'.

---

[39] On the potentially oppressive character of inclusion, see Martti Koskenniemi, *The Gentle Civilizer of Nations. The Rise and Fall of International Law 1870–1960* (CUP, 2001) 131.

[40] Wolff, *Jus gentium*, III, § 310.

Vattel's move away from history distinguished his position from that of nineteenth century publicists as well. Unlike the latter writers, Vattel did not yet depict the need to export the European law of nations as an historical and moral necessity legitimated by Europe's leading role in mankind's progress. The term 'progress', widely used in the mid-eighteenth century, never turned up in Vattel's writings, not even with reference to common topics such as scientific advancement and the comparison between Ancients and Moderns.[41] Vattel indirectly referred to progress as he relied on the Leibniz-Wolffian concept of perfecting (*perfectionnement*) to define the struggle for perfection as a fundamental principle of ontology and morals: just as every monad strives for perfection, so too do individual humans and entire nations.[42] However, 'perfecting' was only meant as 'self-perfecting' and did not imply any collective advancement, which held particularly true in international relations. In Vattel's view, each nation's duty to improve itself derived solely from self-interest. Perfection was not the destination of the states system or humanity at large but the ideal condition in which one state became most wealthy and powerful so as to succeed in the struggle for survival against potentially hostile neighbours in the international state of nature.[43] It was exactly to put a restraint to this struggle that Vattel laid down his theory of the repression of international crimes. His intolerant attitude towards Barbary, while premised on the ahistorical conception of international relations as a perpetual state of nature, was to provide arguments for nineteenth century writers who regarded the eradication of North African piracy as a significant step in the advancement of civilisation.

Custom versus Reason: Vattel on the Legal Effects of Barbary Warfare

As much as Vattel attempted to contrast the Barbary corsairs' warfare with the 'war in due form' and pass them off as pirates, he was aware that his

---

[41] Dieter Gembicki and Rolf Reichardt, 'Progrès' in Rolf Reichardt (ed), *Handbuch politisch-sozialer Grundbegriffe in Frankreich 1680–1820* (Munich, Oldenbourg, 1993) vols 14 and 15, 118–28.

[42] Emer de Vattel, *Défense du système Leibnitien contre les objections et les imputations de M. de Crousaz* (Leiden, Jean Luzac, 1741) I, 2; *DG*, I, 2, § 14.

[43] Vattel used the following words as he introduced the section of the *Droit des gens* devoted to the nations' moral obligations: 'The following maxims will appear very strange to cabinet politicians; and such is the misfortune of mankind, that, to many of those refined conductors of nations, the doctrine of this chapter will be a subject of ridicule. Be it so; but we will, nevertheless, boldy lay down what the law of nature prescribes to nations' (*DG*, II, 1, § 1).

view would hardly impact on state practice. The main problem with the repression of the corsairs was the engaging in a war against them would be expensive and counterproductive for many powers interested in weakening each other through Barbary privateering. These powers were keen on maintaining friendly relations with the corsairs and willing to take on the occasional risk of becoming themselves a target as long as other continental competitors suffered considerable losses. As Vattel wrote his *Droit des gens*, there existed no historical precedent of collective measures by major European powers to repress the Barbary corsairs. Around 1750, such measures had become even less likely as the great powers would not join forces unless the European equilibrium itself was in danger – a threat that Barbary certainly did not pose.

Vattel himself had to acknowledge the great powers' tolerant policy towards Barbary, even though he totally disagreed with it. He noted that 'to prevent endless discussions and quarrels', European courts assimilated the corsairs' maritime expeditions with lawful warfare and accorded it some legal effects, at least as far as the licence to seize movables was concerned. As a result, he admitted that

> [a]t present, it would be in vain to claim a ship taken by the Barbary corsairs, and sold to a third party, or retaken from the captors; though it is very improperly that the piracies of those barbarians can be considered as acts of regular war.[44]

Here Vattel took care not explicitly to endorse the European courts' practice of acknowledging Barbary prizes as lawful. He merely reported on this practice, in an attempt to accommodate it without patently contradicting his previous aggressive statements on Barbary and anti-piracy repression. Interestingly, though, Vattel made clear that the acknowledgement of Barbary prizes was not a mere custom, but a custom sanctioned by the voluntary law of nations. It was indeed by virtue of the voluntary law of nations that, more generally, expeditions undertaken by regular armies were regarded as lawful even if deprived of any just cause or pretext. Vattel thus implied that the Barbary corsairs, acting under sovereign commission, could be assimilated into the same category as regular armies. He admitted that acknowledging Barbary prizes was a practice sanctioned by reason and prudence so as to avoid disputes over the ownership of booty. This had indeed been one of the main reasons that former publicists like

---

[44] Ibid III, 13, § 196.

Grotius and Bynkershoek considered the Barbary corsairs as lawful enemies.

However, Vattel was not satisfied with Grotius' and Bynkershoek's pragmatic approach. He maintained that while the Barbary corsairs were currently allowed to wage war and take booty, they might still forfeit their lawful combatant status if they enslaved captives. Such conduct gravely jeopardised the very foundations of the law of nature and nations and could not be tolerated. Despite his appeals to state practice regarding the corsairs' entitlement to the ownership of captured goods, Vattel was not willing to withdraw his thesis on the necessity of repressing grave international crimes.

Vattel had no doubt that 'enormous offences against the law of nations' such as the enslavement of captives should be punished.[45] In his view, captives might not be enslaved unless personally responsible for capital crimes, as enslavement was in principle 'contrary to human nature' and could only be justified as an alternative to death penalty.[46] Belligerents refusing to release all captives after peace was concluded would thereby manifest a willingness to perpetuate the state of war with them, hence captives were entitled to flee whenever the occasion arose and enjoyed the right of postliminy once returned to their homeland.[47] Their own sovereign might not be able to come to their rescue, but they retained their natural freedom and the right to escape captivity as if hostilities were still ongoing.

Vattel insisted that grave international crimes such as the enslavement of captives should not be tolerated by the 'society of nations'. Without any enforcement, the civilised prescriptions of the voluntary law of nations concerning the conduct of hostilities would be deprived of certainty and predictability, and would thereby become ineffective. Assuming that states were rational entities, Vattel argued, they had to endorse the enforcement of international law and co-operate to carry it out. Once they agreed on the necessity of observing the civilised rules of war, states were supposed to also agree on all conditions required to preserve these rules. These conditions included the repression of the lawbreaker to provide security and deter the wrongdoer and others from committing further

---

45 Ibid III, 9, § 173.

46 Ibid III, 8, § 152.

47 Ibid III, 14, §§ 217–219. Vattel hypothesised that, for the sake of peace, the prisoners' sovereign should not interfere and actively engage in rescuing them after signing a peace treaty, be it iniquitous or not. He was supposed to re-enter his obligations to protect them and vouch for their right of postliminy only when they came back under his jurisdiction.

injuries. Behind this idea of the repression of international crimes lay no cosmopolitan conception of the international community, but only the interest of most nations in moderating war and safeguarding a minimum level of international order. It was largely with regard to this concern that Vattel urged all peoples to reject and abolish usages like the enslavement of prisoners which hindered reconciliation and led to the escalation of warfare.[48]

Acknowledging Barbary prizes represented both a wise and unavoidable move for Vattel. He was writing for practitioners and policymakers who needed feasible guidelines to deal with the Barbary corsairs, rather than sermons about the latter's 'barbarity' and blameworthiness eliciting a universal right to castigate them. And if for Vattel it was all about making a virtue of necessity, others thought otherwise. Some authors not only tolerated the Barbary customs of war – including the licence to enslave, absolutely denied by Vattel – but also attributed to such customs the same validity and rationality status as European customs enjoyed. The Danish lawyer Martin Hübner, author of a celebrated treatise on the seizure of neutral shipping published in The Hague in 1759, did away with any prejudices against Barbary as follows:

> It is notorious that the Turks, and especially the Barbary Republics on the Coast of Africa, live in a perpetual war with Portugal, Spain and several other Christian states; although the sea-robbers of these republics, following ancient customs, do not commit any wrong by taking possession, by force and wherever they can, of vessels belonging to those states, nonetheless the sea-robbers never pick a quarrel with friend and neutral vessels over the ownership of the latter's freight. ... In doing so, the sea-robbers simply follow the prescriptions of the universal law of nations. Everybody knows that ... the navy of the Ottoman Empire and its vassals is a little thing compared with that of our great maritime powers. This is a further reason that induces the Turks to behave in the manner described above. Like for like, the customs that are received in the vast empire of the Muslims are not less compulsory, nor less respectable, than those that have been deemed suitable elsewhere.[49]

---

48 Ibid III, 14, § 222.

49 Martin Hübner, *De la saisie des bâtiments neutres, ou du droit qu'on les Nations belligérantes d'arrêter les navires des peuples amis* (2 vols, The Hague, 1759) vol I, pt II, ch 2, § 11. Translation by the author. Original text: 'Il est notoire que les Turcs, & surtout les Républiques Barbaresques sur la Côte de l'Afrique, vivent dans une Guerre perpétuelle avec le Portugal, l'Espagne & plusieurs autres Etats Chrétiens; si bien que les Ecumeurs de mer de ces Républiques, montées à l'antique, ne font pas faute de s'emparer à force ouverte, partout où ils le peuvent, des Bâtiments appartenant à ces Etats, & même d'en mettre les équipages à la chaîne. Néanmoins ils ne cherchent jamais querelles aux navires

Hübner here reasserted the pluralist conception of the laws of war, according to which the Barbary corsairs acted lawfully when seizing European shipping and putting their crews in chains. As Grotius had put it, Barbary privateers remained lawful belligerents although they applied an old-fashioned and brutal conduct of war. Surely, Hübner was not keen on the practice of enslaving captives and simply claimed that the Barbary corsairs were not liable for this conduct and must be granted impunity, but the latter was exactly the key legal point.

Apart from the issue of enslavement, Hübner's main aim in the excerpt above was to criticise the European powers' practice of seizing non-contraband enemy goods on neutral vessels. He did so by contrasting this practice with the opposite usage of the Ottomans and the Barbary corsairs. Actually, Hübner was not entirely coherent as he first used a universalist vocabulary to argue that the corsairs paid respect to neutral flags because they followed the prescriptions of the 'universal law of nations', whereas later in the paragraph he defended the corsairs by an apparently contrary argument based on cultural relativism. He stated that all customs being equally worthy, those of the Muslims were no less respectable than those of the Europeans.

This stance displayed the strain between universalist and relativist approaches that had coexisted in the pluralist doctrine, and also within individual doctrines, of the laws of war since its inception. While the pluralist doctrine had mainly emerged out of a pragmatic concern with the settlement of prize disputes, it could not get rid of significant theoretical issues. Was Barbary warfare to be tolerated simply because there was no criterion to decide which custom was the most rational? Or should it rather be tolerated because, for authors who had little difficulties justifying an unrestrained *ius belli* and the *ius infinitum*, there was nothing in Barbary warfare that inherently violated the law of nature? Realist writers like Bodin, influenced by early-modern sceptical philosophy, were inclined to think that Barbary warfare had nothing inherently unjust to it. Natural lawyers like Grotius, who believed in the existence of some basic natural principles regulating the conduct of all civilised peoples, mostly justified Barbary warfare out of a practical necessity. This did not prevent them

amis & Neutres sur la propriété de leurs Cargaisons. … [I]ls suivent là-dedans tout uniment les Arrêts du Droit des Gens Universel. On sait que … la Marine Guerrière de cet Empire & de ses Vassaux, est peu [de] chose vis-à-vis de celle de nos grandes Puissances Maritimes. Autant de raisons qui doivent engager les Turcs à ses conduire comme nous venons de le dire. … Coûtumes pour Coûtumes, celles qui sont reçues dans le vaste Empire des Musulmans ne sont pas moins obligatoires, ni moins respectables, que celles que l'on a jugé à propos d'adopter ailleurs.'

from taking on a discriminatory attitude towards the 'barbarian' based on universalist arguments on other occasions.[50]

If Hübner's narrative seemed affected by some inconsistencies, it nevertheless managed to condense the most significant points brought forward by those who questioned the superiority of Europe over Barbary, especially those points framed in terms of international politics: the state of perpetual war involving North Africans and Iberians, which ruled out the characterisation of the Barbary corsairs as pirates; the interests of France, Britain, and the Dutch Republic in maintaining friendly relations with the Ottomans for the sake of trade and to cause damage to European competitors; and the inferiority of the Ottoman navy, which prevented the Sultans from cultivating their dreams of primacy in the Mediterranean and consequently forced them to abide by the 'universal law of nations'. It was particularly indicative of the topicality of Hübner's position, and of the enduring validity of the pluralist paradigm of the laws of war, that in 1774, France's navy minister Antoine de Sartine acknowledged the existence of a specific maritime law of Barbary which should be respected by Europeans even though it might diverge from their customs.[51] Sartine was particularly referring to the principle, already praised by Hübner, that a neutral flag protects the enemy's goods. This principle, vital to the French trade in the Mediterranean and then observed by the North African vessels in contrast to European practice, was eventually to be approved by the 'civilised nations' with the Paris Declaration of 1856.[52]

As Vattel called for the repression of the Barbary corsairs, he was going both against the doctrinal mainstream and against the practice of most European states. Less indulgent than Hübner, he insisted that although the corsairs might be granted the licence to prey on foreign vessels and gain ownership of the movables captured, they could not acquire estates and, most importantly, did not possess any rights over captives, who were detained on a merely provisional basis. As a result, Vattel moved away from pragmatic pluralists like Grotius and Bynkershoek. He also opposed the tolerant view of just war doctrinarians like Pufendorf and Samuel von Cocceji. Vattel rejected the implication contained in their theory that the Barbary corsairs, not unlike their European counterparts, might be seen as

---

[50] This is well illustrated in Georg Cavallar, 'Vitoria, Grotius, Pufendorf, Wolff and Vattel: Accomplices of European Colonisation and Exploitation or True Cosmopolitans?' (2008) 10 *Journal of the History of International Law* 181.

[51] Christian Windler, 'Diplomatie et interculturalité. Les consuls français à Tunis, 1700–1840' (2003) 50 (4) *Revue d'histoire moderne et contemporaine* 63.

[52] *Declaration Respecting Maritime Law, signed at Paris*, 16 April 1856, 115 CTS 1–3, art 2.

just enemies and thus acquire an 'unlimited right' that warranted the enslavement of captives. In Pufendorf's view, it was far from clear whether the Europeans alone could be entitled to just enemy status and thus exercise the *ius infinitum*. Vattel did not get rid of the 'unlimited right', but attributed it to Europeans only.

Harsh Punishment for 'Uncivilised' International Offenders

The whole section of the *Droit des gens* devoted to the laws of war was built upon the contraposition between 'barbarian nations' and 'civilised' or, as Vattel more frequently put it, 'polished nations'.[53] This was particularly evident as far as punishment of the transgressors of the laws of war was concerned. While 'civilised' international offenders should be punished mildly and according to the principle of individual responsibility, for example by depriving them of some territories by a peace treaty, barbarian robber nations like the Barbary corsairs and the Tartars could be punished harshly and collectively.

In accordance with Wolff, Vattel grounded the right to punish exclusively on the right to security.[54] Vattel denied that the right to wage war, and to punish the enemy if necessary, derived from any logical, theological or metaphysical connection between offence and retribution.[55] It uniquely stemmed from the state's right to self-preservation. Once war had broken out, Vattel argued, just belligerents should restrain themselves to repelling the attacker, in conformity with the natural law principle that it is licit to repel force by force, without taking offensive steps that were not required for the sake of national security.[56] Yet punishment might be rightfully meted out to pursue a 'just and important' cause against pirates and robber nations, and also against 'civilised' warmongers and war criminals.[57]

Vattel maintained, for instance, that devastating a city of great strategic importance was 'warranted by the laws of war' if it refused to surrender, or

[53] Jean Barbeyrac had already employed the adjective *civilisé*, which was to become predominant in the nineteenth century, while Vattel still preferred *policé*, but both expressions corresponded to the Latin *moratus* used by Grotius. See Hugo Grotius, *De iure belli ac pacis libri tres,* I, 1 § 12, 1; Hugo Grotius, *Le droit de la guerre et de la paix* (2 vols, Jean Barbeyrac ed, Amsterdam, 1724) I, 1, § 12.

[54] *DG*, III, 9, § 162.

[55] Ibid II, 18, § 339.

[56] This principle was rooted in Roman law. See *Digesta* 9.2.45.4 (Paul. *lib. X ad Sab.*).

[57] *DG*, IV, 2, § 6.

if no other means were available to force a perfidious enemy to 'make war with humanity, or punishing him for some instance of outrageous conduct.'[58] It was for this reason that Vattel regarded the British bombings of France's coastal cities during the Nine Years' War as an inevitable and legitimate response to French privateering that was disrupting the trade of Britain. However, even in this case, as in any other military confrontation between 'polished peoples', Vattel assumed that retaliation should not be aimed at harming the enemy nation as a whole, but exclusively to punish its sovereign and attain victory. Also, European sovereigns should normally be punished gently. They might be forced to turn some of their border provinces over to the victors and provide a guarantee that no aggressive war will be undertaken in the future.[59]

This did not apply to 'uncivilised' international criminals. Vattel believed that severe punishment was the only means available effectively to stop barbarian peoples accustomed to live on plundering since centuries, and thus protect collective security.[60] Here is an illuminating passage in which Vattel pleaded for harsh punishment and for collective responsibility to apply in a collective struggle against a barbarous robber nation, such as the Uzbeks.

> [T]here is another case where the nation in general is guilty of the crimes of its members. That is, when, by its manners, and by the maxims of its government, it accustoms and authorises its citizens indiscriminately to plunder and maltreat foreigners, to make inroads into the neighbouring countries, &c. Thus, the nation of the Uzbeks is guilty of all the robberies committed by the individuals of which it is composed. ... All nations have a right to enter into a league against such a people, to repress them, and to treat them as the common enemies of the human race.[61]

This passage illustrates how Vattel's position was affected by a strong bias against 'uncivilised' international offenders and in favour of 'civilised' ones. He put forward a questionable justification for collective punishment of robber nations based on a problematic notion of collective responsibility, and of deterrence. In addition, he seemed to ignore the fact that regardless of whether robber nations might be deterred from waging aggressive war, European sovereigns hardly might. When subject to 'punitive' measures upon military defeat, European sovereigns simply

58 Ibid III, 8, §§ 168 and 169.
59 Ibid IV, 1, § 6.
60 Ibid II, 6, § 78.
61 Ibid II, 6, § 78.

continued to plot against their former enemies and make preparations for the next conflict. As a result, these sovereigns' immunity from harsh penalties could not be justified under Vattel's own doctrine of international punishment as based on collective security. His privileging of European warlike sovereigns over 'uncivilised' robber nations was groundless.

One of Vattel's aims in writing the *Droit des gens* was to elaborate a system of international law based on sovereign freedom, equality, and mutual respect. It was with this project in mind that he dismissed Wolff's cosmopolitan idea of the world state as potentially despotic, oppressive, and apologetic of universal monarchies. Yet Vattel re-introduced oppression and despotism by other means. He ended by conferring upon ad-hoc military coalitions engaged in the repression of international crimes a power comparable to that of the police organs of a world state. While pleading for universal tolerance, enlightened governments, the respect for sovereignty, and a non-discriminatory notion of the enemy, Vattel eventually justified military intervention and repression as international legal instruments at the disposal of arbitrary coalitions formed by the 'most polished' nations. In doing so, he declared an end to the pluralist view of the laws of war and prepared the ground for nineteenth century narratives advocating for the civilisers' right to enforce international law. In the case of Barbary, Vattel's intolerant attitude anticipated that of the great powers, which after centuries of indulgence had each grown irritated by Barbary privateering by the end of the eighteenth century. Open hostility broke out on occasion of the Barbary Wars fought by the United States.[62] By the 1830s, the Barbary issue was largely settled by the French occupation of Algeria.[63]

62 Daniel Panzac, *Barbary Corsairs. The End of a Legend 1800–1820* (first published 1999, Leiden – Boston, Brill, 2005) 270–292.

63 That Vattel's intolerant attitude can be situated at the beginning of a historical trend leading to nineteenth century armed conflict in North Africa is confirmed by the fact that the occupation of Algeria was preceded by decades of progressive interference by France, especially through the exercise of consular jurisdiction, in the affairs of the Barbary Regencies. See Christian Windler, *Diplomatie et interculturalité*, 90–91.

PART TWO

ENEMIES OF MANKIND WITHIN EUROPE

CHAPTER FOUR

GUILTY SOVEREIGNS: WARMONGERS AND VIOLATORS OF THE LAWS OF WAR

This chapter shifts the focus of the investigation from Barbary to Europe. It illustrates Vattel's attack on sovereigns who systematically abuse the right to make war (in shorthand, warmongers) and on sovereigns who are responsible for egregious or systematic breaches of the laws of war. Vattel stipulated that both of these types of enemy of mankind jeopardised collective security and tranquillity and must therefore be punished, with the caveat that penalties should be aimed solely at special and general deterrence, not retribution. This corresponded to a utilitarian and 'enlightened' approach to punishment that was being advanced by many of Vattel's contemporaries. He also put forward the modern idea that sovereigns responsible for international crimes should be punished as individuals. He insisted, however, that 'barbarian' warlike nations, with whom gentle manners were allegedly ineffective, might be punished collectively.

The chapter then turns to Vattel's criminalisation of sovereigns' violations of the laws of war. This criminalisation was based on the assumption that the laws of war possessed a clear legal status within the voluntary law of nations and required strict observance, whilst in earlier writers' opinion they might easily be derogated either 'by the right of war' or where the sovereign is fighting a just war. As he wrote his *Droit des gens* in the heyday of 'polished' warfare, Vattel put forward a demanding doctrine that restrained belligerents' broad discretion in choosing the means of injuring the enemy and the boundaries of hostilities. Nonetheless, he maintained that in exceptional cases, the civilised rules of warfare might be overruled: first for military necessity, as the highest duty of nations was to ensure national security, no matter what is required, and second for the repression of an enemy of mankind guilty of violating the civilised rules of warfare in the first place. In a common struggle against the enemy of mankind, the customary laws of war might be superseded on a provisional basis for the sake of their own survival. Repressing grave breaches of the laws of war, not unlike repressing abuses of the *ius ad bellum*, was necessary to safeguard a minimum level of collective security and tranquillity.

From Barbary to Europe

The Barbary corsairs did not represent the main target of Vattel's doctrine of international law enforcement. While his hostility towards the corsairs was unequivocal, he certainly did not expect his zero-tolerance approach to the Barbary issue to be translated into practice in the foreseeable future. If the threat of North African privateering had not sufficed to motivate the great powers to join forces in the heyday of Ottoman expansion, collective anti-piracy action had become entirely implausible now that the Sublime Porte was in decline and control of the Mediterranean was a much less sensitive issue. By the mid-eighteenth century, the major threats to international order came from within Europe. In 1758, in the middle of the Seven Years' War, Vattel's major concern was not with maritime marauders, but with those cultivated Christian princes who would not hesitate to turn entire regions of Europe into a battlefield for the sake of glory and power. With his doctrine of international law enforcement, Vattel especially aimed to justify collective action against such princes and sought a minimum level of international security and tranquillity on European soil.

When Vattel articulated this doctrine, he took inspiration from a peculiar example of international law enforcement (here mixed with constitutional law enforcement) in Europe. It was the Holy Roman Empire's collective security system, an originally medieval device which was applied to deal with breaches of the general peace within the Empire. When Vattel was finalising his *Droit des gens*, in 1757, the imperial collective security system had recently been activated against Frederick II of Prussia in response to his aggression against Saxony in August 1756, which triggered the Seven Years' War.[1] On that occasion, the Imperial Diet had qualified Frederick as an enemy of the Holy Roman Empire and demanded that all Imperial Estates, along with France and Sweden as guarantor powers of the Peace of Westphalia, counter him collectively.

As a diplomatic envoy at the service of Prussian-occupied Saxony, Vattel was very much concerned about Prussian expansionism in those years. He explicitly endorsed the activation of the imperial collective security system against the King of Prussia in a formal letter of protest against the invasion of Saxony, which he addressed to the Mayor and the Council of Bern in February 1757. In this letter, Vattel declared all Prussian military

---

[1] Karl Otmar von Aretin, *Das Alte Reich, 1648–1806* (Stuttgart, Klett – Cotta, 1993–1997) vol 3, 92 and 93.

operations to be illegitimate and in open violation of the law of nations.[2] He defended the Imperial Diet's decision to declare Frederick an outlaw, and argued that it was in the interest of all states to join forces and repress those who, like the King of Prussia, trampled on the basic rules of international law.[3]

Vattel might doubt whether the imperial troops, who were so quickly patched together, could really prevent the powerful Prussian army from attaining victory, yet he still viewed the activation of the imperial collective security system as a significant event. It validated his doctrine that those abusing the right to make war should be treated as common enemies of all and be repressed by an international coalition.

The Collective Security System of the Holy Roman Empire

The idea of a common war on behalf of the Holy Roman Empire against the peace-breaker had relevant precedents. Historically, the imperial execution (*Reichsexekution*) constituted an act whereby the Emperor, as overlord responsible for averting feuds and preserving the public peace, responded to internal or external threats by declaring war against the 'enemies of the Holy Roman Empire' upon the Imperial Estates' approval.[4] Indeed, because the Emperor's own resources were limited and he needed the Estates' financial and military support, the *Reichsexekution* soon became an entirely collegial resolution, with power gradually shifting from the imperial authority to the Diet. This reflected the general change in the Empire's balance of power from the first half of the sixteenth century onwards. By then, the Emperor on a number of matters had to come to terms with the Diet and the princely-influenced Imperial Cameral Court, both of which had already emerged as consolidated institutions. This was especially true for security matters. If in 1519 the Emperor only needed to ask for the prince-electors' consent to wage any foreign war he pleased, by 1648 he was required to seek the approval of the whole Diet.[5] Moreover, the Emperor's power was restrained by the electoral capitulation whereby he ought to confirm all privileges granted by his

---

[2] Edouard Béguelin, 'En souvenir de Vattel' in *Recueil de travaux offert par la Faculté de Droit de l'Université de Neuchâtel à la Société Suisse des Juristes* (Neuchâtel, Attinger, 1929) 35–176, 172.

[3] Ibid 173.

[4] Peter H Wilson, *The Holy Roman Empire 1495–1806* (London, Macmilllan, 1999) 52.

[5] Ibid 53.

predecessors upon his accession to the throne. Due to this mutated balance between Emperor and Estates, imperial executions could hardly be imposed by any party to the detriment of others. On several occasions, parties found no agreement on the *Reichsexekution* in response to a common threat, and therefore the collective security system was simply not activated.

Whether an imperial war could be waged depended not only on the balance of power within the Empire and on the gravity of the common threat, but also on foreign interferences. This is particularly true of the Holy Roman Empire's relations with its most powerful neighbour, France. In 1544, for instance, Holy Emperor Charles V managed to have both France and the Ottoman Empire qualified as enemies of the empire and of Christendom in the Diet of Speyer.[6] On that occasion, he secured the backing of the Protestant princes: they perceived the Ottoman and French threat as not just a threat to Habsburg interests, but indeed a threat to their own. At that point, France was still considered by Protestant princes as a common enemy of the Germans, not unlike the Ottoman Empire. But in the aftermath of the Thirty Years' War their attitude changed as they regarded France as a rescuer of German Protestantism. As a result, the Imperial Diet in the Franco-Dutch War of the 1670s shrunk from issuing an official declaration of war against the French.[7] At that time the Holy Roman Empire took part in the hostilities de facto, but no imperial declaration of war was issued, because many in the Holy Roman Empire wished to maintain their ties to France.

The Issue of Security in Pufendorf's Critique of the Holy Roman Empire

In his 1667 critique of the *Present State of Germany*, Samuel Pufendorf had mocked the imperial institutions for their incapacity to gather the consent and resources necessary to maintain peace within the Holy Empire and wage war in the name of all of its states.[8] Because imperial power was firmly in the hands of the Catholic Habsburgs, open opposition by German

---

[6] Klaus Müller, 'Zur Reichskriegserklärung im 17. und 18. Jahrhundert' (1973) 90 *Zeitschrift der Savigny-Stiftung für Rechtsgeschichte, Germanistische Abteilung* 246, 249.

[7] Ibid 248 ff.

[8] Samuel Pufendorf (under the pseudonym: Severinus de Monzambano), *De statu Imperii Germanici liber unus* (Geneva, 1667) V, 2, 7, and 8. On the relationship between protection and obedience in the Holy Roman Empire, see Anne Orford, 'Jurisdiction Without Territory. From the Holy Roman Empire to the Responsibility to Protect' (2009) 30 *Michigan Journal of International Law* 981.

Protestant princes was not a rare phenomenon. The Protestant princes were able to reject exceptional levies, and thereby prevent the Emperor from waging war, and were also able to establish military alliances with foreign powers, notably Sweden and France, against him, as had occurred in the Thirty Years' War and in the League of the Rhine formed in 1658. At that time the Holy Roman Empire was clearly split by confessional divisions, and a powerful and legitimate authority able to decide on war and peace was absent. Although the power of the House of Austria was soon to increase again, thanks to the victories over the Ottomans, the imperial institution would never regain its former legitimacy and prestige.

This state of affairs was sanctioned by the provisions of the Treaty of Münster concerning the use of force against the peace-breaker. Far from acknowledging the Emperor as the sole authority competent over this matter, the drafters stated that 'all Partys in this Transaction shall be oblig'd to defend and protect all and every Article of this Peace against any one.'[9] This denied the Emperor any special status and conferred the right to repress the violator of the peace upon all signatories. The parties to the treaty were sovereigns and refused the pre-eminence of the Emperor, who definitively ceased to possess particular rights based on his traditional role as the guarantor of peace and justice.

The imperial institutions were further weakened by the concessions made by the new Emperor Leopold I in his electoral capitulation of 1658. Commenting on this text and on the Westphalian treaties, Pufendorf famously declared the Holy Roman Empire to have become an irregular body without an actual head.[10] The Emperor had been largely deprived of his competence over security matters. As far as the repression of the peace-breaker in accordance with the Treaty of Münster was concerned, the Emperor had no special prerogative. Nor was there any need of the imperial authority in this respect. The violator of the treaty was no longer regarded as the infringer of the imperial peace, but rather as the breaker of a general compact among sovereign states, some of which did not even belong to the Empire. In this curious mixture of constitutional and international law, the greatest responsibility for preserving peace within the Empire fell upon foreign powers. Indeed, the German states did not trust the Emperor, and did not themselves possess the military strength and

[9] *Treaty of Peace between France and the Empire, signed at Münster*, 14(24) October 1648, 1 CTS 319, 354, art CXXIII.

[10] Pufendorf, *De statu Imperii Germanici*, VI, 9.

political cohesion necessary to respond to grave breaches of the treaty. While this opened the door to foreign intrusions, it also set up a convenient balance of power between Austria, France and Sweden that provided the German princes with considerable leeway.

Differences in power aside, all signatories to the Treaty of Münster were put on the same plane: each had the obligation to maintain peace and, if needed, to repress the peace-breaker. The Emperor was deprived of his former status as supreme feudal lord and of rights related to that status, most importantly the unconditioned *ius ad bellum*. He was not authorised to make alliances or engage imperial troops in a war unless he had obtained the approval of all Imperial Estates summoned in a Diet.[11] Given the Emperor's loss of authority, Pufendorf remarked that if recourse to force was required to repress the peace-breaker, it should no longer be regarded as a punitive measure taken by a superior against a felon, but as an act of war.

> For here the finding of fault is imposed on an offender not as a command from above, but as something freely consented to by him and somehow mutually agreed to. And the penalty is imposed not as on a subject convicted of violating a civil law, but as an act of war against the violator of a treaty.[12]

Once it was assumed that the German princes – despite the persistence of the imperial institutions and the resulting bonds – had an absolute right to make war, then they should be regarded as sovereign moral persons living with each other in a condition of natural freedom, which they might decide to restrain at their own discretion by submitting to treaties with foreign powers or by observing certain customs. At any rate, even when states committed acts of aggression in violation of the treaty they could not be branded as criminals because, in Pufendorf's view, the notions of crime and punishment could not be applied as long as no superior authority was there to define crime and administer justice.[13] This was no longer the case in the Holy Roman Empire. Those states acting in repression of the peace-breaker might take any forceful measures required to re-establish peace, but they were not allowed to indict the enemy as a criminal.

Given the situation in 1667, Pufendorf's critique was entirely justified. However, developments brought about soon after by the common

---

[11] *Treaty of Peace between Sweden and the Empire, signed at Osnabrück*, 14(24) October 1648, 1 CTS 198, 241, art VIII (1).

[12] Pufendorf, *De statu Imperii Germanici*, V, 28.

[13] Samuel Pufendorf, *De jure naturae et gentium* (first published 1672, Charles H Oldfather and William A Oldfather trans, Oxford, Clarendon, 1934) VIII, 3, § 7.

struggles against Louis XIV made it partly obsolete as far as collective security was concerned. Louis' image in Germany was ruined by his persistent military adventurism and brutal conduct of war, especially in the War of the Grand Alliance, while the Habsburg Emperor's position was strengthened by his victories over the Ottomans. Thus in 1689 the Imperial Diet, by then a permanent body, found no impediment to declaring France an 'enemy of the empire' with explicit reference to the precedent created by the Diet of Speyer of 1544.[14] The analogy between the imperial declaration of war of 1544 and that of 1689 is striking: in both situations the French were allied with the Ottomans while the integrity of the Holy Roman Empire, threatened on several fronts, seemed to depend on the unified effort of Emperor and Estates. On both occasions the imperial authority, represented by authoritative personalities such as Charles V and Leopold I respectively, was in a position of relative strength and was able to take advantage of the international conjuncture to impose the Habsburg agenda.

In the late seventeenth century, in light of growing anti-French sentiment, Gottfried Wilhelm Leibniz opposed the Pufendorfian doctrine and instead put forward a conception of the Holy Roman Empire as a defensive alliance that could be effective through a more intensive collaboration among the Estates to grant both internal and external security.[15] According to Leibniz, the constitution of the Empire was supported by the balance of power at the continental level, and both the imperial constitution and the balance of power operated to preserve peace in Germany and Europe. At that stage the topic of security, both internal and external, was very much in vogue in the Holy Roman Empire, and debates in the Diet led to the issuance of the *Reichsexekutionsordnung* of 1673 and the *Reichsdefensionalordnung* of 1681.[16] Security within the Holy Roman Empire was then boosted by the increasing cooperation between the local authorities with a view to enforce extraterritorial crime repression. Externally, the imperial collective security system, revived on the occasion of the conflict against Louis XIV and the Ottomans, was activated in specific anti-Bourbon terms in the War of the Spanish Succession in 1702, and again in the War of the Polish Succession in 1734.[17] Both in the Holy Roman

---

14 Müller, 'Zur Reichskriegserklärung', 256.

15 See Karl Härter, 'Sicherheit und Frieden im frühneuzeitlichen Alten Reich: Zur Funktion der Reichsverfassung als Sicherheits- und Friedensordnung 1648–1806' (2003) 30 *Zeitschrift für historische Forschung* 413, 417.

16 Ibid.

17 Müller, 'Zur Reichskriegserklärung', 257.

Empire and in Europe as a whole, maintenance of peace and security were at that time conceived of as an endeavour to be carried out collectively if it was to be successful.[18] The Leibnizian Vattel still shared this view when drafting his *Droit des gens* in the 1750s.

Frederick II of Prussia as a Notorious Warmonger

When Frederick II acceded to the throne in May 1740 and set out to make Prussia a great power, his aggressive foreign policy posed a serious threat to the collective security system of the Holy Roman Empire. Frederick nearly delivered a deadly blow to the imperial institutions. His first sensational deed was to breach the Pragmatic Sanction and open hostilities against Austria, Prussia's main rival, in December 1740. The Pragmatic Sanction, signed by, amongst others, his father Frederick William I in 1728, should have allowed Maria Theresa of Austria, daughter of Holy Roman Emperor Charles VI, to inherit the Habsburg lands without foreign interference at the latter's death. In December 1740, two months after Charles died, Frederick II's troops attacked and occupied the rich region of Silesia, then belonging to the Habsburg possessions, on the basis of a fictitious dynastic claim built up by Prussian minister Podewils, the central point being that Frederick William I had been deceived when he signed the Pragmatic Sanction.[19] Further, as critics might argue that one of Frederick II's ancestors, the Great Elector Frederick William of Brandenburg, had already renounced his pretensions over Silesia back in 1685, the claim stated that this act of renunciation was void and did not bind Frederick II.[20] Contemporary observers were aware that such pretexts were 'no more than a fig-leaf to cover an act of blatant aggression, and indeed were never seen by Frederick [II] himself as more than that.'[21] With 80,000 troops ready to move, huge monetary resources, and certain that the French would join him in the anti-Habsburg campaign, the ambitious Prussian king could wait no longer. Moreover, he was encouraged to take action as the Austrians were suffering from financial difficulties and had cut a sorry figure during their recent war against the Ottomans.[22]

---

18 Härter, 'Sicherheit und Frieden', 421.

19 Derek McKay, Hamish M Scott, *The Rise of the Great Powers 1648–1815* (London – New York, Longman, 1983) 176.

20 Matthew S Anderson, *The War of the Austrian Succession, 1740–1748* (London – New York, Longman, 1995) 59.

21 Ibid.

22 Ibid 61.

Frederick already manifested his ambitions of conquest in the run-up to his accession to the throne, especially on the occasion of territorial disputes. Although he was praised for carrying out progressive reforms domestically, most importantly the abolition of torture, and for his patronage of the arts, his international conduct and reputation did not resonate with this. Out of his country, '[t]he vision of the philosopher prince, intent on filling his court with savants, poets and ballet dancers, did not survive the autumn [of 1740].'[23] Even Voltaire, one of Frederick's greatest admirers, heavily criticised him, if secretly, from 1740 onwards. Voltaire ascribed to the King of Prussia entire responsibility for the bloodshed of the War of the Austrian Succession, and blamed him for his duplicity as attested to by the recurrent Austro-Prussian rapprochements.[24] Indeed, when Frederick opened the War of the Austrian Succession, he established a new pattern for international morality, according to which war no longer depended on dynastic disputes but was simply waged for the sake of glory and power.[25] Frederick himself had no difficulty admitting that what he sought through war was personal glory.[26]

However, not all agreed on demonising Frederick. In the early 1740s he found large support in occupied Silesia, a state with a strong Protestant majority, and even in the public opinion of enemy countries like the United Kingdom, where George II's engagement in the war in defence of Hanover was unpopular. In fact, many British subjects feared French hostility and assistance to the Jacobites, and were sympathetic with Frederick's decision to attack Catholic Austria in alleged defence of Protestant Silesia.[27] However, Frederick ended by alienating these sympathies as his policies turned out to diverge from the interests of the *Corpus Evangelicorum*, the group of Protestant Imperial Estates. He lost much confession-based endorsement upon attacking Saxony, whose Electors held a perpetual presidency over the *Corpus*, as well as Mecklenburg at the start of the Seven Years' War.[28]

---

[23] Christopher Duffy, *Frederick the Great: A Military Life* (London, Routledge & Kegan Paul, 1985) 21.

[24] Ibid 45–46.

[25] Johannes Kunisch, *Friedrich der Grosse. Der König und seine Zeit* (Munich, Beck, 2004) 171 and 175.

[26] Julian Swann, 'Politics and the State in Eighteenth-Century Europe' in Timothy CW Blanning (ed), *The Eighteenth Century: Europe 1688–1815* (OUP, 2000) 11, 17.

[27] Anderson, *The War of the Austrian Succession*, 80.

[28] Peter H Wilson, 'Prussia's Relations with the Holy Roman Empire, 1740–1786' (2008) 51 (2) *The Historical Journal* 337, 350.

Within intellectual circles, the Prussian King had long escaped overt criticism from his *protégés* and particularly from the Huguenots gathered around the Berlin Academy of Sciences and its secretary, Vattel's friend Samuel Formey.[29] In 1741, immediately after the War of the Austrian Succession broke off, Vattel, in the dedicatory epistle of the *Défense du Système Leibnitien*, still reiterated the apologetic leitmotif that had characterised filo-Prussian Huguenot literature since the foundation of the Berlin Academy by Frederick I. Indeed, as Vattel lauded Frederick II's religious tolerance and enlightened spirit in the *Défense*, Vattel expected that Frederick would jettison aggressive foreign policies upon securing Silesia. Most importantly, Vattel was hoping to secure a diplomatic post through Frederick's good graces.

This was a short-lived delusion. By the summer of 1743, Vattel had to face the fact that Frederick paid little attention to his diplomatic and philosophical talent, and would not grant him either a diplomatic position or a professorship. After he shelved his project of grounding an academy in Neuchâtel and taking on a chair of philosophy and natural law, Vattel headed for Dresden to take his chances at the court of another renowned patron of arts and culture, Saxony's prince-elector Frederick Augustus II, then also King of Poland under the name of Augustus III.[30] Vattel thus went over to the enemy camp, as Augustus had sided with Austria in the meantime.

The Reichsexekution *against Frederick II*

Already in 1744, in the middle of the War of the Austrian Succession, there were rumours that the Elector Augustus, Vattel's employer, would in his capacity as Imperial Vicar declare Frederick II of Prussia as an enemy of the Holy Roman Empire and formally depose him.[31] Because fear and uncertainty spread among the German princes as to whether Frederick would really content himself with Silesia, they might have vouched for the conferral of extraordinary powers upon the Imperial Vicar Augustus so that he could lead the common struggle against the 'enemy of the Holy

---

[29] André Bandelier, *Des Suisses dans la République des Lettres. Un réseau savant au temps de Frédéric le Grand* (Geneva, Slatkine, 2007) 18.

[30] Béguelin, 'En souvenir de Vattel', 44–45. The Neuchâtel Academy would eventually see the light of the day in 1838, under the auspices of Frederick William IV of Prussia.

[31] Anderson, *The War of the Austrian Succession*, 135.

Roman Empire' (*hostis Sacri Imperii*). Yet this strategy did not work in the War of the Austrian Succession. Augustus lacked not only leadership capability but also the external support necessary to enforce any effective measures against the King of Prussia. International backing had become literally indispensable in any German conflict since the Peace of Westphalia had named France and Sweden as guarantors of the imperial peace and established a tight connection between the imperial collective security system and the European balance of power. In the 1740s, when the imperial institutions seemed to crumble under the blows of power politics, endorsement by foreign powers was essential to determine whether the lesser German princes and Estates might consent to declaring an imperial war against a powerful monarch, or whether these princes and Estates would do better to win the monarch over to avoid being aggressed themselves.

As the invasion of Silesia did not produce a coherent anti-Prussian sentiment among the European powers, any project of declaring Frederick II an outlaw during the War of the Austrian Succession by means of the *Reichsexekution* had miserably failed. Since Frederick's main opponent, Austria, happened to be the common enemy of France, Bavaria and Spain as well, he easily had these powers vouch for the rise of Prussia to great power status as long as the resulting alteration of the balance of power was to the detriment of the Habsburgs only. As much as Frederick's allies in the long run also ended by fearing him and regretting this alliance, which eventually led to the Austro-French rapprochement and the diplomatic revolution of 1756, in the early 1740s they still prioritised the weakening of Austria and viewed the growth of Prussia as a positive development. As a result, Frederick managed to split Europe into two fronts and thereby prevented the formation of continental anti-Prussian coalitions. So the War of the Austrian Succession, far from turning into a common struggle against Frederick as an imperial peace-breaker, remained a confrontation driven by *raison d'Etat* and fomented by particular rivalries such as Prussia/Austria, France/Great Britain, and Russia/Sweden.

The pattern of the imperial war was resumed in what has been regarded by commentators as the continuation of the War of the Austrian Succession, the Seven Years' War. The Peace of Aix-la-Chapelle of 1748, of which the only major disposition consisted of the recognition of the Prussian conquest of Silesia, could hardly represent more than a truce, as it had left many powers unsatisfied and willing to take up arms again as soon as the occasion had arisen.[32] Far from implementing the arms reduction required by the treaty, the European powers undertook an arms rush, with the Austrians acting especially effectively to fill the military gap between them and the Prussians.

From 1748 onwards, international tensions spread as the French and the British strengthened their positions at the mouth of the Saint Lawrence River, preparing for the final European struggle for the North American colonies.[33] Initially smoothed over by diplomacy, the confrontation overseas escalated in 1754, paving the way for the *renversement des alliances* and the Seven Years' War in Europe. Meanwhile, on the Continent, Wenzel Anton von Kaunitz, then in charge of Austrian foreign affairs, was striving for a French alliance that he deemed necessary to recover Silesia, and was therefore attempting to drift Louis XV away from Frederick II. The latter actually facilitated Kaunitz's task by seeking a British alliance. Fearful of an invasion by Russia, of losing French support owing to the Austrian diplomatic moves, and of the hostility of his German neighbours, Frederick turned to Britain and ensured its help by the Westminster Convention of 16 January 1756.[34] Aware of these developments, Louis XV no longer hesitated to sign the First Treaty of Versailles with Austria on 1 May 1756. This alliance between what had hitherto been considered as the grimmest 'natural enemies' of Europe sanctioned the so-called Diplomatic Revolution.

Although France and Britain had long been skirmishing in America, and had even declared war on each other, large-scale war operations commenced in Germany. Fearing a combined Austro-Russian attack on Prussia, Frederick II had contemplated a blitzkrieg plan to invade Saxony and Bohemia. He drafted a manifesto stating a number of pretexts for war and blaming Austria, and opened hostilities before the deadline of the ultimatum he gave was over in order to anticipate French and Russian intervention.[35] His troops entered Saxony on 29 August 1756 and took possession of its capital Dresden soon after.

Plans to declare Frederick an outlaw by means of the imperial ban (*Reichsacht*) were being considered in Vienna as early as 1756, as a consequence of his aggression on Saxony on 29 August of the same year, which

---

[32] Franz AJ Szabo, *The Seven Years War in Europe, 1756–1763* (Harlow, Pearson – Longman, 2008) 15–17.
[33] Lucien Bély, *Les rélations internationales en Europe, XVIIe–XVIIIe siècles* (Paris, PUF, 1992) 518.
[34] Ibid 531–5.
[35] Szabo, *The Seven Years War in Europe*, 19.

amounted to a blatant violation of the imperial peace, the *Allgemeiner Landfrieden*. To be sure, Kaunitz assumed that Frederick would make a mockery of both the imperial ban and troops. Frederick never hid his contempt of the imperial institutions, which he deemed to be an antiquated political relic and a hindrance to Prussian expansion, and surely looked forward to crushing the imperial troops and displaying Prussia's military supremacy. Traditionally assigned defensive tasks within the Empire's collective security system, imperial troops were disorganised, inefficient, and small in number compared to the great powers' standing armies. This resulted in the celebrated defeat at Roßbach in November 1757 that would become a classical theme in German historians' narratives on the decay of the Holy Roman Empire. By then, the imperial troops represented an outmoded military patchwork, the strategic relevance of which largely consisted in relieving pressure on Austria by keeping the Prussian forces engaged at the Eastern borders of Brandenburg and Saxony.[36]

And yet Kaunitz needed the imperial war to be formally declared and carried out to justify the Austrian cause and ensure foreign support, especially from France and Sweden. Indeed, following Frederick's aggression against Saxony, Kaunitz had little trouble finding sympathisers in Germany and abroad. Despite the King of Prussia's diplomatic somersaults directed at depicting his war as a necessary preventive measure to protect German Protestantism from the ambitions of Catholic Austria – a view that was untenable for the sole reason that the assaulted Saxony was the most authoritative member of the *Corpus Evangelicorum* – the Imperial Estates condemned the Prussian recourse to force unanimously.[37] While the Protestant princes had no interest in going along with Austria's wish to recover Silesia, they nonetheless fully agreed on driving the Prussians out of Saxony. Needless to say, Kaunitz was the first to stress that the current war was not for the benefit of Austria, but for the Empire as a whole.

On 20 September 1756, Holy Roman Emperor Francis I took the first step by decreeing that all officials and subjects of the King of Prussia were formally discharged from their duties towards the King.[38] Although at that stage Francis I acted without previously ensuring the Diet's approval and thereby forced the electoral capitulation, the Estates endorsed his anti-Prussian policy and gave their formal consent to Francis' declaring imperial war against Prussia and raising an imperial army in January 1757.

---

[36] Aretin, *Das Alte Reich*, 98.
[37] Ibid 89.
[38] Ibid 92.

Shortly after, France and Sweden also asserted their willingness to fulfil their obligations under the Peace of Westphalia and take part in the hostilities to repress Frederick as a peace-breaker. Dangerously isolated on the continent, Frederick attempted to destabilise and divide the enemy coalition by spreading terror among the populations of Franconia and the Upper Palatinate. Yet this policy, far from discouraging the Imperial Estates from continuing the war, augmented the general hostility towards him.[39]

In addition to Frederick's disregard for the law of nations and 'civilised' conduct of warfare, the German princes were motivated to participate in the struggle against him by fear of the consequences of Prussia's success compared to Austria's. A Prussian victory would have jeopardised the liberties of the neighbouring territories, and probably would have meant the total obliteration of the Holy Roman Empire, which Frederick II viewed as an obstacle to the rise of Prussia. Conversely, an Austrian success would have preserved the liberties of the German princes and Estates, only implying political changes that they under the present circumstances were willing to accept, though not necessarily changes which they desired, such as the dismemberment of the Kingdom of Prussia and perhaps the return of Silesia to the House of Habsburg. In a time when the struggle for power between Austria and Prussia seemed to determine the political destiny of much of Central-Eastern Europe, the best way for the lesser states to maintain their liberties was to keep the imperial institutions and their peace-keeping function alive. At that stage, the German princes despite their obligations towards the overlord were still enjoying de facto sovereignty. The framework of the Holy Roman Empire allowed them to benefit from absolute internal freedom, and ensured external protection. Recognising this, even the Protestant rulers put aside their suspicions of Austria's power politics and aligned themselves with it for the sake of the common good.

Vattel's Letter of Protest against the Invasion of Saxony

Vattel first manifested his critical attitude towards Prussia's aggressive policies with his choice to move to Dresden in the middle of the War of the Austrian Succession and offer his services to Frederick's sworn enemy,

[39] Ibid 93.

Saxony's Premier Minister Count Heinrich von Brühl. As the Seven Years' War broke out and Frederick ordered the Prussian troops to tear down two of Count Brühl's castles, Vattel in a letter sent to Brühl early in 1758 stressed that Frederick's actions violated the mores and ethics of the warfare of civilised nations. Vattel mentioned in this letter that he in his *Droit des gens* to be published soon would provide good arguments to address Prussia's contempt for the law of nations. He would contend that 'all powers shall join to chastise a power that wishes to introduce such pernicious customs'.[40] Vattel was referring to his doctrine of the repression of international crimes, in particular to a paragraph of the *Droit des gens* in which he claimed that those who, like Frederick, without any necessity lay waste to 'temples, tombs, public buildings, and all works of remarkable beauty' declare themselves the 'enemies of mankind'.[41] To be sure, Vattel could not afford publicly to declare Frederick as an 'enemy of mankind' in the *Droit des gens*, but he did so privately, or by indirect means. In another letter sent to Brühl in 1759, Vattel anticipated that he would publish an anonymous satirical piece in which to 'make our enemy [Frederick] feel sick of his own fury for military glory by commending his brother [Prince Henry].'[42] This piece was to be printed secretly and appear in the *Journal Encyclopédique* so that 'the King of Prussia will not fail to see it'.[43]

The same critical attitude towards contemporary Prussian bellicism was implicitly reasserted by Vattel in his *Dialogue entre Pierre le Grand et Charles XII sur la gloire des conquérans* of 1760.[44] In this imaginary dialogue, he criticised the populace's naïve admiration for military leaders, and distinguished 'the generous captain who fights out of love for his motherland' from the 'bloodthirsty warrior who, in his barbarous cruelty, sacrifices men's lives for his own ambition'.[45] The former, Vattel claimed, had an absolute obligation to defend his country and therefore was permitted to resort to otherwise illicit means of warfare in cases of extreme necessity, like Peter the Great did. Yet the 'unjust conqueror who ravages

---

40 Emer de Vattel, Letter to Heinrich von Brühl, 16 February 1758, quoted in Béguelin, *En souvenir de Vattel*, 57.

41 *DG*, III, 9, § 168.

42 Emer de Vattel, Letter to Heinrich von Brühl, 7 December 1759, quoted in Béguelin, *En souvenir de Vattel*, 59.

43 Ibid.

44 Emer de Vattel, *Dialogue entre Pierre le Grand et Charles XII sur la gloire des conquérans* in Emer de Vattel, *Mélanges de littérature, de morale et de politique* (Neuchâtel, 1760) 1–19.

45 Ibid 5.

provinces and kingdoms' for personal glory could not be excused. In Vattel's view, such a warmonger was more blameworthy than a pirate.[46]

Throughout the Seven Years' War, however irregularly and scarcely remunerated due to Saxony's financial distress,[47] Vattel never ceased to observe his obligations towards the Elector Augustus and advocate for his rights against Prussia.[48] Hired as an envoy to Bern in 1749, Vattel was later directly involved in the shaping of Saxon foreign policy when he was appointed as a privy councillor of Augustus and a member of the Cabinet on Foreign Affairs.[49] In this capacity, Vattel spoke out in defence of the Saxon cause and challenged Prussian war propaganda in his hometown Neuchâtel, at that time subject to the King of Prussia. In one of the numerous letters sent to Brühl in that period, Vattel told that by confronting the Prussians in Neuchâtel he had drawn their hostility and hatred, yet he was proud of it 'as long as they treat Saxony shamefully'.[50] In an unpublished piece written at that time, Vattel particularly set out to demonstrate 'how much it is important for the honour, the interests, and the security of the Empire and of the Allies to procure just and prompt satisfaction for Saxony' after it had been injured by Prussia.[51]

For the purposes of the present chapter, the most relevant critique of Prussian bellicism by Vattel is found in the letter of protest of February 1757 that he addressed to the Mayor and the Council of Bern to contest

---

46 Ibid 5–6.

47 As Vattel feared the Seven Years' War's impact on Saxon national coffers and hence on his already precarious financial situation, he at some point envisaged to give up his diplomatic mission for Saxony, yet even then he wished to keep distance from Prussia. This was confirmed by the fact that Vattel attempted to secure a post at the French court, where Louis XV, pressured by Madame Pompadour, was getting rid of influential filo-Prussian elements like Marquis d'Argenson and Count Machault D'Arnouville. Vattel's unsolicited application was unsuccessful, though. The French reply was that his services were not requested in Paris at the moment, though they would remain very useful to France, as well as Saxony, had he kept his present position: Bély, *Les rélations internationales en Europe*, 542; Béguelin, *En souvenir de Vattel*, 52.

48 Literary evidence of Vattel's commitment to defending the interests of his master was given in the *Mémoire sur les affaires de Courlande* (Warsaw, 1763), in which Vattel advocated for Augustus' and his son's rights over the Duchy of Courland and Semigallia against the descendants of Duke Ernst Johann von Biron. See Christoph Good, *Emer de Vattel (1714–1767): Naturrechtliche Ansätze einer Menschenrechtsidee und des humanitären Völkerrechts im Zeitalter der Aufklärung* (Baden-Baden, Nomos, 2011) 15.

49 Béguelin, *En souvenir de Vattel*, 58; Christoph Good, *Emer de Vattel*, 14.

50 Emer de Vattel, Letter to Heinrich von Brühl, 15 February 1759, quoted in Béguelin, *En souvenir de Vattel*, 56.

51 Emer de Vattel, Letter to Heinrich von Brühl, 27 December 1759, quoted in Béguelin, *En souvenir de Vattel*, 59.

Frederick's recent invasion of Saxony.[52] Attached were two pieces alleging that the conduct of the King of Prussia towards Saxony was 'deprived of any rightful ground and directly contrary to the sacred rules of the law of nations'.[53] It was argued that irrespective of the fictitious character of the pretexts with which Frederick had sought to cover up the invasion, he should at least have notified the Saxons of his demands in due time and allowed them the possibility of providing for satisfaction prior to Frederick's opening of hostilities. His failure to do so attested to the attack on Saxony being premeditated and to the complaints brought forward as pretexts being irrelevant with respect to the war. From the outset, Vattel stated, the King of Prussia's aim was to conquer rich Saxony and take possession not only of its material resources, but also of its army – an intolerable practice which was unprecedented among Christian princes. If rulers abused the right to make war in this manner, Vattel argued, no true peace would ever be possible. This point was reasserted, with implicit reference to Frederick's conduct in the Seven Years' War, in the *Droit des gens*, as Vattel stated that

> To march an army into a neighbouring country by which we are not threatened, and without having endeavoured to obtain, by reason and justice, an equitable reparation for the wrongs of which we complain, would be introducing a mode pregnant with evils to mankind, and sapping the foundations of the safety and tranquillity of states.[54]

In his letter of protest against the invasion of Saxony, Vattel remarked that Frederick had not only abused the right to make war; he had also breached the laws of war, the sanctity of which had to be preserved if war was not to degenerate into barbaric fury.[55] It was in the common interest of all nations to join and repress the sovereigns responsible for such misconduct. Vattel noted that this had also been the view taken by the Imperial Diet in the recent outlawing of Frederick II as an enemy of the Empire – a view shared by the 'most respectable powers of Europe':

> It is certainly recommended for the interest and the safety of nations to repress he who tramples on rules [i.e. the rules of the law of nations] which constitute the unique foundation of their tranquillity, and without which

[52] Emer de Vattel, Letter to the Avoyer and Council of Bern, 28 February 1757 (Staatsarchiv Bern, Deutschland-Buch H H) 679, reprinted in Béguelin, *En souvenir de Vattel*, 172–173.

[53] Béguelin, *En souvenir de Vattel*, 172.

[54] *DG*, III, 4, § 62.

[55] Béguelin, *En souvenir de Vattel*, 173.

> everything would become prey to the strongest and the most daring. This is what the most respectable powers of Europe have felt; it is what motivated the decree that has recently been issued by the Diet of the Empire.[56]

Here Vattel put forward the idea, later reasserted in the *Droit des gens*, that the modern customs of war represented a fundamental achievement of civilisation and should be preserved for the sake of the common security and tranquillity of nations. For this reason, the Imperial Estates and the 'most respectable' powers of Europe had taken action against the warmonger and war criminal Frederick II. In the past, other powers had done the same to repress aggressive sovereigns threatening collective security.

It may be noted, however, that compared with some of the grand alliances of the past, such as the alliance against Louis XIV in the Nine Years' War, the anti-Prussian coalition of 1757 appeared less inclusive, and was crippled from the outset by the absence of Britain, which sided with Frederick. Yet Vattel implied that this exception did not delegitimate the anti-Prussian coalition. He seemed to make the pragmatic assumption that unanimous consent on the use of force at the international level, not unlike unanimous consent on resistance against the domestic tyrant, was an ideal condition that might only be aspired to. Unanimity, in foreign as well as internal affairs, could not be seen as a casting criterion to decide if a ruler was to be regarded as an enemy of mankind, nor did it indicate how he should be punished.

The kind of universal consent reached by the Grand Alliance in the Nine Years' War, engaging all European powers against Louis XIV, was the product of a specific constellation that posterity could only strive for. Under normal circumstances, the international arena was split by complex alliances aimed at maintaining the balance of power. Here, those who Vattel labelled as warmongers and war criminals were mostly repressed not because they abused the right to make war and violated the laws of war, but because they disturbed the international equilibrium. Indeed, Vattel himself maintained that preserving the balance of power was a legitimate motive to wage war in its own right.[57] At any rate, whatever the reason for the allies joining forces, the bottom line for Vattel was that a

---

[56] Ibid. Translation by the author. Original text: 'Il est certainement de l'intérêt et du salut commun des Nations, de réprimer celui qui foule aux pieds des règles, qui font l'unique fondement de leur repos, et sans lesquelles tout deviendrait la proie du plus fort et du plus audacieux. C'est ce qu'ont senti les plus respectables Puissances de l'Europe; c'est ce qui a dicté le décret qui vient d'émaner de la diète de l'Empire.'

[57] *DG*, III, 3, § 49.

coalition needed to be formed to neutralise the threat. Again, Vattel was concerned not about international justice as such, but about international justice as a means to achieve international order.

As a result, Vattel focused more on the coalition's military effectiveness than on its motives, legitimacy, and unanimity. This became clear in a passage of the *Droit des gens* in which he argued that just as the Nine Years' War, waged by all European powers against Louis XIV, was entirely justified, so was the later War of the Spanish Succession, although in the latter conflict Louis was no longer alone, but rather was supported by the followers of Philip V of Spain and by the Bavarians.[58] Pragmatic as usual, Vattel accounted for the fact that the War of the Spanish Succession was the conflict that most threatened international stability in the age of Louis XIV, and was accordingly seen by Louis' opponents as a most rightful struggle to protect the freedom of the European states from Bourbon despotism. Here, Louis allegedly deserved to be treated as an 'enemy of mankind' though he was not the 'common enemy of all'. In Vattel's view, establishing universal consent was less important than promptly responding to major threats to the 'common' security and well-being of nations, as defined by the 'most respectable' powers depending on the circumstances.[59]

Vattel's Conception of Individual Responsibility for International Crimes, and Its Limitations

In the critique of Frederick II's conduct of war there emerged two important aspects of Vattel's enemy of mankind doctrine: first, that enemies of mankind could be spotted not only in barbarian countries but also in Europe's royal courts; and second, that European sovereigns violating the law of nations must be punished based on the principle of individual responsibility, as opposed to collective responsibility applying to barbarian enemies of mankind.

For Vattel, European sovereigns could be deemed individually responsible for international misconduct because they alone determined their countries' foreign policy and decided on matters of war and peace. Conversely, lower state officials, the civilian population, and the military at large were mostly blameless, and they were certainly not liable for their

58 *DG*, III, 3, § 45.

59 Emer de Vattel, Letter to the Avoyer and Council of Bern in Béguelin, 'En souvenir de Vattel', 173.

country being engaged in a war of aggression. Vattel postulated that in eighteenth century Europe, civilians simply did not partake in hostilities, at least in land warfare, while all state officials and troops were supposed to obey superior orders.[60] Individual soldiers might disregard the usages of war and thus incur in penalties, but could not be blamed for taking part in an aggressive war and for the resulting damages.[61] Consequently, sovereigns alone were to blame for aggressive war and its ramifications, at least when they qualified as notorious warmongers and posed a serious threat to collective security. In an emotional paragraph, Vattel declared these sovereigns to be guilty before their enemies, their own subjects, and 'mankind as a whole'.[62]

Actually, Vattel's idea that sovereigns alone were liable for international crimes was of little practical consequence. On some occasions, he plainly contradicted this idea, most importantly when he justified the killing of war captives. He did so with reference to a famous episode in Swiss history, the *Escalade* of 1602, in which the Duke of Savoy Charles Emmanuel I unsuccessfully attempted to conquer Geneva through a surprise attack.[63] After the Swiss repulsed the Savoyard attackers, those Savoyards captured by the Swiss were executed the next day. Commenting on this event, Vattel claimed that because the Savoyards had assaulted Geneva by surprise, hence without previously declaring war, and without any pretext, the Genevans had been right in sentencing all Savoyard prisoners to death. Yet Vattel did not mention Charles Emmanuel I at all. Whereas Vattel argued the Savoyard troops were executed lawfully, he implied that those responsible for ordering the assault on Geneva did not deserve any form of punishment.

Vattel's apology for the execution of the Savoyard prisoners clearly opposed his assumption that because troops follow superior orders as a matter of principle, they could not be judged for participating in unjust wars.[64] In the case of the *Escalade*, the superior orders defence was indeed supposed to apply, as the Genevans did not blame the Savoyard prisoners for committing war crimes but only for carrying out an unjust assault, for which troops were clearly not liable under the law of nations. And even if the Savoyards had been charged with war crimes as well, this would have

---

60 *DG*, III, 11, § 187; III, 15, §§ 226 and 231.
61 Ibid III, 11, § 184.
62 Ibid.
63 Ibid III, 4, § 68.
64 Ibid III, 11, § 187.

not warranted any collective punishment. Indeed, Vattel maintained that when undisciplined troops violated the laws of war, they should be punished based on the principle of individual responsibility.[65] In Vattel's discussion of the *Escalade*, no mention was made of any violations of the civilised customs of warfare by troops, while the *actus reus* was merely represented by the lack of apparent motives for opening hostilities and by the omission of the declaration of war. As this constituted a kind of conduct for which the sovereign alone was responsible, Vattel's justification of the execution of Savoyard troops had no legal basis whatsoever.

As far as the 'punishment' of sovereigns was concerned, Vattel argued that it should only be aimed to extract from that sovereign 'sufficient security for the time to come'.[66] This could be done, and usually was done, within the framework of a normal peace treaty. Only if the defeated sovereign refused to comply with the coalition's reasonable requests would a 'complete and decisive victory' be required to tame him.[67] Even in the case of unconditional surrender, Vattel did not contemplate any right of the allies to annex or dismember the entire enemy state, change its government, or establish new laws. In particular, he did not justify the collective use of force to replace warmongers with peace-loving sovereigns or, as Kant would later propose, to compel the defeated nation to accept a new constitution 'unfavourable' to war.[68] Vattel did not allow this as he assumed that the nation alone, through Estates or other representatives, was entitled to choose or approve of its sovereign, and hence the coalition's states were not permitted to interfere.[69] And because the coalition's powers were not allowed to replace the enemy nation's sovereign or constitution with new ones that the coalition states might control or influence, it was not expedient for them to punish harshly a sovereign who would probably remain in power, and might attempt to retaliate against them. Vattel thus concluded that civilised warmongers deserved special treatment regardless of the heinousness of their conduct. This point was not about justice or dignity, but about the collective security of Europe.

Nonetheless, Vattel's stigmatisation of European warmongers as individuals guilty before 'mankind as a whole' remains relevant in one

---

65 This Vattel implied in *DG*, III, 8, § 145, where he discussed rape committed by troops.

66 Ibid IV, 2, § 6.

67 Ibid.

68 Immanuel Kant, *Rechtslehre* (first published 1797, Wilhelm Weischedel ed, *Kants Werke*, vol 8, Frankfurt am Main, Suhrkamp, 1977) § 60.

69 On this inalienable right of the nation see *DG* I, 3, §§ 28 ff.

important respect. By claiming that warmongers were guilty before mankind, Vattel depicted mankind itself as a rights-bearing entity in a way which was unprecedented in former literature, and which went beyond Wolff's abstract speculations on the 'world state'. For Vattel, the 'rights of mankind' – at least the rights to security and tranquillity – were enforceable rights. The responsibility of sovereigns before mankind had implications for collective security measures and the right of intervention. To be sure, by 'mankind' Vattel here simply meant the 'society of nations' rather than human kind as the totality of humans. That is why in more sober passages he spoke of the 'right of nations', not of 'mankind', against a common enemy.[70] Still, it is central that Vattel possessed a concrete notion of the international community and called on all states to contribute to its security and thus defend the rights of literally all nations.

Vattel came to this conclusion based on a domestic analogy, through which he assimilated the disturbance of international order with the disturbance of the state's internal order. Contemporary criminal law doctrine argued that crime represented a disruption of public order and tranquillity, and must be punished first because it directly harmed the victims, and second because it indirectly harmed all citizens more generally by creating a feeling of insecurity, scandal, and by inducing imitation.[71] In the international sphere, only the second motive was central for Vattel. He claimed that grave international offences ought to be punished collectively because, by affecting individual states, such offences actually disturbed the tranquillity of all states and might throw international society into turmoil. This was particularly true as nations already lived in a perpetual state of reciprocal fear and potential warfare. Absent a superior authority, Vattel claimed, all states should join forces to punish grave international offences and preserve the world public order.

Vattel stigmatised warmongers not because they acted 'unjustly', but because by abusing their right to make war they destabilised the world public order and possibly the public order in their own countries – just as, on a smaller scale, violent domestic offenders disturbed domestic tranquillity. Vattel thus agreed with the argument of utilitarian criminal law

70 Ibid II, 15, § 222; III, 3, § 49.

71 François Lorry, *Code pénal, ou recueil des principales ordonnances, édits et déclarations sur les crimes et délits* (2nd ed, Paris, Desaint et Saillant, 1755) 6; Pierre-François Muyart de Vouglans, *Institutes au droit criminel, ou principes généraux sur ces matières, suivant le droit civil, canonique, et la jurisprudence du Royaume* (Paris, Le Breton, 1757) I, § 3, p 19; Jean Antoine Soulatges, *Traité des crimes* (Toulouse, Antoine Birosse, 1762) tome premier, I, p 46.

theory, soon to be popularised by Beccaria, that retribution produces more harm than good and must be abandoned in favour of a security-oriented approach.[72] If for Beccaria retribution was embodied by the *Ancien Régime* criminal justice system, for Vattel it was embodied by the just war doctrine, especially in its radical version by writers such as Heinrich von Cocceji.

Vattel turned away from this doctrine towards a theory of international law enforcement grounded on the common utility of all states. As he did so, he took care not to displease those powerful princes who were fed up with just causes and rather enjoyed entertaining themselves with low-intensity conflict in Europe. To validate his own enemy of mankind doctrine, Vattel counted on their own particular interests and in the assumption that war, even if taken as a game, was no longer entertaining when some of the players did not play by the rules. When this occurred, all other players together should force these troublemakers to forfeit, and inflict on them appropriate penalties to dissuade them from breaking the rules again.

Warmongers and Collective Security according to Wolff and Vattel

Vattel did not criminalise aggression as such, but only the systematic recourse to aggression by notorious warmongers jeopardising the 'common security and well-being of nations'. This was especially clear, given that he followed Wolff in admitting that even those waging war on mere 'pretexts' should normally be regarded as lawful enemies as a result of the impunity accorded to them by the 'voluntary law of nations'.[73] In addition, Vattel argued, it would not be fair to declare princes waging war on pretexts to be outlaws, for by the very act of formulating pretexts, even if those pretexts were flawed, these princes at least manifested some formal reverence for the law of nations.[74] Hence, Vattel implied, Frederick II of Prussia could not be regarded as an international offender for attacking Silesia in the War of the Austrian Succession, because he took the trouble

[72] Cesare Beccaria, *Dei delitti e delle pene* (first published 1764, Franco Venturi ed, Turin, Einaudi, 1965) § 12.

[73] As to the differentiation between 'justificatory reasons' and 'pretexts' for war, see Christian Wolff, *Jus gentium methodo scientifica pertractatum* (first published 1749, Joseph H Drake trans, Oxford, Clarendon 1934) VI, § 624; *DG*, III, 3, § 32.

[74] *DG*, III, 3, § 33.

to make his pretexts public in a manifesto.[75] On the other hand, Vattel stressed that princes should not abuse the licence to make war on pretexts. If a prince did so, he gave 'all nations cause to hate and suspect him' and authorised them to join and fight him as an enemy of mankind.[76] This entailed that whilst Frederick might be excused for invading Silesia in the War of Austrian Succession, despite the groundlessness of his pretexts, he could not be pardoned for doing the same to Saxony in the Seven Years' War, as by the latter act he proved to be a habitual warmonger posing a threat to the security of all of his neighbours.

Vattel actually admitted that not all belligerents were concerned with their international reputation enough to articulate pretexts for war. Many waged war without any reason or pretext whatsoever. They might thus be characterised as 'monsters' and 'enemies of mankind', unworthy of human dignity and deserving of being exterminated like ferocious beasts. Vattel did not rule out that a few modern European sovereigns, not unlike the barbarian conquerors of old, might be defined in these terms. He suggested indeed that 'monsters of mankind' waging war for pleasure might still be found 'in polished ages and among the most civilised nations'.[77]

> Nations that ... seem to delight in the ravages of war, who spread it on all sides, without reasons or pretexts, and even without any other motive than their own ferocity, are monsters, unworthy the name of men. They should be considered as enemies to the human race, in the same manner as, in civil society, professed assassins and incendiaries are guilty, not only towards the particular victims of their nefarious deeds, but also towards the state, which therefore proclaims them public enemies. All nations have a right to join in a confederacy for the purpose of punishing and even exterminating those savage nations. Such were several German tribes mentioned by Tacitus—such those barbarians who destroyed the Roman empire: nor was it till long after their conversion to Christianity that this ferocity wore off. Such have been the Turks and other Tartars—Genghis Khan, Timur Bec or Tamerlane, who, like Attila, were scourges employed by the wrath of Heaven, and who made war only for the pleasure of making it. Such are, in polished ages and among the most civilized nations, those supposed heroes, whose supreme delight is a battle, and who make war from inclination purely, and not from love to their country.[78]

75 Ibid II, 18, § 335.
76 Ibid.
77 Ibid III, 3, § 34.
78 Ibid.

In this passage stigmatising past and present warmongers, Vattel appropriated Grotius' and Wolff's argument that a war of aggression carried out without the slightest pretext was literally inhuman.[79] This war that transgressed the 'law of humanity', as Wolff put it, was called a 'feral war' (*bellum ferinum*) as it was so ferocious and ruthless that it resembled more a fight between animals than a military confrontation.[80] In Wolff's opinion, those who waged war with such brutality could not be deemed human beings endowed with reason. Their behaviour was both unlawful and contrary to human nature.

The notion of 'feral warfare' went back to Aristotle. In his *Nicomachean Ethics*, Aristotle defined 'brutishness' as a rare feature of the human character that could be detected almost uniquely among 'barbarians' who had the tendency to make war like beasts.[81] It is important to note that modern commentators, beginning with Grotius, would not follow in Aristotle's steps to claim that feral belligerents could be spotted only among 'barbarians' and 'savages'. Grotius recalled that Seneca used the concept of 'brutishness' (*feritas*) even with reference to civilised yet tyrannical rulers, such as the tyrants Apollodorus of Agrigentum and Phalaris of Cassandra.[82] Nonetheless, Grotius assumed that in modern times, 'war for the war's sake' had become a matter of purely philological concern. It was a phenomenon typical of ancient times, when the *vetus ius gentium* was still in place on the whole earth and all nations made use of an unrestrained licence to use force. That is why he mentioned 'feral warfare' only briefly and then went on to discuss and criticise in more detail the conduct of those who waged war on the basis of at least some alleged pretext, such as Brennus, Hannibal and Attila.[83]

Wolff revisited the feral war concept when he discussed the topic of collective security in the world-state, the *civitas maxima*. In this context, the warmonger who waged war without any purported motive embodied a threat to international security that had to be met by all nations jointly. Wolff defined this type of warmonger as a 'monster of mankind' and

---

79 Hugo Grotius, *De iure belli ac pacis libri tres* (first published 1625, Francis W Kelsey trans, Washington, Carnegie Endowment, 1913) II, 22, § 2.

80 Wolff, *Jus gentium*, VI, §§ 626–627; Wolff, *Institutiones juris naturae et gentium* (first published 1750, Marcel Thomann ed, Hildesheim, Olms, 1969) IV, 7, § 1171. See also Johann Heinrich Samuel Formey, *Principes du droit de la nature et des gens. Extrait du grand ouvrage latin de M. de Wolff* (Amsterdam, 1758) IV, p 298.

81 Aristotle, *Nicomachean Ethics* (David Ross trans, OUP, 2009) VII, 1.

82 Seneca, *De ira* (Robert A Kaster trans, University of Chicago Press, 2010) II, 5.

83 Grotius, *De iure belli ac pacis*, II, 22, § 3.

claimed that the right to repress him rested with all nations in common.[84] In addition, Wolff morally disqualified the 'monster of mankind' as an abnormal individual gaining pleasure from violence and incapable of forming a correct idea of the good.[85] It is important to note, however, that Wolff argued that this individual should be punished only because he represented a threat to international tranquillity, and not as a result of his moral corruption. Wolff – followed in this by Vattel – saw punishment as a means to provide society, be it domestic or international, with security, not as a reaction to immoral behaviour.[86] Here, both Wolff and Vattel rejected Grotius' opinion that a breach of natural law was punishable as such, regardless of its consequences.[87] They defined punishment simply as an act of coercion for the sake of future security, and particularly aimed to amend the offender's behaviour (*poena emendatrix*) and deter others from offending (*poena exemplaris*).[88] Retributive justice was certainly contemplated by the contemporary criminal justice system,[89] but was clearly rejected by natural lawyers in the mid-eighteenth century such as Wolff, Vattel, and Rutherforth.[90]

Thus, Wolff pleaded for collective action against warmongers not because they acted immorally, but because by doing so they threatened the 'common security of nations' (*securitas communis Gentium*).[91] Significantly, this emphasis on security rather than retribution meant that warmongers ought not to be repressed harshly, or any more harshly than other 'enemies of mankind'. Wolff maintained that penalties, both domestic and international, should be exercised to preserve peace, and thus should vary in severity depending on the degree of the threat and the circumstances.[92] 'Enemies' and 'monsters of mankind' certainly deserved punishment,

---

84 Wolff, *Jus gentium*, VI, § 627.

85 Ibid VI, § 626; Christian Wolff, *Psychologia empirica* (first published 1732, Jean Ecole ed, Hildesheim, Olms, 1968) II, 1, 1, § 561.

86 Wolff, *Jus gentium*, VI, §§ 636 ff.

87 Grotius, *De iure belli ac pacis*, II, 20, § 40.

88 Wolff, *Institutiones juris naturae et gentium*, I, 3, § 93; *DG*, I, 13, § 169.

89 Pierre-François Muyart de Vouglans, *Institutes au droit criminel*, VIII, 2, p 390.

90 Thomas Rutherforth, *Institutes of Natural Law* (Cambridge, Bentham, 1754–56) vol 2, ch 18, § 3. For retribution as the aim of punishment in the criminal justice system, see Pierre-François Muyart de Vouglans, *Institutes au droit criminel*, VIII, 2, p 390.

91 Wolff, *Jus gentium*, VI, §§ 629, 652, 965 ff.

92 This is the reason why Wolff claimed that the extent of the right to punish both at national and international level could not be defined and thus remained virtually 'unlimited': Christian Wolff, *Jus naturae methodo scientifica pertractatum* (first published 1740–48, Marcel Thomann ed, Hildesheim, Olms, 1969) vol 8, VIII, 3, § 636; Wolff, *Jus gentium*, V, § 80; Wolff, *Institutiones juris naturae et gentium*, I, 3, § 94.

but they might even be pardoned if the majority of nations thought this to be expedient for the sake of international peace and security.

Far from dismissing 'war for war's sake' as a matter of purely philological concern, Vattel radicalised both the Grotian and Wolffian views on the topic. If Grotius had blamed Attila simply for waging war for ambition and other vicious motives, Vattel went further to claim that Attila fought for pleasure alone, driven by his degenerated nature. Attila thus belonged to the category of 'monsters of mankind' just as Apollodorus of Agrigentum and Phalaris of Cassandra. Vattel believed that these 'monsters' were more hateful than pirates, who at least acted for economic gain.[93] For him, the difference between those who waged war on some concrete motives and those who did it out of brutality did not seem to be trivial.

To be sure, Vattel was not concerned about real instances of 'feral war' in the 1750s. He rather recovered this topos for pedagogic purposes. In his day, the most dreadful threat to international security was no longer embodied by barbarian nations like the Huns, the Mongols, or the Crimean Tartars, and not even by maritime marauders like the Barbary corsairs, but rather by warlike European rulers pursuing personal glory. This is why Vattel claimed that the monster of mankind label could be applied not only to ancient barbarians but also to European sovereigns.[94] If they systematically abused the right to make war, they could thus be characterised as enemies of mankind, just as the barbarian conquerors of old.

The stigmatisation of warlike sovereigns in the *Droit des gens* can be associated with similar narratives which were much in vogue in the age of Louis XIV, when the latter was depicted as a warlike and fanatical despot by non-French writers as well as the French Huguenots whom he persecuted. Not unlike Vattel, these writers recurrently characterised the Sun King as a threat to the security and freedom of Europe as a whole. In the dedicatory epistle of the 1706 French translation of Pufendorf's *De jure naturae et gentium*, Huguenot writer Jean Barbeyrac praised the King of Prussia Frederick I, founder of the Royal Academy of Science at Berlin, for ruling with justice and wisdom, in contrast to those contemporary 'conquerors, or scourges of mankind, who take pleasure in ravaging the earth, and in spreading terror and fright everywhere'.[95] Vattel would likewise

---

93 *DG*, III, 4, § 67.

94 Ibid III, 3, § 34.

95 Samuel Pufendorf, *Le droit de la nature et des gens* (2 vols, Jean Barbeyrac ed, Amsterdam, 1706) I, Dedicatory Epistle.

depict Louis XIV as a threat to international security, although Vattel was cautious enough not explicitly to name the Sun King a 'scourge' or 'enemy of mankind'.

The Laws of War in the Droit des gens

In the chapter of the *Droit des gens* devoted to the 'law of nations during wartime', Vattel expounded a set of legal rules which were applicable to armed conflict regardless of the justice of the cause.[96] Such rules, customary in nature and commonly observed in contemporary European warfare, were rationalised and universalised by Vattel through the idea of the voluntary law of nations, the law based on reason and utility upon which all states, as moral and rational entities, supposedly agreed. In particular, Vattel claimed that under the voluntary law of nations belligerents were not permitted to kill or mistreat captives and surrendered enemy persons, or to harm those not actively participating in hostilities, like women, children, the elderly, the sick, clergymen, intellectuals, labourers, and peasants.[97] In addition, belligerents were not to poison enemy leaders, or treacherously assassinate them by inducing infiltrators or bribed hostiles to commit treason.[98] If most of these rules had been laid down in codes of chivalry and treatises on moral theology since the Middle Ages, Vattel was the first publicist to present them as legal and enforceable – not merely moral – obligations, binding on all belligerents irrespective of the just cause for war.[99]

Regarding material damages that might occur during fighting, Vattel was less strict. He assumed that a victim state in pursuit of security was entitled to demand from the aggressor war reparations and weaken him so as to prevent further attacks. Vattel thus had to justify all means necessary to this end, except those 'absolutely contrary' to the law of nature, such as poisoning and murdering. Vattel declared the destruction of churches, monuments, and tombs as acts worthy of an 'enemy of mankind', yet he

---

96 *DG*, III, 8. The title given by Vattel to this chapter, *Droit des Nations dans la guerre*, could also be translated as 'right of nations in wartime', yet because the rules that Vattel proposed there were both permissive and prohibitive, the broader translation 'law of nations in wartime' is more appropriate.

97 Ibid III, 8, §§ 140, 145, 146, 147, 149, 157.

98 Ibid III, 8, § 155.

99 See, for instance, Robert C Stacey, 'The Age of Chivalry' in Michael Howard (ed) *The Laws of War. Constraints on Warfare in the Western World* (Yale University Press, 1994) 27.

specified that they became licit in the context of sieges and other operations necessary to secure victory.[100] In addition to the allowances based on military necessity, Vattel also permitted belligerents to take booty, impose contributions on civilians, and destroy properties and commodities in order to obtain reparation, satisfaction, and 'to punish the enemy for some gross violation of the law of nations'.[101]

Conscious of the ramifications of these permissions, Vattel attempted, if not entirely convincingly, to give a narrow interpretation of military necessity and of the right to take extreme measures for the sake of punishment. In particular, he made it clear that punitive measures were rarely justified against the civilised. Here, he recalled that Louis XIV behaved unlawfully when he ordered the bombing of Genoa in 1684, which was unwarranted by the requirements of military necessity and constituted a targeting of the Genoese citizenry as a whole as if they were a pirate nation.[102] Moreover, Louis had been responsible for further episodes of brutal warfare unjustified by military necessity, most importantly the ravaging of the German region of the Palatinate in 1674 and 1689. Vattel expressed indignation at those episodes, which had outraged public opinion both in Germany and internationally. To clarify what should be truly understood under military necessity, he set the conduct of the French army in the Palatinate against an opposite example of harsh warfare entirely justified by strategic needs: Peter the Great's recourse to scorched earth tactics in the Great Northern War.[103]

> The tsar Peter the Great, in his flight before the formidable Charles the Twelfth, ravaged an extent of above fourscore leagues of his own empire, in order to check the impetuosity of a torrent which he was unable to withstand. ... A prince who should, without necessity, imitate the tsar's conduct, would be guilty of a crime against his people: and he who does the like in an enemy's country, when impelled to it by no necessity, or induced by feeble reasons, becomes the scourge of mankind. In the last century, the French ravaged and burnt the Palatinate. All Europe resounded with invectives against such a mode of waging war.[104]

For Vattel, Peter the Great's ravaging of Russian lands represented an extreme attempt to hold off the Swedes, while the devastations of the

100 *DG*, III, 9, § 168.
101 Ibid III, 8, §§ 164 and 166.
102 Ibid III, 9, § 167.
103 Ibid.
104 Ibid.

Palatinate by the French army amounted to indiscriminate atrocities not serving the aims of the war. Such acts might generate an absolute and enduring hostility incompatible with the civilised law of nations and the 'war in due form' paradigm. They brought about a situation of perpetual conflict, open or latent, preventing any lasting peace.[105] Here Vattel surely took care not to irritate the French court, which he hoped would be his employer one day, and therefore did not explicitly mention Louis XIV when critiquing the French conduct in the Palatinate. In the end, Vattel cautiously put all blame for that conduct on a 'haughty and unfeeling minister', the Marquis de Louvois, Louis' Secretary of War. By doing so, Vattel got away with his implication that Louis, as the sovereign and ultimate responsible for the conduct of the French army, qualified as an enemy of mankind.

Compliance with the Laws of War in the Eighteenth Century

In the first half of the eighteenth century, general compliance with the rules of warfare was enhanced by the spreading sense of international politesse and, most importantly, by their beneficial impact on the states' exchequer. By now it was necessary to wage war with moderation as increasing professionalisation and technological improvements had made standing armies a very expensive toy for sovereigns. As financial requirements were rapidly rising for territorial states that needed to improve their bureaucratic apparatus, princes could no longer afford to suffer enormous losses on the battlefield. Neither could they allow themselves to have their cities plundered and their lands ravaged by foreign invaders or local troops. This concern was common to all European monarchs in the first half of the eighteenth century and gradually determined a change in their attitude towards warfare, especially in relation to the protection of civilians. Vattel also noted that 'by protecting the unarmed inhabitants, keeping the soldiery under strict discipline, and preserving the country, a general procures an easy subsistence for his army, and avoids many evils and dangers.'[106]

---

[105] Kant would famously reassert this argument in *Zum ewigen Frieden* (first published 1795, Wilhelm Weischedel ed, Frankfurt am Main, Suhrkamp, 1977) Sixth Preliminary Article.

[106] *DG*, III, 8, § 147.

As Vattel wrote his *Droit des gens*, moderation at war was advised also because, due to the current homogeneous distribution of power in Europe and to the nature of eighteenth century warfare, sovereigns could rarely expect more from their military ventures than some minor territorial gains. Under these circumstances, the old just war rhetoric had become obsolete. Sovereigns renounced degrading their opponents as heretics or sinners and rather expressed, in ceremonials and diplomatic exchanges, their common belonging to the aristocratic elite of Europe.[107] As they freed themselves of the constraints represented by religious authorities and confessional politics, rulers found legitimacy and acknowledgement within the international society of aristocracy. As a result of the reciprocal acknowledgement of Europe's sovereigns as free and equal parties, the just war doctrine collapsed due to its emphasis on the just cause.

The view of eighteenth century warfare as humane and moderate rapidly became a historiographic myth, partly as a consequence of contemporary narratives by writers like Montesquieu, Voltaire, and Vattel praising European politesse during war.[108] This myth has recently been relativised by historians who have contended that eighteenth century battles actually remained bloody enough. Yet even these critics do not contest that the eighteenth century did see a considerable transformation both in the practice and theory of warfare, which often resulted, if not in diminished casualty rates, then at least in enhanced protection for civilians.[109] In this regard, it is significant that the trend towards restraining warfare occurred much more quickly in state practice than in legal doctrine. The most authoritative scholars in the first half of the eighteenth century, Bynkershoek and Wolff, did not account at all for the current transformations in the reality of warfare and still refused to put any clear limits on the means of injuring the enemy.[110] Yet in practice, some significant exception aside, unrestrained warfare disappeared from the battlefields of Europe at the end of the age of Louis XIV and was not to return until the Napoleonic Wars. Rather, the problem with eighteenth century humanised warfare

107 Matthew S Anderson, *War and Society in Europe of the Old Regime 1618–1789* (New York, St Martin's, 1988) 189.

108 Voltaire, *Le siècle de Louis XIV* (first published 1751, Jaqueline Hellegouarc'h ed, Paris, Librairie Générale Française, 2005) 128; Montesquieu, *De l'esprit des lois* (first published 1748, Victor Goldschmidt ed, Garnier-Flammarion, Paris 1979) X, 3; *DG*, III, 8, § 158.

109 Christopher Duffy, *The Military Experience in the Age of Reason* (London, Routledge, 1987) 32.

110 Cornelius van Bynkershoek, *Quaestionum juris publici libri duo* (first published 1737, Tenney Frank trans, Oxford, Clarendon, 1930) I, 1; Wolff, *Jus gentium*, VII, §§ 825, 846, 877, 882.

was that while it applied to Europe, it did not always apply to the colonies.[111]

The Status of the Laws of War in the Pre-Vattelian Doctrine

Vattel has been regarded by several commentators as one of the founders of international humanitarian law.[112] He certainly did not invent the term, and did not even employ the expression 'laws of war' with consistency. On some occasions he did use this expression in the modern sense, as a body of rules regulating and moderating warfare, but not consistently. Actually, in some passages of the *Droit des gens*, Vattel by the 'laws of war' (*lois de la guerre*) still meant the *ius belli* in its Roman acceptation, that is, the belligerent's right to take measures that despite their heinousness were legalised by the state of war, such as ravaging enemy territory and spreading terror among civilians. Here Vattel equated the 'laws of war' with the 'right of arms', which one later editor of the *Droit des gens* in a footnote straightforwardly defined as the 'right of the strongest'.[113] Vattel had no troubles preserving this notion of *ius belli* because his major preoccupation was not with the possibility that belligerents might resort to harsh means of warfare on the claim of military necessity – a possibility inherent in warfare – but rather with the likelihood that belligerents might mutually disqualify each other as unjust enemies under the just war doctrine. While military necessity could hardly be regulated, the attitude of belligerents towards each other could be, and should be.

It was with Vattel that the distinction between *ius ad bellum* and *ius in bello* turned into a contraposition: the former was obliterated, as the emphasis by now was on the modalities, as opposed to the causes, of warfare. To be sure, the distinction between *ius ad bellum* and *ius in bello* had already been sketched by earlier authors, first by Renaissance writers on military law, such as Pierino Belli. Belli distinguished quite neatly between the right to make war, along with the normative corpus concerning this right, from the right of belligerents in wartime.[114] This distinction was

---

111 Harold E Selesky, 'Colonial America' in Howard (ed), *The Laws of War*, 59.

112 Robert Kolb, 'La validité du modèle de Vattel après 1945' in Yves Sandoz (ed), *Réflexions sur l'impact, le rayonnement et l'actualité du 'Droit des gens' d'Emer de Vattel* (Brussels, Bruylant, 2010) 137, 159–163.

113 *DG* (Paul Pradier-Fodéré ed) III, 15, § 228, n a.

114 Diego Quaglioni, *La disciplina delle armi tra teologia e diritto. I trattatisti dello "ius militare"* in Claudio Donati and Bernhard R Kroener (eds), *Militari e società civile nell'Europa dell'età moderna* (Bologna, Il Mulino, 2007) 447, 448.

grounded on the formalist concept of public war as laid down in Justinian's *Digest*, according to which legitimate sovereigns might wage war at their own discretion independently of the justice of the cause (the ancient *ius fetiale* representing a literary relic by the time the *Digest* was drafted). In turn, the revival of this formalist idea of public war had become central in Belli's lifetime as modern state sovereignty emerged. At that stage, lesser political authorities had to forfeit the right to make war – most importantly the right of reprisal and right of resistance against the tyrant – with which they were vested under now-defunct feudal law.

Although in early modern times opinions were still divided as to the opportunity of preserving the requirement of the 'just cause', jurists in principle agreed that only public war waged on a sovereign's command could be defined as war proper. As a consequence, when the state was not at war under the sovereign's command, peace ought to reign, as was synthesised through the Ciceronian formula, appropriated by modern lawyers, that 'there is no medium between war and peace'.[115] Building on this very postulate, Alberico Gentili and Christian Wolff were those who most clearly set apart *ius ad bellum*, *ius in bello*, and *ius post bellum*. They did not explicitly employ such wording, but did work with the same concepts: Gentili divided his *De iure belli* into three books dealing with the causes, conduct, and conclusion of war respectively, and Wolff took a similar line by separating *Jus belli Gentium*, *Jus Gentium in bello*, and *Pax & pactio pacis*.[116] Vattel also followed suit when distinguishing the 'right to make war' (*droit de faire la guerre*) from the 'right of nations in wartime' (*droit des Nations dans la guerre*) and from nations' rights and duties regarding the 'restoration of peace' upon termination of the hostilities.[117]

Yet Gentili's and Wolff's *ius in bello* had nothing to do with Vattel's, and not even with international humanitarian law, for that matter. What immediately attracts attention in the international legal treatises by Gentili, Grotius, Pufendorf, Wolff, Bynkershoek, and most of their disciples, is the permissive character of the law of war, which mostly remained a 'right of war' in the ancient sense. For these authors, the mere presence of the state of war conferred on the warring parties a broad licence to

115 Cicero, *Philippicae* (David R Shackleton Bailey trans, Harvard University Press, 2009) VIII, 4.

116 Alberico Gentili, *De iure belli libri tres* (first published 1598, Coleman Phillipson ed, Oxford, Clarendon, 1933); Wolff, *Jus gentium*.

117 *DG*, III, 1; III, 8. In all these acceptations the word *ius* or *droit* referred to the normative corpus governing the conduct of the belligerents rather than to their subjective rights.

perform acts normally unlawful in peacetime, as long as these acts corresponded to what military necessity dictated. Vattel also reiterated this idea of the 'right of war', but put forward a narrower interpretation of military necessity and spelled out clearer restraints on the conduct of warfare.

Conversely, Gentili, Grotius, Pufendorf, and Wolff vouched for almost any means of injuring the enemy in a state of war.[118] Whether they worked with a formal concept of war based on the legal equality of belligerents (Gentili and Pufendorf), or maintained a substantial notion of 'just cause' (Grotius and Wolff), all of these writers put emphasis on what warring parties were allowed to do (almost anything) instead of what was forbidden (almost nothing). In the writings of Pufendorf and Wolff, prohibitive rules often suffered broad exceptions and even became irrelevant as a result of the just enemy's 'unlimited right' of injuring the enemy.[119]

The apparently progressive concept of a 'solemn war' introduced by Gentili and reasserted by Grotius changed nothing in this regard. While their idea that public enemies had equal rights and should not discriminate against each other became useful for later authors like Vattel for building up a system of the *ius in bello*, that idea meant something different to Gentili and Grotius. According to Grotius, the 'solemn war' was not at all a chivalrous confrontation as the name may suggest. It was simply described as a formally declared public war resulting in the impunity of all warring parties and the right to appropriate all goods seized on the battlefield. The focus was not on restraining hostilities during wartime, but on legitimating the conduct of all belligerents so as to prevent disputes over the booty as well as vengeful tendencies in the post-war period. The occurrence of a 'solemn war' thus conferred upon belligerents the right to do whatever it took to pursue safety and obtain redress. While in earlier

---

[118] Gentili, *De iure belli libri tres*, II, 6 (where poisoning is allowed in 'wars of extermination'), 18 (where torture is allowed as a means of punishment and to terrorise a nation); Grotius, *De iure belli ac pacis*, III, 4, 5, 6, 7 (on the rights of belligerents during a 'solemn war'); Samuel Pufendorf, *De jure naturae et gentium* (first published 1672, Charles H Oldfather and William A Oldfather trans, Oxford, Clarendon, 1934) VIII, 6, § 18; Wolff, *Jus gentium*, VII, §§ 825, 846, 877, 882. See also Richard Zouche, *Iuris et iudicii fecialis, sive Iuris inter gentes, et quaestionum de eodem explicatio* (first published 1650, Erskine Holland ed, Washington, Carnegie Institution, 1911) pt I, sections XI, XV, XVI; Johann Gottlieb Heinecke, *Elementa juris naturae et gentium* (Halle, 1738) II, § 201. The harsh conception of the laws of war and the idea of a *ius infinitum* was partly shared also by Jean-Jacques Burlamaqui, *Principes du droit politique* (Amsterdam, 1751) pt IV, ch 5, § 7.

[119] Samuel Pufendorf, *De jure naturae et gentium*, VIII, 6, § 18; Wolff, *Jus gentium*, VI, § 754.

natural law doctrine this right was granted to the 'just enemy' alone, Grotius pleaded for a 'bilateral' law of war according the right to all warring parties.[120]

Radical naturalists, such as Heinrich von Cocceji, certainly continued to link the right to take up arms to the substantial justice of the cause, whilst legalists à la Gentili derived this right from the fulfilment of formal criteria, namely, sovereignty and the declaration of war. Nevertheless, the consequences of both of these approaches for the *ius in bello* were the same: both the 'just enemy' of the naturalists and the 'regular enemy' of the legalists were permitted to resort to any means necessary to victory. The difference was that while the legalists directly assumed that the 'regular enemy' might carry on hostilities with absolute arbitrariness in the first place, the doctrinarians of the just war first insisted that armed response against the aggressor be immediate and proportionate.[121] Naturalists themselves eventually returned to the ancient idea of the 'right of war' as they vested the just enemy with an 'unlimited right' to injure the opponent.

The seemingly opposing narratives of 'just' and 'regular' warfare finally came to similar results. And this could not be otherwise, since 'regular war' and 'just war' were two sides of the same coin, the Roman idea of 'public war', and they preserved its ambivalences. In particular, regular war as was described both by Gentili and Grotius was a re-conceptualisation of the Roman 'public war' through the idea of a war which was 'just on both sides' (*bellum ex utraque parte iustum*).[122] To be sure, in contrast to Gentili, Grotius shrunk from embracing a straightforwardly formalist interpretation of the Roman 'public war'. He therefore attempted to overcome Gentili's realism and thereby reconcile the ideas of public war and just cause with each other.

In the chapters of *De iure belli ac pacis* following the discussion on the 'solemn war', especially, Grotius restated the medieval tradition in an attempt to counterbalance the realist and Roman law-based views of Ayala and Gentili respectively. In these chapters, Grotius discussed the *temperamenta belli* traditionally prescribed by theology and morals, and

120 For a detailed analysis of the bilateral conception of the law of war, see Peter Haggenmacher, *Grotius et la doctrine de la guerre juste* (Paris, PUF, 1983) 203–223.

121 Diego Quaglioni, *La disciplina delle armi tra teologia e diritto*, 449.

122 The idea of a war that is 'just on both sides' had been developed by medieval lawyers (see Haggenmacher, *Grotius et la doctrine de la guerre juste*, 203–223) and had recently been reasserted by Francisco de Vitoria, *Relectio de iure belli* (first published 1539, Anthony Pagden and Jeremy Lawrance eds, CUP, 1991) q 2, art 4.

he called on belligerents to battle with moderation and humanity. Although he believed that the formalist account of war, centred on impunity and the rights of the victor, was necessary to provide stability for the post-war scenario, he was aware that formalism made too many allowances to disputing parties.

However, Grotius was not willing to confer any strictly legal status upon the *temperamenta belli*. He maintained that belligerents in a 'solemn war' were allowed to resort to any means available to attain victory, except rape and, partly, poisoning and assassination. Indeed, Grotius pointed out that poisoning and assassination were not absolutely contrary to the law of nature as they had originally been banished by high-ranking state and military officials merely out of interest in protecting themselves from the evils of war.[123] As a result of his critique and relativisation of the traditional laws of war, Grotius can hardly be described as a 'humanitarian' author in the modern sense. Rather, his most remarkable contribution to the modern *ius in bello* lay in his restatement of the *temperamenta belli*, which he however believed to be binding in conscience only.

A similar evaluation can be given of Wolff's approach. In his 'voluntary law of nations', he mostly dealt with postliminy, truces, and the manner of acquiring ownership of the booty, but did not deal with humanitarian prescriptions.[124] He proved even less humanitarian in spirit than Grotius by failing to propose an antidote for his hazardous concept of the 'unlimited right of the offended against the offender'. Though Wolff deserved credit for his attempt to systematise international law and neatly distinguish *ius in bello* from *ius ad bellum*, some of the reflections he articulated in his *Jus gentium* sounded more noxious to international peace than even the most radical political realism. Although Wolff's book as a whole can be seen as a seminal doctrinal work, it was probably just as well that it received little attention from practitioners.

Novelty of Vattel's Approach to the Laws of War

Unlike his predecessors, Vattel put forward a more coherent normative system of the early modern law of war. Vattel's theory regulated the treatment of captives and prohibited, amongst others, poisoning, murdering, plundering, ravaging, and the killing of civilians not involved in military

123 Hugo Grotius, *De iure belli ac pacis*, III, 4, §§ 15–19.
124 Wolff, *Jus gentium*, §§ 887 ff.

operations.[125] Taken singly, most of these norms had been touched upon by legal doctrine for centuries and constituted no novelty, but in the *Droit des gens* they took on an unprecedented and cohesive role. In an attempt to make them concretely applicable, Vattel liberated them from the Grotian erudite adornments and the Wolffian deductive excesses. He prioritised examples from modern history over those from biblical and ancient narratives, and preferred to appeal to prudence rather than deductive reasoning. In doing so, he did not randomly collect the laws of war as they had been laid down by his predecessors in the hope that princes would comply, but instead restricted himself to retaining and rationalising only those norms that were in force when he wrote the *Droit des gens*. His aim was to lay out the natural legal foundations of the customs of war commonly followed by civilised nations in the mid-eighteenth century.

If eighteenth century customs of war were to preserve their validity, they had to be presented as resting on a minimum content of natural law that was necessary to govern international relations. Vattel thought it imperative to demonstrate how the rules of warfare as grounded on immutable reason must be obeyed even if state practice diverged and international hostility escalated, involving the society of nations at large. This move towards rationalising Europe's customs of war was supposed to amend the collusion of natural and customary norms which affected Grotius' system, in particular his problematic three-step construction of the law of war. Grotius in *De iure belli ac pacis* answered the question of what was licit during hostilities first by making recourse to strict natural law, which permitted nearly anything if the cause was just; second, he exposed what was rightful in a 'solemn war' (and even here he maintained that almost any means of warfare was licit); and finally, considering the brutality of 'solemn war', he resorted to morals and Christian charity to prohibit a number of misconducts, though only *in foro interno*.

Vattel disagreed with Grotius' premises and was critical of his reasoning. In particular, Vattel no longer accepted the Grotian assumption that warfare among individuals and warfare among states could be treated in the same manner. Vattel believed that if strict natural law, designed to regulate relationships among natural persons in the state of nature, was directly applied to states without any mediation, the ramifications could be ruinous. At the international level, the phenomenon of moralising conflict and criminalising the enemy would assume incontrollable

125 *DG*, III, 8–9.

proportions, generating perpetual hostility, and preventing long-lasting reconciliation.

Wolff moved away from this paradigm, but he did so in a way that Vattel did not accept. Wolff dropped the Grotian equation of states and human individuals only to lay down a more permissive natural law for states – which went exactly against Vattel's own project. Wolff merely resorted to the idea of a special international law applicable to states so as to free them from the prescriptions binding natural persons, as he believed that sovereigns needed to be given a free hand to do whatever national security required. He created a specific sphere of the law of nature for states to unleash their domestically-restrained hostility in the international arena. Ultimately, his natural law theory came dangerously close to that of Hobbes.[126] Vattel responded by emphasising the role of the laws of war instead.

Civilised Warfare and Its Enemies

Vattel commenced his project of a treatise on the law of nations in the late 1740s, towards the end of the War of the Austrian Succession.[127] He usually referred to this conflict when he wished to give evidence of the civilised customs of war in force in his day.[128] Still traditionally justified through dynastic claims, at least on paper, the War of the Austrian Succession represented for him the pattern for wars conducted within reasonable limits dictated by humanity, political wisdom, and great powers' general fear of substantive alterations of the balance of power. Given these premises, hostility in the War of the Austrian Succession was relatively restrained, and acts of chivalry were not uncommon. In the *Droit des gens*, credit was given to the Duke of Cumberland for his gentlemanliness at war, and to Louis XV for generously relinquishing all territories conquered by his army for the sake of a long-standing peace at Aix-la-Chapelle. In general, Vattel presented Britain and France as gentle powers deserving of the utmost credit for the progress of civilisation and the observance of the laws of war in the period between the Treaty of Utrecht and the beginning of the Seven Years' War.

---

126 Thomas Hobbes, *Leviathan* (first published 1651, Richard Tuck ed, CUP, 1991) I, 14.
127 Béguelin, 'En souvenir de Vattel', 123.
128 *DG* III, 8, §§ 151 and 158; III, 9, § 163.

> Let us, in this particular, bestow on the European nations the praise to which they are justly entitled. Prisoners of war are seldom ill-treated among them. We extol the English and French; we feel our bosoms glow with love for them, when we hear the accounts of the treatment which prisoners of war, on both sides, have experienced from those generous nations.[129]

The other side of the coin was that the War of the Austrian Succession in many respects revealed the very end of the golden age of polished warfare. Vattel seemed to have become fully aware of this at the time of the Seven Years' War, when he drafted his letter of protest against the Prussian invasion of Saxony, complaining not only about the King of Prussia's act of aggression, but also about his conduct of warfare.[130] Indeed, Frederick had already given evidence of his neglect for the law of nations at the end of the War of the Austrian Succession, upon signing the Peace of Aix-la-Chapelle, as he broke his promise to return all Saxon prisoners of war and enlisted them in his own army instead.[131] He resumed this practice in the Seven Years' War, as he forcefully recruited Saxon soldiers for his army after promising to free them under the Treaty of Dresden. During the same conflict, Frederick further trampled on the laws of war by imposing heavy contributions from the Saxon population and by resorting to ravaging and vandalising as a means of warfare.[132] In a case that drew attention from the international public opinion, Frederick had Elector Augustus' hunting lodge of Hubertusburg destroyed – an act which observers perceived as contrary to the customs of war of 'polished' nations.[133] Frederick also ordered the ravaging of the estates of Count Brühl, then Vattel's patron, 'with the explicit instruction that it was to be made to appear as if the king knew nothing of the deed.'[134] Witnessing these acts, even some of Frederick's allies admitted that his conduct did not conform with the canons of the civilised nations and, in the wording of British envoy Andrew Mitchell, attested to a 'meanness that I am really ashamed to narrate.'[135] To be sure, the anti-Prussian coalition was not without blame either,

129 Ibid III, 8, § 150.

130 Emer de Vattel, Letter to the Avoyer and Council of Bern in Béguelin, 'En souvenir de Vattel', 172–173.

131 Anderson, *The War of the Austrian Succession*, 105 and 153.

132 Duffy, *Frederick the Great*, 294.

133 Ibid 110.

134 Szabo, *The Seven Years War*, 39–40.

135 Andrew Mitchell, *Memoirs and Papers* (London, 1850) vol 1, 165, quoted in Szabo, *The Seven Years War*, 39–40.

especially as it had engaged light troops, such as Pandurs, Hussars, and Cossacks, in guerrilla warfare that sometimes resulted in atrocities.[136]

As Vattel laid down his doctrine of international law enforcement, he attempted to provide a doctrinal framework for dealing with all such breaches of the law of nations. The fact that in his day the laws of war, despite some significant exceptions, were usually observed to a higher extent than in former ages did not stop him from elaborating a theory justifying the repression of the lawbreakers. On the contrary, he felt that exactly because the laws of war had recently developed into one of the highest achievements of civilisation, their safeguard was all the more indispensable. As international law had revealed its civilised and humanitarian nature, international law enforcement now really made sense.

[136] Duffy, *Frederick the Great*, 294. The first theories of irregular warfare (*petite guerre*) appeared at this very time: Thomas-Auguste Le Roy de Grandmaison, *La petite guerre, ou traité du service des troupes légères en campagne* (Paris, 1756); Louis Michel de Jeney (Mihály Lajos Jeney) *Le partisan, ou l'art de faire la guerre avec succès selon le génie de nos jours* (The Hague, Constapel, 1759). On the deployment of light and irregular troops in the eighteenth century, see also Duffy, *The Military Experience*, 268.

CHAPTER FIVE

DISTURBERS OF THE BALANCE OF POWER

Chapter four has dealt with warmongers and violators of the laws of war as enemies of mankind jeopardising collective security and tranquillity. This chapter explores a further typology of enemy of mankind: the disturber of the balance of power. By 1758, the balance of power doctrine had already been subject to scholarly criticism, especially as a result of Frederick II of Prussia's dramatic entrance onto the international stage. At that point, it was no longer self-evident that international equilibrium would further collective security, or at least collective security as envisaged by Vattel, that is, a device which protected lesser states from ambitious great powers seeking territorial expansion. Nonetheless, Vattel maintained an optimistic conception of the balance of power doctrine.

Dismissive of international institutionalism as utopian and counterproductive, Vattel was confident that systems of alliances of the kind formerly used to oppose projects of universal monarchy, most importantly against Louis XIV, could still be effective to counter enemies of mankind in the mid-eighteenth century. In addition, Vattel attempted to rationalise the traditional balance of power theory by integrating it into the Wolffian paradigm of collective security. Despite these efforts, Vattel's conception of the balance of power remained problematic, as it vested the great powers with a virtually unrestrained licence to repress the disturber of the balance, or to turn the balance in their favour.

Law and Politics in Vattel's Conception of the Balance of Power

In the mid-eighteenth century, the principle of equilibrium was commonly perceived as one of the cornerstones of Western statecraft. It had become central in international affairs at least since the Thirty Years' War (1618–1648), and had been recognised as an axiom of foreign policy since the Treaty of Utrecht in 1713.[1] The recognition of this principle in modern

[1] *Treaty of Peace and Friendship between France and Great Britain, signed at Utrecht*, 11 April 1713, 27 CTS 477, 482, art 6. For a historical discussion of the balance of power

international politics was based on the idea that once confessional disputes had been put aside, the nations of Europe revealed themselves as parts of a homogeneous cultural and political system in which the tranquillity of one member depended on that of the others, and the tranquillity of the community as a whole depended on the preservation of international equilibrium. For Vattel and his contemporaries, Europe was no longer 'a confused heap of detached pieces', but 'a kind of republic', the members of which co-operated to maintain order and freedom.[2] This quasi-republic was governed by a balance of power according to which no state was allowed 'absolutely to predominate, and prescribe laws to the others', as Vattel put it.[3]

This reasoning belonged to the realm of political prudence, not law, and lent itself to various if not contradictory interpretations.[4] Equivocal and only vaguely prescriptive, the principle of equilibrium seemed unreliable as a tool for clearly determining the legal rights and duties of sovereigns at the international level; some writers advocated it to preserve the status quo, others championed the equilibrium to subvert the present state of affairs.[5] Vattel justified the principle of the balance as a device to preserve a minimum level of collective security and tranquillity. That is why he characterised the disturber of the balance as an enemy of mankind deserving of repression by all nations.[6]

This tendency to legalise or 'naturalise' the prudential principle of equilibrium can be explained by two main factors: first, the assumption that the balance of power represented the most convenient device to further all nations' security and freedom, to moderate hostility, and to hold in check those ambitious great powers which were interested in territorial expansion. Vattel defended the principle of equilibrium to delegitimate annexations and wars of conquest, especially when they affected lesser states like his home-country, Switzerland. Second, the principle of balance might claim some normative value from its basis in an analogy between politics and physics. For scholars used to adopting concepts and methods

doctrine, see Herbert Butterfield, 'The Balance of Power' in Herbert Butterfield and Martin Wight (eds), *Diplomatic Investigations: Essays in the Theory of International Politics* (London, Allen & Unwin, 1966) ch 6.

2 *DG*, III, 3, § 47.

3 Ibid.

4 Ibid III, 3, § 42.

5 Federico Chabod, 'Principio dell'equilibrio e aspirazioni alla pace in Europa fra Settecento e Ottocento' (first published 1939) in Federico Chabod, *Idea di Europa e politica dell'equilibrio* (Luisa Azzolini ed, Bologna, Il Mulino, 1995) 33, 44.

6 *DG*, III, 3, § 44.

of the natural sciences in order to increase the cogency of their theories, the doctrine of the balance of power was warranted by the assimilation of the states system with a system of physical bodies resting or moving in accordance with invariable laws. Once this analogy was granted, the conclusion was that if tranquillity, that is, the state of rest of the international system, was to be maintained, every major alteration of the balance of power had to be met by the exertion of an equal and opposite force, which might require all nations affected by the alteration to join forces against the disturber of the equilibrium. Vattel accordingly stipulated that the hegemonic ambitions of the most powerful on the continent, be it Austria or France, could only be countered and neutralised by a sum of opposing forces, led by Britain as the holder of the political balance.[7]

This said, there might be legitimate reasons for power growth.[8] Vattel stated that because war may only be waged to respond to or to prevent an actual injury, one nation's growth in power did not justify the recourse to force by other states unless that nation also manifested aggressive intentions.[9] This was especially true if the suspected state refused, upon its neighbours' official request, to give them sufficient guarantees that it would not attack them, in which case the neighbour acquired the legal right to launch a pre-emptive strike.[10] For in a natural condition in which no superior authority was there to grant the public peace, every nation had the right to resort to war as a means to provide for its own security once peaceful means were exhausted. Further, pre-emptive use of force against a suspected aggressor was authorised where neighbouring states had sought a guarantee of non-aggression, had not received a reply from the suspected aggressor, and strategic considerations compelled them to avert an invasion at any cost.

This right to pre-emptive war did not appear problematic to Vattel if the suspected offender was a recidivist. In reference to Louis XIV's notorious bellicism, for instance, Vattel claimed that the 'presumption [of guilt] becomes nearly equivalent to certainty, if the prince who is on the point of rising to an enormous power has already given proofs of imperious pride and insatiable ambition.'[11] Thus, notorious international offenders should

---

7 Ibid III, 3, § 48.
8 Ibid III, 3, § 42.
9 Ibid III, 3, § 43.
10 Ibid III, 3, § 44.
11 Ibid.

be presumed guilty, their past offences amounting to evidence of bad faith in the assessment of any future behaviour.

Pre-emptive collective actions might be lawful against first offenders too. This certainly would occur if a growing power denied its neighbours adequate guarantees upon their demand. The convenience of collective military action would still be assessed according to the principles of prudence and sound politics, but the natural right to security constituted a sufficient legal basis for neighbouring states to form a coalition and repress the disturber of the balance of power. It was by putting forward a legal doctrine of domestic and international security that Vattel transferred the principle of the equilibrium from the plane of politics to that of international law proper. The right to security implied the right to repress and, if necessary, punish aggressive growing powers.

Leibniz's Attack on Louis XIV as the Disturber of the European Equilibrium

German polymath Gottfried Wilhelm Leibniz, whose natural law theory had a major impact on those of Wolff and Vattel, was among the first writers to endorse the principle of international equilibrium as inspired by the analogy between the states system and the physical world. Leibniz's favourite target was Louis XIV, judged to be as much of a warlike despot as his ally Mehmed IV, the Ottoman Sultan.[12] Leibniz labelled the King of France as a *Mars Christianissimus*, a bellicose tyrant who wielded Catholic religion as a tool of oppression and waged war merely for glory, without any regard for the most elementary principles of the law of nations.[13] In this connection, Leibniz particularly denounced the atrocities committed by French troops in the Palatinate. He accused them of making war like barbarians and appealed to all European states to fight back whatever the cost.[14]

An experienced diplomat, Leibniz had no difficulties claiming that the only means to respond effectively to the threat represented by imperialist despots was the balance of power, as opposed to both the just war

---

[12] Gottfried Wilhelm Leibniz, *Mars Christianissimus* (Cologne, 1684) 80; Gottfried Wilhelm Leibniz, *Essais de théodicée* (first published 1710, Jacques Brunschwig ed, Paris, Garnier-Flammarion, 1969) § 166.

[13] Leibniz, *Mars Christianissimus*, 9, 32, 33, 63, 64.

[14] André Robinet, *G.W. Leibniz. Le meilleur des mondes par la balance de l'Europe* (Paris, PUF, 1994) 238–240.

doctrine and the utopian peace projects.[15] Notably, he dismissed Saint Pierre's project of a perpetual peace on the ground of its being too idealistic or, in the worst of hypotheses, conducive to universal tyranny.[16] Vattel was to reaffirm these Leibnizian theses to criticise the idea of the world state as possessing the potential to lead to world-wide despotism – an argument later picked up by Kant too.[17] Leibniz also asserted, followed in this again by Vattel, that the balance of power had to be secured by diplomacy and a system of defensive alliances to be activated as soon as growing powers manifested aggressive intentions.[18] In an age in which the perspective of substantial territorial gains was often curtailed by military equilibrium, Leibniz believed the art of diplomacy to be central in predisposing the warring parties to seek mediation and accept compromises, instead of fighting to the bitter end. For this to occur, traditional diplomatic relations had to be re-thought. Whilst Louis XIV had developed diplomacy as an instrument to increase France's political influence in the international arena, it was now time to make diplomacy work for peace.

The conceptions of world order of both Leibniz and Vattel, especially their reliance on the balance of power and their rejection of utopian cosmopolitanism, were grounded not only on political realism, but also on metaphysics. Vattel elaborated such metaphysical reflections in the *Défense du système Leibnitien*, an early work that he published in 1741 to make a name for himself in the academic scene.[19] In this apologetic book, written in support of Leibniz's *Theodicy* against the critiques of Swiss Calvinist theologian Jean-Pierre de Crousaz, Vattel reasserted the Leibnizian idea that the world was governed by a universal harmony pre-established by God, in which evil existed only as a condition for the greater

---

[15] Ibid 79. For his own part, Leibniz lay himself open to the charge of idealism because he believed in the possibility of an ecumenical and political alliance among all Christian peoples, as well as between Europe and China.

[16] Ibid 198.

[17] *DG* (Paul Pradier-Fodéré ed) Préface, 59; Immanuel Kant, *Zum ewigen Frieden* (first published 1795, Wilhelm Weischedel ed, Frankfurt am Main, Suhrkamp, 1977) Zusatz, Von der Garantie des ewigen Friedens.

[18] Robinet, *G.W. Leibniz*, 79.

[19] Emer de Vattel, *Défense du système Leibnitien contre les objections et les imputations de M. de Crousaz* (Leiden, Jean Luzac, 1741). On the circumstances under which the book was published, see Edouard Béguelin, 'En souvenir de Vattel' in *Recueil de travaux offert par la Faculté de Droit de l'Université de Neuchâtel à la Société Suisse des Juristes* (Neuchâtel, Attinger, 1929) 35–176, 44. By publishing the *Défense*, Vattel also aimed to convince his sovereign, Frederick II of Prussia, of the opportunity to ground a scientific academy in Neuchâtel, in which Vattel would then obtain a professorship. This attempt, however, was unsuccessful.

good.[20] If closely examined, Vattel argued, all evil, war, and disorder brought upon mankind represented a challenge for humans to achieve higher degrees of moral and intellectual perfection.[21]

Vattel did not discuss international politics in his *Défense*. Yet it is plausible that for him, as had already been apparent in Leibniz's case, the balance of power in international relations was ontologically justified because it contributed to maintain or re-establish international order, in accordance with the principle of universal harmony. Indeed, for Vattel and other natural lawyers, the doctrine of the balance was one of those theories the appeal of which very much stemmed from its ostensible correspondence with an a priori idea of harmony and world order. The cosmic order maintained by the natural laws of morals and physics had to be reflected by some form of order in international relations. That eighteenth century writers like Vattel insisted on defending the balance of power despite its hegemonic ramifications was partly due to an unfaltering belief in the inherently rational character of the idea of equilibrium, which reflected the order of the universe, be it created by the Christian God or by a clockmaker.

The Critique of the Balance of Power Theory in Wolff's Jus gentium

By the late 1740s, when Prussia was emerging as a great power and bringing about a major change in Europe's balance of power, the most authoritative follower of Leibniz, Christian Wolff, was finalising his masterpiece on international law, the *Jus gentium methodo scientifica pertractatum*.[22] In this treatise, Wolff aimed to establish an innovative and entirely rational system of the law of nations, independent from international politics, history, and the opinion of ancient and modern authorities. Wolff certainly shared most of the theses previously put forward by his predecessors, especially Grotius and Pufendorf, but disagreed with their methods on the basis that they lacked scientificity.[23] In the eyes of his famed disciple, Vattel, Wolff succeeded in his attempt to rationalise international law, establish its distinctive categories, and distinguish it from natural

20 Vattel, *Défense*, 54.

21 Ibid 53.

22 Christian Wolff, *Jus gentium methodo scientifica pertractatum* (first published 1749, Joseph H Drake trans, Oxford, Clarendon 1934).

23 Marcel Thomann, 'Introduction' in Christian Wolff, *Jus gentium methodo scientifica pertractatum* (first published 1749, Marcel Thomann ed, Hildesheim, Olms, 1972) XXVII.

law proper.[24] The latter project had lately been attempted by other jurists, but Vattel had no doubt that the first systematic treatment of the modern law of nations had to be credited to Wolff.[25] He had moved away from the classical idea of the *ius gentium* to inaugurate the conception of international law as a body of norms specifically regulating the conduct of sovereign states.[26]

The balance of power was one of those subjects in which Wolff struggled to provide purely rational and legal answers for an essentially political issue which happened to be very topical in his day. Due to his personal circumstances, he was surely the last person who would have accused Prussia of currently causing an alteration in the balance of power. Prussia's sovereign, Frederick II, had indeed been responsible for re-appointing Wolff to a professorship at the University of Halle, and later even made him a privy councillor, after Wolff had been driven out by Frederick William I over charges of impiety.[27] The rehabilitation of Wolff had been praised all over Europe, and had contributed to the image of Frederick II as a reformer and enlightened sovereign, tolerant in religious matters. To thank Frederick, Wolff dedicated to him the bulky *Jus naturae* that appeared in eight volumes during the 1740s.[28] In these dedications Wolff expressed his sincere admiration for the wise domestic policies of his benefactor. Only a few statements imperceptibly hinted at some disappointment about Frederick's militarism. Wolff limited himself to suggesting that after so many victories (in the recent War of the Austrian Succession) nothing could have increased Frederick's reputation more than restoring the primacy of domestic policy.[29] This might imply that the

---

24 *DG* (Paul Pradier-Fodéré ed) Préface, 53–54.

25 In those years, a rational distinction between the law of nations and natural law was attempted, for instance, by François Richer D'Aube, *Essai sur les principes du droit et de la morale* (Paris, Brunet, 1743) Préface, VIII.

26 Peter Haggenmacher, *Grotius et la doctrine de la guerre juste* (Paris, PUF, 1983) 609; Peter Haggenmacher, 'L'état souverain comme sujet du droit international, de Vitoria à Vattel' (1992) 16 *Droits. Revue française de théorie juridique* 11.

27 Wilhelm Schrader, 'Christian Wolff' in *Allgemeine Deutsche Biographie* (Bayerische Akademie der Wissenschaften ed, Leipzig, Duncker & Humblot, 1898) vol 44, 12. Talks about calling Wolff back to Halle had already begun in the last years of Frederick William I's reign, as it became patent that the ousting of Wolff had adversely affected the reputation of the university and also of the Prussian monarchy (ibid).

28 Christian Wolff, *Jus naturae methodo scientifica pertractatum* (8 vols, first published 1740–48, Marcel Thomann ed, Hildesheim, Olms, 1969). Wolff also dedicated his *Institutiones juris naturae et gentium* of 1750 to Frederick II's brother, prince August William of Prussia.

29 Wolff, *Jus naturae*, vol 8, Dedicatio.

Prussian King should now focus on fulfilling his duties towards his citizens rather than going after glory on Europe's battlefields.

Under no circumstances would Wolff have stigmatised Prussia's foreign policy as disruptive of the balance of power in those years. Even placing Wolff's personal situation to one side, he was openly sceptical of the balance of power doctrine, and was one of its strongest critics. Wolff admitted that a proportionate distribution of power in the international arena might be useful, but this was a consideration based on political convenience, not law.[30] He actually remarked that those who would shout at balance-threatening unifications or aggrandizements of kingdoms were not likely to be true victims, but rather potential invaders.[31] Moreover, Wolff was adamant that the argument for the preservation of international equilibrium should never be used to threaten individual nations or prevent them from extending their own territory by legitimate means, notably by the right of succession.[32] Based on Wolff's premises, even the Grand Alliance formed to disrupt the Bourbon plans for a universal monarchy in the War of the Spanish Succession could be questioned.

Having dismissed the balance of power as a political instrument, Wolff shifted attention to a further situation which might elicit collective intervention: the abuse of the *ius ad bellum* by 'disturbers of the peace' (*perturbatores pacis*).[33] Here Wolff seemed to leave aside the issue of international equilibrium to instead rely exclusively on collective security as a means to rescue states aggressed by warmongers. Indeed, in his theory of the enforcement of international law based on the analogy between the domestic commonwealth and the *civitas maxima*, the principle of equilibrium was out of place. In the domestic sphere, the balance of power represented a device to preserve a fair and well-functioning administration, but did not find any application in matters of security properly so-called. Because security within the domestic commonwealth was simply about repressing crime (at least according to the contemporary understanding), Wolff attempted to apply the same to the world-state as well.

Wolff's reasoning was premised on the classical idea that humans were sociable creatures in need of the help of their fellow human beings, and that nature itself had established a global society for them to each benefit

30 Wolff, *Jus gentium*, VI, § 646.
31 Ibid § 649.
32 This Wolff called the *obligatio ad studium potentiae*: ibid I, § 70. See also ibid VI, § 648.
33 Ibid VI, § 652; VII, § 965.

from mutual assistance.[34] This might not be a novel idea, and yet Wolff was alone in drawing out all the consequences of a the universal society concept and coming up with the notion of the *civitas maxima* as a state-like commonwealth of mankind. Earlier scholarship either advanced only an unrealistic idea of this universal society or straightforwardly rejected it. Vitoria and Suárez belonged to the first strand: they hypothesised a world commonwealth through an analogy with the universal Church.[35] On the opposite strand were those inspired by Hobbes who simply denied that even a universal society of mankind (let alone a universal state) had ever existed. In any case, most early-modern writers claimed that regardless of the original state of mankind, once ownership had been introduced and humanity had been divided into independent polities, universal solidarity had been significantly restrained in favour of national interests. Governments had then replaced the benevolence towards the neighbour originally commanded by the necessary law of nature with the less general but stronger bonds of civil society.

While Wolff might agree on the details of this historical evolution, he did not see how it could possibly limit the ambitions of reason, which allegedly directed humans towards perfecting themselves and striving for more suitable and civilised forms of political organisation, also at the global level. Pushing deductive reasoning to extremes, Wolff took the world state—ideal, yet thinkable in analogy with the domestic commonwealth—as a meta-reality to grant the coherence of his system of the law of nations and the logical possibility of international legal norms. If the law of nations, defined in modern terms as the law regulating international relations, was to be regarded as law proper, a world state had to be imagined as enacting that law. To be sure, the construction of a state-like society of mankind was rejected by many, Vattel included, due to its speculative character.[36] The untimely meditations on the *civitas maxima* caused Wolff to be mocked by commentators until cosmopolitanism was revived in the early twentieth century.

Nevertheless, the Wolffian world-state theory deserves a closer examination, as it had significant ramifications in terms of collective security and the repression of international offences. Wolff began the discussion of

---

[34] Ibid Prolegomena, §§ 7–8.

[35] Francisco de Vitoria, *De potestate civili* (first delivered 1528, Anthony Pagden and Jeremy Lawrance eds, CUP, 1991) q 3, a 4; Francisco Suárez, *De legibus ac Deo legislatore* (first published 1612, Gwladys L Williams trans, Oxford, Clarendon, 1944) bk II, ch 17.

[36] *DG* (Paul Pradier-Fodéré ed) Préface, 58.

his utopian *civitas maxima* by claiming that norms ought not to be derived from facts.[37] He criticised previous natural lawyers on the basis that they did not provide a firm foundation for international law and had allowed normative principles to collide. In particular, he was unsatisfied with Grotius' emphasis on customs and opinions and with Pufendorf's reduction of the law of nations to strict natural law following the Hobbesian model. For Wolff, both of these approaches allowed for the arbitrary interpretation of normative sources: the humanist Grotian model lacked conceptual clarity and lent itself to endless discussions about opinions and examples, often ending in unresolved contradictions, while the Pufendorfian theory traced back international law to principles produced by natural law that were too strict to be applied in the international sphere.

In response to Grotius and Pufendorf, Wolff contended that for there to be international law proper it must be conceived of as analogous to positive, domestic law. He said that although humankind was divided into free and equal self-governing polities, it could still be ideally regarded as a larger political, supranational entity. Mankind could be characterised as the sum of all human beings politically organised into national commonwealths that were in turn unified in the *civitas maxima*. Positivists and political realists might well argue that the world-state was a pure fiction, but Wolff replied that they likewise resorted to a fiction – the nation-state – the immovable mover of modern law and politics.[38] And indeed he did not criticise them for relying on it. Quite the contrary, he intended to convince his readers that to some extent it was possible to apply the inherently fictional concept of state to the realm of world affairs too. He believed that, just in mathematics, the philosophy of international law (no less than political philosophy) must rely on some axiom where to start, if any compelling conclusions are to be formulated. For the theory of the state and international law alike, this axiom was constituted by the notion of state.

Wolff claimed that his own use of axioms was legitimate, provided that he was able to draw from them the key elements for the demonstration of other propositions 'which must be admitted without hesitation.'[39] These propositions – derived by deductive reasoning and based on the axiomatic existence of the *civitas maxima* – were the norms that made up international law. His claim was that if international legal norms existed, which,

---

37 Wolff, *Jus gentium*, Prolegomena, § 13.
38 Ibid Prolegomena, § 21.
39 Ibid.

Wolff said, was confirmed by experience, their condition of possibility had to exist too. Further, since in his opinion the condition of the possibility of a body of laws was constituted by a political authority legitimated by public consent, a universal international law was not possible unless a democratic world polity could be conceived as enacting it. The universal society was supposed to share common goals as well as laws agreed upon by all nations and approved by a fictitious ruler. These enactments, imaginary yet rational, made up the 'voluntary law of nations'.[40]

Wolff's Doctrine of Just War and Collective Security

The main reason motivating nations to join a universal commonwealth was collective security. Under 'common security of nations' (*securitas communis Gentium*), Wolff meant a system by which all nations within the universal commonwealth protected each other both from bellicose states inside the commonwealth and from the few rogue states that refused to enter the *civitas maxima* and comply with its norms.[41] Such aggressive and rebellious states should be repressed as soon as they resorted to force unlawfully or made manifest preparations for an attack. This fulfilled the traditional just war requirement that war might rightfully be waged only when a wrong has been suffered or is likely to be inflicted.[42] By this doctrine of collective security, Wolff attempted to reconcile the Hobbesian security paradigm – here applied to the international sphere – with the just war doctrine.

Wolff additionally posited that a counter-attack against the lawbreaker might be launched when necessary 'for the purpose of preserving the equilibrium.'[43] Yet he was not referring to the political balance of power, which he strongly criticised because it might hinder legitimate territorial aggrandizements and also justify illicit expansionism as long as the latter did not significantly alter the force ratio between the big powers. By 'equilibrium' Wolff simply meant military equilibrium, that is, the maintenance of a given force ratio between the aggressor and the allies acting in

---

40 Ibid Prolegomena, § 12.

41 Ibid Prolegomena, §§ 9–13. Wolff's conception of collective security was developed by twentieth century writers, especially by Hans Kelsen, who was very much familiar with Wolff's work: Hans Kelsen, *Collective Security under International Law* (Washington, United States Government Printing Office, 1957) 3.

42 Wolff, *Jus gentium*, VI, § 617.

43 Ibid VI, § 651.

response, so that 'an equal force can be opposed to an unjust force.'[44] Wolff's contention in that passage was that military assistance to victims of an act of aggression was licit only in the event that they were not in a condition to repel the attack on their own.

While maintaining a certain military equilibrium constituted a legitimate aim of those engaged in a 'just war', no state had the right to open hostilities for the sake of preserving the political balance of power in the first place. There was a right and duty on all nations to defend the common security, and this might involve promoting international equilibrium, especially by means of alliances, as long as this could be done without infringing upon the right of others. Yet no military action was justified unless the suspected aggressor committed an actual wrong or was likely to commit it.[45] If he did, he declared himself an enemy of all nations (*hostis gentium omnium*), and solely for this reason they had 'the right to repel unjust force by force, so that the common security may be defended and preserved.'[46]

In terms of strict law, the right to punish pertained to all nations as a whole and could be exercised by any of them if they so wished. On the other hand, it was not feasible for literally every nation to take up arms. Nor was it convenient, since war ought not to escalate and end by producing more harm that it was meant to prevent. Wolff thus specified that only proportionate regional-scale responses were recommended against the unlawful aggressor, and he therefore suggested that they be performed by those who had 'the most interest' in diminishing the power of the disturber of public security.[47] Apparently, he was not willing to push his conception of world-state-sponsored punitive war to extremes. Fearing the ramifications of theorising a universal right to punish, he turned his potentially revolutionary theory of the common security of nations into a justification of regional collective defence.

Vattel on the Balance of Power and Collective Security

Vattel disagreed with the Wolffian dismissal of the balance of power theory. For Vattel, the doctrine of international equilibrium was a necessary complement to international law, since justice and political prudence

44 Ibid VI, § 646.
45 Ibid VI, §§ 650–651.
46 Ibid VI, § 652.
47 Ibid.

went hand in hand. Therefore, after zealously repeating Wolff's opinion that a state's territorial aggrandizement must be tolerated if lawful, Vattel reminded his readers that history contained far too many instances of sovereigns hiding their imperialist goals behind unfounded claims to succession or election. What would have been the destiny of Europe's freedom, he asked, had not Henry II of France and the German Protestant princes joined forces to oppose Charles V in the 1550s?[48] Based on this and other historical examples, Vattel contended that no state had ever significantly increased its power without also furnishing the grounds for legitimate grievance to its neighbours. Hence, he suggested, '[l]et the other nations be watchful and alert in repressing that growing power, and they will have nothing to fear.'[49] Here, he justified pre-emptive warfare against potential disturbers of the international equilibrium, and presented the balance of power as the most appropriate and rational device to preserve international tranquillity.

Most legal and political writers in the mid-eighteenth century shared Vattel's trust in the balance of power. German scholar Ludwig Martin Kahle, for instance, had recently pleaded for the balance in Europe in his work, *De trutina Europae*, which had appeared in Latin in 1744 and had been translated into French by Vattel's closest friend and philosophical interlocutor, Samuel Formey.[50] In summing up Kahle's opinion, Formey stated that the balance of power was the 'fundamental principle of public affairs in Europe.'[51] Vattel would not go that far, but shared the bulk of Kahle's and Formey's theses on the balance as one of the most convenient instruments to ensure international tranquillity.[52] A further optimistic account of international equilibrium published in those years and probably known to Vattel was provided by David Hume in his essay *Of The Balance of Power*.[53] This piece, along with other political essays by Hume, had been published in two French editions, and had been reviewed, again by Formey, in the *Nouvelle Bibliothèque Germanique* in 1754.[54] Asserting

48 *DG*, III, 3, § 42.
49 Ibid.
50 Ludwig Martin Kahle, *La balance de l'Europe considérée comme la règle de la guerre et de la paix* (Samuel Formey trans, Berlin – Göttingen, 1744 [trans of *De Trutina Europae. Tam quam praecipua pacis bellisque norma* (Göttingen, 1744)].
51 Ibid A3.
52 *DG*, III, 3, § 47.
53 David Hume, 'Of the Balance of Power' (Edinburgh, 1752) in David Hume, *Essays Moral, Political, and Literary* (Thomas H Green and Thomas H Grose eds, Aalen, Scientia, 1964) 348–56.
54 Michel Malherbe, 'Introduction' in David Hume, *Essais et traités sur plusieurs sujets* (Michel Malherbe ed, Paris, Vrin, 2009) vol 2, 11.

his position less diplomatically than Vattel would, Hume had claimed that the doctrine of equilibrium, founded on 'common sense and obvious reasoning,' had allowed Europe to repress the 'violent and haughty race' of the House of Austria as well as another formidable enemy, equally animated by a 'spirit of bigotry and persecution', Louis XIV.[55] Examining these successful struggles of the past, Hume favourably looked on Britain as the nation holding the balance of power and having a special responsibility for the preservation of peace in Europe. Indeed, because Britain's international position had strengthened in the last decades, he was even more optimistic about the functioning of the balance than some of his countrymen were around 1700, when they counted more on the mutual hostility between Austria and France than on the unified front of the Grand Alliance led by Britain.[56]

Vattel would subscribe to Hume's defence of the balance of power based on successful historical precedents, yet would disagree with Hume's theoretical premises. While Hume combined his advocacy for international equilibrium with a marked scepticism about the normative force of the 'law of nature and nations', Vattel believed that the balance of power was not an alternative to natural and international law, but rather their necessary complement.[57] He postulated that international equilibrium alone did not suffice to grant collective security if the basic principles of the law of nations were not respected in the same breath.

Vattel asserted his doctrine to be realist, and it certainly was. Yet it was normatively unsatisfactory as well, especially considering that there was no clear rule to decide whether a sovereign ought to be regarded as a disturber of international peace.[58] By and large, Vattel justified the formation of an international coalition waging pre-emptive war in cases where a sovereign notoriously accustomed to trampling on the law of nations was making preparations for an act of aggression, especially by raising troops and gathering them at the borders. The only fundamental criterion that should be observed prior to launching a pre-emptive strike was that the suspected aggressor's intent to harm be 'manifest'. This might sound vague, but given the lack of a superior authority legitimated to establish the

---

[55] Hume, 'Of the Balance of Power', 353.

[56] See, for instance, Anon, *The Balance of Power: or, A Comparison of the Strength of the Emperor and the French King* (London, 1709) 8–9.

[57] On Hume's position, see Martti Koskenniemi, 'The Advantage of Treaties. International Law in the Enlightenment' (2009) 13 (1) *Edinburgh Law Review* 27, 29.

[58] On the normative vagueness of the balance of power doctrine, see Heinz Duchhardt, 'The Missing Balance' (2000) 2 *Journal of the History of International Law* 67.

validity of evidence in the international sphere, it is not surprising that Vattel resorted to traditional legal concepts, such as *notorius* and *manifestus*, simply to point out that aggression must be undisputable in the eyes of all, or at least the majority of nations, before a penalty is meted out against the aggressor. Vattel pursued a similar argument when he addressed the topic of tyranny and reasserted Bartolus' thesis that the right of resistance only arises when tyranny is 'manifest'.[59]

Still, the use of the term 'manifest' seemed less problematic in the case of tyranny than in the case of repression as a penalty for international crimes. Indeed, Vattel specified that resistance against the tyrant could and should be legitimated by a formal deposition of the prince by parliaments and tribunals acting as organs representing the people and giving lawful expression to their general will. Yet at the international level, the neighbouring countries willing to act against the 'manifest' aggressor were likely to do so for their own national interest only, not for the public good, and to be concerned less about consent than about forming a strong military alliance. If the lawful deposition of a manifest tyrant by parliament expressed the consent and unity of a domestic community, the repression of a manifest aggressor by a coalition of the willing at most expressed the mood of the multitude in the international arena.

To clarify his concept of the 'manifest' disturber of international equilibrium, Vattel, like Hume, examined various historical examples. Vattel first made reference to the War of the Spanish Succession 1701–14, caused by French and Austrian ambitions over the Spanish Empire at the death of Charles II of Spain. On that occasion, conflict arose because both Philip of Anjou, grandson of Louis XIV, and the Archduke Charles, son of Leopold I of Austria, claimed Charles II's inheritance. The struggle ended with a compromise, sealed by the Treaties of Utrecht and Rastatt, whereby Philip retained the Spanish throne and the overseas territories of the Empire, while Charles obtained the Spanish Netherlands, Sardinia, Naples, and Milan. This conflict had been viewed by contemporary observers as the greatest threat to the stability of the balance of power in modern history. In the run-up to the conflict, Vattel argued, several nations of Europe were understandably worried about the potential unification of France and Spain under the same crown, since Louis XIV had been responsible for

59 On Bartolus' doctrine of the right of resistance, see Diego Quaglioni, *Politica e diritto nel Trecento italiano. Il "De Tyranno" di Bartolo da Sassoferrato (1314–1357). Con l'edizione critica dei trattati "De Guelphis et Gebellinis", "De regimine civitatis" e "De tyranno"* (Florence, Olschki, 1983) 185 (on the *tyrannus apertus et manifestus*).

triggering most European conflicts in the previous forty years and displayed hostile intentions once again.[60] In Vattel's view, the alliance of the Austrians, the British, the Dutch, and the Russians, amongst others, against France was justified insofar as Louis was a notorious warmonger who the coalition expected would seize every opportunity available to expand Bourbon power. Vattel indeed affirmed that recourse to force against a suspected aggressor must be had considering his character, habits, and past behaviour. The right of all nations to take repressive action was all the 'more evident against a sovereign, who, from an habitual propensity to take up arms without reasons, or even so much as plausible pretexts, is continually disturbing the public tranquillity.'[61]

In a further argument relating to the War of the Spanish Succession, Vattel contended that if two autonomous powers such as France and Spain aimed to be unified, their goal could not be but dominate over their neighbours. Still, Vattel remarked, once Philip of Anjou acceded to the Spanish throne at the end of the conflict he proved to be not the imperialist despot that his opponents supposed him to be. Thus their fear of a Bourbon imperialist policy in Europe, initially legitimate, turned out to be groundless in the end. This comment indicated that, even though Vattel endorsed the doctrine of the balance of power, he did not do so unconditionally and was willing to admit its weaknesses. International equilibrium was a useful political device, but history showed that it had not always been applied properly.

Louis XIV remained a candidate for enemy of mankind status nevertheless. In his discussion on the War of the Spanish Succession, Vattel simply asserted that with hindsight, the presumption of guilt pronounced against the Bourbons on that specific occasion was probably unfounded, but he did maintain that it had been manifest in the eyes of those who actually experienced that struggle. The allied powers had acted in good faith when they characterised Louis as a warlike despot and therefore certainly waged a lawful war. The Sun King had only himself to blame if the greater part of Europe joined forces to stop him. Yet even on this point Vattel, for the sake of his diplomatic career, cautiously avoided formulating any overt criticism of Louis' policies, or of Bourbon policies more generally. Vattel thus attempted to criticise without displeasing, offsetting stigma by laud. To make his point on the repression of the disturbers of the balance of power,

---

60 *DG*, III, 3, § 44.
61 Ibid III, 3, §§ 49–50.

Vattel ultimately preferred to mention 'another case more evident': that of Charles V.[62]

When Vattel was drafting his *Droit des gens*, authoritative voices had already risen against the doctrine of international equilibrium and revealed its hidden implications from the points of view of law, politics, and economics. Vattel was not conversant with the critical theses of Johann Heinrich Gottlob von Justi, whose essay *Die Chimäre des Gleichgewichts von Europa* came out in 1758, but was very much familiar with Wolff's reservations about the balance of power – which he simply avoided to address.[63] Vattel was equally acquainted with Montesquieu's critique of the balance of power, in which the age of European equilibrium was characterised as one in which hostilities never ceased. For Montesquieu, peace could by then be defined as a state of 'general effort of all against all' in which sovereigns fearful of each other unleashed arms races destined to result in renewed continental wars.[64] Domestically, the militarisation of society and the increasing relevance of war as determinant of politics might restrain political freedom and pave the way for despotism. Eventually, European subjects would probably end by being deprived of their citizenship and property rights and turned into the slaves of their rulers, as was typical among Tartar tribes.[65]

For Vattel, these preoccupations were groundless. He agreed with Montesquieu that the militarisation of society was undesirable because it might be instrumental to despotism. And yet Vattel believed that this militarisation had little to do with the doctrine of international equilibrium, and could be avoided if only princes would resume the old custom of discharging troops in peacetime.[66] This would re-establish a concrete distinction between war and peace and enhance mutual trust and friendly international relations. Vattel contended that if standing armies were kept at a minimum while states relied on mercenary troops and local militias, arms races would be much less likely. This had been a dominating pattern in European warfare from the Middle Ages until the Thirty Years' War. Re-actualising it, Vattel claimed, would be necessary for small republics

---

62 Ibid III, 3, § 45.

63 Johann Heinrich Gottlob von Justi, *Die Chimäre des Gleichgewichts von Europa* (Altona, 1758).

64 Montesquieu, *De l'esprit des lois* (first published 1748, Victor Goldschmidt ed, Paris, Garnier-Flammarion, 1979) XIII, 17.

65 Ibid.

66 *DG*, III, 3, § 50.

and princedoms, such as Neuchâtel, to win back political independence vis-à-vis great powers that owed their hegemonic position to the overwhelming military strength of their standing armies. A well-functioning balance of power would do the rest, increasing the sovereigns' reliance on mutual assistance and discouraging them from embarking on unnecessary preventive wars.

A further reason why the balance of power did not have to lead to hostile sentiments was that it should not be idealistically aimed at eliminating disparities of power between states. Vattel criticised the view that for there to be political order in Europe all countries should be equally powerful – a view that the Duke of Sully had attributed to Henry IV of France, who allegedly put it forward in the context of his *Grand Dessein* for a perpetual peace in Europe. Vattel dismissed that conception of the balance of power as abstract and based on a purely quantitative idea of equilibrium.[67] Instead, he advocated for the maintenance of the status quo. In his opinion, a correctly understood balance of power should not aim at establishing a utopian equality, but rather should preserve the current power relationships, legitimated by prescription or peace treaties, and only allow for slight territorial changes.[68] This justified contemporary state practice. For all the numerous wars fought on European soil since the age of Louis XIV, the map of Europe as it was drafted at Westphalia was never significantly altered.

As Vattel criticised the abstract idea of international equilibrium as based on power equality, he rejected all the more the broader project, allegedly articulated by Henry IV, of securing perpetual peace in Europe by means of a permanent confederation – an idea entirely at odds with Vattel's conception of the world public order. For Vattel, international tranquillity was best secured by individual states acting in concert rather than by international institutions which deprived states of sovereignty and were likely to carry out hegemonic projects. Vattel's aversion to the institutionalisation of international law was patent in his critique of the Wolffian notion of the *civitas maxima*, and also in his sceptical remarks about the aptness of international conferences to achieving international order. Sarcastically, Vattel defined the Congress of Cambrai in 1724 and the Congress of Soissons in 1728 as 'tedious farces acted on the political theatre, in which the principal performers were less desirous of coming to an

67 Ibid III, 3, § 48.
68 Vattel discussed prescription in *DG*, II, 11, § 147.

accommodation than of appearing to desire it.'[69] This opinion is not surprising, considering that the period of apparent peace resting on the Franco-British entente from the end of the Great Northern War until the early 1730s was in fact a cold war, with all European sovereigns remaining on the look-out for open confrontations, arranging plots and shifting alliances.[70] For Vattel, the congresses of Cambrai and Soissons, far from contributing to international stability, simply signalled a baroque taste for absurd disputes and empty rhetoric in the little theatre of European foreign affairs in the run-up to the Wars of the Polish and Austrian Successions.

Whether involving real or cold wars, international relations for Vattel remained, more often than not, conflictual. Despite his rhetoric on the society of nations and the unity of mankind, he largely maintained a Hobbesian vision of the international arena, and was neither able nor willing to conceive of permanent conflict resolution models based on multinational convergence. Vattel strongly affirmed the principles of the law of nations to be universal, yet he admitted that states tended to dissent on a case by case interpretation and application of such principles. In his eyes, the preservation of the balance of power was one of the few issues that concerned all states and might bring together domestic interests and international justice.

Treaties and Treaty Breakers

While Vattel was firmly against the institutionalisation of international law, he was open to the modalities of international law enforcement and of the preservation of international equilibrium. In general, enforcement measures against enemies of mankind might be taken by ad-hoc coalitions which would be dissolved as soon as the threat was over.[71] As far as the balance of power was concerned, though, Vattel noted that the most suitable means for preserving it was to form alliances 'to oppose the more powerful potentate' already present in peacetime.[72] Should this fail to discourage a powerful state from pursuing expansionist policies, all other non-coalition nations were called on to join the coalition and fight against that state.

---

69 Ibid II, 18, § 331.

70 Derek McKay and Hamish M Scott, *The Rise of the Great Powers 1648–1815* (London – New York, Longman, 1983) 126.

71 *DG*, II, 13, § 198.

72 Ibid III, 3, § 48.

However, at times (and actually more often than Vattel was willing to admit), alliances might occasion general war instead of preventing it. He himself posited that since treaties of alliance, and international treaties more generally, generated a perfect obligation for every signatory to respect the treaty's terms, the violation of even one article of it amounted to an injury. It therefore elicited the injured party's right to resort to armed force – provided that party had no other means to safeguard their interests – in order to coerce the insolvent into furnishing reparation or satisfaction.[73] In the absence of a common superior, Vattel argued, the duty to observe international agreements and the right to repress the treaty-breaker directly stemmed from natural law, notably from the maxim *pacta sunt servanda* as the necessary condition for peace and security, both at the domestic and international level. This dictate was approved by international consent as well, since all nations were supposed to agree that for peace to be possible and long-lasting, treaty obligations should be observed, and treaty breaches justified recourse to force in retaliation. According to Vattel, the Europeans' opinion and practice supported this view, as did those of the Arab nations, as attested to in the Quran, in which the prophet Mohammed recommended that his disciples keep their word and observe agreements.[74] In light of this universal consent, the natural duty to comply with international treaties and the right to use force against the treaty breaker could be regarded as norms belonging to the voluntary and customary law of nations as well. Vattel had little doubt that the sovereigns who violated international treaties sapped 'the foundations of the peace and common safety of nations', and should be repressed as enemies of mankind.[75]

In fact, since determining the lawfulness of a treaty breach was an arduous task in the international sphere, Vattel maintained that sovereigns who at least provided a reasonable pretext for breaking a treaty could be pardoned. Only those who violated a treaty on 'evidently frivolous' pretexts, or without furnishing any pretext whatsoever, might properly be labelled as enemies of mankind and be repressed by a multinational force.

---

[73] Ibid II, 12, §§ 163–164. Vattel asserted that public treaties, pacts and conventions were essentially the same because they were signed by sovereigns or their plenipotentiaries. The only significant distinction was drawn between agreements supported by the sovereign and those made by officials acting on their own. This differentiation was based on that formulated by the Romans between *foedus* and *sponsio* (ibid II, 12, §§ 152–153; II, 13, §§ 206 ff.).

[74] Ibid II, 12, § 163* (Paul Pradier-Fodéré ed); II, 15, § 219. Still, Mohammed was later rebuked together with Tamerlane at *DG*, II, 17, § 273.

[75] Ibid II, 15, § 222.

Here, Vattel asserted the same logic already used when differentiating between sovereigns waging aggressive war for pleasure and ambition alone, and those who at least bothered to formulate some pretexts.

> It is the sovereign who violates his engagements on pretences that are evidently frivolous, or who does not even think it worth his while to allege any pretence whatever, to give a colourable gloss to his conduct, and cast a veil over his want of faith,—it is such a sovereign who deserves to be treated as an enemy to the human race.[76]

When sovereigns breached a treaty for either frivolous pretexts or under no pretext whatsoever, they indicated a complete lack of respect for the law of nations and thus indirectly harmed all states, which had a strong interest in this law being observed. A treaty breach resulting in an act of aggression, in particular, evidenced a sovereign's disposition to harm that should be stopped before it could escalate and should also prompt other rulers to behave in the same manner by imitation or fear.

At any rate, the decision of whether collective action should be waged in retaliation for treaty breach had to be weighed up by 'prudence and wise policy'.[77] Like Cicero, Vattel put forward the utilitarian argument that the formula *pacta sunt servanda* was not rational in itself, but rather necessary for the preservation of human society, both domestic and international. This maxim was fundamental to the maintenance of security, property rights, and social and diplomatic relations. It was sacred and inviolable insofar as it furthered the prosperity and tranquillity of nations.[78] This actually entailed that the *pacta sunt servanda* maxim could be superseded if the interests of mankind, or of the majority of (civilised) nations, so required. Moreover, Vattel argued, it could be overruled if its rigorous application allowed an injury to occur, or a grave offence against the law of nations to go unpunished. A void international agreement, for instance, was one through which a sovereign alienated a province of his country against the nation's will as expressed by the parliament or the states-general. Another type of treaty deprived of validity was one that had been stipulated on an unjust ground, as in the case of an offensive alliance against an innocent nation.[79]

---

76 Ibid.

77 Ibid II, 13, § 200.

78 Ibid II, 15, § 218.

79 Ibid II, 12, §§ 160, 161, 168. In accordance with state practice and most part of the natural law tradition, Vattel stated that alliances against non-Christians and among Christians of different confessions were permitted (ibid II, 12, § 162; II, 15, § 230).

Most importantly, the *pacta sunt servanda* maxim could be neglected by any individual nation if its own security was endangered. Since the fundamental duty of a sovereign was to protect their subjects, a sovereign might disregard international obligations where the necessity to respond to internal as well as external threats so demanded. This was a collision between the sovereign's absolute duty to protect his country and his less compulsory international obligations. Vattel had no doubt that in the case of real, not simulated, necessity an exception to the *pacta sunt servanda* obligation arose that gave the sovereign a licence to break a treaty with impunity.[80] More specifically, the breach of an international treaty might be justified by the *rebus sic stantibus* clause.[81] On this legal basis, if a nation was threatened by unforeseeable events or calamities which may cause its ruin or dissolution, it could not be held accountable for neglecting the terms of a treaty or a military alliance. This had been true, for instance, of the United Provinces during the War of Devolution of 1667–68, as they turned their back on their former ally Louis XIV and sided with their traditional enemy, Spain. On that occasion, the United Provinces acted lawfully as the Sun King had clearly broken the Franco-Dutch alliance the first by carrying on an imperialist agenda that posed a serious threat to Dutch freedom.

80 Ibid II, 12, § 170.
81 Ibid II, 17, § 297.

CHAPTER SIX

TYRANTS

This chapter deals with a figure of enemy of mankind relevant to both public law and international law: the tyrant. It demonstrates that Vattel's main concern in his treatment of the issue of tyranny and the right of resistance was to combine two seemingly opposite strands of the doctrine: the monarchomach tradition and Hobbes' theory. In principle, Vattel put forward a conception of civil war as a 'war in due form', which must be waged in compliance with the laws of war. He thus assimilated civil strife with international armed conflict. Vattel did so by relying on Hobbes' argument that both the tyrant and the rebel in a civil war must be seen as adversaries confronting each other in the state of nature, where there is no criterion for right and wrong. The centrality of this paradigm cannot be overstated, and today's international lawyers still have to deal with it when attempting to expand international humanitarian law into instances of internal armed conflict.

On the other hand, Vattel admitted that tyrants may be punished as ordinary criminals when they committed egregious violations of the law of nature and nations. Here Vattel recovered from the monarchomach tradition the idea that heinous tyrants might rightfully be toppled and may also be assassinated if necessary, while foreign powers should provide assistance to the tyrannised nation. Yet the ultimate motive by which Vattel justified intervention by foreign states was not the moral duty to assist an oppressed nation, much less the duty to repress the tyrant as a transgressor of the law of nature, but rather the need to protect the 'society of nations' at large from the ramifications that tyranny in one country might have at the international level. Once again, Vattel was primarily concerned about collective security, and with the function that international intervention could fulfil in terms of special and general deterrence.

Tyranny as a Legal Issue: The Bartolian Paradigm and Its Re-elaboration in the Vindiciae contra tyrannos

One crucial element of Vattel's theory of international law enforcement was the idea that collective action should be taken to punish acts committed by a sovereign not only against foreign nations, but also against a sovereign's own subjects. He postulated that there were some offences that – due to their extreme heinousness – adversely affected not only the victims, but mankind at large, and therefore had to be punished regardless of where and by whom they were committed. Tyranny belonged to this category.

Vattel provided a detailed treatment of tyranny in his *Questions de droit naturel*, a commentary on the Wolffian *Jus naturae* that he wrote in the early 1750s and published in 1762.[1] The *Questions* were meant to settle some thorny issues of natural and public law left open or unsatisfactorily answered by Wolff. In this work, Vattel provided some examples of situations in which popular resistance against the tyrant was permitted.[2]

> As far as concerns undertakings that are manifestly tyrannical and capable of ruining the state, for instance, if the prince endeavoured to reduce his subjects to slavery; if he made them die, despite their innocence, without any trial; if he deprived them of their property, without any evident pretext; if he made an attempt, publicly and violently, on the pudicity of women; if he wished to burn and destroy a city without any reason, or deliver the state to its enemies; is it possible to assume that the people has promised him a resigned obedience in cases of such nature? ... Our first principle opposes such a monstrous doctrine.[3]

Here Vattel described the tyrant as a ruler who acted irrationally or merely for his own interest, as opposed to the public good. The tyrant denied the fundamental rights of his subjects – life, freedom, and property – and disrespected the basic moral norms of society. These might seem like traditional topoi, but the fact that Vattel forcefully asserted them to justify the right of resistance was not entirely trivial at a time in which writers would rarely make use of the legal notion of tyranny. Rather, mainstream

---

[1] Emer de Vattel, *Questions de droit naturel* (The Hague, 1763).

[2] Vattel did not have the Bartolian notion of 'manifest' tyranny at first hand, and indeed ignoring Medieval sources was not uncommon for eighteenth century writers. In the *Questions de droit naturel* Vattel did not mention Bartolus, while in the *Droit des gens* he only referred to him through intermediate sources, notably Bodin. See, for instance, *DG*, II, 3, § 40* (Paul Pradier-Fodéré, ed).

[3] Vattel, *Questions de droit naturel*, VIII, § 1041. Translation by the author. Original text: 'Pour ce qui est des entreprises manifestement tyranniques & capables de perdre l'Etat, par exemple, si le Prince entreprenait de réduire ses sujets en esclavage; s'il les faisait périr, quoiqu'innocents, sans aucune forme de procès; s'il enlevait leurs biens, sans prétexte apparent; s'il attentait publiquement, & avec violence, à la pudicité des femmes; s'il voulait brûler & détruire une ville sans raison, ou livrer l'Etat aux ennemis; est-il possible de supposer que le peuple lui a promis une docile obéissance, pour des cas de cette nature? ... Notre premier principe s'oppose à une doctrine si monstrueuse.'

writers in the mid-eighteenth century usually restricted themselves to discussing 'despotism' as the oriental version of tyranny.[4] They might depict European rulers as 'despots' by association, but not as 'tyrants' in the legal sense, as implying the existence of a right of resistance.[5] Even apart from their fear of rulers' reactions, mid-eighteenth century writers abandoned the notion of tyranny because they dropped Aristotelian politics, one of the main concerns of which was tyranny, and also dismissed Aristotle's cyclical vision of history, according to which any form of monarchy was destined to degenerate into tyranny at some point. Enlightenment writers tended to reject this cyclical understanding in favour of the idea of historical progress. The few anti-conformist authors insisting on the traditional notion of tyranny were also those who still relied on Aristotle's cyclical conception of history, as is well exemplified by Rousseau.[6] All early-modern writers had trouble dealing with the problem of tyranny. This became apparent already from the sixteenth century, when Machiavelli, and partly Bodin, attempted to get rid of the traditional category of tyranny to endorse state power. There, an inescapable incompatibility emerged between the duty to obey and the right to resist. Such incompatibility even peaked in the seventeenth century with the contraposition between Hobbesian-authoritarian and Lockean-liberal accounts of political power.[7]

Tyranny as a legal problem was in essence medieval, and would remain extraneous to legal and political modernity. In the Middle Ages, the question of the tyrant played a pivotal role in feudal law and had been

[4] The French term *despotisme* came up in non-political contexts in 1698 and started soon to be used with reference to Louis XIV's government, thereby spreading in the political rhetoric: Hella Mandt, 'Tyrannis, Despotie' in Otto Brunner, Werner Conze and Reinhart Koselleck (eds), *Geschichtliche Grundbegriffe* (Stuttgart, Klett – Cotta, 1990) vol 6, 651, 675; Davide Monda, 'Contro un 'Sole' dispotico. Assolutismo e dispotismo nella Francia di Luigi XIV' in Domenico Felice (ed), *Dispotismo. Genesi e sviluppo di un concetto filosofico-politico* (Naples, Liguori, 2001) vol 1, 165.

[5] In addition, not all writers agreed that such association could be made. Even in the age of Louis XIV, some influential authors denied that 'in the perfectly polished states' of Europe there existed any despotic form of government: Jacques-Bénigne Bossuet, *Politique tirée des propres paroles de l'Ecriture Sainte* (first published 1709, Geneva, Droz, 1967) bk VIII, art 2, prop 1.

[6] Jean-Jacques Rousseau, *Du contrat social* (first published 1762) in Jean-Jacques Rousseau, *Œuvres complètes* (Bernard Gagnebin and Marcel Raymond eds, Paris, Gallimard, 1969) vol 3, III, 10; Aristotle, *The Politics* (Stephen Everson ed, CUP, 1988) III, 8.

[7] To be sure, these two accounts had something in common: a few anti-tyrannical implications could be spotted in Hobbes' writings, while Locke's outspokenly liberal political philosophy actually contained some authoritarian elements.

thoroughly addressed by jurists of that era, first by John of Salisbury, who provided a celebrated justification of tyrannicide in his *Policraticus* to reassert the sovereign's submission to God and the Church, and later by Bartolus de Saxoferrato in his treatise *De tyranno*, in which he laid down a detailed doctrine of tyranny that would remain paradigmatic for later medieval and early-modern writers.[8] In the 1350s, Bartolus worked out this doctrine to contrast the expanding might of the Italian *signorie*, notably that of the Visconti, and to call on the imperial and ecclesiastical universal powers to liberate Italy from oppression. Here the tyrant was perceived not only as the enemy of the communes, but also as a subverter of the world order established by God.[9] The medieval obsession with tyranny emerged from a complex context that was theological, legal, political, and anthropological all at once, and within which the individual was subordinate to political power only as long as that power mirrored the cosmic order.[10] In this context, the tyrant qualified as an individual who sinned by privileging his own ambitions and passions over the good of the community, and abused earthly power in a manner gravely contrary to divine and natural law.

Importantly, Bartolus specified that resistance was licit only in cases of 'manifest' tyranny – an idea that early-modern writers, including Vattel in both the *Droit des gens* and the *Questions*, were to reaffirm.[11] Indeed, the use of categories such as 'manifest' and 'notorious' in medieval and modern scholarship with reference to tyranny is not surprising, as those categories belonged to the tradition of the *ius civile* and were simply transferred to the domain of public law. However, it cannot be denied that the concept of 'manifest' might raise some issues, especially in writers like Vattel who not only discussed 'manifest' tyranny, but also justified foreign intervention in the event of 'manifest' tyranny. If transferring the 'manifest' concept from the province of civil law to that of public law might prove problematic, the likelihood of doctrinal and practical problems was even greater if one attempted to transfer it to the domain of international law.

---

[8] Harold J Berman, *Law and Revolution. The Formation of the Western Legal Traditions* (Harvard University Press, 1983) 281–2; Quaglioni, *Politica e diritto nel Trecento italiano. Il "De Tyranno" di Bartolo da Sassoferrato (1314–1357). Con l'edizione critica dei trattati "De Guelphis et Gebellinis", "De regimine civitatis" e "De tyranno"* (Florence, Olschki, 1983) 17 ff.

[9] Quaglioni, *Politica e diritto*, 37.

[10] On the medieval conception of law, see Paolo Grossi, *L'ordine giuridico medievale* (Rome – Bari, Laterza, 1997).

[11] Bartolus de Saxoferrato, *De tyranno* (written 1355–57) in Quaglioni (ed), *Politica e diritto*, 175–213, q V ff.

The concept of 'manifest' tyranny was actually less problematic for Bartolus. He lived in a time in which there existed universal last instance deciders, such as the Pope and the Emperor; a time in which 'manifest' truth was deemed attainable. According to the medieval scientific and theological paradigm, truth – in theology, philosophy, politics, and law – pertained to the human discourse as a reflection of divine truth. On the issue of tyranny, Bartolus did not rule out that disagreements might arise regarding the occurrence of a specific case of tyranny, but he maintained that such disagreement was accidental, and a proper examination of the case would settle any dispute.

The right to resist became markedly more difficult to justify as the medieval paradigm fell apart. As the modern notion of sovereignty emerged and the Reformation broke through, the legitimacy of universal authorities previously claiming, and sometimes abusing, the right to approve of anti-tyrannical resistance collapsed, and establishing 'Truth' in political and religious matters had become a hard task. Preoccupied with the ramifications of Bartolus' doctrine of tyranny for state power in the age of confessional strife, Bodin almost obliterated the topic entirely, suggesting that a tyrant *ex defectu tituli*, or usurper, should be regarded as a lawful ruler if one hundred years had elapsed since his seizure of power. In addition, Bodin strongly advised subjects against forcefully opposing the tyrant *ex parte exercitii*, that is, the abuser of legitimate political power.[12] In return, Bodin projected the figure of the unjust ruler into the distant Orient, denying that Europe had ever experienced the intolerable equation of ownership and political power typical of Asian peoples, notably the Ottomans.[13] As Bodin attempted to neutralise the Bartolian doctrine for the sake of the state's political stability after the St Bartholomew's Day massacre, his concept of tyranny became an archaic relic that could no longer be integrated into a modern conception of power.[14] Within a (virtually) absolutist paradigm of sovereignty, the legitimacy of the people's right to resist, along with foreign powers' right to intervene, had become

[12] Jean Bodin, *Six livres de la République* (first published 1576, Aalen, Scientia, 1977) II, 4 and 5.

[13] Moralising criticism aside, many European writers in the sixteenth century held the Ottomans in high esteem for their political organisation, stability, and military strength. See Hans Sturmberger, 'Das Problem der Vorbildhaftigkeit des türkischen Staatswesens im 16. und 17. Jahrhundert und sein Einfluß auf den europäischen Absolutismus' in *XIIe Congrès International des Sciences Historiques*, Rapport IV (Vienna, 1965) 201–209.

[14] Margherita Isnardi Parente, 'Signoria e tirannide nella "République" di Jean Bodin' in Domenico Felice (ed), *Dispotismo. Genesi e sviluppo di un concetto filosofico-politico* (Naples, Liguori, 2001) vol 1, 127, 140.

highly problematic. Political writer Etienne de la Boétie—whose *Discours de la servitude volontaire* was published posthumously by his friend Montaigne in 1576, the same year in which Bodin's *République* came out—was equally sceptical about the right of resistance in its medieval version. De la Boétie advanced a theory of civil disobedience against the tyrant, yet stressed that forceful resistance was not expedient and should be avoided for the sake of public peace.[15] Reliance on absolutist power was theorised around the same time by Libertines like Pierre Charron, and later, based on a similarly individualist and sceptical epistemology, by Hobbes.[16]

And yet reliance on absolutist power represented but one type of response, if the most successful historically, to religious conflict. On the opposite corner stood monarchomachs like François Hotman, Theodore Beza, and Philippe du Plessis Mornay, who aspired to goals similar to those pursued by the absolutists, yet radically differed in the means to achieve them.[17] This difference of modality was apparent, for example, when writers such as monarchomach Hotman and absolutist Bodin, both starting from a common interest in defending the ancient freedom and fundamental laws of the 'Franks', came to opposite conclusions about how to give effect to this. Whilst Bodin took on the Roman and canon law concepts of *princeps legibus solutus* and *suprema potestas* to underpin monarchical power, monarchomachs like Hotman recovered mythologies of the people's sovereignty to challenge it.[18] Calvinist monarchomachs no longer believed in a universal Church like most medieval writers, but still believed in God's Truth as embodied by the Calvinist religion.[19] This epistemological framework still granted the application of Bartolus' category of 'manifest' tyranny, especially in instances of confessional confrontations in which there could be no doubt as to where Truth lay. It was not an accident that the modern theory of regicide was emblematically set out within the monarchomach tradition in the *Vindiciae contra tyrannos*,

---

15 Étienne de la Boétie, *Discours de la servitude volontaire* (first published 1576, Miguel Abensour ed, Paris, Payot, 1976) 199.

16 On the political thought of early modern sceptical philosophers, see Roman Schnur, *Individualismus und Absolutismus. Zur politischen Theorie vor Thomas Hobbes (1600–1640)* (Berlin, Duncker & Humblot, 1963), and Annamaria Battista, *Alle origini del pensiero politico libertino* (Milan, Giuffrè, 1989).

17 On the Huguenot doctrine of the right to resist, see Quentin Skinner, *The Foundations of Modern Political Thought* (CUP, 1978) vol 2, 302–348. See also Mario Turchetti, *Tyrannie et tyrannicide de l'Antiquité à nos jours* (Paris, PUF, 2001) 423 ff.

18 François Hotman, *Francogallia* (first published 1573, John H Salmon trans, CUP, 1972) 221 and 235.

19 Skinner, *The Foundations of Modern Political Thought*, vol 2, 240.

plausibly composed by either Philippe du Plessis Mornay or Hubert Languet and published in Basel in 1579, in the context of Huguenot reaction to religious persecution under the Valois monarchy.[20] Drawing on Cicero, the Bible, canon law, and historical examples, the author provided an unprecedented and influential treatment of the right to resist, culminating in a doctrine of intervention and of the individual citizen's right to kill the tyrant – a doctrine that Vattel would confront; partly accepting and partly dismissing it.[21]

The author of the *Vindiciae* also provided a paradigmatic justification of international intervention for humanitarian purposes. Earlier scholars had usually refrained from theorising a right or duty to assist oppressed foreign nations lest this would legitimise undue intromissions and spread conflicts instead of bringing them to an end. The author of the *Vindiciae* took account of the ramifications of international intervention, but advocated for it nevertheless, as he assumed that in the wake of the St Bartholomew's Day massacre no compromise with the Valois monarchy was possible anymore.[22] The author also admitted that foreign powers were rarely motivated by charity when they came to the rescue of a tyrannised people.[23] However, he argued, this did not invalidate the normative argument, supported by Scripture and theology, which required that foreign princes assist a people oppressed by tyranny. By linking together examples from the Old Testament with a universalist view of the Church as Christ's body, the author claimed that Christian masters were bound not only to protect their own subjects but also to expand the 'true faith' and render assistance to all believers in need, castigating tyrants anywhere, because 'where the glory of God and the kingdom of Christ is concerned, no limits, no frontiers, no barriers, ought to restrict the zeal of pious princes'.[24]

The arguments set out in the *Vindiciae* in the late 1570s, in the midst of the Wars of Religion, were premised on the assumption that France's public peace and tranquillity were irreparably compromised. Therefore, for the author, the risk of his doctrine of intervention backing imperialist endeavours disguised as acts of international solidarity was less

20 Ernest Barker, 'The Authorship of the *Vindiciae Contra Tyrannos*' (1930) 3 *Cambridge Historical Journal* 164.

21 Philippe du Plessis Mornay, *Vindiciae, contra tyrannos* (George Garnett ed, CUP, 1994) IV.

22 Skinner, *The Foundations of Modern Political Thought*, vol 2, 304.

23 Du Plessis Mornay, *Vindiciae*, IV, 173–4.

24 Ibid IV, 176.

threatening than a defeat in the ongoing Wars of Religion. After all, foreign rulers had been involved in French civil infighting from the outset, and the author's apology for foreign intervention was simply aimed at legitimising the English, German, and Dutch support to the Huguenots that was already in place. The author's only reservation about intervention was that foreign princes should not take advantage of hostilities to subjugate the people that they were supposed to help.[25]

The medieval account of tyranny revived by the monarchomachs during the Wars of Religion was dismissed by political scientists and absolutist thinkers who in those same years were laying down the foundations of political modernity on a markedly statist basis. Natural lawyers, from Grotius onwards, attempted to find a middle way in order to harmonise the Bartolian doctrine within their modern conceptions of sovereignty, at the cost of patent shortcomings. Vattel set out to provide a workable synthesis between the Bartolian opinion, which he inherited from the monarchomachs, and the Hobbesian realist approach. He thus advanced an original notion of civil war and the right of resistance that would remain paradigmatic in international legal doctrine until the twentieth century.

Vattel on Tyranny

Vattel seemed to have little in common with radical theorists of tyranny such as the monarchomachs. Vattel was politically moderate, supportive of principality as the form of government approved by the people of his native town, and was not a republican hardliner à la Rousseau. That Vattel was not favourably disposed towards popular resistance and changes of regime was confirmed in a letter that he addressed to his friend Formey in October 1749. Therein, Vattel strongly condemned the recent *Henzi-Verschwörung*; an attempt by a faction of citizens of Bern to bring down the local aristocracy that held nearly absolute power in the city.[26] He maintained that this faction had no right to replace the aristocracy with a republic, and he denied, more generally, that rebellion against political authorities could be justified based on the argument of the best constitution. In a footnote to a posthumous edition of the *Droit des gens*, Vattel straightforwardly dropped the question of the best constitution and

[25] Ibid IV, 183–4.

[26] Emer de Vattel, Letter to Johann Heinrich Samuel Formey, 10 October 1749 in *Varnhagen Collection* (Jagiellonian Library, Kraków) 270.

asserted that he would not 'examine which of these sorts of government [democracy, aristocracy, or monarchy] is the best. It will suffice to say in general that the monarchic government seems preferable to every other, depending on the sovereign's power being limited and not absolute.'[27] Even when princes ruled in an authoritarian manner, Vattel claimed, they were entitled to govern as long as they accomplished their basic public duties and were committed to the state's welfare and tranquillity.

Vattel was actually fascinated by the idea of a 'philosopher king' who embodied firm authority and wisdom. This is best illustrated by Vattel's enthusiasm about the early 'enlightened' policies of Frederick II after his accession to the throne of Prussia, which induced Vattel to dedicate the *Défense du système Leibnitien* to him in the hope of receiving a call to Berlin.[28] Even when Vattel later criticised Frederick for his military adventurism, he continued to admire his conduct of domestic affairs, notably his criminal law reforms, religious tolerance, and his welcoming policy towards the Huguenot community.[29] In the *Droit des gens*, Vattel praised these enlightened and tolerant policies as he affirmed that 'the states of the king of Prussia', including the Principality of Neuchâtel, were countries in which social peace and wealth ideally coexisted with and were boosted by the 'universal tolerance of all religions'.[30] Vattel highly valued the policies implemented by the Prussians in Neuchâtel, especially the abolition of torture there.[31] While the King of Prussia might qualify as an 'enemy

---

27 *DG*, I, 1, § 3* (Paul Pradier-Fodéré ed). Translation by the author. Original text: 'Nous n'examinerons pas non plus laquelle de ces diverses sortes de gouvernement est la meilleure. Il suffira de dire en général que le gouvernement monarchique parait préférable à tout autre, moyennant que le pouvoir du souverain soit limité et non absolu'.

28 Emer de Vattel, *Défense du système Leibnitien* (Leiden, 1741). See in particular the dedicatory epistle where Vattel greatly lauded the Prussian 'philosopher king'.

29 On Berlin as a privileged destination for Swiss intellectuals in the eighteenth century, see André Bandelier, 'De Berlin à Neuchâtel: la genèse du *Droit des gens* d'Emer de Vattel' in Martin Fontius (ed) *Schweizer im Berlin des 18. Jahrhunderts* (Berlin, Akademie-Verlag, 1996) 45–56.

30 *DG*, I, 12, § 135.

31 Emer de Vattel, Letter to Johann Heinrich Samuel Formey, 8 November 1755 in *Varnhagen Collection* (Jagiellonian Library, Kraków) 270. Tetsuya Toyoda's survey on the historical background of the *Droit des gens* – a survey that is illuminating in many respects – seems to exaggerate the significance of the popular discontent in Neuchâtel over Prussian sovereignty. See Tetsuya Toyoda, 'La doctrine vattelienne de l'égalité souveraine dans le contexte neuchâtelois' (2009) 11 *Journal of the History of International Law* 103. Although some complaints did take place, they never reached the point of contesting Frederick II's titles to govern the principality [Ulysse Guinand (ed), *Histoire du gouvernement de Neuchâtel, sous la domination Prussienne, depuis 1707 jusqu'au 1832* (Lausanne, 1833) 34 ff]. Vattel in his private correspondence of the 1740s and 1750s expressed his scepticism about any regime change in his native town, and he by no means hinted at such solution in the *Droit des gens* or in other writings.

of mankind' in that he disturbed the peace of Europe and sponsored brutal warfare, his qualities as a ruler remained untouched by that conduct.

That tyranny was no longer a topical issue did not entail that it should not be discussed. Especially in lesser principalities subject to foreign domination like Neuchâtel, the debate over the aims and limits of rightful political power ought to be kept alive to prevent sovereigns from abusing their position at some point and possibly eroding local freedoms and privileges. De la Boétie had already pointed out that one central reason why tyranny can assert itself is that a tyrant's subjects possess the habit of obedience to him, while they should instead pay critical attention to the tyrannical drifts of monarchical power.[32] A similar admonishment to look out for abuses of power was given by Vattel in his treatment of tyranny and of other crimes committed by sovereigns. Indeed, he advanced his theory of the repression of international crimes in an age which saw comparatively fewer violations of the law of nations than previous epochs. It thus seems that for Vattel, the closer humanity moved towards its goal of civilising both domestic and international affairs, the harder it must fight to secure this goal.

It was at the very stage when tyranny apparently disappeared from the political landscape of Europe that Vattel warned against overconfidence and put forward a clear endorsement of the right to resist. In the *Droit des gens*, he addressed tyranny as follows, reasserting some of the considerations already drafted in the *Questions de droit naturel*.

> A subject ought patiently to suffer from the prince doubtful wrongs, and wrongs that are supportable. ... [E]very citizen has tacitly engaged to observe this moderation; because, without it, society could not exist. But when the injuries are manifest and atrocious,—when a prince, without any apparent reason attempts to deprive us of life, or of those things the loss of which would render life irksome, who can dispute our right to resist him? Self-preservation is not only a natural right, but an obligation imposed by nature, and no man can entirely and absolutely renounce it.[33]

Vattel here resorted to the Bartolian doctrine as it was re-elaborated in modern writings, especially the *Vindiciae*.[34] He took up the notion of 'manifest tyranny', required for popular resistance to be legitimate, as well as the distinction between the tyrant de facto (*tyrannus ex parte exercitii*)

---

[32] De la Boétie, *Discours de la servitude volontaire*, 215.
[33] *DG*, I, 4, § 54.
[34] Du Plessis Mornay, *Vindiciae*, 48, 140, 141.

and the mere usurper (*tyrannus ex defectu tituli*).[35] Vattel especially stressed that the prince might be lawfully put down only if his acts were patently and unbearably tyrannical, as the commonwealth's peace and tranquillity would be severely threatened if subjects were authorised to resist in response to the slightest injuries. Yet this might sound generic, and it was not made any clearer by the fact that the overarching criterion to justify or condemn resistance remained an under-defined 'good of the whole'. Concrete examples like those illustrated in the *Questions de droit naturel* were lacking in the *Droit des gens*.[36] Vattel here attempted to link the 'good of the whole' to the maxims of 'sound statecraft', arguing that arbitrary administration would inevitably foment unrest and was therefore deeply contrary to the tyrants' own interest, but this was presumably not very convincing.

Also, who was to judge whether tyranny was 'manifest'? This question, relatively unproblematic for Bartolus, had become a legitimate one during the Wars of Religion, and even more so in the mid-eighteenth century, as sceptics arguing for epistemological subjectivism might wonder if there existed any 'manifest' or 'evident' knowledge at all. To prevent objections, Vattel had to spell out what he concretely meant by 'manifest' tyranny. He did so by resorting to constitutional arguments. Drawing on Bodin's opinion, he posited that although sovereigns were above domestic law in their public capacity, they remained strictly bound to the country's fundamental laws that determined the extent and manner of exercising political power.[37] Vattel then proceeded by following a contractualist pattern, arguing that princes were supposed to receive their authority from the nation and were under an obligation to respect and defend its constitution, any modifications to which had to be approved by its representatives.[38] This was premised on the tacit condition to the *pactum subjectionis* that the

35 Bartolus, *De Tyranno* in Quaglioni, *Politica e diritto*, q V, 185.

36 Vattel, *Questions de droit naturel*, VIII, § 1041.

37 Bodin, *République*, I, 8. To be sure, the international lawyer Vattel also put emphasis on the ruler's subjection to the law of nations, whose role was minimised by Bodin instead, who tended to conceive of the law of nations as a cynical *ius belli* and assumed that the sovereign's licence in foreign affairs need rather be limited, if vaguely enough, by the laws of God and nature. See Margherita Isnardi Parente, 'Introduzione' in Jean Bodin, *I sei libri dello Stato* (Turin, Utet, 1964) vol 1; Diego Quaglioni, *I limiti della sovranità* (Padua, Cedam, 1992) 123–139.

38 *DG*, I, 4, §§ 34 and 47; Vattel, *Questions de droit naturel*, VIII, § 391. If pressed by urgent matters, the prince was permitted to make exceptions to the constitution, but he should ask for the nation's approval and ratification immediately thereafter. Moreover, the fundamental laws could be modified only if unanimous consent by the people could be ascertained: Vattel, *Questions de droit naturel*, VIII, §§ 120 and 815.

sovereign had to govern with a view to the people's welfare and happiness.[39] If the sovereign seriously violated this clause, he would commit 'a criminal abuse' that would entitle the people to resume their primeval sovereignty.[40] If the sovereign was guilty of breaching fundamental laws, he was to be deprived of both the right and title to govern.[41]

For Vattel, the prince was also strictly bound to any pledge he publicly made, though it was practically impossible to ascertain beforehand to what extent the subjects had to tolerate infringements of privileges, exemptions, or immunities that he had sworn to respect when acceding to the throne.[42] This judgment was left to the people's discretion. Vattel only pointed out that subjects should first listen to prudence and then consider carefully if it was truly necessary to topple the tyrant by force. History had indicated that peoples who were traditionally fond of their freedom (like the Swiss) were more likely to succeed in their struggle against oppression than those who have been accustomed to living under the yoke of despotism for centuries. If resistance was surely convenient and legitimate for the former, it was far less so for the latter.[43]

The Tyrant as an Enemy of Mankind and the Right of Resistance

One peculiarity of Vattel's approach was that for him only the tyrant *ex parte exercitii*, and not the bare usurper, qualified as an enemy of mankind deserving of repression by an international coalition. Whilst the former was an actual oppressor, the latter did not necessarily act against the law, and might even acquire a fully legitimate title to sovereignty through long

39 Vattel, *Questions de droit naturel*, VIII, §§ 60 and 91.

40 *DG*, I, 4, § 46.

41 Ibid I, 4, § 51.

42 Vattel, *Questions de droit naturel*, VIII, §§ 126 and 145. Vattel believed that having recourse to customary law alone was not enough to protect particular privileges and statutes vis-à-vis the monarchical power, therefore a contractualist underpinning was required. Dissenting with Wolff, he regarded the prince's promise to rule for the sake of general good as 'perfect', hence enforceable. Such enforceability was allegedly guaranteed by the fact that the pledge was undertaken with 'solemnity' and sealed by an oath, where the presence of God as witness was no longer needed and the will of the contracting parties sufficed for a strict obligation to arise. See also Hugo Grotius, *De iure belli ac pacis libri tres* (first published 1625, Francis W Kelsey trans, Washington, Carnegie Endowment, 1913) II, 13, § 3, 3.

43 *DG*, I, 4, § 51. Despotic regimes could be overturned even if established by the people's free consent in ancient times, for subjects could no longer be supposed to agree on such decision and were not bound to their forefathers' choice (Vattel, *Questions de droit naturel*, VIII, § 269).

possession and the nation's tacit consent, as Bodin had taught.[44] Prudence advised that the usurper be left in charge as long as he ruled without misusing power.[45] To be sure, where prescription claims were unfounded, Vattel maintained that the usurper's title to govern might be contested, and foreign powers allied to the former rulers acquired the right to resort to force to re-install those deposed authorities.[46] However, Vattel did not furnish a general rationale in favour of the right of foreign powers to intervene to restore dethroned rulers. In addition, the right to intervene lapsed as soon as the rebellious nation through its representatives formally deposed the ruler, or clearly manifested the will to do so, thereby retrieving its original sovereignty. In this instance, any intervention by third countries would count as a grievous breach of international law.

Vattel pointed out that a nation resuming full sovereignty after being oppressed by a tyrant was not authorised by this alone to take revenge on him for the abuses that he committed while in power. Neither should foreign states arrogate the right to meddle in that nation's affairs and punish the tyrant without its approval. Vattel recalled that historically, those who held and acted otherwise did so to the detriment of domestic and international tranquillity. He thus strongly reasserted the 'natural' principle that the person of the sovereign be regarded as 'sacred and inviolable'. This was a slippery slope argument: justifying the assassination of the tyrant could bring about fanaticism and instigate private individuals to take justice in their hands, with the result that wise sovereigns might be killed along with oppressors. The assassination of Henry IV of France by the Catholic fanatic François Ravaillac in 1610 exemplified this danger.[47]

Actually, Vattel did not stress the sacredness of the person of the sovereign to contest the idea that princes abusing their power might be lawfully killed. They might do so, provided that the assassination was commanded by the people's representatives. Rather, Vattel contended that the right to kill the sovereign could not be claimed by private individuals acting arbitrarily, as had been regrettably claimed by the Calvinist author of the *Vindiciae* and by Spanish Jesuit Juan de Mariana.[48] The requirements

---

44 *DG*, I, 5, § 59; Bodin, *République*, II, 5; Isnardi Parente, 'Signoria e tirannide nella *République* di Jean Bodin', 137.

45 *DG*, I, 4, § 54.

46 Ibid II, 12, § 196.

47 Ibid I, 4, § 50.

48 Vattel, *Questions de droit naturel*, VIII, § 60; Juan de Mariana, *De rege et regis institutione libri tres* (Toledo, 1599) [George Albert Moore trans, *The King and the Education of the King*, Washington, Country Dollar Press, 1944] VII; du Plessis Mornay, *Vindiciae*,

posed in the *Vindiciae* for the individual's right to resist on God's command, including 'a mind empty of all ambitions' and 'authentic and earnest zeal', must have sounded anachronistic if not delirious to Vattel, who like many of his contemporaries characterised religious enthusiasm as socially dangerous and conducive to superstition, fanaticism, and oppression.[49] He was clearly hostile to institutionalised religion, and especially disapproved of its influence on law and politics – a position well illustrated in his powerful attack on the papacy in the *Droit des gens*.[50] For Vattel, the discourse of religious fanatics claiming the right to kill the tyrant in God's name furnished evidence of how harmful was the use of religious arguments in political and legal issues.[51]

Vattel's anticlericalism first publicly emerged in his *Défense du système Leibnitien*, an apology for the Leibnizian philosophy that he published in 1740 to refute the theology of Jean-Pierre de Crousaz, labelled by Vattel as a 'rigid sectarian of Calvin'.[52] Yet Vattel's antipathy towards 'fanatical' theologians had actually developed since the early 1730s, when he turned from theology to philosophy and left Bale, where he had been a disciple of the theologian and pastor Pierre Roques, for Geneva, where he became familiar with the philosophies of Leibniz and Wolff.[53] It was in Geneva that Vattel, disappointed at the alleged corruption of the *Vénerable classe*, the local consistory, came to the conclusion that priests and theologians had better not deal with matters political.[54]

Vattel's anticlericalism did not prevent him from asserting, from a utilitarian standpoint, that religion contributed to the state's political stability. From this perspective, the prince should respect and even promote religion – including the freedom of religion, which was a natural right – as long as this favoured state interests. In most cases, Vattel admitted, the citizens worshipping God with sincerity and devotion also obeyed the civil authority.[55]

Politics however maintained an unquestionable primacy over religion. Vattel accordingly posited that in the event of conflict between the state

II, 68. On Mariana's position, see Harald E Braun, *Juan de Mariana and Early Modern Spanish Political Thought* (Aldershot, Ashgate, 2007) 85.

49 Du Plessis Mornay, *Vindiciae* II, 69.

50 *DG*, I, 12, § 146.

51 Ibid I, 12, § 126.

52 Emer de Vattel, *Défense du système Leibnitien* (Leiden, 1741) Préface, XXXVIII ff.

53 Edouard Béguelin, 'En souvenir de Vattel' in *Recueil de travaux offert par la Faculté de Droit de l'Université de Neuchâtel à la Société Suisse des Juristes* (Neuchâtel, Attinger, 1929) 35–176, 39–41.

54 Emer de Vattel, Letter to Frédéric Ostervald, 19 December 1746, quoted in Edouard Béguelin, 'En souvenir de Vattel', 37. See also above, 20.

55 *DG*, I, 12, §§ 127–128; Vattel, *Questions de droit naturel*, VIII, § 81.

and the followers of a religion, the latter should choose voluntary exile rather than overt resistance to the prince. The freedom of conscience and of religion was a natural right, but trying to enforce it without first being legitimated by the entire nation's consent would mean infringing upon the rights of fellow citizens to keep a sovereign whom they believed entitled to govern. Vattel posited that open resistance in that case was illicit. Only private disobedience might sometimes be rightful, in the case that a fanatical ruler ordered his subjects to commit 'manifestly' atrocious and inhuman acts. In this instance, disobedience was required, at least morally. Vattel, for instance, praised those French military officials who in August 1572 disobeyed the orders of their sovereign, Charles IX, by refusing to slay their Huguenot fellow citizens on occasion of the St Bartholomew's Day massacre.[56]

Vattel's discussion of the St Bartholomew's Day massacre confirmed that commands in gross violation of the law of nature might be disobeyed, yet they did not justify open rebellion. Vattel merely contended that all soldiers were morally bound to ignore Charles IX's orders, not that they should rise against him on the grounds that he had become a manifest tyrant when he commanded the slaughter of the Huguenots. Vattel claimed that while under the circumstances disobedience was certainly praiseworthy, it was 'more difficult to determine in what cases a subject may not only refuse to obey, but even resist a sovereign, and oppose his violence by force.'[57] Here Vattel reasserted Etienne de la Boétie's argument that resistance and civil disobedience were two separate issues.[58] Disobedience to Charles' barbarous orders was rightful, but active resistance should be carried out only if it was in the interest of the whole country and did not undermine its security and tranquillity. For Vattel, the duty to repress a tyrannical enemy of mankind decayed if resistance was likely further to destabilise the country and thereby would turn out to be detrimental to national interest.

'Manifest tyranny' for Vattel ultimately meant a governmental conduct that injured the majority of the population. In the *Questions de droit naturel*, he stipulated that resistance was allowed if 'all citizens, or at least the greater part of them' agreed on toppling the tyrant, since it was a principle agreed upon by all contractors to the social pact that 'the opinion of

---

56 *DG*, I, 4, § 54.

57 Ibid.

58 De la Boétie, *Discours de la servitude volontaire*, 199.

the majority would be taken as the general will.'[59] So, when a 'manifest' abuse of power urged the greater part of the population to consent to enforcing the right of resistance, every citizen was allowed to take up arms. In this event, the prince was expressly or tacitly dethroned as the nation as a whole was supposed to regain possession of its original sovereignty. The prince thus turned into a public enemy who might rightfully be killed by his former subjects by the right of war.[60]

As civil power was supposed to be conferred upon the ruler with the tacit reservation that it should be employed in favour of the public good, failure by the ruler to comply with this condition re-established the state of nature, and potentially of war, between the nation and him. When he was faulted for violating fundamental laws, liberties, and privileges, or for egregiously misgoverning and leading the country to ruin, the whole nation was allowed to resist. In this case, its representatives were entitled to formally declare the *pactum subjectionis* void, as the Dutch had done through a formal Act of Abjuration to liberate themselves from Philip II's oppressive regime in 1581.[61] Vattel also noted that tyrants of the worst sort might be not only rightfully deposed but also assassinated.[62]

Vattel was aware that advancing the idea of national consent did not suffice to avert all critique. The idea of the general will might fit small countries like Switzerland but, as Rousseau would later admit, was hardly applicable to larger political entities.[63] Even if resistance was legitimated by the pronouncements of magistrates and massive popular revolts, factions would probably form nevertheless, unveiling the abstract character of the general will. Vattel thus suggested that to avoid unrest in a country, all disputes between sovereign and subjects should be resolved through arbitration. He proudly recalled that the princes and city of Neuchâtel had been settling their disputes in just such a civilised manner since 1406, when they declared the Canton of Bern as perpetual judge over their litigation.[64] Yet Vattel was certainly aware that this did not settle the major issue. It was improbable that arbitration, which had long turned into a marginal phenomenon in international affairs by the eighteenth century,

[59] Vattel, *Questions de droit naturel*, VIII, §§ 60 and 91.
[60] *DG*, I, 4, § 51.
[61] Ibid.
[62] Ibid.
[63] Rousseau, *Contrat social*, III, 8.
[64] *DG*, I, 4, § 52.

could still be applicable in momentous disputes involving the key interests of the great powers.[65]

Vattel's Assimilation of Civil War with International Armed Conflict

Vattel attempted to neutralise the conflict between the right to resist and the duty to obey by resorting to a formalist notion of civil war. His aim was to assimilate civil strife with international 'war in due form', and apply to the former the rules which governed the latter. Doctrinally, the 'war in due form' paradigm was based on the idea, first put forward by medieval and early-modern theologians, that public war between entities with no common superior on earth might be deemed 'just' on both sides, at least *in foro externo*.[66] Vattel endorsed this reasoning to posit that in a war between sovereign states, under normal circumstances, all parties were equally entitled to use force, should not discriminate against each other, and thus had to comply with the laws of war regardless of the justice of the cause. He argued that the same should apply to civil war.

Prior to the publication of the *Droit des gens*, civil war was usually considered in terms of either dynastic legitimacy or moral justice. The former was emphasised by theorists of absolutism, who tended to deny insurgents any right to take up arms.[67] Moral justice, instead, was highlighted by natural law theorists who contemplated resistance in the event of 'unbearable tyranny', based on the teaching of Aristotle, Aquinas and Bartolus.[68] In the middle between absolutism and just war doctrine stood Hobbes. Although Hobbes dwelt on absolutist rationales, he started from individualist premises. Given these premises, he concluded by justifying resistance as a means of self-defence against a ruler who pretended obedience without granting protection.[69]

---

65 On the marginal role of arbitration in the eighteenth century, see Wilhelm Grewe, *The Epochs of International Law* (Michael Byers trans, Berlin, de Gruyter, 2000) 363–366. See also Hans Staub, *Die völkerrechtlichen Lehren Vattels im Lichte der naturrechtlichen Doktrin. Ein Beitrag zur Gründungsgeschichte des Völkerrechts* (Naumburg an der Saale, Lippert & Co, 1921) 102.

66 Peter Haggenmacher, *Grotius et la doctrine de la guerre juste* (Paris, PUF, 1983) 203–223.

67 Bodin, *République*, II, 5; Balthazar Ayala, *De iure belli et officiis bellicis et disciplina militari libri tres* (first published 1582, John Westlake ed, Washington, Carnegie Endowment, 1912) I, 2.

68 Bartolus, *De tyranno*; Thomas Aquinas, *Summa theologiae* (60 vols, Thomas Gilby et al trans, London, Eyre and Spottiswoode, 1964–73) II–II, q 42, a 2. Aquinas in turn referred to Aristotle, *Politics*, III, 5, and to Aristotle, *Nicomachean Ethics* (David Ross trans, OUP, 2009) VIII, 5.

69 Thomas Hobbes, *De cive* (first published 1642, Richard Tuck ed, CUP, 1998) XII, 3.

In the Hobbesian view, a prince in violation of the social pact might certainly be killed, but then he should be properly called an 'enemy', not a 'tyrant'.[70] As ethics was a matter of taste and there was no moral standard to judge whether the ruler acted justly or unjustly, the concept of tyranny itself made no sense. For Hobbes, there were no 'tyrants' or 'wise princes' but simply 'sovereigns' and 'enemies'. This postulate constituted the condition of the possibility of assimilating civil war with international armed conflict.

The potentially revolutionary ramifications of Hobbes' individualism were largely disregarded by most commentators, who were apparently committed to stigmatising his authoritarian views.[71] Hobbes' destiny was more or less the same as Machiavelli's: their names were cursed for centuries, while their theories nevertheless continued to re-emerge in different forms and disguises, the self-righteous being those who eventually put them into practice in the most radical way.[72] The increasing aversion towards Hobbes was first due to the general phenomenon that in the heyday of modern natural law, from Grotius' *De iure belli ac pacis* up to Vattel's *Droit des gens*, political realism lost ground to naturalist normativism. Once the nation-states had asserted themselves over their churches and local authorities, the justifications of power based on pure effectiveness which had previously been useful for enhancing the commonwealth's unity against internal and external enemies turned out to be counterproductive. Instead, the substantial conceptions of sovereignty set out by natural lawyers proved a suitable device to justify the state's growing intrusiveness into religion, the economy, and the private spheres of subjects, where such spheres already existed. Suffice it to consider the Wolffian underpinnings of the Prussian *Allgemeines Landrecht* of 1794.[73]

And yet, although several natural law theories literally became political theologies and came to justify state power by making it a divinity (Hegel's *Philosophy of Right* with its normative descriptivism was the last

70 Ibid.

71 Pufendorf was one of the few writers to publicly recognise Hobbes' merits, but kept distance from the most radical consequences of the Hobbesian theory. For a detailed analysis of Hobbes' influence on Pufendorf, see Fiammetta Palladini, *Samuel Pufendorf discepolo di Hobbes* (Bologna, Il Mulino, 1990).

72 Frederick II of Prussia, for instance, straightforwardly applied Machiavellian principles to international affairs immediately after publishing his *Anti-Machiavel* in 1740.

73 *Allgemeines Landrecht für die preussischen Staaten* (2 vols, Berlin, 1794). The Wolffian underpinnings of the *Allgemeines Landrecht* are emphasised by Alfred Dufour, 'Religion, Eglise, Etat dans la pensée d'Emer de Vattel' (2002) 3–4 *Revue historique neuchâteloise* 169, 175.

outstanding expression of the stream inspired by Hobbes' *Leviathan*), other theoretical approaches, closer to the Lockean model, came to opposite results and provided grounds for lawful resistance and revolution.[74] Incidentally, this also explains the remarkable influence of Vattel's *Droit des gens* – or at least of the liberal arguments contained therein – on the American revolutionary and constitutional debates of the 1770s and 1780s.[75] Yet, beyond any differences between individualist (Hobbes), organicist (Rousseau), and eclecticist (Vattel) perspectives, the fact remains that as far as a theoretical legitimation of the right of resistance was concerned, modern natural lawyers had nothing to add to what had been stated by Bartolus. This was inherent in the very notion of the right of resistance, which involved the paradox of justifying the most unjustifiable in the eyes of the moderns, that is, waging war against the great pacifier, the state. In Europe, this taboo was broken as late as 1949, when in the wake of unprecedented historical events the new German constitution was approved with an explicit provision for the right to resist.

Most modern natural lawyers merely insisted that recourse should be had to common sense as a means to determine if tyranny was 'unbearable'. Towards the final stages of the natural law tradition, with one eye to the classical doctrines and the other to the American revolutionary experience, Kant would still argue in his early lectures on natural law that whereas it might be justifiable for a people to rise up against the tyrant in extreme circumstances, the tyrant could not be blamed for repressing the upheavals by force.[76] In principle, the ruler was always right in crushing a revolt because his fundamental duty was to secure the country's peace and tranquillity. Rebels, instead, were deemed to act not only illegally with respect to positive law but also unjustly under the law of nature, as resistance was a practice that could not be generalised if social order was ever to be preserved. Nevertheless, Kant admitted that there might arise cases where insurgency proved morally legitimate although it infringed upon both positive law and strict natural law. This only history could tell. If any

74 Thomas Hobbes, *Leviathan* (first published 1651, Richard Tuck ed, CUP, 1991); Georg Wilhelm Friedrich Hegel, *Grundlinien der Philosophie des Rechts, oder Naturrecht und Staatswissenschaft im Grundrisse* (first published 1821, Johannes Hoffmeister ed, Hamburg, Meiner, 1955).

75 Jesse Reeves, 'The Influence of the Law of Nations Upon International Law in the United States' (1909) 3 *American Journal of International Law* 547.

76 Immanuel Kant, *Naturrecht Feyerabend* (lectures delivered 1784) in Immanuel Kant, *Gesammelte Schriften* (Gerhard Lehmann ed, Berlin, Deutsche Akademie der Wissenschaften, 1979) 1317, 1391–1392.

attempts to resistance and revolution revealed themselves to be a posteriori contributors to a nation's political progress and to humanity's general advancement, then, and solely then, those events could be supposed to have been legitimate.[77] Far from clarifying the issue, this position left it to the judgement of posterity, shifting the plane of the discourse from law to the philosophy of history.

In his later political essay on the *Perpetual Peace*, looking at the revolution going on in France, Kant put the question of resistance in more concrete terms. In the fifth preliminary article, where he stated the principle that 'no state shall by force interfere with either the constitution or government of another state', he also remarked that 'very different would it be, if a revolution should divide a state into two parts, each of which should pretend to be the whole'.[78] In this case, '[t]o lend assistance to one of the parties cannot then be esteemed an interference with the government, it being then in a state of anarchy.'[79] Kant thus argued that civil war – as a confrontation between two entirely independent entities, as distinct from mere sedition – could be assimilated with international conflict lawful on both sides. This idea was to fit well with the realist conception of the law of nations that Kant would soon bring forward in his legal masterpiece, the *Science of Right*.[80]

Kant was not responsible for a 'Copernican revolution' of the law of nations. He did deserve credit for articulating an idealist and yet rational view of international relations, but he pulled back to more traditional positions after seeing that the French Revolution was actually not the great civilising endeavour that he and many others hoped for. The man who had to be credited (or criticised, depending of the viewpoint) for a pragmatic approach to the law of nations was Vattel, whose work Kant belittled in the *Perpetual Peace* but almost plagiarised in the later *Science of Right*.[81]

Actually, in the *Perpetual Peace* Kant already relied on the Vattelian doctrine, despite the irony of his criticism of it. The fifth preliminary article of

---

[77] Immanuel Kant, *Idee zu einer allgemeinen Geschichte in weltbürgerlicher Absicht* (first published 1784, Wilhelm Weischedel ed, *Kants Werke*, vol 11, Frankfurt am Main, Suhrkamp, 1977) 31–50.

[78] Immanuel Kant, *Zum ewigen Frieden* (first published 1795, Wilhelm Weischedel ed, Frankfurt am Main, Suhrkamp, 1977) Fifth Preliminary Article.

[79] Ibid.

[80] Immanuel Kant, *Rechtslehre* (first published 1797, Wilhelm Weischedel ed, *Kants Werke*, vol 8, Frankfurt am Main, Suhrkamp, 1977) §§ 53 ff.

[81] Kant, *Zum ewigen Frieden*, Second Definitive Article.

the *Perpetual Peace* represented a hymn to pragmatism and, above all, a plain copy of Vattel's opinion on civil war – a major turning point in international legal doctrine. Most pre-Vattelian writers, and lately Wolff, had believed that the justice of the cause was the casting criterion in deciding whether an internal conflict qualified as mere sedition or as civil war,[82] and hence whether insurgents ought to be treated as ordinary criminals or lawful combatants. This position simply reiterated the just war paradigm and did not offer any solution to settle the problem of the right of resistance in practice. On the other hand, absolutist thinkers like Bodin and Ayala obliterated the substantial 'justice of the cause' only to insist on the legitimacy of the ruler and systematically privilege order over freedom. By aprioristically discriminating against rebels, these authors did not seem to be realists either. Their position might be effective in cases of mere sedition, but not necessarily in the case of civil war proper, when a country was neatly split and the ruler was no longer able to grant general security and safety.

It is no wonder that Bodin's and Ayala's paradigms, based on an abstract absolutisation of 'legitimate' sovereign power, was never effective in pacifying countries plagued by internal infighting. Their absolutist doctrine was sometimes translated into practice, but only in the long term. This means that the doctrine did not contribute to bringing civil war itself to an end in the first place – which was the main concern of these writers: in France, the Wars of Religion ended with a compromise sanctioned by the Edict of Nantes of 1598 and the power of the French monarchy was consolidated only later, by Richelieu and Louis XIV; in the Low Countries, the United Provinces managed to assert their independence from Spain to the great displeasure of royalists like Ayala; in Britain, the English Civil War led to the Commonwealth and the Protectorate, while the monarchy was first restored in 1660, and this did not occur without a radical transformation in the relationship between the King and Parliament. On all of these occasions, civil war could have ended either way – so the issue of political legitimacy was not as clear as Bodin and Ayala wished it to be – and the absolutisation of royal power did not always prove to be the best solution for achieving domestic tranquillity. This illustrates much about the idealistic character of Bodin's and Ayala's conception of civil war as centred on the preservation of the *status quo*.

82 Christian Wolff, *Jus gentium methodo scientifica pertractatum* (first published 1749, Joseph H Drake trans, Oxford, Clarendon 1934) VIII, § 1012.

Hobbes on Tyrants and Rebels as Equal Warring Parties

Hobbes literally revolutionised the concept of civil war. In opposition to Bodin and Ayala, Hobbes claimed that political legitimacy does not derive from dynastic legitimacy—and not even from the ruler's respect of customs, privileges, and fundamental laws—but from the ruler's capability of providing protection.

> The obligation of subjects to the sovereign is understood to last as long, and no longer, than the power lasteth by which he is able to protect them. For the right men have by nature to protect themselves, when none else can protect them, can by no covenant be relinquished.[83]

Hobbes transferred the classical principle of private self-defence to the domain of public law, with enormous consequences for the modern doctrine of the right of resistance.[84] If the ruler was not able to provide protection, the social pact became void, the state of nature resumed, and the subjects were permitted to resist the ruler as if against an enemy with whom they were at war. Here the first central idea by which Hobbes innovated the doctrine—compared to the medieval doctrine on resistance and to its later elaborations by Calvinist monarchomachs—was that political obligation may decay as a result of the sovereign's failure to provide security, not as a result of his failure to abide by divine law and broad natural law principles, or by the country's customs and constitution. The second fundamental point was that a sovereign failure to provide security as such resuscitated the state of nature, and this resuscitation represented an essential logical condition for the right of resistance to arise. No right of resistance was conceivable in the civil state. Actually, for Hobbes there existed no right of resistance as such—and indeed he avoided this term—but instead only an unlimited right that individuals may exert in the state of nature. Hobbes' construction here became a tenet of modern contractualism. Although later writers like Locke, Vattel and Kant would criticise Hobbes for characterising the state of nature as nearly lawless, they all reasserted his idea that the right of resistance was possible only after the state of nature had been resumed, notably as a result of a sovereign's misconduct.[85] The resulting civil war was an exceptional condition—a

[83] Hobbes, *Leviathan*, XXI, 21.

[84] For an analysis of the right of resistance in Hobbes' writings, see Susanne Sreedhar, *Hobbes on Resistance: Defying the Leviathan* (CUP, 2010).

[85] John Locke, *Two Treatises of Government* (first published 1690, Peter Laslett ed, CUP, 1988) XVIII, 205; *DG*, I, 4, § 51; Kant, *Naturrecht Feyerabend*, 1374.

condition of war—in which tyrant and rebels confronted each other as enemies. Civil war radically overturned the existing legal and political order, as there was no middle way between the civil state and the state of nature. On this point, Hobbes, Locke, Vattel, and Kant moved away from the medieval doctrine of resistance. Bartolus indeed assumed that resistance against the tyrant – not unlike a reprisal or a just war waged by a vassal against the overlord – was a normal act taking place within a political and legal order that remained essentially immutable.[86] Modern contractualists innovated by rejecting this view. The revolutionary potential of modern contractualist theories lay exactly in the radical distinction between the civil state as a normal state, and the state of nature as an exceptional state.

Hobbes' idea that upon the resumption of the state of nature all parties to a civil war confronted each other as enemies holding an equal 'right to everything' was key to obliterating the Roman law dichotomy enemy *versus* criminal, which royalists Bodin and Ayala had used to criminalise rebels.[87] Hobbes maintained that a ruler incapable of granting social peace forfeited his political legitimacy; hence such ruler's labelling of rebels as criminals had no legal effects. This ruler might well treat the rebels as ordinary criminals in an attempt to regain total control of the country, but the rebels might in turn pursue their own struggle to topple him, for in the state of nature self-preservation represents the only standard for action and '[t]he notions of right and wrong, justice and injustice, have there no place.'[88]

It is not surprising that, despite the ruler's failure to provide protection, Hobbes saw no difficulty in attributing to him the licence to carry on the struggle against the rebels. Hobbes postulated that rebels, regardless of their number, could never be regarded as the primeval possessors of sovereignty who might depose the ruler at their discretion. Once the first social covenant had been (supposedly) stipulated, the people could not regain their original rights. Conversely, the people without a ruler were deemed a mere multitude, a motley crowd of individuals who had nothing in common but their existence in the state of nature. This individualist and nominalist stance clearly differentiated Hobbes from organicist

86 Quaglioni, *Politica e diritto*, 37.

87 Hobbes, *Leviathan*, XIV, 4. Unlike Ayala, though, Bodin did not use the dichotomy criminal *versus* enemy to disqualify foreign political entities, like the Barbary Republics, whose sovereignty and lawful belligerency he acknowledged. See above, 50–4.

88 Hobbes, *Leviathan*, XIII, 13.

theorists of popular sovereignty like Althusius and Rousseau. The two latter thinkers assumed sovereignty to be primordially vested in the people as a whole, and to be merely delegated to the ruler, which implied that in the case of tyranny the ruler turned into a criminal while the subjects resumed sovereignty.[89] While Althusius and later Rousseau maintained that in cases of internal infighting justice always lay with the people, which they metaphysically depicted as inherently superior to the ruler, Hobbes claimed that internal infighting generated a state of nature in which no criterion of justice existed anymore, hence ruler and subjects became enemies on a footing of equality. Ruler and subjects might well battle to death but could not disqualify each other as criminals proper.

Hobbes' proposition that tyrant and subjects confronted each other as enemies, not as criminals, was profoundly innovative, yet it did not originate from a humanitarian spirit, and nor could it contribute to the moderation of hostilities. Hobbes posited that the state of nature was one of nearly unrestrained licence, as exemplified by the English Civil War and the Thirty Years' War. This conception of the state of nature was radically different from Vattel's later description of the condition of international freedom between states, regulated by civilised manners and customs of warfare. For Vattel, the equality of belligerents implied a moderation of hostilities. For Hobbes, instead, the fact that tyrant and rebels might regard each other as equal parties did not prevent them from waging total war to annihilate each other. Analogously, when Pufendorf, relying on the Hobbesian paradigm of political enmity, declared the Barbary corsairs to be public enemies proper, and not pirates, he did not mean that they should therefore be treated more gently. Common to Hobbes and Pufendorf was the conviction that war was governed by strict natural law only, which elicited the Hobbesian 'right to everything' and the Pufendorfian just enemy's 'unlimited right'. In their view, belligerents' natural freedom could not be restrained by customs, treaties, or politesse.

Vattel's View of Civil War as a Matter of Effectiveness

Vattel deserved credit for thinking Hobbes' premises through to their ultimate consequences in a humanitarian perspective during the age of polished warfare. Vattel contended that if warring parties viewed each other

---

[89] Johannes Althusius, *Politica methodice digesta* (first published 1603, Frederick S Carney ed, Boston, Beacon, 1964) XXXVIII; Rousseau, *Contrat social*, ch I, § 7.

as legal enemies, they should accordingly observe the customs of war while fighting. He stipulated that this held true in international armed conflict as well as internal ones, as long as the latter qualified as civil war proper.

To define civil war, Vattel dropped the traditional arguments based on political legitimacy and moral justice, and instead relied on the Hobbesian anti-essentialist paradigm and on the political common sense of his days. Vattel described civil war as a state of affairs in which a faction was militarily strong enough to oppose government troops and take control over part of the country's territory. By this fact alone, that faction could be considered as a sovereign entity.

> A civil war breaks the bonds of society and government, or, at least, suspends their force and effect: it produces in the nation two independent parties, who consider each other as enemies, and acknowledge no common judge.[90]

With the underpinning of Hobbes' political theory, Vattel became the first international lawyer to define civil war as a pure matter of effectiveness, regardless of substantial justice and dynastic legitimacy. The progressive abandonment of discriminating attitudes towards the public enemy represented the fundamental aim of Vattel's argumentation. He was convinced that the principles of the 'war in due form' governing international conflict should also apply to internal strife and regulate the relations between all disputing parties, including foreign powers if they were involved. With regard to the *ius in bello*, there ought to be no difference between the international and domestic levels. Both regulars and irregulars should regard each other as lawful enemies and renounce all conduct which was contrary to the laws of war, such as pillaging, mistreating prisoners and civilians, breaking capitulations and employing improper weapons. Legal restraints also extended to the *ius post bellum*. If the rebellion was crushed, Vattel warmly advised sovereigns to be clement and concede amnesty to insurgents for the sake of national reconciliation and tranquillity. If, on the contrary, the rebellion was successful and resulted in a regime change, Vattel recommended, for the same reason, that rebels not take vengeance on the former ruler and restrict themselves only to depriving him of power.[91]

---

90 *DG*, III, 18, § 292.
91 Ibid I, 4, § 54.

Humanity, Security, and the Right of Intervention

When civil war was understood as a 'war in due form', foreign powers also had particular rights and duties mostly independent of the justice of the cause. Once civil war broke out, these powers should first limit themselves to offering diplomatic mediation, and abstain from any military or economic intervention in favour of any of the parties.[92] However, if diplomatic efforts revealed themselves to be ineffective, as normally happened, foreign powers were permitted to take part in hostilities either on behalf of their official allies, if formal agreements had been stipulated to this effect beforehand, or, lacking this framework, on behalf of the factions whose cause they held to be the more founded. As for allies, Vattel specified that they might tacitly or expressly reserve the right to withdraw support if entering the conflict would excessively jeopardise their own safety, or if their allies waged a manifestly unjust war.[93] The decision to participate in hostilities should be made with considerations not only for international obligations, but also, and more importantly, national interest.

Yet Vattel stressed that foreign powers' actions based on these considerations should never encroach upon a nation's right to choose its own destiny. Thus, foreign powers were not allowed to meddle in a civil war to assist a monarch who had been dethroned with the approval, whether tacit or express, of the greater majority of the subjects. Foreign governments were authorised to support a ruler against his people in doubtful cases only, when it was hard to distinguish between sovereigns and tyrants, patriots and rebels. Vattel contended that it was particularly in these circumstances that 'the *voluntary* law of nations reigns among states' and all parties 'engage in a formal war'.[94] When either party carried on a 'manifestly' just war, the voluntary law of nations lapsed, and foreign powers were no longer allowed to align themselves with the unjust enemy.

This was especially the case where a tyrant violated the law of nature and nations to such an extent that he turned into a 'monster' and enemy of mankind. In this event, foreign powers were authorised to come to the rescue of the oppressed people and liberate it from a tyrannical ruler who might rightfully be killed like a 'savage beast'.

> As to those monsters who, under the title of sovereigns, render themselves the scourges and horror of the human race, they are savage beasts, whom

[92] Ibid III, 18, § 296; Wolff, *Jus gentium*, II, § 258.
[93] *DG*, III, 6, §§ 85–87.
[94] Ibid II, 12, § 196.

> every brave man may justly exterminate from the face of the earth. All antiquity has praised Hercules for delivering the world from an Antæs, a Busiris, and a Diomede.[95]

Because such a tyrant guilty of horrendous crimes infringed upon the 'rights of humanity' at large, foreign powers had the right to intervene against him, even in the absence of the oppressed population's express consent, if the failure to protest was motivated by fear of repression.[96] Here, the casting criterion to authorise intervention was not consent, nor the opinion of the majority, but the moral duty on all nations to repress 'manifest' and egregious violations of the law of nature and nations. If the account of civil war and the right of intervention as based on effectiveness might be valid in doubtful instances, when the voluntary law of nations 'reigned', this was no longer the case when tyrants qualified as enemies of mankind.

A paradigmatic case in which foreign nations were permitted to rescue a people tyrannised by an enemy of mankind was represented by religious persecution. In this event, foreign states had a strong interest in intervening to repress a fanatical prince who, as well as tyrannising his subjects, might pose a major threat to international security and tranquillity.

> When a religion is persecuted in one country ... to an intolerable excess ... it becomes a case of manifest tyranny, in opposition to which all nations are allowed to assist an unhappy people. A regard to their own safety may also authorise them to undertake the defence of the persecuted sufferers. ... All distinctions of states and nations are to be disregarded, when there is question of forming a coalition against a set of madmen who would exterminate all those that do not implicitly receive their doctrines.[97]

Here Vattel referred to the tyrannical conduct of a famous 'King of France', Louis XIV, guilty of persecuting the Huguenot minority in his country. Vattel described the Sun King as a 'mad' and fanatical tyrant and the coalition's wars against the King as morally laudable endeavours. This humanitarian ideal had been a classical leitmotif of theories of the right of resistance since the *Vindiciae*. Yet Vattel maintained that foreign powers were allowed to take action against a tyrannical persecutor not only to rescue an oppressed people, but 'also', and actually more decisively, to

95 Ibid II, 4, § 56.

96 Vattel referred to the enemy of mankind literally violating the 'rights of humanity' at *DG*, III, 8, § 158.

97 Ibid II, 5, § 62.

prevent religious strife from spilling over, with 'a regard to their own safety'.[98] Ultimately, even the humanitarian motivation turned out to be a utilitarian one, since for him every human action was determined by self-interest, and 'all motivation comes down, in the end, to utility'.[99] While Vattel, in his treatment of the right of intervention, still indulged in traditional humanitarian rhetoric, his main theses were not grounded on humanitarian arguments but on the principles of utility and security. Vattel's utilitarian perspective on the right of intervention, like his conception of civil war as a matter of effectiveness, signalled a major paradigm shift away from the just war theory and towards a 'modern' doctrine of the law of nations.

---

[98] Ibid.

[99] Emer de Vattel, 'Essai sur le fondement du droit naturel' in Emer de Vattel, *Pièces diverses, avec quelques lettres de morale et d'amusemens* (Paris, 1746) § 21, reprinted in Emer de Vattel, *Droit des gens* (Paul Pradier Fodéré ed, Paris, 1863) 1–32. This utilitarian position was close to that of Jean-Jacques Burlamaqui, *Principes du droit naturel* (Geneva, 1747) pt I, ch 5, § 4; pt II, bk 4, § 10.

CONCLUSION

Collective Security and the Necessity of International Law Enforcement

Vattel laid down his enemy of mankind theory to assert the principle that international law needs some form of enforcement to respond to international crimes if international law itself is to be preserved. This idea was shelved in the nineteenth century (except when enforcement targeted non-state actors such as pirates and slave-traders), but has been reaffirmed in the past one hundred years. Indeed, Vattel's advocacy for the repression of heinous international crimes has, directly or indirectly through the medium of later publicists familiar with it, contributed to the shaping of a modern doctrine of *jus cogens*, war crimes and crimes against humanity, and to the doctrine of military intervention for humanitarian purposes.[1] Today, the issue of enforcement is still felt with a sense of urgency, especially as concern grows over the widespread lack of compliance with international humanitarian law worldwide.[2] In addition, the paradigm that compliance with international law must be achieved through enforcement measures has recently found additional applications outside international criminal law, in areas such as international environmental law and, more problematically, in the sanction mechanisms of the IMF and WTO.[3] While the Vattelian doctrine had no impact on the latter developments, reading it today is still helpful for developing an understanding about which historical and doctrinal circumstances contributed to the issue of enforcement in international law, and for analysing the reasons why this issue persists in international legal discourse.

---

[1] Robert Kolb, 'La validité du modèle de Vattel après 1945' in Yves Sandoz (ed), *Réflexions sur l'impact, le rayonnement et l'actualité du 'Droit des gens' d'Emer de Vattel* (Brussels, Bruylant, 2010) 137.

[2] International Committee of the Red Cross, *Report on Strenghtening Legal Protection for Victims of Armed Conflicts* (2011) 12–13 <http://www.icrc.org/eng/resources/documents/report/31-international-conference-strengthening-ihl-report-2011-10-31.htm>.

[3] Anne Orford, 'Trade, Human Rights and the Economy of Sacrifice' in Anne Orford (ed), *International Law and its Others* (CUP, 2006) 156; Karen N Scott, 'Non-Compliance Procedures and Dispute Resolution Mechanisms under International Environmental Agreements' in Duncan French (ed), *International Law and Dispute Settlement. New Procedures and Techniques* (Oxford and Portland, OR, Hart, 2010) 225.

The modernity of Vattel's approach is particularly evident in his focus on security as the ground of international law enforcement. His collective security theory was reasserted by later writers and was integrated in the traditional doctrine of the balance of power, with the caveat, however, that the doctrine of the balance must be deemed a political doctrine, not a legal one – a distinction that Vattel had rejected as he equated utility with justice. In the aftermath of the two World Wars, the collective security theory gained central importance because it underpinned both the establishment of collective security mechanisms within the League of Nations, and later the United Nations, and the creation of international human rights law. Publicists in the second half of the twentieth century emphasised the necessity of enforcing a minimum level of public order in the domestic sphere as well as a minimum world public order at the international level, to be achieved, if necessary, through economic sanctions and the use of force, and especially to prevent conflicts which might involve the deployment of weapons of mass destruction.[4] The idea of collective security and a minimum world public order, either unsuccessfully implemented or not implemented at all in the Cold War era, forcefully re-emerged in the doctrines of humanitarian intervention in the 1990s, and later the responsibility to protect from the 2000s onwards, accompanied by theories calling on 'well-ordered' nations to liberate the world from rogue states.[5]

The scarce successes and the legitimacy issues which plague most contemporary attempts to enforce international law and collective security measures are hardly surprising. Vattel's own theory was from the outset affected by severe limitations in terms of feasibility and legitimacy. He claimed that all nations were necessarily concerned about 'manifest' heinous international crimes, and he assumed that a coalition of the willing would build up spontaneously in the face of a common threat. Yet this never happened in Vattel's lifetime and will probably never happen. In the eighteenth century all states, when threatened, simply secured the most convenient alliances and in doing so caused the international community to split up into two compact fronts, both claiming to be waging a war in self-defence or to defend fundamental rights. Vattel was confident that the

4 Myres S McDougal, *Law and Minimum World Public Order* (Yale University Press, 1961) 59–96.

5 A paradigmatic theory of international 'decency' *versus* outlawry was advanced by John Rawls, *The Law of Peoples* (Harvard University Press, 1999). For a critical view on the doctrine of humanitarian warfare, see Anne Orford, *Reading Humanitarian Intervention. Human Rights and the Use of Force in International Law* (CUP, 2003).

most powerful 'polished' nations would finally join in a common struggle against the universal enemy for the sake of civilisation, but this confidence in the civilising mission of the great powers, already questionable then, has long gone.

Re-reading Vattel's collective security doctrine illuminates how little the structure of international law has changed since 1758. Far from breaking with the former paradigm of world order based on the balance of power and the Concert of Europe, the institutionalisation of collective security in the twentieth century simply established a new and no less problematic international equilibrium based on the legalised, if mildly constrained, hegemony of the great powers.[6] This is a revised version of the eighteenth and nineteenth centuries pentarchy and does not alter the fundamentally hegemonic structure of international law. Vattel was among the apologists for this international order, and his enemy of mankind theory constituted a tool to universalise and enforce it. Though the actors and the language of power change, moving beyond state boundaries, hegemonic politics and the balance of power still appear as the dominant principles shaping international law and order and determining what counts as criminal behaviour and deserves punishment.

Pluralism, Universality, and Natural Law

As Vattel abandoned the pluralist tradition of the laws of war to criminalise Barbary warfare, he asserted the idea that European international law constituted a standard of civilisation.[7] This idea supported his broader project of rationalising, universalising, and enforcing Europe's international law. Vattel's standard of civilization was also reaffirmed in later decades, when the hypothesis of a law of nations embracing all humanity had already gone out of favour. His rhetoric of civilisation and anti-piracy struggle was taken up by nineteenth century writers, particularly those seeking justifications for the United States' Barbary Wars and for France's colonial adventure in North Africa.[8] In rejecting the traditional tolerant

---

[6] Gerry Simpson, *Great Powers and Outlaw States. Unequal Sovereigns in the International Legal Order* (CUP, 2004) 193.

[7] This expression is especially borrowed from Gerrit W Gong, *The Standard of "Civilisation" in International Society* (Oxford, Clarendon, 1984).

[8] Ann Thomson, *Barbary and Enlightenment* (Leiden, Brill, 1987) 123 ff.

paradigm to promote the enforcement of the European law of nations as a rational and universal law, Vattel furthered an authoritarian and influential idea of civilisation and of international law and order.

Vattel's universalist and anti-pluralist argument against Barbary gives evidence of the key function of natural law in his system, especially in the repression of international crimes. Natural law both furnished good reasons (or rather pretexts) to outlaw North African privateering and accorded the corsairs' opponents a broad licence to repress them. The latter point derived from Vattel's assumption that when international security was threatened by an enemy of mankind and the voluntary law of nations was at risk or powerless to address the threat, strict natural law was concretely applicable and might supersede the voluntary law of nations itself. Vattel took this stance in analogy to former natural law theories, notably those of Hobbes and Locke, positing that natural law came into effect again anytime that positive laws ceased to fulfil their function of protecting the individuals to whom they applied.[9] Hobbes and Locke were especially thinking of the case of tyranny, in which the subjects of the tyrant (at least if threatened by death, Hobbes required) were deemed to re-enter the state of nature and re-acquire their primeval right to self-defence. Basing his theory on the domestic analogy, Vattel maintained that in a state of international emergency provoked by an enemy of mankind trampling upon the voluntary law of nations, the recourse to natural law eliciting all nations' right to collective self-defence became imperative to obtain a minimum level of international security. This in turn was essential to re-establish the laws of war and the voluntary law of nations as the normal legal framework, which returned once the common threat had been repelled.

Vattel's argument that natural law must uphold a key role in international relations soon disappeared from textbooks, but natural law in fact crept into nineteenth century 'positivist' and crypto-naturalist doctrines.[10] Naturalist argumentations, while often indirectly formulated, shaped—as they still shape—the understanding and the vocabulary of sovereign freedom and equality, self-defence, crimes against humanity, human rights, and humanitarian intervention. In addition, the Vattelian idea that

9 Thomas Hobbes, *Leviathan* (first published 1651, Richard Tuck ed, CUP, 1991) XXI, 21; John Locke, *Two Treatises of Government* (first published 1690, Peter Laslett ed, CUP, 1988) Second Treatise, XVIII, 205.

10 Martti Koskenniemi, 'Miserable Comforters. International Relations as New Natural Law' (2009) 15 (3) *European Journal of International Relations* 395, 403.

the state of emergency, be it domestic or international, brings about exceptional circumstances under which the normal legal framework no longer applies has been frequently reasserted throughout the modern age and can still be seen at work in contemporary debates on 'illegal enemy combatants' or 'illegal immigrants'. To be sure, Vattel, unlike some contemporary theorists, argued that the state of exception is not normless but simply governed by an alternative normativity.[11] While the prescriptions of natural law as regards the conduct of war remained fairly indefinite when compared to the voluntary law of nations, they still provided a normative framework. Moreover, the natural obligations that applied to the state of emergency were just as compulsory as the voluntary or positive law. They belonged to strict and enforceable natural law (*ius naturale stricte dictum*) as opposed to the non-enforceable prescriptions of morals (*ius naturale late dictum*).[12] In this regard, there remains a considerable difference between the early-modern (or medieval, for that matter) concept of exception as a state regulated by natural law and the contemporary notion of exception as a normative vacuum.

The Two-Tiered Approach to International Law Enforcement

The main target of Vattel's enemy of mankind theory were not North-African corsairs, but deviant European sovereigns, whom Vattel regarded as truly capable of jeopardising international order. Nonetheless, he demanded that uncivilised international criminals such as the Barbary corsairs and the Tartars be repressed more severely than the civilised and even exterminated if necessary. The unequal treatment of civilised and uncivilised illustrated that as much as the Vattelian theory of international law enforcement was grounded on enlightened criminal law principles, it turned out to possess a hegemonic and oppressive character.

---

[11] Carl Schmitt, *Politische Theologie* (first published 1922, Berlin, Duncker & Humblot, 1970) 13 ff; Giorgio Agamben, *Homo sacer. Il potere sovrano e la nuda vita* (Turin, Einaudi, 1995) 190; Giorgio Agamben, *Stato di eccezione* (Turin, Bollati Boringhieri, 2003) 93. Regarding contemporary international terrorism and the alleged necessity of applying extraordinary measures to counter it, both at the domestic and international level, Philip Bobbitt has advanced a milder version of legal exceptionalism arguing that the goal of these measures 'is in fact the *preservation* of the rule of law': Philip Bobbitt, *Terror and Consent. The Wars for the Twenty-First Century* (New York, Anchor, 2009) 366 (emphasis in original). This argument reasserts Vattel's position on the long-term preservation of the laws of war.

[12] Immanuel Kant, *Naturrecht Feyerabend* (lectures delivered 1784) in Immanuel Kant, *Gesammelte Schriften* (Gerhard Lehmann ed, Berlin, Deutsche Akademie der Wissenschaften, 1979) 1317, 1374.

While nineteenth century publicists might agree with Vattel on the harsh treatment of the barbarians, they entirely rejected his statement that European sovereigns could be criminalised. Yet the statement became fashionable again from the first half of the twentieth century. At that stage, the emergence of total warfare required the abandonment of the unrestrained *ius ad bellum* and recommended a more severe attitude towards war crimes and, later, towards state-sponsored human rights violations as well, be they committed against foreigners or nationals. In particular, developments in international criminal law – from the incrimination of German Emperor William II at Versailles through to the trials of heads of state like Augusto Pinochet and Slobodan Milošević, and the creation of the International Criminal Court – have sanctioned Vattel's opinion that even sovereigns can be liable for international crimes.[13]

It is far from clear whether such trials, often open to criticism as an expression of political interests or victor's justice, represent a satisfactory option for dealing with war crimes and human rights abuses.[14] This comes as no surprise, as some of the biases that affect international justice today have already affected former conceptions of international law enforcement in the past, Vattel's included. Though the actors of international politics and their relative strengths may change, the privileged status of the great powers and their leaders' immunity from an international justice that they themselves impose on others remain unaltered. While Vattel's discriminatory rhetoric against the uncivilised has now become politically incorrect, his two-tiered approach to the repression of international crimes still constitutes a structural feature of international law.

---

[13] Because Vattel strongly criticised any institutionalisation of international law, he can hardly be seen as a theorist justifying the establishment of permanent international tribunals. Yet the principles underpinning such tribunals still largely resonate with his arguments. Significantly for current debates, Vattel insisted that repressive action should be taken to punish not occasional violations of the law of nations, but only manifest and recurrent ones (*DG*, II, 5, § 70) – an idea later reasserted in the definition of crimes against humanity. A further Vattelian argument that still permeates today's doctrine is that the international community is called on to repress crimes committed by sovereigns not only against foreigners but also against their own subjects, which entailed the right of intervention for humanitarian purposes.

[14] Scholarship has pointed out that these trials do not fully meet the ends of retribution and satisfaction for the victims, nor (which was Vattel's concern) of preventing further offences in terms of special and general deterrence. Nor, thus far, do they seem successfully to exert the broader pedagogic function of building and communicating narratives of justice that meet the expectations of suffering local populations. See Mark A Drumbl, *Atrocity, Punishment, and International Law* (CUP, 2007) 173–179.

The Return of the Enemy of Mankind?

The enemy of mankind concept has long been neglected by legal scholarship as a result of the virtual disappearance of the enemy of mankind par excellence – the pirate – from the international arena during the nineteenth and twentieth centuries.[15] However, in the past few years the concept has become fashionable again, both among lawyers discussing the recent revival of piracy, and also among a few authors – sometimes in the fields of literary critique and security studies – eager to depict early-modern piracy as a precedent for today's international terrorism.[16] In their search for precedents, some of these latter scholars have placed under the category of enemy of mankind not only pirates, but a number of other offenders and antagonists in modern history, such as revolutionaries, anarchists, and even ordinary criminals.[17] While this approach might be informative from the viewpoint of cultural and literary history – because it is true that all of these offenders were labelled as enemies of mankind at some point – it is less relevant legally. These authors present each of these offender types as yet another instance of the 'absolute enemy' and the discriminated against, and thereby come to generic conclusions that do not throw light upon the legal ramifications of the enemy of mankind concept itself, particularly in international legal doctrine. This book has attempted to fill this gap in contemporary scholarship by focusing on Vattel's doctrine, which constituted a turning point in the elaboration of a modern notion of the enemy of mankind.

By investigating the enemy of mankind theory, the book has drawn attention to a topic traditionally neglected also by commentators on

[15] Thus, the doctrine of piracy has often been defined as 'obsolete' or 'obsolescent': DHN Johnson, 'Piracy in Modern International Law' (1957) 43 *Transactions of the Grotius Society* 63. From the mid-nineteenth century onwards, the concept of piracy has been less relevant for cases of sea-robbery proper than for situations of civil war in which insurgents, as well as foreign citizens assisting them, were labelled as pirates by the government. See, for instance, Raoul Genet, 'La qualification de "pirates" et le dilemme de la guerre civile' (1937) 3 *Revue internationale du droit des gens* 12; Hersch Lauterpacht, 'Insurrection et piraterie' (1939) 46 *Revue générale de droit international public* 513; Carl Schmitt, 'The Concept of Piracy' (2011) 2 *Humanity* 1, 27 (1st edn 'Der Begriff der Piraterie' (1937) 6–7 *Völkerbund und Völkerrecht* 351).

[16] Daniel Heller-Roazen, *The Enemy of All* (New York, Zone Books, 2009); Bobbitt, *Terror and Consent*, 133; Michael Kempe and Oliver Gänswein, 'Die Rückkehr der Universalfeinde' (2010) 32 *Zeitschrift für Neuere Rechtsgeschichte* 2, 91–106. The analogy between piracy and terrorism has rightly been contested by several legal scholars. See, for instance, Eugene Kontorovich, 'The Piracy Analogy' (2004) 45 *Harvard International Law Journal* 183.

[17] Isaac Land (ed) *Enemies of Humanity. The Nineteenth-Century War on Terrorism* (Basingstoke, Palgrave Macmillan, 2008).

Vattel's work. The few scholars mentioning the theory have tended to understate it as a purely rhetorical exercise in Vattel's state-centred international legal system, or have misrepresented it as a move back to the just war doctrine.[18] Those dismissing the enemy of mankind theory as irrelevant have lost sight of the importance of international law enforcement for Vattel. They have depicted him as an advocate of an unrestrained *ius ad bellum*, who is at most concerned with the balance of power.[19] On the other hand, those characterising Vattel's enemy of mankind theory as a mere re-elaboration of the just war doctrine have failed to see that his aim was to justify collective security measures, not retribution against the wrongdoer or assistance to victims of aggression.

In fact, international law enforcement constituted one of Vattel's key concerns and a major point of originality in his work. International law enforcement represented a necessary condition for preserving a minimum level of collective security and tranquillity, without which sovereign 'rights' themselves, including the *ius ad bellum*, would become meaningless. That is why Vattel did not content himself with calling on sovereigns to preserve the balance of power, but put forward a broader theory of international law enforcement demanding the repression of all forms of misconduct detrimental to the 'common security and well-being of nations'.

Vattel's enemy of mankind theory constituted a 'modern' and 'enlightened' international legal project, grounded on the notions of security and utility. At the same time, it was a project deeply rooted in the Western legal and philosophical tradition. In stating that international law had to be enforced for the sake of collective security and utility, Vattel consciously reasserted Cicero's equation of *iustitia* and *utilitas*. For Vattel, as well as for Cicero, the ultimate essence of law was to preserve the basic conditions without which human society would be impossible, or unthinkable. This utilitarian conception of law—classical, modern, and anti-medieval—lay at the basis of Vattel's theory of international law enforcement.

---

18 Simone Zurbuchen, 'Vattel's *Law of Nations* and Just War Theory' (2009) 35 *History of European Ideas* 408; Gabriella Silvestrini, 'Justice, War, and Inequality. The Unjust Aggressor and the Enemy of the Human Race in Vattel's Theory of the Law of Nations' (2010) 31 *Grotiana* 44; Gabriella Silvestrini, 'Vattel, Rousseau et la question de la justice de la guerre' in Vincent Chetail and Peter Haggenmacher (eds), *Vattel's International Law in a XXIst Century Perspective* (Leiden – Boston, Nijhoff, 2011) 110.

19 This was Carl Schmitt's view in *The Nomos of the Earth* (1st published 1950, New York, Telos, 2003) 165–168.

Because it describes Vattel's enemy of mankind theory as a 'modern' doctrinal and political project, the book questions Ian Hunter's description of the *Droit des gens* as a 'diplomatic casuistry' as opposed to a 'theory of international law'.[20] In this respect, the book comes closer to the position of Emmanuelle Jouannet, who presents the *Droit des gens* as a theory of 'classical' (meaning modern) international law. However, while Jouannet focuses on Vattel as a theorist of sovereignty and the voluntary law of nations, this book focuses on another aspect of Vattel's thought. It investigates the conditions for sovereignty and the voluntary law of nations to be preserved as expressions of European civilisation, and for preventing the international society from plunging back into a barbaric condition.

To make his enemy of mankind theory a truly 'Enlightened' one, Vattel only lacked an appropriate philosophy of history. It was Kant who took this task upon himself. He argued that the observance of international law is required not only to attain 'future' security, but also for the sake of a 'perpetual' peace. Thus, in his Sixth Article for Perpetual Peace, Kant demanded that belligerents abstain from heinous hostile acts that would make peace after war unachievable, and a general and perpetual peace utopian.[21] Kant made the same move in the *Rechtslehre*, in which he defined the 'unjust enemy' as a belligerent who commit acts which, if universalised, would make peace impossible and 'perpetuate the state of nature' among nations.[22] Whereas Vattel accepted the international state of nature as an ineliminable fact and only sought to regulate it, Kant attempted to overcome it, at least in the hypothetical terms of a philosophy of history, and in the non-enforceable terms of morals. This historical and moral awareness—both united in a secular eschatology—fundamentally distinguished Kant's position from Vattel's.[23]

History and morals conferred a radical character to the discourse of Kant, and even more so to the narratives by revolutionaries à la

---

20 Ian Hunter, 'Vattel's *Law of Nations*: Diplomatic Casuistry for the Protestant Nation' (2010) 31 *Grotiana* 108; Ian Hunter, 'Law, War, and Casuistry in Vattel's *Jus Gentium*' (2011) 28 (2) *Parergon* 87.

21 Immanuel Kant, *Zum ewigen Frieden* (first published 1795, Wilhelm Weischedel ed, Frankfurt am Main, Suhrkamp, 1977) Sixth Preliminary Article. Here Kant, not unlike Vattel, spoke of 'future peace' (*künftiger Frieden*), yet he assumed that the latter in turn represented a precondition for a truly perpetual peace.

22 Immanuel Kant, *Rechtslehre* (first published 1797, Wilhelm Weischedel ed, Frankfurt am Main, Suhrkamp, 1977) § 60.

23 See also Immanuel Kant, *Die Religion innerhalb der Grenzen der bloßen Vernunft* (first published 1793, Wilhelm Weischedel ed, Frankfurt am Main, Suhrkamp, 1977) III, I Abteilung, IV.

Robespierre, who assumed historical progress to be necessary and inevitable (not only hypothetical), and the moral right of Revolution to be absolute here and now (not only a posteriori).[24] In those times of revolutionary domestic and international armed conflict, the enemy of mankind concept, which Vattel endeavoured to integrate into a realist and utilitarian conception of the world order, was morally loaded again and took on an unprecedented polemical connotation.

Both Vattel's utilitarian approach and Robespierre's moralist position were 'modern'. In today's political rhetoric, the enemy of mankind concept is still articulated in both utilitarian narratives, with an emphasis on security, and moralist ones, with reference to ideas of civilisation and humanitarian warfare. Regardless of the political agendas and the theoretical underpinnings of the enemy of mankind concept, the basic function of the concept has remained unaltered, that is, to justify the disqualification of alleged international criminals and rogue states where consent is lacking and more traditional friend/enemy discourses no longer provide the degree of legitimacy necessary for the struggle. In this respect, Cicero, Vattel, Robespierre, and even present statesmen have applied the enemy of mankind concept in a similar way. However, it is especially when hostility and division within mankind run deepest and there seems to be no criterion for right and wrong that appeals to fear easily replace arguments, and enemies of mankind proliferate.

24 Maximilien Robespierre, *Rapport fait au nom du Comité de salut public sur la situation politique de la République*, 27 brumaire an II (17 November 1793) in Marc Bouloiseau and Albert Soboul (eds), *Œuvres de Maximilien Robespierre* (Ivry, Phénix, 2000) vol 10, 167, 176.

BIBLIOGRAPHY

Vattel

Défense du système Leibnitien contre les objections et les imputations de M. de Crousaz (Leiden, Jean Luzac, 1741).

'Essai sur le fondement du droit naturel' [in *Pièces diverses, avec quelques lettres de morale, et d'amusemens* (Paris, 1746)], reprinted in Emer de Vattel, *Droit des gens* (Paul Pradier-Fodéré ed, Paris, Guillaumin, 1863) 1–32.

Pièces diverses, avec quelques lettres de morale, et d'amusemens (Paris, 1746).

Letter to Frédéric Ostervald, 7 November 1746 in Edouard Béguelin, 'En souvenir de Vattel' in *Recueil de travaux offert par la Faculté de Droit de l'Université de Neuchâtel à la Société Suisse des Juristes* (Neuchâtel, Attinger, 1929) 35–176.

Letter to Johann Heinrich Samuel Formey, 13 January 1749 in Nachlass Formey (Berlin, Staatsbibliothek) K 39.

Letter to Johann Heinrich Samuel Formey, 10 October 1749 in *Varnhagen Collection* (Jagiellonian Library, Kraków) 270.

'Réflexions sur le Discours de M. Rousseau touchant l'origine de l'inégalité parmi les hommes' (first published 1755) in Emer de Vattel, *Amusemens de littérature, de morale et de politique* (The Hague, 1765) 79–89.

Letter to the Avoyer and Council of Bern, 28 February 1757 (Staatsarchiv Bern, Deutschland-Buch H H) 679, reprinted in Edouard Béguelin, 'En souvenir de Vattel' in *Recueil de travaux offert par la Faculté de Droit de l'Université de Neuchâtel à la Société Suisse des Juristes* (Neuchâtel, Attinger, 1929) 35–176, 172–173.

Droit des gens, ou principes de la loi naturelle appliqués à la conduite des nations et des souverains (London, i.e. Neuchâtel, 1758).

Droit des gens, ou principes de la loi naturelle appliqués à la conduite des nations et des souverains (Paul Pradier-Fodéré ed, Paris, Guillaumin, 1863).

Droit des gens, ou principes de la loi naturelle appliqués à la conduite des nations et des souverains (first published 1758, with an introduction by Albert de Lapradelle, Washington, Carnegie Institution, 1916).

The Law of Nations, or, Principles of the Law of Nature Applied to the Conduct and Affairs of Nations and Sovereigns (first published 1883, Bela Kapossy and Richard Whatmore eds, Indianapolis, Liberty Fund, 2008).

'Dialogue entre Pierre le Grand et Charles XII sur la gloire des conquérans' in Emer de Vattel, *Mélanges de littérature, de morale et de politique* (Neuchâtel, 1760) 1–19.

Mélanges de littérature, de morale et de politique (Neuchâtel, 1760).

Questions de droit naturel (The Hague, 1763).

Mémoire sur les affaires de Courlande (Warsaw, 1763).

Letter to Johann Heinrich Samuel Formey, 14 December 1764 in Varnhagen Collection (Jagiellonian Library, Kraków) 270.

Amusemens de littérature, de morale et de politique (The Hague, 1765).

Letter to Johann Heinrich Samuel Formey, 21 September 1765 in *Varnhagen Collection* (Jagiellonian Library, Kraków) 270.

Letter to Johann Heinrich Samuel Formey, 14 July 1767 in *Varnhagen Collection* (Jagiellonian Library, Kraków) 270.

Historical Sources

Alciati, *De verborum significatione libri quatuor* (Lyon, Sebastiano Grifo, 1530).
——, *Responsa* (first published 1561, Frankfurt am Main, Vico, 2004).
Althusius, Johannes, *Politica methodice digesta* (first published 1603, Frederick S Carney ed, Boston, Beacon, 1964).
Anon, *The Balance of Power: or, A Comparison of the Strength of the Emperor and the French King* (London, 1709).
Appian, *Roman History* (Horace White trans, London, Heinemann, 1912–3).
Aquinas, Thomas, *Summa theologiae* (60 vols, Thomas Gilby et al trans, London, Eyre and Spottiswoode, 1964–73).
Aristotle, *Nicomachean Ethics* (David Ross trans, OUP, 2009).
The Politics (Stephen Everson ed, CUP, 1988).
Ayala, Balthazar, *De iure belli et officiis bellicis et disciplina militari libri tres* (first published 1582, John Westlake ed, Washington, Carnegie Endowment, 1912).
Baldus de Ubaldis, *Super toto Codice* (1545 Lyon edn).
In infortiatum, digestum novum, et instituta commentaria (1577 Lyon edn).
Bartolus de Saxoferrato, *De tyranno* (written 1355–57) in Diego Quaglioni (ed), *Politica e diritto nel Trecento italiano* (Florence, Olschki, 1983) 175–213.
——, *Commentaria* (9 vols, Giovanni Polara ed, Rome, Il Cigno Galileo Galilei, 1996–98, reprint of 1526 Venice edn).
Beccaria, Cesare, *Dei delitti e delle pene* (first published 1764, Franco Venturi ed, Turin, Einaudi, 1965).
Bellone, Marcantonio (ed), *Decisiones rotae Genuae de mercatura et pertinentibus ad eam* (Genoa, Ternoni, 1582).
Bentham, Jeremy, *Principles of International Law* in John Bowring (ed), *The Works of Jeremy Bentham* (Edinburgh, William Tait, 1838–1843) vol 2, 535–572.
Bodin, Jean, *Six livres de la République* (first published 1576, Aalen, Scientia, 1977).
——, *I sei libri dello stato* (3 vols, Margherita Isnardi Parente and Diego Quaglioni eds, Turin, Utet, 1964–1997).
Boétie, Étienne de la, *Discours de la servitude volontaire* (first published 1576, Miguel Abensour ed, Paris, Payot, 1976).
Bossuet, Jacques-Bénigne, *Politique tirée des propres paroles de l'Ecriture Sainte* (first published 1709, Geneva, Droz, 1967).
Burlamaqui, Jean-Jacques, *Principes du droit naturel* (Geneva, 1747).
Principes du droit politique (Amsterdam, 1751).
Bynkershoek, Cornelius van, *De dominio maris dissertatio* (first published 1703, Ralph Van Deman Magoffin trans, OUP, 1923).
——, *Quaestionum juris publici libri duo* (first published 1737, Tenney Frank trans, Oxford, Clarendon, 1930).
Carpzov, Benedict, *Practica nova imperialis Saxonica rerum criminalium in tres partes divisa* (first published 1638, Leipzig, 1709).
Casaregi, Giuseppe Maria, *Il consolato del mare* (Lucca, 1720).
Cicero, *In Verrem* (Albert C Clarck ed, Oxford, Clarendon, 1917).
——, *De officiis* (Walter Miller trans, London, Heinemann, 1913).
——, *Philippicae* (David R Shackleton Bailey trans, Harvard University Press, 2009).
——, *De finibus* (Leighton D Reynolds trans, Oxford, Clarendon, 1998).
——, *De re publica* (Clinton W Keyes trans, London, Heinemann, 1928).
——, *De legibus* (Clinton W Keyes trans, London, Heinemann, 1928).
Chambrier d'Oleires, Jean Pierre, *Questions de droit des gens et observations sur le traité du Droit des gens de M. de Vattel* in *Mémoires de l'Académie royale des sciences et belles-lettres depuis l'avènement de Frédéric Guillaume II au trône, 1788–1789* (Berlin, Georg Decker, 1793).

——, *Questions de droit des gens. Suite des observations sur le traité du Droit des gens de M. de Vattel* in *Mémoires de l'Académie royale des sciences et belles-lettres depuis l'avènement de Frédéric Guillaume II au trône, 1790–1791* (Berlin, Georg Decker, 1796).

Cocceji, Heinrich von, *Theses ordinariae ex jure naturae & gentium de jure postliminii* (Heidelberg, 1673).

——, *De postliminio in pace, et amnestia* (Frankfurt/Oder, 1691).

——, *Disputatio iuris gentium publici de armis illicitis* (Frankfurt/Oder, 1698).

——, *De sacro-sancto talionis iure* (Frankfurt/Oder, 1705).

——, *Dissertatio iuris gentium publici de iusto proeliorum exitu* (Frankfurt/Oder, 1706).

——, *Prodromus iustitiae gentium sive exercitationes duae* (Frankfurt/Oder, 1719).

——, *Grotius illustratus, seu Commentarii ad Hugonis Grotii libros tres* [4 vols, Samuel von Cocceji ed, Wrokław (Breslau) 1744–52].

Cocceji, Samuel von, *Introductio ad Henrici L. B. de Cocceji Grotium illustratum* (Halle, 1748).

Codex Theodosiani (Theodor Mommsen and Paul M Meyer eds, Berlin, Weidmann, 1905).

Coke, Edward, *Institutes of the Lawes of England* (first published 1628, Clark, NJ, Lawbook Exchange, 2001).

Constitutio Criminalis Carolina (first published 1532, Osnabrück, Biblio-Verlag, 1973).

Covarruvias, Diego, *In regulae peccatum: De regulis iuris, lib. VI admodum breves commentarji* (first published 1554) in Diego Covarruvias, *Opera Omnia* (Turin, 1594) vol 2.

Cussy, Ferdinand de, *Phases et causes célèbres du droit maritime des nations* (Leipzig, Brockhaus, 1856).

Diderot, Denis, 'Droit naturel' in Denis Diderot and Jean-Baptiste le Rond D'Alembert (eds), *Encyclopédie, ou, Dictionnaire raisonné des sciences, des arts et des métiers* (first published 1751–80, Elmsford, NY, Pergamon Press, 1985) vol 5, 115–116.

Dumont, Jean, *Corps universel diplomatique du droit des gens* (8 vols, Amsterdam – The Hague 1731).

Florus, Lucius Annaeus, *Epitome de Tito Livio bellorum omnium annorum DCC libri* (Edward S Forster trans, London, Heinemann, 1929).

Formey, Johann Heinrich Samuel, *Principes du droit de la nature et des gens. Extrait du grand ouvrage latin de M. de Wolff* (Amsterdam, 1758).

General and Definitive Treaty of Peace between France, Great Britain and the Netherlands, signed at Aix-la-Chapelle, 18 October 1748, 38 CTS 301–323.

Gentili, Alberico, *De legationibus libri tres* (first published 1585, Ernest Nys ed, OUP, 1924).

——, *De iure belli libri tres* (first published 1588–89, Coleman Phillipson ed, Oxford, Clarendon, 1933).

——, *Hispanicae advocationis libri duo* (first published 1613, Frank F Abbott ed, OUP, 1921).

Grotius, Hugo, *De iure belli ac pacis libri tres* (first published 1625, Francis W Kelsey trans, Washington, Carnegie Endowment, 1913).

——, *De iure belli ac pacis libri tres* (first published 1625, Robert Feenstra ed, Aalen, Scientia, 1993).

——, *Le droit de la guerre et de la paix* (2 vols, Jean Barbeyrac ed, Amsterdam, 1724).

——, *De iure praedae commentarius* (written 1604, first published 1868, Gwladys L Williams trans, Oxford, Clarendon, 1950).

Gunnerus, Johann Ernst, *Vollständige Erklärung des Natur- und Völkerrechts nach den Grundlagen des Herrn Hofrath Darjes* (first published 1752, Vienna, 1786).

Hegel, Georg Wilhelm Friedrich, *Grundlinien der Philosophie des Rechts, oder Naturrecht und Staatswissenschaft im Grundrisse* (first published 1821, Johannes Hoffmeister ed, Hamburg, Meiner, 1955).

Heinecke, Johann Gottlieb, *Elementa juris naturae et gentium* (Halle, 1738).

Hobbes, Thomas, *De cive* (first published 1642, Richard Tuck ed, CUP, 1998).

——, *Leviathan* (first published 1651, Richard Tuck ed, CUP, 1991).

Hotman, François, *Quaestionum illustrium liber* (Geneva, 1573).

——, *Francogallia* (first published 1573, John H Salmon trans, CUP, 1972).

Hübner, Martin, *De la saisie des bâtiments neutres, ou du droit qu'on les Nations belligérantes d'arrêter les navires des peuples amis* (2 vols, The Hague, 1759).

Hume, David, 'Of the Balance of Power' (Edinburgh, 1752) in David Hume, *Essays Moral, Political, and Literary* (Thomas H Green and Thomas H Grose eds, Aalen, Scientia, 1964) 348–56.

Isidore of Seville, *Etymologiarum sive originum libri XX* (Stephen A Barney ed, CUP, 2010).

Institutiones Iustiniani Augusti in *Corpus iuris civilis* (Paul Krüger and Theodor Mommsen eds, Berlin, Weidmann, 1911) vol 1.

Digesta Iustiniani Augusti in *Corpus iuris civilis* (Paul Krüger and Theodor Mommsen eds, Berlin, Weidmann, 1911) vol 1.

Codex Iustinianus in *Corpus iuris civilis* (Paul Krüger ed, Berlin, Weidmann, 1911) vol 2.

Jeney, Louis Michel de (Mihály Lajos Jeney), *Le partisan, ou l'art de faire la guerre avec succès selon le génie de nos jours* (The Hague, Constapel, 1759).

Justi, Johann Heinrich Gottlob von, *Die Chimäre des Gleichgewichts von Europa* (Altona, 1758).

Justinian, *The Civil Law, Including the Twelve Tables* (SP Scott ed, Cincinnati, Central Trust Company, 1932).

Kahle, Ludwig Martin, *La balance de l'Europe considérée comme la règle de la guerre et de la paix* (Samuel Formey trans, Berlin – Göttingen, 1744 [trans of *De Trutina Europae. Tam quam praecipua pacis bellisque norma* (Göttingen, 1744)].

Kant, Immanuel, *Naturrecht Feyerabend* (lectures delivered 1784) in Immanuel Kant, *Gesammelte Schriften* (Gerhard Lehmann ed, Berlin, Deutsche Akademie der Wissenschaften, 1979) 1317–1394.

——, *Idee zu einer allgemeinen Geschichte in weltbürgerlicher Absicht* (first published 1784, Wilhelm Weischedel ed, *Kants Werke*, vol 11, Frankfurt am Main, Suhrkamp, 1977) 31–50.

——, *Zum ewigen Frieden* (first published 1795, Wilhelm Weischedel ed, Frankfurt am Main, Suhrkamp, 1977).

——, *Rechtslehre* (first published 1797, Wilhelm Weischedel ed, *Kants Werke*, vol 8, Frankfurt am Main, Suhrkamp, 1977) [Mary Gregor trans, *The Science of Right* in *The Metaphisics of Morals* (CUP, 1996)].

Köhler, Heinrich, *Juris socialis et gentium ad jus naturale revocati specimina VII* (2nd ed, Jena, 1737).

Lampredi, Giovanni Maria, *De licentia in hostem liber singularis, in quo Samuelis Cocceji sententia de infinita licentia in hostem exponitur et confutatur* (Florence, 1761).

Legnano, Giovanni da, *Tractatus de bello, de represaliis et de duello* (written 1360, Thomas E Holland ed, OUP, 1917).

Leibniz, Gottfried Wilhelm, *Mars Christianissimus* (Cologne, 1684).

——, *Essais de théodicée* (first published 1710, Jacques Brunschwig ed, Paris, Garnier-Flammarion, 1969).

Le Roy de Grandmaison, Thomas-Auguste, *La petite guerre, ou traité du service des troupes légères en campagne* (Paris, 1756).

Livy, *Ab urbe condita* (Benjamin O Foster, London, Heinemann, 1919).

Locke, John, *Two Treatises of Government* (first published 1690, Peter Laslett ed, CUP, 1988).

Lorry, François, *Code pénal, ou recueil des principales ordonnances, édits et déclarations sur les crimes et délits* (2nd ed, Paris, Desaint et Saillant, 1755).

Mably, Gabriel Bonnot de, *Le droit public de l'Europe* (2 vols, Geneva, 1746).

Machiavelli, Niccolò, *Il principe* (first published 1513, Delio Cantimori ed, *Il Principe e altre opere politiche*, Milan, Garzanti, 1976).

——, *Discorsi sopra la prima deca di Tito Livio* (first published 1513–21, Delio Cantimori ed, *Il Principe e altre opere politiche*, Milan, Garzanti, 1976).

Mariana, Juan de, *De rege et regis institutione libri tres* (Toledo, 1599) [George Albert Moore trans, *The King and the Education of the King* (Washington, Country Dollar Press, 1944)].

Montesquieu, Charles-Louis de Secondat, Baron de, *De l'esprit des lois* (first published 1748, Victor Goldschmidt ed, Garnier-Flammarion, Paris 1979).
Muyart de Vouglans, Pierre-François, *Institutes au droit criminel, ou principes généraux sur ces matières, suivant le droit civil, canonique, et la jurisprudence du Royaume* (Paris, Le Breton, 1757).
Ompteda, Ludwig von, *Litteratur des gesammten sowohl natürlichen als positiven Völkerrechts* (Regensburg, Montag, 1785).
Ordonnance de la marine (first published 1681, Paris, Les Libraires Associés, 1755).
Plato, *Republic* (Robin Waterfield trans, OUP, 1994).
Plessis Mornay, Philippe du, *Vindiciae, contra tyrannos* (George Garnett ed, CUP, 1994).
Pliny the Elder, *Natural History* (Harris Rackham trans, London, Heinemann, 1942).
Plutarch, *Agesilaus and Pompey* in *Parallel Lives* (Bernadotte Perrin ed, London, Heinemann, 1914–26) vol 5.
Pufendorf, Samuel, *Elementorum jurisprudentiae universalis libri duo* (first published 1660, Edwin H Zeydel trans, Oxford, Clarendon, 1931).
——, *De statu Imperii Germanici liber unus* (written under the pseudonym: Severinus de Monzambano, Geneva, 1667) [Michael J Seidler ed, *The Present State of Germany* (Indianapolis, Liberty Fund, 2007)].
——, *De jure naturae et gentium* (first published 1672, Charles H Oldfather and William A Oldfather trans, Oxford, Clarendon, 1934).
——, *De existimatione* in Samuel Pufendorf, *Dissertationes academicae selectiores* (Lund, 1675).
——, *Le droit de la nature et des gens* (2 vols, Jean Barbeyrac ed, Amsterdam 1706).
——, *De officio hominis et civis juxta legem naturalem libri duo* (Gottlieb Gerhard Titius ed, Leipzig, 1709).
——, *Introduction à l'histoire générale et politique de l'univers* (8 vols, Amsterdam, Chatelain, 1743–45) [first German edn *Einleitung zu der Historie der vornehmsten Reiche und Staaten* (Frankfurt am Main, Knoch, 1682); Jocodus Crull trans, *An Introduction to the History of the Principal Kingdoms and States of Europe* (3rd edn, London, Gilliflower and Newborough, 1699)].
Rayneval, Gérard de, *Institutions du droit de la nature et des gens* (2nd ed, Paris, Leblanc, 1803).
Richer D'Aube, François, *Essai sur les principes du droit et de la morale* (Paris, Brunet, 1743).
Robespierre, Maximilien, *Rapport fait au nom du Comité de salut public sur la situation politique de la République*, 27 brumaire an II (17 November 1793) in Marc Bouloiseau and Albert Soboul (eds), *Œuvres de Maximilien Robespierre* (Ivry, Phénix, 2000) vol 10, 167–188.
Rousseau, Jean-Jacques, Letter to Jean le Rond d'Alembert, 20 March 1758 in Jean-Jacques Rousseau, *Œuvres complètes* (Bernard Gagnebin ed, Paris, Gallimard, 1995) vol 5, 1–125.
——, *Du contrat social* (first published 1762) in Jean-Jacques Rousseau, *Œuvres complètes* (Bernard Gagnebin and Marcel Raymond eds, Paris, Gallimard, 1969) vol 3, 347–470.
Rutherforth, Thomas, *Institutes of Natural Law* (2 vols, Cambridge, Bentham, 1754–56).
Selden, John, *De iure naturali et gentium juxta disciplinam Ebraeorum libri septem* (London, 1640).
Seneca, *De ira* (Robert A Kaster trans, University of Chicago Press, 2010).
Soulatges, Jean Antoine, *Traité des crimes* (Toulouse, Antoine Birosse, 1762).
Suárez, Francisco, *De legibus ac Deo legislatore* (first published 1612, Gwladys L Williams trans, Oxford, Clarendon, 1944).
——, *De triplici virtute theologica* (first published 1621, Gwladys L Williams trans, Oxford, Clarendon, 1944).
Tacitus, *Annales* (John Jackson trans, London, Heinemann, 1925–37).
Textor, Johann Wolfgang, *Synopsis juris gentium* (first published 1680, Carl Ludwig von Bar ed, Washington, Carnegie Institution, 1916).
Titius, Gottlieb Gerhard, *De dominio in rebus occupatis* (Braunschweig, 1704).

Treaty of Peace between Sweden and the Empire, signed at Osnabrück, 14(24) October 1648, 1 CTS 198–269.

Treaty of Peace between France and the Empire, signed at Münster, 14(24) October 1648, 1 CTS 319–356.

Treaty of Peace and Friendship between France and Great Britain, signed at Utrecht, 11 April 1713, 27 CTS 477–490.

Treaty of Peace and Amity between France and the Netherlands, signed at Utrecht, 11 April 1713, 28 CTS 39–60.

Treaty of Peace and Amity between France and Savoy, signed at Utrecht, 11 April 1713, 28 CTS 125–134.

Velleius Paterculus, Marcus, *Historiarum ad M. Vinicium consulem libri duo* (Frederick W Shipley trans, Harvard University Press, 1979).

Vitoria, Francisco de, *De potestate civili* (first delivered 1528, Anthony Pagden and Jeremy Lawrance eds, CUP, 1991) 1–44.

——, *Relectio de iure belli* (first delivered 1539, Anthony Pagden and Jeremy Lawrance eds, CUP, 1991) 293–327.

Voltaire, François-Marie Arouet dit, *Le siècle de Louis XIV* (first published 1751, Jaqueline Hellegouarc'h ed, Paris, Librairie Générale Française, 2005).

——, *Essai sur les mœurs et l'esprit des nations* (first published 1756, Henri Duranton ed, *Œuvres complètes de Voltaire*, vols 22–24, Oxford, Voltaire Foundation, 2009–2011).

Ward, Robert Plumer, *An Inquiry into the Foundation and History of the Law of Nations in Europe, from the Time of the Greeks and Romans, to the Age of Grotius* (2 vols, London, Strahan and Woodfall, 1795).

Weidler, Johann Friedrich, *De quaestione iuris gentium utrum praeda Salensibus Afris erepta vindicari possit* (Wittenberg, Eichsfeld, 1735).

Wolff, Christian, *Psychologia empirica* (Frankfurt – Leipzig, Renger, 1732) in Christian Wolff, *Gesammelte Werke* (Jean Ecole ed, Hildesheim, Olms, 1968) pt 2, vol 5.

——, *Jus naturae methodo scientifica pertractatum* (8 vols, first published 1740–48, Marcel Thomann ed, Hildesheim, Olms, 1969).

——, *Jus gentium methodo scientifica pertractatum* (first published 1749, Joseph H Drake trans, Oxford, Clarendon, 1934).

——, *Jus gentium methodo scientifica pertractatum* (first published 1749, Marcel Thomann ed, Hildesheim, Olms, 1972).

——, *Institutiones juris naturae et gentium* (first published 1750, Marcel Thomann ed, Hildesheim, Olms, 1969).

Zouche, Richard, *Iuris et iudicii fecialis, sive Iuris inter gentes, et quaestionum de eodem explicatio* (first published 1650, Erskine Holland ed, Washington, Carnegie Institution, 1911).

Modern Sources

Agamben, Giorgio, *Homo sacer. Il potere sovrano e la nuda vita* (Turin, Einaudi, 1995).

Stato di eccezione (Turin, Bollati Boringhieri, 2003).

Alexandrowicz, Charles H, 'Doctrinal Aspects of the Universality of the Law of Nations' (1961) 37 *British Yearbook of International Law* 506–515.

Allgemeines Landrecht für die preussischen Staaten (2 vols, Berlin, 1794).

Anderson, Matthew S, *War and Society in Europe of the Old Regime 1618–1789* (New York, St Martin's, 1988).

——, *The Rise of Modern Diplomacy 1450–1919* (London – New York, Longman 1993).

——, *The War of the Austrian Succession, 1740–1748* (London – New York, Longman, 1995).

Antony Anghie, 'Vattel and Colonialism' in Vincent Chetail and Peter Haggenmacher (eds), *Vattel's International Law in a XXIst Century Perspective* (Leiden – Boston, Nijhoff, 2011) 237–253.

Aretin, Karl Otmar von, *Das Alte Reich, 1648–1806* (3 vols, Stuttgart, Klett – Cotta, 1993–1997).

Arneil, Barbara, 'Trade, Plantations, and Property: John Locke and the Economic Defense of Colonialism' (1994) 55 *Journal of the History of Ideas* 591–609.

Bandelier, André, 'De Berlin à Neuchâtel: la genèse du *Droit des gens* d'Emer de Vattel' in Martin Fontius (ed), *Schweizer im Berlin des 18. Jahrhunderts* (Berlin, Akademie-Verlag, 1996) 45–56.

——, *Des Suisses dans la République des Lettres. Un réseau savant au temps de Frédéric le Grand* (Geneva, Slatkine, 2007).

Bar, Carl Ludwig von, *History of Continental Criminal Law* (Thomas Sydney Bell trans, Boston, Little Brown, 1916) [trans of *Geschichte des deutschen Strafrechts und der Strafrechtstheorien* (first published 1882)].

Barker, Ernest, 'The Authorship of the *Vindiciae Contra Tyrannos*' (1930) 3 *Cambridge Historical Journal* 164–181.

Bartelson, Jens, *A Genealogy of Sovereignty* (CUP, 1995).

Battista, Annamaria, *Alle origini del pensiero politico libertino* (Milan, Giuffrè, 1989).

Baumgartner, Frederic J, *Declaring War in Early Modern Europe* (New York, Palgrave Macmillan, 2011).

Beaulac, Stéphane, *The Power of Language in the Making of International Law. The Word Sovereignty in Bodin and Vattel and the Myth of Westphalia* (Leiden, Nijhoff, 2004).

Béguelin, Edouard, 'En souvenir de Vattel' in *Recueil de travaux offert par la Faculté de Droit de l'Université de Neuchâtel à la Société Suisse des Juristes à l'occasion de sa réunion à Neuchâtel, 15–17 Septembre 1929* (Neuchâtel, Attinger, 1929) 35–176.

Bély, Lucien, *Les rélations internationales en Europe, XVIIe–XVIIIe siècles* (Paris, PUF, 1992).

Berman, Harold J, *Law and Revolution. The Formation of the Western Legal Tradition* (Harvard University Press, 1983).

Bitterli, Urs, *Die 'Wilden' und die 'Zivilisierten'. Grundzüge einer Geistes- und Kulturgeschichte der europäisch-überseeischen Begegnung* (Munich, Beck, 1976).

Bobbitt, Philip, *Terror and Consent. The Wars for the Twenty-First Century* (New York, Anchor, 2009).

Bödecker, Hans Erich, 'Menschheit' in Reinhard Koselleck (ed), *Geschichtlicher Grundbegriffe* (Stuttgart, Klett – Cotta, 1982) vol 3, 1063–1090.

Bona, Ferdinando, 'Postliminium in pace' (1955) 21 *Studia et documenta historiae et iuris* 249–275.

Bono, Salvatore, *Corsari nel Mediterraneo. Cristiani e musulmani fra guerra, schiavitù e commercio* (Milan, Mondadori, 1993).

Braudel, Fernand, *La Méditerranée et le monde méditerranéen à l'époque de Philippe II* (first published 1949, Paris, Armand Colin, 1966).

Braun, Harald E, *Juan de Mariana and Early Modern Spanish Political Thought* (Aldershot – Burlington, Ashgate, 2007).

Brenton, Lauren, 'Legalities of the Sea in Gentili's *Hispanica Advocatio*' in Benedict Kingsbury and Benjamin Straumann (eds), *The Roman Foundations of the Law of Nations* (OUP, 2010) 270–282.

Bugeaud, Thomas-Robert, *Histoire de l'Algerie Française* (Paris, Morel, 1846–50).

Bull, Hedley et al (eds), *Hugo Grotius and International Relations* (Oxford, Clarendon, 1990).

Bulmerinck, August, *Die Systematik des Völkerrechts* (Dorpat, 1858).

Burkhardt, Johannes, 'Die Friedlosigkeit der Frühen Neuzeit. Grundlegung einer Theorie der Bellizität Europas' (1997) 24 *Zeitschrift für historische Forschung* 509–574.

Butterfield, Herbert, 'The Balance of Power' in Herbert Butterfield and Martin Wight (eds), *Diplomatic Investigations: Essays in the Theory of International Politics* (London, Allen & Unwin, 1966).

Carty, Anthony, *The Decay of International Law* (Manchester University Press, 1986).

——, *Philosophy of International Law* (Edinburgh University Press, 2007).

——, 'Vattel, 17th Century Wars of Religion and the Present' in Yves Sandoz (ed) *Réflexions sur l'impact, le rayonnement et l'actualité du 'Droit des gens' d'Emer de Vattel à l'occasion du 250e anniversaire de sa parution* (Brussels, Bruylant, 2010) 181–194.

Cavallar, Georg, 'Vitoria, Grotius, Pufendorf, Wolff and Vattel: Accomplices of European Colonisation and Exploitation or True Cosmopolitans?' (2008) 10 *Journal of the History of International Law* 181–209.

Chabod, Federico, 'Principio dell'equilibrio e aspirazioni alla pace in Europa fra Settecento e Ottocento' (first published 1939) in Federico Chabod, *Idea di Europa e politica dell'equilibrio* (Luisa Azzolini ed, Bologna, Il Mulino, 1995) 33–62.

Chetail, Vincent and Haggenmacher, Peter (eds), *Vattel's International Law in a XXIst Century Perspective* (Leiden – Boston, Nijhoff, 2011).

Cursi, Maria Floriana, *La struttura del "postliminium" nella repubblica e nel principato* (Naples, Jovene, 1996).

Daston, Lorraine and Stolleis, Michael (eds), *Natural Law and Laws of Nature in Early Modern Europe* (Farnham – Burlington, Ashgate, 2008).

Declaration Respecting Maritime Law, signed at Paris, 16 April 1856, 115 CTS 1–3.

Domingo, Rafael, *Gaius, Vattel, and the New Global Law Paradigm* (2011) 22 (3) *European Journal of International Law* 627–647.

Döring, Erich, 'Heinrich von Cocceji' in *Neue Deutsche Biographie* (Bayerische Akademie der Wissenschaften ed, Berlin, Duncker & Humblot, 1957) vol 3, 300.

——, 'Samuel von Cocceji' in *Neue Deutsche Biographie* (Bayerische Akademie der Wissenschaften ed, Berlin, Duncker & Humblot, 1957) vol 3, 300.

Drumbl, Mark A, *Atrocity, Punishment, and International Law* (CUP, 2007).

Duchhardt, Heinz, *Balance of power und Pentarchie* (Paderborn, Schöningh, 1997).

——, 'The Missing Balance' (2000) 2 *Journal of the History of International Law* 67–73.

Duffy, Christopher, *Frederick the Great: A Military Life* (London, Routledge & Kegan Paul, 1985).

——, *The Military Experience in the Age of Reason* (London, Routledge, 1987).

Dufour, Alfred, 'Religion, Eglise, Etat dans la pensée d'Emer de Vattel' (2002) 3–4 *Revue historique neuchâteloise* 169–192.

Duranton, Henri, 'Humanité' in Rolf Reichardt and Hans-Jürgen Lüsebrink (eds), *Handbuch politisch-sozialer Grundbegriffe in Frankreich 1680–1820* (Munich, Oldenbourg, 2000) vol 8, 1–51.

Edelstein, Dan, *The Terror of Natural Right: Republicanism, the Cult of Nature, and the French Revolution* (University of Chicago Press, 2009).

Fauchille, Paul, *Traité de droit international public: 8ème édition du Manuel de droit international public de M. Henri Bonfils* (Paris, Rousseau et Cie, 1922).

Fenwick, Charles, 'The Authority of Vattel' (1913) 7 *The American Political Science Review* 395–410.

Fillias, Achille, *Histoire de la conquête et de la colonisation de l'Algerie 1830–1860* (Paris, De Vresse, 1860).

Findley, Carter Vaughn, *The Turks in World History* (OUP, 2005).

Fisher, Godfrey, *The Barbary Legend: War, Trade, and Piracy in North Africa, 1415–1830* (Oxford, Clarendon, 1957).

Fögen, Marie Theres, '*Inimici humani generis*. Menschheitsfeinde und Glaubensfreunde in der Spätantike' in Laurent Mayali and Maria M Mart (eds), *Of Strangers and Foreigners* (Berkeley, Robbins Collection, 1993).

Forcellini, Egidio, 'Latro' in *Lexicon totius Latinitatis* (first pubslished 1771, Jacopo Facciolati and Egidio Forcellini eds, Padua, 1871) vol 3, 40.

——, 'Vindicta' in *Lexicon totius Latinitatis* (first pubslished 1771, Jacopo Facciolati and Egidio Forcellini eds, Padua, 1871) vol 4, 998.

Gagnebin, Bernard, *Burlamaqui et le droit naturel* (Geneva, La Frégate, 1944).

Gaurier, Dominique, *Histoire du droit international: auteurs, doctrines et développement de l'Antiquité à l'aube de l'époque contemporaine* (Rennes, Presses Universitaires de Rennes, 2005).

Gembicki, Dieter and Reichardt, Rolf, 'Progrès' in Rolf Reichardt (ed), *Handbuch politisch-sozialer Grundbegriffe in Frankreich 1680–1820* (Munich, Oldenbourg, 1993) vols 14 and 15, 118–28.

Genet, Raoul, 'La qualification de "pirates" et le dilemme de la guerre civile' (1937) 3 *Revue internationale du droit des gens* 12–25.

Göçek, Fatma Müge, *East Encounters West. France and the Ottoman Empire in the Eighteenth Century* (OUP, 1987).

Goffman, Daniel, *The Ottoman Empire and Early Modern Europe* (CUP, 2002).

Gong, Gerrit W, *The Standard of "Civilisation" in International Society* (Oxford, Clarendon, 1984).

Good, Christoph, *Emer de Vattel (1714–1767): Naturrechtliche Ansätze einer Menschenrechtsidee und des humanitären Völkerrechts im Zeitalter der Aufklärung* (Baden-Baden, Nomos, 2011).

Goyard-Fabre, Simone, 'Barbeyrac et la théorie du droit naturel' in Jean Barbeyrac, *Ecrits de droit et de morale* (Simone Goyard-Fabre ed, Paris, Duchemin, 1996) 1–74.

Grewe, Wilhelm, *The Epochs of International Law* (Michael Byers trans, Berlin, de Gruyter, 2000) [trans of *Epochen der Völkerrechtsgeschichte* (first published 1984)].

Grossi, Paolo, *L'ordine giuridico medievale* (Rome – Bari, Laterza, 1997).

Grunert, Frank, 'Theologien der Strafe. Zur Straftheorie von Thomas von Aquin und ihrer Rezeption in der Spanischen Spätscholastik: das Beispiel Francisco de Vitoria' in Hans Schlosser, Dietmar Willoweit (eds), *Neue Wege strafrechtsgeschichtlicher Forschung* (Cologne – Weimar – Vienna, Böhlau, 1999) 313–332.

Guggenheim, Paul, *Emer de Vattel et l'étude des relations internationales en Suisse* (Geneva, Librairie de l'Université, 1956).

Guinand, Ulysse (ed), *Histoire du gouvernement de Neuchâtel, sous la domination Prussienne, depuis 1707 jusqu'au 1832* (Lausanne, 1833).

Haggenmacher, Peter, *Grotius et la doctrine de la guerre juste* (Paris, PUF, 1983).

——, 'L'état souverain comme sujet du droit international, de Vitoria à Vattel' (1992) 16 *Droits. Revue française de théorie juridique* 11–20.

——, 'Le modèle de Vattel et la discipline du droit international' in Vincent Chetail and Peter Haggenmacher (eds), *Vattel's International Law in a XXIst Century Perspective* (Leiden – Boston, Nijhoff, 2011) 1–48.

Härter, Karl, 'Sicherheit und Frieden im frühneuzeitlichen Alten Reich: Zur Funktion der Reichsverfassung als Sicherheits- und Friedensordnung 1648–1806' (2003) 30 *Zeitschrift für historische Forschung* 413–431.

Heller-Roazen, Daniel, *The Enemy of All* (New York, Zone Books, 2009).

Heuss, Alfred, *Die völkerrechtlichen Grundlagen der Römischen Aussenpolitik in republikanischer Zeit* (first published 1933, Aalen, Scientia, 1968).

Holt, Peter H, 'The Treaties of the Early Mamluk Sultans with the Frankish States' (1980) 43 (1) *Bulletin of the School of Oriental and African Studies* 67–76.

Hunter, Ian, 'Vattel's *Law of Nations*: Diplomatic Casuistry for the Protestant Nation' (2010) 31 *Grotiana* 108–140.

——, 'Law, War, and Casuistry in Vattel's *Jus Gentium*' (2011) 28 (2) *Parergon* 87–104.

Ilari, Virgilio, *L'interpretazione storica del diritto di guerra romano fra tradizione romanistica e giusnaturalismo* (Milan, Giuffrè, 1991).

International Committee of the Red Cross, *Report on Strenghtening Legal Protection for Victims of Armed Conflicts* (2011) 12–13 <http://www.icrc.org/eng/resources/documents/report/31-international-conference-strengthening-ihl-report-2011-10-31.htm>.

Isnardi Parente, Margherita, 'Signoria e tirannide nella "République" di Jean Bodin' in Domenico Felice (ed), *Dispotismo. Genesi e sviluppo di un concetto filosofico-politico* (Naples, Liguori, 2001) vol 1, 127–144.

Johnson, DHN, 'Piracy in Modern International Law' (1957) 43 *Transactions of the Grotius Society* 63–85.

Jouannet, Emmanuelle, *Vattel et l'émergence doctrinale du droit international classique* (Paris, Pedone, 1998).
——, *Droit international libéral-providence. Une histoire du droit international* (Brussels, Bruylant, 2011).
——, 'Les dualismes du droit des gens' in Vincent Chetail and Peter Haggenmacher (eds), *Vattel's International Law in a XXIst Century Perspective* (Leiden – Boston, Nijhoff, 2011) 133–150.
Kammel, Frank Matthias, 'Gefährliche Heiden und gezähmte Exoten: Bemerkungen zum europäischen Türkenbild im 17. und frühen 18. Jahrhundert' in Ronald Asch, Wulf Eckart Voß, and Martin Wrede (eds), *Frieden und Krieg in der Frühen Neuzeit* (Munich, Wilhelm Fink, 2001) 503–525.
Kaltenborn von Stachau, Karl, *Kritik des Völkerrechts* (Leipzig, Mayer, 1847).
Keller, Alexis, 'Vattel, la tradition du droit des gens et la question des peuples autochtones' (2006) 56 (4) *Schweizerische Zeitschrift für Geschichte* 387–409.
Kelsen, Hans, *Collective Security under International Law* (Washington, United States Government Printing Office, 1957).
Kempe, Michael and Gänswein, Oliver, 'Die Rückkehr der Universalfeinde' (2010) 32 *Zeitschrift für Neuere Rechtsgeschichte* 91–106.
Kolb, Robert, 'La validité du modèle de Vattel après 1945' in Yves Sandoz (ed), *Réflexions sur l'impact, le rayonnement et l'actualité du 'Droit des gens' d'Emer de Vattel à l'occasion du 250e anniversaire de sa parution – Reflections on the Impact, Influence and Continuing Relevance of the 'Law of Nations' by Emer de Vattel on the Occasion of the 250th Anniversary of Its First Publication* (Brussels, Bruylant, 2010) 137–175.
Kontorovich, Eugene, 'The Piracy Analogy' (2004) 45 *Harvard International Law Journal* 183–237.
Koselleck, Reinhart, *Kritik und Krise. Eine Studie zur Pathogenese der bürgerlichen Welt* (Frankfurt am Main, Suhrkamp, 1973).
Koskenniemi, Martti, *The Gentle Civilizer of Nations. The Rise and Fall of International Law 1870–1960* (CUP, 2001).
——, *From Apology to Utopia. The Structure of International Legal Argument* (2nd ed, CUP, 2005).
——, 'The Advantage of Treaties. International Law in the Enlightenment' (2009) 13 (1) *Edinburgh Law Review* 27–67.
——, 'Miserable Comforters. International Relations as New Natural Law' (2009) 15 (3) *European Journal of International Relations* 395–422.
Kunisch, Johannes, *Friedrich der Grosse. Der König und seine Zeit* (Munich, Beck, 2004).
Land, Isaac (ed), *Enemies of Humanity. The Nineteenth-Century War on Terrorism* (Basingstoke, Palgrave Macmillan, 2008).
Lapradelle, Albert de, 'Introduction' in Emer de Vattel, *Droit des gens, ou principes de la loi naturelle appliqués à la conduite des nations et des souverains* (Washington, Carnegie Institution, 1916).
Lauterpacht, Hersch, 'Insurrection et piraterie' (1939) 46 *Revue générale de droit international public* 513–549.
Le Fur, Louis, 'La théorie du droit naturel depuis le XVIIe siècle et la doctrine moderne' (1927) 18 (3) *Recueil des cours de l'Académie de droit international de La Haye* 259–442.
Lesaffer, Randall (ed), *Peace Treaties and International Law in European History. From the Late Middle Ages to World War One* (CUP, 2004).
Lowe, Vaughan and Staker, Christopher, 'Jurisdiction' in Malcolm D Evans (ed), *International Law* (3rd ed, OUP, 2010) 313–39.
Luban, David, 'A Theory of Crimes against Humanity' (2004) 65 *Yale Journal of International Law* 85–167.
Lutz, Heinrich, *Ragione di stato und Christliche Staatsethik im 16. Jahrhundert* (Münster, Aschendorff, 1961).
Maffi, Alberto, *Ricerche sul postliminium* (Milan, Giuffrè, 1992).

Malherbe, Michel, 'Introduction' in David Hume, *Essais et traités sur plusieurs sujets* (Michel Malherbe ed, Paris, Vrin, 2009) vol 2.
Mallarmé, André, 'Emer de Vattel' in Antoine Pillet (ed) *Les fondateurs du droit international* (Paris, Giard & Brière, 1904) 481–601.
Mancuso, Francesco, *Diritto, stato, sovranità. Il pensiero politico-giuridico di Emer de Vattel tra assolutismo e rivoluzione* (Naples, Edizioni Scientifiche Italiane, 2002).
——, '*Le Droit des gens* come apice dello *jus publicum europaeum*? Nemico, guerra, legittimità nel pensiero di Emer de Vattel' (2009) 38 *Quaderni Fiorentini per la storia del pensiero giuridico moderno* 1277–1310.
Mandt, Hella, 'Tyrannis, Despotie' in Otto Brunner, Werner Conze and Reinhart Koselleck (eds), *Geschichtliche Grundbegriffe* (Stuttgart, Klett – Cotta, 1990) vol 6, 651–706.
Manning, William Oke, *Commentaries on the Law of Nations* (first published 1839, London, Sweet, 1875).
McDougal, Myres S, *Law and Minimum World Public Order* (Yale University Press, 1961).
McKay, Derek and Scott, Hamish M, *The Rise of the Great Powers 1648–1815* (London – New York, Longman, 1983).
Meylan, Philippe, *Jean Barbeyrac (1674–1744) et les débuts de l'enseignement du droit dans l'ancienne Académie de Lausanne. Contribution à l'histoire du droit naturel* (Lausanne, Rouge, 1937).
Monaco, Lucia, *Persecutio piratarum* (Naples, Jovene, 1996).
Monda, Davide, 'Contro un 'Sole' dispotico. Assolutismo e dispotismo nella Francia di Luigi XIV' in Domenico Felice, *Dispotismo. Genesi e sviluppo di un concetto filosofico-politico* (Naples, Liguori, 2001) vol 1, 165–188.
Moschetti, Cesare Maria, 'Pirateria' in Francesco Calasso (ed), *Enciclopedia del diritto* (Milan, Giuffrè, 1958–95) vol 33, 873–911.
Mössner, Jörg Manfred, *Die Völkerrechtspersönlichkeit und die Völkerrechtspraxis der Barbareskenstaaten* (Berlin, de Gruyter, 1968).
Muir-Watt, Horatia, 'Droit naturel et souveraineté de l'État dans la doctrine de Vattel' (1987) 32 *Archives de philosophie du droit* 71–85.
Müller, Klaus, 'Zur Reichskriegserklärung im 17. und 18. Jahrhundert' (1973) 90 *Zeitschrift der Savigny-Stiftung für Rechtsgeschichte, Germanistische Abteilung* 246–259.
Neff, Stephen C, *War and the Law of Nations. A General History* (CUP, 2005).
Nettement, Alfred, *Histoire de la conquête d'Alger* (Paris, Lecoffre, 1856).
Nussbaum, Arthur, *A Concise History of the Law of Nations* (2nd ed, New York, Macmillan, 1954).
Orford, Anne, *Reading Humanitarian Intervention. Human Rights and the Use of Force in International Law* (CUP, 2003).
——, 'Trade, Human Rights and the Economy of Sacrifice' in Anne Orford (ed), *International Law and its Others* (CUP, 2006) 156–196.
——, 'Jurisdiction Without Territory. From the Holy Roman Empire to the Responsibility to Protect' (2009) 30 *Michigan Journal of International Law* 981–1015.
——, *International Authority and the Responsibility to Protect* (CUP, 2011).
Palladini, Fiammetta, *Samuel Pufendorf discepolo di Hobbes* (Bologna, Il Mulino, 1990).
Panizza, Diego, 'Political Theory and Jurisprudence in Gentili's *De iure belli*' (Working paper No 15, New York, Institute for International Law and Justice, 2005), <http://www.iilj.org/newsandevents/documents/Panizza.pdf>.
Panzac, Daniel, *Barbary Corsairs. The End of a Legend 1800–1820* (Leiden – Boston, Brill, 2005).
Parker, Geoffrey, 'Early Modern Times' in Michael Howard (ed) *The Laws of War. Constraints on Warfare in the Western World* (Yale University Press, 1994) 40–58.
Parry, Clive (ed), *The Consolidated Treaty Series* (231 vols, Dobbs Ferry, NY, Oceana Publications, 1969–86).

Pérotin-Dumon, Anne, 'The Pirate and the Emperor. Power and the Law on the Seas, 1450–1850' in James D Tracy (ed), *The Political Economy of Merchant Empires. State Power and World Trade 1350–1750* (CUP, 1991) 196–227.

Phillipson, Coleman, 'Emer de Vattel' in John Macdonell (ed), *Great Jurists of the World* (Boston, Little, Brown, & Company, 1914) 477–504.

——, 'Introduction' in Alberico Gentili, *De iure belli libri tres* (first published 1588/89, Coleman Phillipson ed, Oxford, Clarendon, 1933).

Quaglioni, Diego, *Politica e diritto nel Trecento italiano. Il "De Tyranno" di Bartolo da Sassoferrato (1314–1357). Con l'edizione critica dei trattati "De Guelphis et Gebellinis", "De regimine civitatis" e "De tyranno"* (Florence, Olschki, 1983).

——, *I limiti della sovranità. Il pensiero di Jean Bodin nella cultura politica e giuridica dell'età moderna* (Padua, Cedam, 1992).

——, *La sovranità* (Rome – Bari, Laterza, 2004).

——, *La disciplina delle armi tra teologia e diritto. I trattatisti dello "ius militare"* in Claudio Donati and Bernhard R Kroener (eds), *Militari e società civile nell'Europa dell'età moderna* (Bologna, Il Mulino, 2007) 447–462.

Rawls, John, *The Law of Peoples* (Harvard University Press, 1999).

Reeves, Jesse, 'The Influence of the Law of Nations Upon International Law in the United States' (1909) 3 *American Journal of International Law* 547–561.

——, 'La communauté internationale' (1924) 3 *Recueil des cours de l'Académie de droit internationale de La Haye* 1–94.

Reibstein, Ernst, *Völkerrecht. Eine Geschichte seiner Ideen in Lehre und Praxis* (Freiburg – Munich, Alber, 1957).

——, 'Die Dialektik der souveränen Gleihheit bei Vattel' (1958) 19 *Zeitschrift für ausländisches öffentliches Recht und Völkerrecht* 607–636.

Remec, Peter P, *The Position of the Individual in International Law According to Grotius and Vattel* (The Hague, Nijhoff, 1960).

Rivier, Alphonse, *Lehrbuch des Völkerrechts* (2nd ed, Stuttgart, Ferdinand Enke, 1899).

Robinet, André, *G.W. Leibniz. Le meilleur des mondes par la balance de l'Europe* (Paris, PUF, 1994).

Roelofsen, Cornelis G, 'Grotius and the International Politics of the Seventeenth Century' in Hedley Bull, Benedict Kingsbury, and Adam Roberts (eds), *Hugo Grotius and International Relations* (Oxford, Clarendon, 1990) 95–131.

Rose, Peter, 'Cicero and the Rhetoric of Imperialism. Putting the Politics back into Political Rhetoric' (1995) 13 (4) *Rhetorica* 359–399.

Rossel, Virgile (ed), 'Lettres intimes d'Emer de Vattel' (1902) 25 *Bibliothèque universelle et revue suisse* 36–54.

Roth, Andreas, '*Crimen contra naturam*' in Lorraine Daston and Michael Stolleis (eds), *Natural Law and Laws of Nature in Early Modern Europe* (Farnham – Burlington, Ashgate, 2008) 89–104.

Rousseau, Charles, *Principes de droit international public* (Paris, Sirey, 1953).

Rubin, Alfred P, *The Law of Piracy* (first published 1988, Irvington-on-Hudson, NY, Transnational Publishers, 1998).

Ruddy, Francis S, 'The Acceptance of Vattel' in Charles H Alexandrowicz (ed), *Grotian Society Papers: Studies in the History of the Law of Nations* (The Hague, Nijhoff, 1972) 177–96.

——, *International Law in the Enlightenment: The Background of Emmerich de Vattel's* Le Droit des Gens (Dobbs Ferry, NY, Oceana Publications, 1975).

Russell, Frederick H, *The Just War in the Middle Ages* (CUP, 1975).

Sahlins, Peter, *Natural Frontiers Revisited. France's Boundaries since the Seventeenth Century* (1990) 95 *The American Historical Review* 1423–1451.

Sandoz, Yves (ed), *Réflexions sur l'impact, le rayonnement et l'actualité du 'Droit des Gens' d'Emer de Vattel – Reflections on the Impact, Influence and Continuing Relevance of the 'Law of Nations' by Emer de Vattel* (Brussels, Bruylant, 2010).

Schermaier, Martin Josef, '*Res communes omnium*. The History of an Idea from Greek Philosophy to Grotian Jurisprudence' (2009) 30 *Grotiana* 20–48.

Schmitt, Carl, *Politische Theologie* (first published 1922, Berlin, Duncker & Humblot, 1970).

——, 'The Concept of Piracy' (2011) 2 *Humanity* 1, 27–29 (1st edn 'Der Begriff der Piraterie' (1937) 6–7 *Völkerbund und Völkerrecht* 351–354).

——, *The Nomos of the Earth* (1st published 1950, New York, Telos, 2003).

Schnur, Roman, *Individualismus und Absolutismus. Zur politischen Theorie vor Thomas Hobbes (1600–1640)* (Berlin, Duncker & Humblot, 1963).

Schrader, Wilhelm, 'Christian Wolff' in *Allgemeine Deutsche Biographie* (Bayerische Akademie der Wissenschaften ed, Leipzig, Duncker & Humblot, 1898) vol 44, 12–28.

Schröder, Peter, 'Vitoria, Gentili, Bodin: Sovereignty and the Law of Nations' in Benedict Kingsbury and Benjamin Straumann (eds), *The Roman Foundations of the Law of Nations* (OUP, 2010) 163–186.

Scott, Karen N, 'Non-Compliance Procedures and Dispute Resolution Mechanisms under International Environmental Agreements' in Duncan French (ed), *International Law and Dispute Settlement. New Procedures and Techniques* (Oxford and Portland, OR, Hart, 2010).

Selesky, Harold E, 'Colonial America' in Michael Howard (ed), *The Laws of War. Constraints on Warfare in the Western World* (Yale University Press, 1994) 59–85.

Silvestrini, Gabriella, 'Justice, War, and Inequality. The Unjust Aggressor and the Enemy of the Human Race in Vattel's Theory of the Law of Nations' (2010) 31 *Grotiana* 44–68.

——, 'Vattel, Rousseau et la question de la justice de la guerre' in Vincent Chetail and Peter Haggenmacher (eds), *Vattel's International Law in a XXIst Century Perspective* (Leiden – Boston, Nijhoff, 2011) 110–129.

Simpson, Gerry, *Great Powers and Outlaw States. Unequal Sovereigns in the International Legal Order* (CUP, 2004).

——, 'Enemies of Humankind' in Jennifer Gunning et al (eds), *Law, Ethics and Society* (Aldershot, Ashgate, 2006) 85–94.

——, *Law, War and Crime. War Crimes Trials and the Reinvention of International Law* (Cambridge, Polity, 2007).

Skinner, Quentin, *The Foundations of Modern Political Thought* (2 vols, CUP, 1978).

Souza, Philip de, *Piracy in the Graeco-Roman World* (CUP, 1999).

Sreedhar, Susanne, *Hobbes on Resistance: Defying the Leviathan* (CUP, 2010).

Staub, Hans, *Die völkerrechtlichen Lehren Vattels im Lichte der naturrechtlichen Doktrin. Ein Beitrag zur Gründungsgeschichte des Völkerrechts* (Naumburg an der Saale, Lippert & Co, 1921).

Stolleis, Michael, *Geschichte des öffentlichen Rechts in Deutschland* (Munich, Beck, 1988–1999) 3 vols [trans of vol 2, *Public Law in Germany 1800–1914* (New York, Berghahn Books, 2001); trans of vol 3, *A History of Public Law in Germany 1914–1945* (OUP, 2004)].

Sturmberger, Hans, 'Das Problem der Vorbildhaftigkeit des türkischen Staatswesens im 16. und 17. Jahrhundert und sein Einfluß auf den europäischen Absolutismus' in *XIIe Congrès International des Sciences Historiques*, Rapport IV (Vienna, 1965) 201–209.

Swann, Julia, 'Politics and the State in Eighteenth-Century Europe' in Timothy CW Blanning (ed), *The Eighteenth Century: Europe 1688–1815* (OUP, 2000) 11–51.

Szabo, Franz AJ, *The Seven Years War in Europe, 1756–1763* (Harlow, Pearson – Longman, 2008).

Thomson, Ann, *Barbary and Enlightenment. European Attitudes Towards the Maghreb in the Eighteenth Century* (Leiden, Brill, 1987).

Thomson, Janice E, *Mercenaries, Pirates, and Sovereigns* (Princeton University Press, 1994).

Toyoda, Tetsuya, 'La doctrine vattelienne de l'égalité souveraine dans le contexte neuchâtelois' (2009) 11 *Journal of the History of International Law* 103–124.

Tuck, Richard, *The Rights of War and Peace: Political Thought and the International Order from Grotius to Kant* (OUP, 1999).

Turchetti, Mario, *Tyrannie et tyrannicide de l'Antiquité à nos jours* (Paris, PUF, 2001).
Twiss, Travers, *The Law of Nations Considered as Independent Political Communities* (2nd ed, Oxford, Clarendon, 1875).
Vollenhoven, Cornelis van, *The Three Stages of the Law of Nations* (The Hague, Nijhoff, 1912).
Watson, Adam, *International Law in Archaic Rome* (Johns Hopkins University Press, 1993).
Westlake, John, *Chapters on International Law* (first published 1894) in *The Collected Papers of John Westlake on Public International Law* (Lassa Oppenheim ed, CUP, 1914).
Wheaton, Henry, *Elements of International Law, with a Sketch of the History of the Science* (Philadelphia, Carey, Lea & Blanchard, 1836).
——, *Histoire des progrès du droit des gens en Europe et en Amérique depuis la Paix de Westphalie jusqu'à nos jours* (4th ed, Leipzig, Brockhaus, 1865).
Wilson, Peter H, *The Holy Roman Empire 1495–1806* (London, Macmilllan, 1999).
——, 'Prussia's Relations with the Holy Roman Empire, 1740–1786' (2008) 51 (2) *The Historical Journal* 337–371.
Windler, Christian, *La diplomatie comme expérience de l'autre. Consuls Français au Maghreb (1700–1840)* (Geneva, Droz, 2002).
——, 'Diplomatie et interculturalité. Les consuls français à Tunis, 1700–1840' (2003) 50 (4) *Revue d'histoire moderne et contemporaine* 63–91.
Wortley, Ben A, 'Pirata non mutat dominium' (1947) 24 *British Yearbook of International Law* 258–272.
Ziegler, Karl-Heinz, *Das Völkerrecht der Römischen Republik* in Hildegard Temporini (ed), *Aufstieg und Niedergang der Römischen Welt* (Berlin – New York, de Gruyter, 1972) vol 1, 68–114.
——, 'The Peace Treaties of the Ottoman Empire with European Christian Powers' in Randall Lesaffer (ed), *Peace Treaties and International Law in European History* (CUP, 2004).
Zurbuchen, Simone, 'Vattel's *Law of Nations* and Just War Theory' (2009) 35 *History of European Ideas* 408–417.

NAME INDEX

SUBJECT INDEX

www.ingramcontent.com/pod-product-compliance
Lightning Source LLC
LaVergne TN
LVHW020652300926
849161LV00004B/911
* 9 7 8 9 0 0 4 2 5 4 3 4 3 *